MUSIC APPRECIATION

ITS HISTORY AND TECHNICS

by Percy A. Scholes

Edited for American readers
by WILL EARHART

M. WITMARK & SONS

NEW YORK

Printed in the United States of America by
J. J. LITTLE & IVES COMPANY, NEW YORK

THE study of music, rightly undertaken, can be of the highest educational value. We are in error if we dismiss it as a recreation, or seclude it as a remote and technical study which is out of relation to the rest of our intellectual life. Its range is not less wide than that of literature; it appeals to the same faculties of emotion and judgment; it is, allowing for the necessary difference of medium, subject to the same general aesthetic principles. Its history, far too much neglected in our schools, is an essential part of the history of our civilization. The mental training offered by analytical study of its construction and texture is closely parallel to that afforded by the natural sciences. Its problems of style are as interesting and varied as those presented by any literary form. Above all, it is a language with a poetry as noble as that of Dante or Racine, of Shakespeare or Milton. All the arguments which can be used for the inclusion of Language and Literature in our ordinary scheme of education may be used with equal force in the case of Music. Its worth has been attested by almost every educational writer from the time of Plato; and the only reason why it is not already established in our schools is that English music is but now recovering from a century of apathy and neglect, in which its tradition, once amongst the greatest in Europe, was allowed to fall into oblivion. From this dark, unprofitable period we have now emerged; and it is high time that our national gift of music, which has once more come into its own in executance and in composition, should be duly recognized in the training grounds of our schools and colleges."

—From an Official Document issued by the National Board of Education for England and Wales in 1923.

"It is unphilosophical to say that exercises in vocal music may not be so directed and arranged as to produce those habits of feeling of which these sounds are the type. Happiness, contentment, cheerfulness, tranquillity—these are the natural effects of music."

"But it is said, the time spent would be quite inadequate to the end proposed; that the labor of a life is needed to form the musician. The answer to this objection is, that it mistakes the end proposed,

v

which is not to form the musician. Let vocal music, in this respect, be treated like the other branches of instruction. As many probably would be found to excel in music as in arithmetic, writing, or any of the regular studies, and no more. All cannot be orators, nor all poets, but shall we not, therefore, teach the elements of grammar, which orators and poets in common with all others use? It should never be forgotten that the power of understanding and appreciating music may be acquired, where the power of excelling in it is found wanting."

"Now, the defect of our present system, admirable as that system is, is this, that it aims to develop the intellectual part of man's nature solely when, for all the true purposes of life, it is of more importance, a hundredfold, to feel rightly than to think profoundly.
"If the committee have erred in attaching so much importance to vocal music as a part of public instruction, they can only say they err with Pythagoras, and Plato, Milton and Luther, Pestalozzi, and Fellenberg. Finer spirits than these the world hath not bred. In such company there will be consolation."

—From a report submitted in 1837 to the School Board of Boston, Mass., by a special committee appointed by the Board to consider a petition relative to introducing instruction in vocal music into the Boston Public Schools. The petition was the direct outgrowth of the work of Lowell Mason, who became the first teacher of music in Boston's schools and in any public school in the United States. The complete text of the report from which the above excerpts are taken may be found in *History of Public School Music in the United States;* Edward Bailey Birge; published by the Oliver Ditson Co.

AMERICAN EDITOR'S PREFACE

IN preparing the American edition of this book by Dr. Scholes —which I first read in typewritten form in Switzerland in 1934—numerous alternatives relative to the extent and nature of the proposed editorial revision naturally presented themselves. What these were, and the decisions made with respect to them, may be of interest to the American reader, and may also be of direct help through preparing his receptive attitude for the pages he is about to read.

One question of moment was that of adding to the historical and critical review of the study of Musical Appreciation as found mainly in England, a similar review of it as it is found in the United States. That plan, though it came the more insistently to mind because Dr. Scholes himself had included a brief sketch of the movement in the United States, was finally abandoned. One reason for abandonment was that the addition, if the review were at all thorough, would more than equal in amount the contents of the original book: and another reason was that the American reader knows the facts of the situation in his own country very well anyway. Of course, there would be another value in such a plan, namely that of affording opportunity for a comparative study in one book of aims and methods in the two countries. But against this would be the destruction of a unity that pervades the book now despite the differences that may be noted in English opinion. Moreover, the very comparisons hypothesized would inescapably take place in the mind of every American reader anyway; for knowing American musical appreciation, his reading of a form and spirit of appreciational study that somehow differs from his own will freshen comparison more than another rehearsal of his own formulas. In short, if quickening of thought comes from contact with another culture, the American editor's disinclination to make a hybrid out of this work may claim place as a natural virtue and as unconscious wisdom!

But while no large interpolations or additions could well be made without distorting the form of the book and destroying its unity, the possibility remained that the whole might be subject to some interpretative or subsumptive comment that would be of definite value. For many conflicting views from many separate sources are brought forward in the text; and these are intentionally left, as Dr. Scholes hints in his Preface, to resolve themselves as best they may in the reader's mind. The inevitable result, however, of thus presenting multifarious materials to the mind is to induce in it an effort toward finding some general principles to which the unordered and often conflicting elements can be related. To use a figure of speech, a catalytic agent, it would appear, might be needed; and since this would be sought with some difficulty by the reader, an attempt to supply it by the American editor appeared reasonable. Such an addition could not well be confined, however, for the reasons already stated, to interpolations or footnotes, and so it was decided to incorporate it in an additional Preface. That is now being done, and much of the matter of the ensuing paragraphs is devoted to the attempt.

A great many of the divergent views found herein, then, might be reconciled, or might at least be put on a common basis for discussion, if, reaching behind matters of materials and methods objectively considered, they were referred to æsthetic and psychological grounds. The child, for instance, or the student of whatever age, is conceived in much of the book as listening to some piece of music or other which it is desired he shall come to appreciate. He is held before our thought as attending to tones that are in vibration in the air, and there is much discussion as to the kinds of tonal designs or forms that will best capture his aural attention, and as to what may or may not be said to him in order to ensure his aural attention. But this standpoint implies that the various contributing writers conceive music as tones actually sounding, and think of the ear only as engaged in receiving them. A different view, that at first glance seems little more than quibbling with words, but that is potent to produce basic changes in our outlook, is gained when we follow a line of thought best stated, perhaps, by H. S. Goodhart-Rendel. This author points out [1] that sounds are not the material of musical art, in as much as a composer may produce a work of musical art without a single tone having been sounded; and another musician may then receive and enjoy the work by looking at the score, again without a tone being sounded. Not tones, but *ideas of tones* are thus the material of musical art.

Under this conception the work of the teacher of appreciation—and for that matter, the work of any teacher in connection with any subject—appears in a new light. Not the physical senses, but an intelligence and an affective disposition that lie beyond them, are being addressed. Not present sounds, but long memories of sounds that once came through the ear to haunt the mind are the goal of the teacher's effort; not present attention, however quick and alert, to the surface of the music, but something akin to complete absorption *in* the music and complete absorption *of* the music—or parts of it—is sought.

When this point of view is applied to many of the controversies that are waged in *Part II* of the book, *The Alleged Case Against Musical Appreciation,* and elsewhere in the book's pages, some approach to a solution of the arguments is gained. Not methods and materials used by the teacher, but the teacher's power to penetrate, by some form of pedagogical magic, the core of the pupil's sentient being, will determine the degree of success or failure. The question is not whether music is "a thing to be talked about" or not (see page 39). It may be talked about diviningly—and divinely!—with the result that the talk echoes in our understanding and feeling with almost the power and quality of the music itself, or it may be talked about so pedantically and undiscerningly that the hearer is taken far out of the charmed circle throughout which the voice of the music itself resounds. The teacher of appreciation may deal in fact (page

[1] In his book *Fine Art;* Oxford University Press, 1934. The same thought is expressed in an article *Music and Mind,* by Will Earhart, in the *Music Clubs Magazine* for January-February 1933; and again the thought is stated in the book, *The Meaning and Teaching of Music,* Earhart, M. Witmark and Sons, 1935.

58), but only in fact that the teacher makes musically mean-
ingful, and not in *hard* fact, for that term connotes a mode of
presentation [1] that is undivining and non-penetrative. Technical
terms (page 60) may be used or abused: only a teacher who holds
in one hand the glowing chalice of music, while reaching down
with the other to extend helpful "terms" to the student, will
rightly use them. Whether appreciation of music is best developed by hearing or by doing, and whether teachers of music
should therefore all teach all students, always, to sing or to play
is, again, a matter of a mode and a degree of teaching, not a
choice of subject-matter. Certain it is that many teachers of
voice and instruments do not teach their pupils to listen, understand, remember, and dwell in loving understanding with the
treasures of music with which they may have been dealing. The
constant procession of students who abandon technical study because of its musical aridity, the dull, mechanical playing of many
students who continue to "take lessons", and the hard unmusi-
calness of many who succeed in gaining a good or even a brilliant technique of performance, all attest to that fact. On the
other hand, we all know equally of teachers of "doing"
who are apostles also of musical light and life. That teachers
of Appreciation reveal similar lack of possession of power is not
surprising. Rather it is but additional testimony to the fact that
in any field we may become lost in externalities. Nevertheless,
since the externalities, in the form of piano keyboards, violin
strings, and fingers, are more numerous and obstructive in the
case of an approach through specialized technique than they are
in the case of a direct approach through the ear, it is probable
that, as between two teachers of equal understanding and
power, advantage in the development of a responsive musical-
ness in the student would lie with the Appreciation teacher.
Certain it is that the teacher of a technique, if he does develop
appreciation in the pupil, does it only by turning away momentarily from the technique itself in order to adopt the very modes
of explanation and enlightening exposition that are normal to
the teacher of Appreciation. If he does that, then one must con-

[1] Short "e", please!

cede that advantage shifts to him: for the music that is to be
thus affectionately dwelt upon in mind, will reside there in a
much more positive way (having been an experience for more
than the organs of hearing) than will music the acquisition of
which enlisted the ear alone.— And yet even here is a minor disadvantage: for the concept gained through playing may easily
be *obscured under* kinesthetic memories instead of being rein-
forced by them; and the concept that, in contrast, is aural alone,
will, in that case, be purer musically, even though it be of less
material texture.

The approach to music through form history, biography, anecdotes, is beset by the same danger. Figuratively speaking, those
material facts are the trees, rivers, plains, and hills that compose
the complete landscape; but if we bend our attention too nar-
rowly and intently upon them we shall certainly miss the landscape. On the other hand, it would be a foolish mistake to try
to grasp the landscape without seeing them at all. That would
be one of those efforts in the direction of "airy fantasy" (see
page 57) that have so often vitiated efforts toward evoking an
appreciative attitude. Such efforts, indeed, would be comparable
to an attempt to have the hearer grasp the meaning of an ora-
tion without listening to the orator's words. Nevertheless, to
revert to our original figure, those externals, taken singly and
separately, do not constitute the landscape; and in that sense
Ernest Newman is right when he contends that even the most
essential of them, namely, Form, does not inescapably reveal the
heart of the matter. We can console ourselves, however, with
the reflection that music is in no worse case in this respect than
is any other phase of life. In politics the issues lie hidden behind
the candidates and the flux of external events; and back of the
forms and appurtenances of religion lies the living Word that
we seek. That we often miss it, because, due to some shortcoming in ourselves or in those who would communicate with
us, our attention is short-circuited and directed to objects that lie
in the outer confines of the promised land, is proof only that
teachers and learners are still imperfect. Probably, however
(again to return to our figure), attention to the components of

the landscape should follow a favorable impression of the landscape as a whole, and should not precede that vision. Here in America, at least, this procedure is widely followed; although one cannot say precisely how widely because no statistical survey is at hand to inform us. It has the merit of following the pedagogical maxim, "the whole before the parts", and it subscribes to the psychological belief that learning is more successful when it pursues the "whole-part" than when it pursues the "part-whole" direction. It would appear, moreover, to be more in harmony with what we know about interest. It need hardly be said, however, that the "whole" should not, for young children, be a large one.

This same matter of attention in relation to response is still further illuminated by another idea from the field of æsthetics. It is a distinction between perceptive and intuitive attention, and therefore bears upon the quality of attention rather than upon the nature of its object or upon the direction of its movement. Prall [1], in defining the difference between the two modes of attention, uses an illustration that appears as though made for our hand. He reminds us that "if attention is characteristically perceptive and not intuitive", the deeper processes of æsthetic response "remain largely in abeyance, as when in musical dictation one hears so well as to write out accurately what was perceived through the ears and the sense for rhythm, without in the least feeling the formal or sensuous or expressive beauty of the dictated passage."

The whole question of whether one subject-matter or another leads toward appreciation of music appears, in the light of this thought, to be beside the point. Belief in its truth colored all the statements preceding; and acceptance of it would immediately reveal the reason why, as Dr. Scholes points out, one teacher succeeds when using one kind of subject-matter, and another teacher fails with that kind, but succeeds with something of quite diverse nature. The difference is in the teacher, not in the subject-matter. One teacher is himself deeply responsive to one

[1] D. W. Prall, in his book, *Aesthetic Judgment*, published by Thomas Y. Crowell Company.

kind of appeal and his feeling enables him to speak in words and in tones of voice that do not so much produce knowledge in his hearers as have the effect of a revelation to them. Sometimes this responsiveness on the part of the teacher is to dramatic or "programmatic" features associated with the music, and then his pupils reveal equally an eager responsiveness to such dramatic appeals. Sometimes it is rather for the human interests that cling about composers or compositions, and again the teacher will find himself successful, in the sense of arousing enthusiastic interest in those factors. In cases that are rarer (one must reluctantly believe) the responsiveness is to the sheer beauty of tone and of striving, swelling, subsiding, reiterative or adventurous, tonal forms: and then the sensitive responses called forth from pupils are those which the true musician wishes to see awakened. And finally, there is at times an absence of any of these enthusiasms; and then there remain—facts.

Still another idea from the field of æsthetics bears upon another phase of discussion found in the book, namely, that which would determine whether phonograph ("gramophone") records should receive preference, or whether voices and instruments in direct presentation are preferable and should be used, even when transcriptions from the composer's original scoring are thereby entailed. Dr. Scholes and the majority of the teachers quoted prefer the phonograph to transcriptions, and some prefer it even to any direct performance, unless that be of very excellent quality. Against this conclusion we have no disposition to argue; but it is remarkable that the entire discussion is conducted without any reference to the æsthetic importance of sheer tone alone in the appeal of music, apart from its design or from any so-called expressive quality it may possess. For this matter of the sensuous appeal of *material* [1] in all art—tone in music, color in painting, word-sounds in poetry, the kind of metal or of fabric used in crafts—is important.[2] In this case it bears directly upon

[1] The point of view advanced by H. S. Goodhart-Rendel, quoted approvingly a little earlier, is not forgotten or abandoned. It is merely convenient now to consider physical Tone, before it passes over into idea, as the material of music.

[2] In a hasty check of this statement, five books on aesthetics that were within easy reach were just now drawn from the shelves. Their authors, Edmund

the question of the use of the phonograph, and is connected, moreover, with pedagogical practice, in that the musical receptivity of individuals at various ages, with respect to the comparative values of *material, form,* and *expression,* must also be taken into account. Briefly, there is reason to believe that a young child, because he is in a sensory stage, because his attention-span is too short to hold him to analysis of any but the briefest forms (or perhaps we should say to anything beyond brief factors of design), and because the music that is taught as "expressive" is likely to express qualities of feeling outside of his experience, derives the major part of his musical enjoyment mainly from the *sheer sound* of it. It is sensuous sound, not form, expression, biography, or musical history, that makes him follow the band down the street. Therefore the primary [1] æsthetic factor in music, *Tone,* is a matter of first importance in work with younger children. Belief in the truth of that statement, it is true, need not entail change in the teacher's preference for the use of the phonograph with little children, for the tone of the later machines and records is now extraordinarily fine and authentic. There was a time, however, when that tone was such as to endanger greatly the attitude of all young hearers toward any music that came out of the gaping horn. Only an older and more experienced listener could, at that time, be trusted to read back of the sounds that came to his ears to the thought and mood that gave the composition value. But even now, and in any case, it appears unwise to choose the one medium of musical expression or the other—or, for that matter, to teach any branch of music whatsoever, especially to young children—without first considering this essential matter of tone-quality.[2] That quality must be good: for it is useless to ask children to like or appreciate what they take no pleasure whatever in listening to as sound.

Possibly it is this very shortcoming with respect to an appraisal

Gurney, George Santayana, E. D. Puffer, D. W. Prall, and Louis Arnaud Reid, all support the point—in some cases, eloquently and at length.

[1] Not the greatest or highest.

[2] It is considered by two contributors to these discussions, although not from this same point of view. See pp. 297 and 302.

of the proper place of tone that sometimes induces the teacher to try to awaken interest by telling programmatic stories, relating biographical anecdotes, or by talking about external characteristics of the music. These teachings of course have their place; but that place is not one which they should occupy in substitution for music itself, but one from which they should vend toward the music and thereby contribute to and enlarge interest in it. The distinction is important; for often the kind and direction of interest aroused in an apathetic class by a baffled teacher is so tangential to the path of the interest that he passionately desires or should desire to arouse that his seeming success must rather be regarded as dismal failure. One teacher who contributes an account of her experience naïvely reveals this very fact. (See pages 258-9.) Her statement in regard to the small boys' interest in "little Handel running after his father's coach" is coupled with another to the effect that "even this interest is better than none." But that amounts to saying only that such interest is better than that which is worse; and the obvious answer is that it is also worse than that which is better. The "better" is, of course, interest in music itself. We see the capacity for such an interest in children in their fondness for music concerning which they have heard no word of explanation or description. That native fondness, indeed, furnishes the basis and justification for all of our later teaching; for were it absent we should be helpless. It should surely, then, not be neglected and left to take care of itself, while we replace it with other and less musical kinds of interest. Particularly would we appear to be unwise if we attempted to build up "programmatic" interest in music on the part of young children;—if our contention is right that those children are in a sensory stage, and therefore hear music as something that brings pleasure as sound and klang and moving pattern received through the ear. Yet, so far as opinion on this point is expressed by contributors to this book, the programmatic idea seems to be regarded as particularly appropriate for use with those same young children. However, many other ways of approaching music with them are suggested—as on page 309, for instance—and, indeed, no conceivable approach fails to find expression in this tolerant compilation. Perhaps all we should say now, therefore, is that because interest is aroused by a music teacher during a music lesson, it is not on that account necessarily pure musical interest.

The admirable discussion by Dr. Scholes on pages 190 to 201 inclusive, and particularly that on the last half of page 201, suggests further one pedagogical dictum that may prove useful to the reader. It was stated to the present writer by Dr. Will Grant Chambers, now Dean of the School of Education of Pennsylvania State College, in approximately this form: "All education is analysis of experience, and may be retarded by over-analysis of a meagre experience, or by under-analysis of a rich experience." The possibility of helpful application of the statement to the teaching of Musical Appreciation is probably obvious, yet it may easily be overlooked or forgotten. How often does the teacher err by giving the children a new and not very large musical experience, and by then hanging an endless amount of expository talk upon that slender experience? On the other hand, why not, as Dr. Scholes advocates, give the children any experience, however rich (for the Creator does— He withholds no part of the earth or sky from the gaze of the smallest child) and then safeguard the values that may be gained by permitting the child to draw out of it only that which he naturally absorbs—in this case the *spirit* of a piece of music that he is yet far too young to analyze or learn about in any detail. The analysis will come later, and will be continuous, year after year, if and when a great experience has been gained. Such large, unanalyzed experience is not advocated here as properly constituting the whole, or even a large part, of that which the teacher of Musical Appreciation should bring to his pupils. It is enough to suggest that it may have place, and to counsel the teacher to reflect that in all teaching this balancing of experience with the analysis of it is one of his most delicate and vital problems.

A few lesser matters of detail remain to be spoken of. In the effort to preserve a very desirable unity of style and thought changes in the body of the work have been limited to matters of mere usage, such as adopting the American ending *"or"* for words that in English end in *"our"*—labor, favor, etc.—and substituting American forms of words for some that, in their English form, would appear alien to American eyes. "While" for "whilst", and "among" for "amongst" are illustrative of these. In the case of quotations, however, changes of this latter class were not made. Perhaps, indeed, they need not have been made anywhere. It was felt, however, that trivialities of speech, as of dress or manners, often erect little barriers between persons who otherwise might enter into quick and friendly intercourse; and so it seemed wise to remove from the main text even the smallest impediments of the kind. But in quotations, this would often have been inadvisable, and so it was thought preferable there to let the British terms stand consistently, and beg the reader to effect the translation. "Music master", "headmaster", "forms", and "time-tables", are instances. They do not instantly summon to our minds, it is true, those warm and familiar entities known to us as music teachers, principals, grades [1], and class schedules. The word "time-tables", indeed, being in America connected with railways rather than with schools, may even seem faintly absurd, or may give us a fleeting (and quite erroneous!) impression of coldly mechanistic school control. But with a little effort we can remember that the words only, and not the children— no, nor the teachers—differ.

Beyond these lesser matters of editorial concern lay somewhat larger ones. Although Dr. Scholes is intimately acquainted with our American schools, and although in this book he frequently speaks, as the reader will discover, of the greater attention given in our schools to Musical Appreciation, his present discussion is nevertheless based almost wholly upon teaching as practiced in British schools and as described by British teachers. The intrinsic value of the discussions is none the less for that. No one can read this rich and ample compendium of thought on ways of developing musical appreciation among the masses without coming to the conviction that British minds have seen as

---

[1] But numerically "Forms" and "Grades" do not match. See pp. 286-7, "VI form."

broadly, deeply, and wisely (whatever the practical outcomes in Great Britain have been) as have any in America. Nevertheless, in the background, as the concrete basis for all the discussion, is the English school: and that school does have different cultural traditions and certainly has an unfamiliar terminology. For the most part the terms have been let stand, because the reader may easily level them by exercising a little quick imagination. To think of the "music master" using a "gramophone" as the music teacher or supervisor—Mr. X, perhaps, with whom you are well acquainted—using the phonograph, will surely not be difficult. When, however, a difference exists that is substantial rather than merely verbal, definitions and explanations are provided in footnotes. The very organization of British schools, for instance, differs from that which obtains in the United States, and unless the American reader is informed on this point his understanding of many passages in the book is likely to be delayed and made difficult. Fortunately G. Kirkham Jones gives an admirable description of London Elementary Schools (which may be accepted as typical) on page 277 of the book: but since the American reader will find himself in need of the information there provided long before he reaches that distant page, he is advised now to read it at the outset—a bit of advice that is repeated in a footnote on an early page. Additional information relative to types of schools found in England is either given in footnotes or is made unnecessary by statements concerning the ages of the pupils that are incorporated in the body of the text.

The general ideas that were put forth in the earlier part of this long introduction do not, it hardly need be said, provide a body of doctrines to which all the discussions in the book can be referred. The book is far too comprehensive for that; and, anyway, an attempt at such completeness of generalization would be pedantic and foolish. If a few of the problems more frequently debated herein are slightly clarified by reference to these touchstones of æsthetic and pedagogical thought, their inclusion will not be wholly unjustified; and more than that the writer of them hardly ventures to hope.

WILL EARHART

PREFACE

THE Preface to this book can be a very short and simple thing. I have thought the time ripe for a book on "Musical Appreciation" of a different type from any yet issued—one that should not lay down any one personal system or method, but should discuss the subject in a comprehensive and ample way, tracing the history of the "Appreciation" idea, answering the chief objections that have been advanced, setting out the broad underlying philosophy of "Appreciation" teaching, debating a large number of detailed points of principle and procedure, and recording the experiences and experiments of practical teachers in a great variety of schools, and, to conclude, attempting a Glossary of all the technical terms that an "Appreciation" teacher or pupil can need to know.

That I have been helped by many good friends (known and unknown to me) will be realized as the book is read.

I have hopes that my compilation may, from the large scope it attempts, be found useful not only in Britain and the British Empire but also in the United States. I am well aware that in some respects American thought and practice on this subject have run ahead of the British, but, on the other hand, a volume wherein so large a body of opinion and experience is collected should be found to contain *something* helpful to all. I call attention to the Analytical Index at the end, which, it is hoped, adds some *reference value* to whatever *reading value* the book may possess.

It is my earnest wish that my book may be influential in encouraging and guiding many who are working for the greater usefulness of Music as a factor in a sane and happy social life.

PERCY A. SCHOLES

CHAMBY, MONTREUX,
SWITZERLAND.

Note:—It has been thought desirable to publish this Glossary as a separate work, so as to give the general public the advantage of it. Its title is *Scholes' Handbook of Musical Terms,* and it is published by M. Witmark & Sons.

CONTENTS

MUSIC APPRECIATION

Its History and Technics

PART I

THE HISTORY OF THE "MUSICAL APPRECIATION" IDEA

CONTENTS OF PART I

HISTORY OF THE APPRECIATION MOVEMENT

THERE are many social movements of value of which nobody has yet troubled to collect the historical data, and this seems to be true of the "Musical Appreciation" movement. The present chapter represents, then, merely a pioneer attempt. Such particulars as I have been able to find are here recorded in the hope that my attention may be called to any omissions, or that some later writer, using my sketch as a basis (which he is quite at liberty to do), may be led to the production of a more exhaustive study of the subject.

1789

Possibly the earliest recognition of the Appreciation principle is in a complaint of DR. CHARLES BURNEY, the great historian of music. In 1789 he reached publication of the third volume of his *History*, and as an introductory chapter to it he offered a thoughtful and valuable *Essay on Musical Criticism*. In this there occurs the following:

"There have been many treatises published on the art of musical composition and performance but none to instruct ignorant lovers of music how to listen or to judge for themselves."

And the idea of the existence of the "ignorant lover" (potentially an "appreciator" of great art, actually an appreciator merely of the simplicities) is carried further as the essay ends:

"There is a degree of refinement, delicacy, and invention which lovers of simple and common Music can no more comprehend than the Asiatics harmony. It is only understood and felt by such as can quit the plains of simplicity, penetrate the mazes of art and contrivance, climb mountains, dive into dells, or cross the seas in search of extraneous and exotic beauties with which the monotonous melody of popular Music has not yet been embellished. What

3

judgment and good taste admire at first hearing, makes no impression on the public in general, but by dint of repetition and habitude. A syllogism that is very plain to a logician, is incomprehensible to a mind unexercised in associating and combining abstract ideas."

It will be seen that the germs of the present day Appreciation movement are latent in this passage.

1826–30

Between thirty and forty years after Burney wrote thus, two attempts were made to provide that desired treatise "to instruct ignorant lovers of music"; the Swiss, HANS GEORG NÄGELI, who had been lecturing to amateurs in various German cities in 1824, issued in 1826 his *Vorlesungen über Musik mit besonderer Berücksichtigung der Dilettanten* ("Lectures on Music, with particular regard to Amateurs"), and FÉTIS in 1830 issued his *La Musique mise à la portée de tout le monde* ("Music brought within everybody's reach"). Of this latter I have traced no fewer than 19 editions: 8 in the original French, 4 in English, 1 in American (if the distinction may be allowed), 2 in Italian, 1 in Spanish, 1 in German, 1 in Portuguese, and 1 in Russian. I am not at all sure, however, that these are all; I have gradually built up the list from books of reference in various languages amplified by observation of continental second-hand booksellers' catalogues, and probably I am not yet at the end of the process. The eagerness with which the musical public of various countries held out its hands for copies of Fétis's book is remarkable. Apparently people were carried away by the novelty of discovering at last a musical author who realized that, in addition to books to guide the composer and the performer, there was a need of books to guide the *listener,* and so publishers competed with one another in getting out editions—sometimes a pirated edition in opposition to an authorized one (Fétis's native Belgium, though it could have imported the original Paris edition, had one authorized edition of its own and two pirated ones).

Mr. C. B. Oldman, of the British Museum, who first called my attention to Nägeli's work, considers it the first of its type ("it should be given pride of place in any history of the Appreciation movement". Nägeli's book was of a considerably less "popular" character than that of Fétis, and so never caught on much, apparently.

The period when there occurred all this Musical Appreciation activity on the part of Fétis was from 1830 to 1858, exactly covering the working lifetimes of Mendelssohn, Chopin, and Schumann. We can readily understand that the new color and emotional tendency of music, with the introduction of attractive short forms, like Chopin's Nocturnes, Mendelssohn's Songs Without Words, and Schumann's Novelettes and the like, had opened up the art to a new public, and that this public would be eager to seize upon a book that might make it still more accessible to them (just as the new musical public that broadcasting has created is to-day glad to get hold of a book which will explain the construction of music, enable it to identify the instruments of the orchestra, and tell it something of the composers).

Fétis, then, I consider to be the first notable Musical Appreciation Author. And he was one of its first Lecturers also. What lectures he gave in France and his native Belgium I do not know, but he came to England to give a series under the title he was the following year to adopt as that of his book, *La Musique mise à la portée de tout le monde*. Only one lecture of the series was delivered, the reason being, I think, that the season was too far advanced. Mendelssohn, aged twenty, was in London at the same time, and Fétis thoughtlessly got the poor boy into trouble. The two of them were one day in St. Paul's Cathedral, at a Festival of the Sons of the Clergy, when Purcell's Te Deum in D was performed—badly. Fétis was writing a series of letters to his son in Paris about his London experiences, which letters were being published periodically in the *Revue Musicale,* and he not only very caustically criticized Purcell's music (which I think had certainly not been given in its original form, but as knocked about by its editor, Boyce), but also stated that *"Mr. Felix Mendelssohn, a young and distinguished German composer, who was with me, received exactly the same impression"*, and added that Mendelssohn simply could not stand the stuff and actually went out rather than hear it to the end! Then the fat was in the fire! An English paper copied this statement out of the *Revue Musicale,* and the courteous and diplomatic young society-favorite had the unhappy task of clearing himself of a charge of having reflected harshly upon the chief composer of a nation that was treating him particularly hospitably.

Incidentally, the brilliant young Mendelssohn (like many professional musicians of to-day) did not in the least grasp the need of enlightening and stimulating the "ordinary listener". He sneered at Fétis's lecture project. *"What is the good of talking so much about music?"* he said. *"It is better to compose well"*— which was certainly a very illogical remark. (What is the good of discussing *Hamlet?* It is better to write good plays." "What is the good of discussing Rembrandt? It is better to paint fine pictures." So we might go on!)[1]

In observing the credit that attaches to Fétis as a pioneer of a new branch of education (the education of the Listener), we must remember one circumstance that enormously enhances that credit. This sympathy with the new and untrained musical public came from one of the best-educated musical men in all Europe. We commonly find the highbrows of to-day unsympathetic towards the Appreciation movement, but that was not the attitude of Fétis. He could put himself in the place of the "ordinary listener", and yet he was, at different times, Professor of Counterpoint and Fugue at the Paris Conservatoire and Principal of the Brussels Conservatoire, was a voluminous composer of masses, operas, and piano music, and was, moreover, the author of important books on composition, piano technique, vocal technique, plain-song, counterpoint and fugue, the harmony of the Greeks and Romans, and other deep technical subjects. His erudite eight-volume *Biographie Universelle des Musiciens* is still indispensable to all serious students of music.

---

[1] "Illogical" indeed! Note on a later page an account of Mendelssohn's own Appreciation Lectures to Goethe. P. A. S.

Before leaving the subject of Fétis and his once popular Appreciation book it may be interesting to see the titles of his chapters and so to grasp what was his idea of helping the listener. As we can now see, he was a trifle too technical, too professional, too academic. He had not yet differentiated quite sufficiently between what we may call "listener-knowledge" and "performer-knowledge". He deserves none the less credit on that account, for if he saw dimly into the subject most of his colleagues in various countries, so far as we know, saw not at all. Here is his scheme of chapters:

FIRST SECTION

Of the Musical System, considered in the three Qualities of Sounds—Intonation, Duration, and Intensity.

I. The object of Music. Its Origin. Its Means.
II. Of the Diversity of Sounds, and of the Manner of Expressing them by names.
III. How we represent Sound in Notation.
IV. Of the Differences of Scales; of the Names given to them, and of the operation called Transposition.
V. Of the Duration of Sounds and Silences in Music; how these are represented in Notation, and how they are Measured.
VI. Of what is called Expression in musical Execution; of its Means and of the signs by which it is indicated in Notation.

SECOND SECTION

Of Sounds considered in their Relations of Succession and Simultaneity, and of the Result of these.

VII. What is the Relation of Sounds to One Another?
VIII. Of Melody.
IX. Of Harmony.
X. Of the Art of Writing Music; Counterpoint, Canon, Fugue.
XI. Of the Manner of Using Voices.
XII. Of Instruments.
XIII. Of Instrumentation.
XIV. Of the Forms of Composition—in both Vocal and Instrumental Music.

THIRD SECTION

Of Performance.

XV. Of Song and Singers.
XVI. Of Instrumental Execution.

FOURTH SECTION

How we analyze the Sensations produced by Music in order
to arrive at Judgments upon it.

XVII. Of the Prejudices of the Ignorant and of those of the Musically Learned.
XVIII. Of the Poesy of Music.
XIX. Of the Analysis of Musical Sensation.
XX. Is it of use to Analyze Musical Sensations?

I have said above that Fétis has not sufficiently distinguished between listener-knowledge and performer-knowledge. Yet if his book be examined it is impossible not to admit that to any intelligent but uninformed music-lover of that day its perusal must have meant a great widening of interest and perception. Books for the Listener, even to-day, necessarily consist largely of summarized elementary information, differing from books for the Performer mainly in the fact that they are more elementary and simpler in expression. Perhaps the most noticeable lack in Fétis's book is that of any comprehensive historical survey of music, such crumbs of historical information as he offers occurring merely incidentally.

However, do not let us overlook the wonder of his achievement. Here, so far back as the 1830's, was a great musical *savant,* primarily occupied in writing for and in training performers and composers, who could yet remember the listeners and regard them also as capable of profiting by training.

In the 1870's

It is not generally remembered that the Rev. John Curwen (1816–80), the founder of the Tonic Sol-fa movement, was also a pioneer in Musical Appreciation. Although his main efforts were concentrated upon the attempt to popularize choral singing, he saw the one-sidedness of a purely vocal curriculum and made at any rate the beginnings of an attempt to supplement it by the intelligent representation of instrumental music. In 1919 his daughter-in-law, Mrs. J. Spencer Curwen, so well known to and so much respected by all musical educators in Britain for about half a century, wrote to me as follows—commenting on an observation I had made which reflected upon the early tonic sol-faists.

"It is quite true that Sol-fa suffered from lack of musicianship in Mr. Curwen's followers. Perhaps 'lack of musicianship' is hardly fair. They knew the vocal classics well. It was rather lack of general culture. John Curwen himself had a much wider outlook. Before I was married (and that is more than forty years ago) I illustrated for him what would now be called an 'appreciation' lecture. He took a Beethoven sonata to pieces, I played the subjects separately, and illustrated each little point that he brought out, and then played the whole movement. We went through the whole sonata in that way. So even in that he was ahead of his generation. He would have been interested in our recent developments."

About 1883

The name of the English musician RIDLEY PRENTICE (1842–95) should be mentioned in any such conspectus as this chapter tries to give. After a distinguished student career at the Royal Academy of Music, he embarked on a campaign of popularization of music in various London suburbs by means of "Monthly Popular Concerts" and "Twopenny Concerts". Simultaneously he was doing much work as pianist and piano teacher, and about 1883 he produced a most excellent series of books for piano students called *The Musician*. That such a series should bear such a name is in itself significant: there are still pianists who have not aspired to the wider qualification. The idea was to give the piano student, from the beginning to the end of his study, a close understanding of the music he practiced. The six grades of the work laid down a repertory advancing in difficulty, every composition in the repertory being treated in a sort of intelligent "annotated program" style. The aim of the work was clearly stated in the preface; it was to be *a Guide and Companion to the Pianoforte Student during his course of study, helping him to understand music better, and consequently to enjoy it more.* That such "understanding" might be given to the listener, as apart from the pianist, and imparted in class and not merely connected with individual lessons, had apparently not occurred to the author: otherwise the ideals by which he was moved and the plans he adopted were very much those of the orthodox "appreciationist" of to-day.

About 1886

We may also count HANS VON BÜLOW among the pioneers of Muscial Appreciation work. The British composer, J. D. Davis, has kindly put on paper for me the record of an incident of which he was witness:

"When a student at the Raff Conservatoire, Frankfort-on-Main, I heard the late Hans von Bülow finish a lecture upon Brahms by playing from memory the *Variations and Fugue upon a Theme by Handel.* As the learned Doctor played he analyzed the whole work: each Variation and the final Fugue—a tour-de-force which has rarely been equaled."

The date of that occurrence was 1886 or thereabouts, that is, a few years later than the date when, in England, Curwen, as we have seen, was doing a little work on these very lines.

1888

It is shortly after the publication of Prentice's able series that we find the beginning of a similar pedagogy in the United States, and it is permissible to wonder whether the fact that this also was connected with piano tuition does not indicate that Prentice's book had some circulation there. The protagonist of the idea in America was W. S. B. MATHEWS, and he went beyond Prentice, since he realized that the piano pupil should be offered opportunities of hearing music beyond that of his own performance. It will be best that I should here quote from the reply kindly sent me by Dr. Frances Clark, of Camden, N. J., to an inquiry I have addressed to her on the genesis and early development of the Musical Appreciation movement in the United States.

"The question you raise in regard to music appreciation, both the name and the thing, is an interesting one. I have kept in pretty close touch with the matter, and have made certain statements in various papers which I have written, but your request has impelled me to look more closely into the facts.

"I have an almost complete eleven-year file (1891-1902) of the magazine, *Music,* edited and published by the late W. S. B. Mathews. This was the first journal or magazine devoted to professionalized music. Some years ago I had an index made of the entire set. On receipt of your letter I went over this index. I did not find the term 'music appreciation' used at all. I then went over the magazines themselves under articles of a title which might have included 'appreciation' but found absolutely no mention of the word.

"So far as I am able to determine (and I have often seen it stated), Mr. Mathews' book in two volumes, *How to Understand Music,* published in 1888, was the first pronouncement of the new idea in studio piano-teaching, namely, that specific works should be heard by the students. His thought was that there should be much hearing of fine classical music played by the teacher or otherwise. This, of course, was a personal matter with Mr. Mathews. He was a brilliant pianist and had led himself into the realm of discovery that music should be heard.

"However, as you will note, he does not use the word 'appreciation'. The first sentence in his preface is: 'As a text book, the present work covers a new ground. Its prime object is to lead the student to a consciousness of music as MUSIC, and not merely as playing, singing, or theory.'"

About 1895–6

Dr. Clark's reference to the fact that Mathews did not use our present-day term, "Musical Appreciation", leads me to remark that I was for a little time under the impression that I had established the fact of its first use in or about 1895.

In the *Musical Times* for August 1895 I found an account of a meeting of the Musical Association in London, at which a touring party of American musicians was received and, under the chairmanship of Sir John Stainer, a paper read by my old friend Professor WALDO S. PRATT, Professor of Music and Hymnology in the Hartford Theological Seminary, Connecticut. The title of the paper was "The Isolation of Music", and the *Musical Times* describes it as "an eloquent appeal for the increased use of music as a part of general culture." The report of the paper includes the following words:

"The lecturer then gave some particulars concerning the efforts being made in America to develop musical appreciation by including it in the educational curriculum."

On turning to the *Proceedings* of the Musical Association, however, and reading the paper in full, I find that the term "musical appreciation" in this passage is used in the general sense and that by "including it in the educational curriculum" is meant merely the inclusion of the subject of music (mostly in the form of singing). Evidently the possibility of a musical curriculum directly based on *the needs of the listener* had at that period not occurred to Professor Pratt and his colleagues, though that they were ready for the idea is clear from the following passage:

"In literary study it is clearly seen that breadth and accuracy of culture depend·chiefly, not on the mere minute preparation of single extracts for elocutionary delivery, but on the intelligent analysis of and the sympathetic familiarity with large numbers of works by many masters, on many subjects, in many styles, and appealing to many susceptibilities. 'Reading', said Lord Bacon, 'maketh a full man'—meaning copious private reading for information and scope. Is it not the same with music? Technique, literary or musical, is a means, not an end. It is a necessary servant of culture, but a sorry object of worship. May we not hope that the goal of their work is not the preparation of isolated pieces for performance, but the cultivation in every student of the power to know for himself at first hand many works, by all sorts of composers, in every known form, even including hundreds that never are and never can be prepared for perfect performance? And the power to read music readily and copiously should be made to lead to an insatiable desire to go on doing so till something of the whole range of musical literature is gone over. To be a somewhat striking performer may coexist with an altogether petty and paltry muscianship, just as many an elocutionist and actor is only a literary tyro or poltroon. . . .

"One more working-out of this analogy between literature and music may be suggested. The ablest teachers of literature know that their highest mission is not to teach prose or poetry in and for themselves, as mere objective products, but to show how in these products humanity has expressed itself, how the author's personality is declared, how the author represents a period, a class, or a tendency of human development, and how in the utterance universal thoughts and sentiments are embodied and universal sensibilities are touched. It is the proud boast of literature that to study it in any proper way is to study and to know *man* in the fullest sense. I cannot but believe that music and musical education will remain somewhat isolated and fruitless until a precisely analogous ambition becomes thoroughly operative there. We may devote ourselves to the mechanics of composition or performance, we may range eagerly over the whole field of musical works and styles, we may become even learned in their formal analysis and technical criticism, and yet these achievements will be but small unless in all this study we are steadily gaining in a vital, hearty, spiritual sympathy with composers and performers as representative men, and through them with the essential life of mankind."

Perhaps it was some memory of Professor Pratt's paper that stirred the Editor of *The Musical Times* the following year (May 1896) to the expression of a definite suggestion in the direction of what we now call "Musical Appreciation", a suggestion very advanced indeed for that day. I quote the passage in full, because of its high importance:

"Considering how widespread is the love of music, it is surprising that while so much is done to educate the performer, little or nothing is done to educate the listener. We venture to urge the point upon those concerned with music as teachers. Many, of course, do not admit that 'listening' is an art to be improved by education. A short time ago, for instance, Mr. F. H. Cowen, in a bright little article on 'The Art of Composition', which appeared in a contemporary, took up this view, and affirmed that the 'lover of music must possess an innate feeling for the beauties of the art to be able to understand and appreciate them'. Now, surely this is only partially true. Love for a thing may come (and very often does) as the *result* of understanding it. What we do not understand is generally repellent. It may be true, as Mr. Cowen affirms, that among the 'educated masses' a greater proportion take an 'intelligent interest' in literature, painting, poetry, &c., than in music; but when Mr. Cowen explains this by saying that 'music appeals to a subtle sense comparatively rare in existence', we fancy the facts are against him. So far from being 'rare', this 'subtle sense' is possessed almost universally. Savages in all parts of the world manifest a positive passion for music; the 'common people' in every land have songs and dance tunes which they transmit from generation to generation, and a complete collection of which would fill several hundred volumes; every street urchin whistles and sings, or buys or makes a musical instrument of some kind and exhibits exemplary patience in learning to play a tune upon it; if a piano-organ appears in a 'slum' a crowd gathers to listen and is even willing to pay for the privilege. Why, from time immemorial every religious sect has recognized the power of music over the hearts of men and utilized it with the most successful results. Think of Luther and his magnificent hymn-tunes; of John Wesley and his; of the Revivalists, such as Moody and Sankey; of the Salvation Army tunes and bands. No, no, Mr. Cowen, it is the *absence* of the musical sense that is rare— not its presence. Says Mr. Cowen: 'Not only the composer, but the intelligent listener must be born, not made.' And this, we think, is just where the mistake comes in. It is, in our opinion, precisely the 'intelligent listener', as distinguished from the raw-material 'lover of music', that has to be 'made', and cannot, in the very nature of the case, be 'born'. Take any one who is 'fond of music'—that is to say, of a 'tune'; and *given time and the proper conditions,* you may make of him, according to his brain power, a more or less 'intelligent listener'. It is just this branch of musical education (upon which the welfare of composers so much depends) that is least attended to in our educational curriculum; and thus, while we have plenty of music-lovers, we have few intelligent listeners. To put the matter in a nut-shell: Every intelligent listener must be a lover of music, but every music-lover is not, necessarily, an intelligent listener." [1]

About 1897

I suggest, tentatively, that the next historic dates are those of the publication of two very popular books, on the two sides of the Atlantic, OLIVERIA PRESCOTT's *About Music and What it is Made of* (London—reproducing lectures given in a girl's school in 1893) and KREHBIEL's *How to Listen to Music* (New York, 1897). These books were valuable efforts, and are, perhaps, still somewhat read, for many public libraries contain them.

1903

Then comes H. G. WELLS, who must, apparently, be looked upon as one of the prophets of Appreciation. In 1903 his series

[1] We may assume the writer of this passage to be the then Editor of the journal, E. F. JACQUES. He was himself in the habit of lecturing on appreciation lines. There is an amusing account in George Bernard Shaw's reprinted music criticisms from *The World* of one of a series of Historical Recitals to which Jacques supplied spoken annotations (the year is 1892—four years before the remarks just quoted appeared in *The Musical Times*):
"On Saturday, at Prince's Hall, Mr. J. H. Bonawitz began a Historical Recital, which must, I think, be going on still, as I had to leave after the sixteenth piece, and there were eleven, including the Appassionata Sonata, yet to come. Besides, there was a running commentary, by the editor of the Musical Times, Mr. Edgar Jacques, who, being clever, popular with his colleagues, and well up in the subject, would have been the very man for the occasion, were he not afflicted with a sense of humor, with which he maintained a cheerful struggle throughout the performance. Not that the recital was uninteresting—by no means; nor was it anybody's fault that the harpsichord jingled like a million bell-wires, or that the effect of the Bach clavichord fugue upon it was execrable, or that the Palestrina *ricercare* had to be played on the most modern of American organs, or that the audience, overcome by the association of reading-desk and organ, was ludicrously solemn. Yet these things were; and when Jacques pleaded that the American instrument was 'something between' the organ in the Albert Hall and the portable organs of Palestrina's day, and frankly gave up the harpsichord as a bad job after the audience had listened to it for half an hour with unsuspicious awe, the twinkling of his eye betrayed the suppressed convulsions within. At last he disappeared from the platform for a while; and, as I seized the opportunity to slip out, I was conscious of a seismic vibration in the building, which convinced me that Jacques, hidden somewhere among the foundations, was having his laugh out. It does not do to have too clever a lecturer on these occasions unless you have all the other arrangements to correspond."

of articles, "Mankind in the Making", appeared in the Fortnightly Review (and possibly simultaneously in some American
journal). In the April issue he discussed school education.
After denouncing piano instruction in schools on account of the
disturbance it causes to the regular curriculum, and insisting that
this type of musical training belongs essentially to the "private
home province", he goes on to say:

"But it is probable that a different sort of music-teaching altogether
—a teaching that would aim, not at instrumentalization, but at
intelligent appreciation—might find a place in a complete educational scheme. The general ignorance that pervades, and in part
inspires these papers, does, in the matter of music, become special,
profound, and distinguished. It seems to me, however, that what
the cultivated man or woman requires is the ability to read a score
intelligently rather than to play it—to distinguish the threads, the
values, of a musical composition, to have a quickened ear rather
than a disciplined hand."

It is rather remarkable that an author who has never shown
any special interest in music, or knowledge of it, should have hit
the musical-educational nail on the head so accurately, and it
will be noticed with interest that the handiest word he can find
to describe the nature of the lessons he advocates is the very one
that soon came to be generally adopted; he speaks of "a teaching
aimed at intelligent *appreciation*."

This article by Wells was at the time quoted and commented
upon in the leading British musical journal, *The Musical Times,*
and may, perhaps, have had more influence than is now remembered—possibly on both sides of the Atlantic.

We now arrive at the beginnings of a definitely, widely, and
officially organized "movement". I will ask Dr. Frances Clark
to take up again her narrative of events in the United States:

1906–7

"In 1906 the College Entrance Examination Board voted to add
music to the list of subjects which may be offered for entrance to
college. This aroused especial attention.

"In 1907 was published the first of a series of six volumes, *The Appreciation of Music,* by Thomas Whitney Surette and Daniel Gregory Mason. So far as I have been able to determine, this is the first time the words 'music appreciation' have been used as the title of a book or an address, or a paper.[1] Here is the first sentence in the preface:

'This book has been prepared in order to provide readers who wish to listen to music intelligently, yet without going into technicalities, with a simple and practical guide to musical appreciation written from the listener's rather than from the professional musician's standpoint.'

"Mr. Edward Bailey Birge, in his admirable work, *History of Public School Music in the United States,* says:

'The term "appreciation", applied to music both in the broad sense of a ruling purpose in school-music and the more restricted sense of a curriculum subject, came into use in the present century. It is conspicuously absent from the discussions and writings of school-music teachers during the preceding epochs. It began to be used at the beginning of the present century to express a broadening conception of what the aim of public school music should be, and about a decade later it became thoroughly identified with studying music by means of listening lessons."

"I have examined the titles of addresses and papers given before the Music Section of the National Educational Association beginning in 1885 to 1906, but do not find the word mentioned at all in it.

"So much for the name.

"Now for the actual leading up to the teaching of appreciation. Mr. Birge mentions a number of interesting developments in the matter of giving oratorios, &c., and mentions the fact of my own series of music history courses in the high school of Ottumwa, Iowa.

[This was from 1903 to 1906.]

"There were doubtless sporadic instances of certain studios teaching music appreciation, following Mathews' music-understanding idea of playing selections for the pupils.

---

[1] Kobbé's *How to Appreciate Music* (New York, 1906) comes very near the same term, however. P. A. S.

"So far as I have ever been able to learn, there was no attempt by anybody at teaching music appreciation in the schools as a regular part of the work, either the grade [1] or secondary, until my own discovery of the applicability of the then perfected records in the fall of 1909. My demonstrations made in individual schools and later in large public groups and meetings in early 1910 led to the establishment of the Educational Department of the Victor Talking Machine Company, which I formed, beginning April 1, 1911.

"In the year 1910 there sprang up in three or four cities some beginning of the work following visits of the professors to my work in Milwaukee. If you have Mr. Birge's book you will find that he gives me full credit on pages 207 and 208.

"As you know, the perfection of the reproducing process did not bear mentionable fruit for this work until 1906, when the Victor Red Seal records of Caruso, Melba, Williams, Schumann-Heink, and Kubelik were released. Now, as you see, it was but three years after the advent of usable records that I began the actual application of using them in education.

"The idea spread very rapidly, and in five years my lists showed over three thousand cities whose work included music appreciation.[2]

"I believe, then, that this is a correct statement of the case:

'1. So far as concerns the idea of students listening to music in contrast to the then standard methods of teaching, the honor must go to W. S. B. Mathews in his above-named book, *How to Understand Music*.

'2. The first use of the term in a text-book or authoritative article is found in the book of Surette and Mason, *The Appreciation of Music*, but that book was also directed toward studio work, with evidently no thought of school work in mind.

'I do not doubt that in the twenty years interim between Mathews' Book of 1888 and the Surette and Mason work of 1907 there was some mention made of the term and the idea, but no instance is on record in public papers or addresses of such work being done, or, at all events, I have not been able to find it.

'3. So far as any application of the idea or thing itself to the teaching of music in the public schools is concerned, I think I may claim the distinction.' "

[1] i.e. Elementary. P. A. S.
[2] I call particular attention to this very remarkable fact. P. A. S.

I add to Dr. Clark's account the names of two or three more American pioneers, given in Professor Birge's book. He says that PETER DYKEMA (now Professor of Music Education in Teacher's College, Columbia University) "introduced the pupils of the Fletcher School in Indianapolis to the Wagner Music Dramas"; that WILL EARHART (now Director of Music in the Pittsburgh Public Schools) "started critical study courses at Richmond, Indiana"; [1] and that MARY REGAL undertook "an appreciation course in the high schools of Springfield, Mass."

Amplifying slightly what Dr. Clark says about the book of Surette and Mason, I may say that I understood it to be intended not merely for "studio work" in the narrow sense of the term but for class work in colleges and universities, and, apparently, even, the higher types of school. The preface states that "with the adoption in 1906, by the College Entrance Examination Board, of musical appreciation as a subject which may be offered for entrance to college, this mode of studying music has established itself firmly in our educational system." (It seems rather astonishing that in 1907 such a remark should be possible as to the effects of a reform that had only been introduced in 1906.) It is volume I of the work, with its supplementary volume of illustrations, that constitutes the essential part of it, and the aim of this is "to lay down a course of study . : . well suited to the needs of schools and colleges, as well as of general readers." Many of us in Britain at once bought this book, and its influence was considerable. The visits during several winters (beginning 1909) of one of its authors, Mr. Surette, in the capacity of a University Extension Lecturer attached to Oxford University,[2] tended to extend the influence of the book. It was probably at that time an entirely novel step for any foreign scholar to take service under a British University Extension Board. Of the popularity of Mr. Surette's teaching I myself had practical evidence. He had for two winters given courses at Rochdale, Lancashire, under the joint auspices of Oxford University and of the Rochdale Workers' Educational Association, and, on his failing to

[1] A fuller account of these courses is given in Appendix E.   W. E.
[2] I think through the influence of Mr. (now Sir Henry) Hadow.   P. A. S.

reappear in the country for a third winter, I was asked to give courses, which I did for a further two or three years. I think it probable that other young musicians in England besides myself got their start as lecturers in this subject through the enthusiasm for it that Mr. Surette had created.

1908–9

In this same year (1909) Mr. BERNARD JOHNSON, B.A., B.Mus., City Organist of Nottingham, coming out of the Albert Hall after a recital, heard a working man say "It's all right for them as understands it; I *don't!*" whereupon he started that admirable practice of giving a preliminary explanation at the piano ("never exceeding five minutes") of any large-scale work he was about to play on the organ—a practice he continued with uninterrupted success for the following quarter-century. Mr. Johnson ranks, then, decidedly, as one of our English pioneers, and, with Mr. Surette and Mr. Johnson both at work, 1909 must be considered an important year in the history of the movement in England.

Jacques's *Musical Times* suggestion seems to have had no outcome. It was only after a further decade had elapsed that such teaching as he advocated began to become common in British schools, and the definite impulse towards it seems to have come from America. A Miss A. LANGDALE, L.R.A.M., of whom I can find out very little, served as a useful link between American and British pioneers for a brief period. In a letter to me Mr. STEWART MACPHERSON generously admits indebtedness to her at the beginning of his public work on behalf of Appreciation. He alludes to an article she published in March 1908 in a paper called *The Crucible.* I have turned this up at the British Museum. *The Crucible* was a Roman Catholic magazine published at Oxford. The article is entitled "A Plea for Broader Treatment of Music in our Schools." The author uses the term "Musical Appreciation" throughout the article and makes reference to courses in American universities. It would appear that she had visited the United States at the very beginning of the definite Musical Appreciation movement there, and was anxious to see it spread to her own country.

It was two months after the appearance of this article (i.e. in June 1908) that the Music Teachers' Association was founded. It grew out of a Reading Club of Mr. Macpherson's own pupils, and Miss Langdale was, I note, a member of the Provisional Committee. A leaflet was issued stating its aims and objects as follows (I have italicized the passages that are relevant to the immediate purpose of the present discussion):

"I. To promote progressive ideas upon the teaching of music, especially with a view to the more educational treatment of the subject in schools.

"II. *To press upon the Heads of Schools, and to stimulate and maintain among teachers, a recognition of the important and often overlooked fact that music is a literature, and should be taught and studied from that point of view.*

"III. *To insist most strongly—as a preparation for the 'art of listening'—upon the necessity of systematic ear-training from early childhood.*

"IV. To promote class-singing, in which singing at sight should be the chief aim.

"V. *To realize that the amount of time at the disposal of the average boy and girl for the overcoming of the technical difficulties of an instrument is, in the nature of things, usually insufficient to enable them to cope with works demanding more than quite elementary powers of execution and therefore that it is desirable to bring them into touch with good music, well played, and simply commented on by the teacher.*"

At the inaugural public meeting of the Association at the Broadwood Rooms (the late Dr. W. H. Cummings in the chair) one hundred members were enrolled. Within a few years they had increased to one thousand. Two main planks in the Association's platform have always been (*a*) the necessity for appreciation study, and (*b*) the importance of training music teachers. The Association has held vacation courses for teachers that may be considered the progenitors of all the various vacation courses held now annually in various parts of England, Scotland, and

Wales,[1] and a Training School for Music Teachers that exists independently of it is a definite result of its propaganda. The monthly journal *The Music Student* (now *The Music Teacher*) was adopted as its organ at an early date, was largely sustained by its members, and has always been the most active exponent of the "appreciation" motive in music teaching. Mr. Macpherson, the founder of this Association, and the author of our most valuable pedagogical literature of the subject, is rightly looked upon as the Father of the Musical Appreciation movement in Britain. It may be convenient to list the chief of his books on Appreciation, giving their dates.

1910. *Music and its Appreciation.*
1910. *The Appreciative Aspect of Music Study.*
1912. (with Ernest Read) *Aural Culture Based on Musical Appreciation.*
1915. *The Musical Education of the Child.*
1923. *The Appreciation Class.*

As I myself have sometimes received from friends of the Appreciation movement undeserved credit owing to an impression that I was one of its founders, I would say that my first book with an "Appreciative" trend, *The Listener's Guide to Music,* was not published until 1919, and that although I had so early as 1900 made tentative experiments in a boys' school, and had from the beginning of the movement in the United States kept myself informed about it, yet I did not, so far as I recall, in any way appear before the public as interested in the subject until about 1910. The credit of initiating the British campaign and of fighting its early battles belongs then to Mr. Stewart Macpherson and his colleagues, to whom we owe a great debt.

Bound up with the Appreciation movement is the movement for providing Concerts for Children. So far as Britain is concerned I take it that the first to provide any regular public-series

[1] The summer holiday course of the Tonic Sol-fa College, held annually since 1876, antedates these, but was restricted in its scope and does not seem to have led to imitation. P. A. S.

of such concerts was the late Gwynne Kimpton, a woman orchestral conductor. Her concerts began in 1911; they were held in the Aeolian Hall, London; annotated programs specially written for children and short introductory talks (Dr. J. E. Borland, Mr. Stewart Macpherson, and once or twice myself) were a feature.

The 1920's

A very promising attempt was made by the Aeolian Company (on both sides of the Atlantic) from 1925 onwards, to help Appreciation work by the provision of a large library of "Pianola" and "Electric Duo-Art" rolls with explanatory matter printed alongside the perforations. I had the honor to be appointed Editor of this series and had the help of the best musical authors (and many composers) of all countries. The economic blizzard that soon set in swept this scheme out of existence after many thousands of pounds had been sunk in it.

About the same date (or a little earlier) Musical Appreciation began to creep into the program of our British music-teaching institutions (Royal Academy of Music, Royal College of Music, Guildhall School of Music, Trinity College of Music, &c.).

At the time of writing the Appreciation movement may be said to have been in existence on both sides of the Atlantic for a quarter of a century. Its fortunes have been checkered. In the United States it was much more heartily welcomed, by both musicians and educationists, than in Britain, where our national conservatism constituted an impediment. As will be realized from the quotations given elsewhere in this book there exist a certain number of leading music critics, well informed on every aspect of our national musical activity except the educational, who even after the lapse of a quarter of a century are ludicrously ignorant of the aims and methods of Musical Appreciation teaching. This condition may, however, be expected to disappear during the coming quarter-century as conversions and retirements occur. Indeed, we may hope in time to be served by a group of critics who have themselves as schoolboys enjoyed the opportunity of making in the school Appreciation Class their first extensive acquaintance with the masterpieces. It is certainly quite time that discussions as to the *value* of Musical Appreciation teaching were dropped and replaced by debate as to methods—in the improvement of which there is probably no finality.

The above synopsis presents, in as clear a way as I find myself able to compass, the genesis and early history of that movement for the Training of Listeners called the Musical Appreciation Movement. It must be recognized that there have probably in every period been individual educationists who have realized the desirability of doing something to interest their pupils and have made their experiments in various directions. Oscar Browning, as a housemaster at Eton, was one of these. He describes his efforts in certain of his books. A convenient summary of them will be found in the following letter contributed by him to *The Athenaeum* in 1920:

My DEAR SIR,—I am induced by your article on "New Year's Suggestions" (*Athenaeum,* January 2nd) to relate what I did many years ago for encouraging the love of art and music among my pupils at Eton, where I was a Master from 1860 to 1875.

I traveled much abroad, and generally returned with a number of artistic photographs. I had these simply framed and lent them to my boys to hang up in their rooms so as to displace the commonplace pictures which their taste had chosen. When they left I often allowed them to take away with them any picture which they had specially preferred; and I know this had a considerable effect in forming their taste. One of my pupils was accidentally drowned at Oxford, and when I visited his parents I found that they had hung in their drawing room the pictures which had adorned his rooms at Balliol, and they were all works of art of which he had made the acquaintance at my house. Also I was every other Saturday at home to my friends, and provided for them first-rate chamber music played by artists from London. These concerts the elder boys were allowed to attend. I knew that a large proportion of my pupils would be wealthy patrons of art and music, and I thought it extremely important that they should be brought up to appreciate the very best in these departments.

This practice was disliked by some of my colleagues, and especially by the Head Master, who thought it effeminate and demoralizing, and it eventually brought about my dismissal. Looking back after more than forty years, I am quite satisfied with the results, and think that the good I did was cheaply purchased by the loss which I suffered. I hope that others will not be deterred from following my example.

Yours faithfully,

OSCAR BROWNING.

Palazzo Simonetti,
  Via Pietro Cavallini, Roma.
January 12th, 1920.

If, however, we are to consider the mere provision in places of youthful education of suitable opportunities for hearing fine music as examples of "musical apprecation" work we must perhaps reckon Milton as the first musical appreciationist, as he is also the Father of the Children's Concert Movement. In his *Tractate of Education* (1644), after recommending the exercise of wrestling, he says:

"The interim of unsweating themselves regularly, and convenient rest before meat, may both with profit and delight be taken up in recreating and composing their travailed spirits with the solemn and divine harmonies of Music heard or learnt; either while the skilful *Organist* plies his grave and fancied descant, in lofty fugues, or the whole symphony with artful and unimaginable touches adorn and grace the well studied chords of some choice composer, sometimes the lute, or soft organ stop waiting on elegant voices either to religious, martial, or civil Ditties; which, if wise men and Prophets be not extremely out, have a great power over dispositions and manners, to smoothe and make them gentle from rustic harshness and distempered passions. The like also would not be unexpedient after meat to assist and cherish Nature in her first concoction, and send their minds back to study in good tune and satisfaction."

HISTORY OF THE ANNOTATED PROGRAM FROM 1768 TO OUR OWN DAYS

As a necessary supplement to the previous section I offer a short sketch of the history of the Annotated Concert Program.

Quite obviously such a program is an effort at "Appreciation" teaching. It is, in fact, nothing but a Musical Appreciation lesson (good or bad) in print. The only reasons I have not inserted the various material of this section in its chronological positions in the previous sections are (*a*) that it would have produced a somewhat confusing result, and (*b*) that the public mind has, curiously, never recognized the identity of the two things, so that there has been little or no apparent influence of the one on the other or the other on the one.

1768

The beginning of the practice of providing elucidations of music in the program of a concert cannot be positively dated. Possibly the earliest example is the program of a concert of Catches and Glees given by Arne at Drury Lane Theatre in 1768. It has a preface explaining the nature of the Catch and the Glee, and the various items are provided with historical and critical notes (see Cummings's *Arne*, 1912).

1783

Fifteen years later (1783) Frederick the Great's Capellmeister, J. F. R. Reichardt, a busy literary man as well as a fine musician, founded in Potsdam a regular Tuesday performance (*Concert-Spirituel*—obviously named after the famous Paris series) and provided in his program both the words of the songs and "historical and aesthetic explanations enabling the audience to gain a more immediate understanding and enabling him to attain his end more easily" (*Allgemeine Deutsche Biographie*). The "end" alluded to was the widening of the taste of the public, for Reichardt introduced a great deal of music previously unheard in that part of Germany.

1790

Seven years after this (1790) the device is found in regular application at Biberach, in Swabia, where an orchestral conductor, J. H. Knecht, introduced it. Fétis and, after him, Grove say that he had been a professor of literature, in which case his view of music was probably a somewhat wider one than that of many conductors of the time; the statement, however, seems open to doubt as it is not mentioned in *Allgemeine Deutsche Biographie*. But Knecht was a man of general and musical learning and very active and enterprising.

1813

The same general intention as that of an Annotated Program is seen in the advance articles that Weber, during his opera conductorships at Prague (1813) and Dresden (1817), used to contribute to the local papers. Wagner's treatise on Beethoven's Ninth Symphony, inserted in his Dresden program in 1846, is a noble example of the same kind of thing.

1836

John Thompson, Reid Professor of Music in the University of Edinburgh from 1841, provided analytical remarks in the program of the Professional Society of Edinburgh from 1836 or earlier, and afterwards did the same in those of the concerts connected with his professorship during the few months for which he held it before his early death. Possibly he was influenced by a letter that had appeared in *The Musical World* of 2 December, 1836, and put its ideas into practice as soon as the opportunity occurred. This letter was written by a well-known London musician of the day, C. H. Purday, and it is worth quotation as it exactly expresses the object presumed to be aimed at by the compilers of such annotated programs to-day.

"The public are not to be blamed for taking little interest in that which they do not understand. Although they know that the composition which has just been performed is the effusion of some such extraordinary mind as that of a Mozart, a Haydn, or a Beethoven, with whose names they are familiar, from the circumstance of having their works so often brought before their notice—but are as ignorant (generally speaking) of the true character, design, and end of those stupendous efforts of genius, as are the Hottentots of their existence: consequently, the performance of them, if listened to at all, is heard with indifference. To effect the object which gave rise to this letter, I would propose that a prologue, if I may use the term, should preface every performance of the works of the great masters, giving a brief and pithy analysis of the composition to be performed, showing its relative character to the mind of the musician, the feelings by which he was actuated in the production of his work, and the circumstances (where known) under which it was brought out: this would, by the novelty, in the first place, attract attention, and by frequent repetition, keep that attention alive and lead us in tracing the mind of the author through the productions of his pen; and the design of his work would thus be made clear to the understanding of the amateur, and infuse in him the desire to become more intimately acquainted with the classical compositions of the great masters."

1845

John Ella, long prominent in London musical life as the director of a chamber music organization, the Musical Union (1845-80), is often spoken of in Britain as the introducer of Annotated Programs. It will be seen that he had been anticipated, but it was probably the utility of his analytical notes over so long a period that formally established the practice, and thenceforward it became a common one.

1856

The most important series of Annotated Programs ever issued in Britain is that supplied for forty years (1856-96) by Sir George Grove for the famous Saturday orchestral concerts at the Crystal Palace. These were admirably adapted for their purpose and were stored up by many regular attendants at the concerts, so that sets of them occasionally come into the market to-day, when they are eagerly bought up by students as offering an exposition of the best musical thought and knowledge of their period applied to performances that were representative of every type of serious orchestral music then current. The articles on the Beethoven Symphonies were afterwards expanded into a book, which remains the standard one on its subject and which perfectly illustrates that combination of a persevering search for every kind of useful information with keen enthusiasm for the music itself which was characteristic of its author.

Since those days the Annotated Program has in Britain greatly declined in value. Its provision is often entrusted either to hack writers or else to highbrow writers who, losing sight of their audience and with the composer's score before them on their study table, produce a minutely detailed analysis such as cannot be followed in listening unless by a trained musician so much in love with detective work as to be willing to put aside artistic pleasure in its favor.

The standard in the United States is, on the whole, higher, and the audiences of the best series of orchestral concerts are ·supplied with much helpful guidance and, moreover, supplied with it in advance, the programs being sent to concert subscribers by mail without charge, whereas in Britain they are usually only obtainable in the concert hall and at a cost of one shilling.[1] A copy of the envelope in which the Boston Symphony Orchestra sends out its program is before the writer: it bears the words "NOTICE TO POSTMASTER: *This envelope contains an advance program, the value of which depends on prompt delivery.*" The late Mr. Philip Hale's annotations on the programs of the concerts of this orchestra from 1891 until his death in 1934 won high admiration for their encyclopedic completeness. They represent one type of such annotations—that which supplies information rather than (primarily) analysis.

It is much to be wished that writers of analytical programs would answer in their mind, before beginning each task, a few obviously fundamental questions, such as whether they are writing for professional musicians or for the general public, whether they mean their notes to be read before the performance begins

---

[1] The management of the Courtauld-Sargent Concert scheme in London now sends its subscribers programs in advance.

or during its course, and so on. If they intend the notes to be read by the general public and while the performance is in progress, then the notes should be very concise and simple and such "pointers" to musical themes should be provided as can readily be identified by the ear.

The above sketch, brief as it is, is thought to be the most complete that has yet appeared—at any rate as regards the early history of the Annotated Program, though some further details of the later history, particularly in Britain, can be found in Grove's *Dictionary* under the heading "Analytical Notes." It is probable that if any competent researcher comes to think the subject worthy of his time and attention other interesting early instances of the application of the idea of annotation will be discovered. I give here what appears to be an isolated example from America. On 12th April, 1787, the Uranian Academy of Philadelphia gave its first concert. Its "Syllabus" placed in the hands of every ticket-holder included brief comments on the pieces performed, rising to the following for the closing item (see Sonneck's *Early Concert Life in America,* Leipzig, 1907).

The HALLELUJAH CHORUS from the Messiah. By Handel.
(Introduced by three bars of Instrumental Music.)

REMARKS

Hallelujah	[Repeated often.]
For the Lord God omnipotent reigneth:	[*Here the voices unite.*]
Hallelujah: (several times) For the Lord God, etc.	[*By the Counter,* Tenor and Bass.]
Hallelujah: (several times) For the Lord God, etc.	[1st, by the treble; 2nd, by the tenor and bass, and then by the counter and tenor, whilst the other parts, through the whole of this passage, are repeating Hall. in every variety.]
The kingdom of this world, is become the kingdom of our Lord, and of his Christ	[Chorus.]

REMARKS

And he shall reign for ever, etc., King of kings, and Lord of lords:	[A beautiful fugue.] [By the Treble and Counter in long notes; whilst the tenor and bass repeat "for ever and ever, Hal." in quick notes with intervals.]
King of kings, and Lord of lords:	[Two or three times in very low notes; by the Treble: whilst the Counter, Tenor, and Bass are repeating, "for ever and ever, Hal." often, in quick notes, with intervals: *The effect is wonderful.*]
And he shall reign for ever and ever (often) King of kings, and Lord of lords:	[Several times: the harmony very full.]
And he shall reign for ever and ever, Hal.	[Often: the last Hal. very slow.]

Amusingly crude as this may be thought, it is nevertheless a true "Appreciation Lesson" in the sense that it is an effort to focus the attention of the listener upon the music and to increase his enjoyment by assuring his observation of its details.

It is needless to remind the reader that the Annotated Program has led to the coming into existence of a type of book based on its methods. Such a book in Germany is Hermann Kretschmar's seven-volume *Führer durch den Konzertsaal* ("Guide through the Concert Room"). In all the chief European languages books on these lines now exist in abundance.

The Phonograph Companies have, of course, adopted the same model for the leaflets they give with many of the records of the classics and of the more serious modern music.

In fact, the educational principle of "Appreciative" guidance is now everywhere admitted—except that if mention is made of its application in actual places of education in Britain, a certain number of leading music critics and "academic" or "high-brow" musicians express their distress (*these same critics, by the way, being in many cases among the authors of our Annotated Programs*).

THE TERM "MUSICAL APPRECIATION"

The term "Musical Appreciation" (the author of which seems to be unknown) has caused so much misunderstanding, in Britain at all events, that it would be very advantageous if we could drop it.

But unfortunately no better term has ever been suggested. At least, I think not, and I have discussed the question with various prominent musical educationists who could propose nothing better. In 1928, in the monthly journal, *The Dominant,* I offered a prize of five pounds for a term which could replace it. I will give the complete list of suggestions I received. Some of what I think the most "far-fetched" of these came from more than one competitor, and others equally "far-fetched" were supported by some logical etymological argument, which, if logic and etymology were in themselves deciding factors, would constitute strong claims to the prize. This is the list:

Musical Knowledge (but the training we give is more than an imparting of knowledge; it is largely a training in perception); *Musical Perception* (but the training we give includes the imparting of a considerable body of knowledge); *Musical Imagination, Musical Sympathy* (but these do not cover the ground and, moreover, would look very self-conscious in a school class-schedule); *Musical Culture* (too wide; it might seem to include performance); *Musical Understanding* (but is it any better a term than "Musical Appreciation?"); *Musical Intimation* (sounds odd but came from a professional psychologist and editor of a general educational journal, and he gives grounds for his choice); *Musical Receptibility, Musical Assimilation* (we can see what the proposers of these terms are driving at, but do they meet the case? Can you see them in the class-schedule or in the published curriculum of the school?); *Musical Enjoyment, Enjoyment of Music* (sound enough suggestions in their way, perhaps, conveying the very idea of "appreciation" without its ambiguity, but should we get value for the effort necessary to float the new name?); *Joy in Music, Pleasure in Music, Love of Music, Loving Music* (not possible class-schedule terms, surely); *Musical Listening* (the best yet, perhaps); *Musical Initiation* (perhaps still better); *Musical Cognition* (but fancy a child saying "I'm going to the Musical Cognition Class"!!); *Musical Self-Assertion, Musical Educement* (the sort of terms that came supported with clever argument, but, inasmuch as the argument could not accompany them in daily use, unsuitable, I think); *The Architecture of Music* (does not by any means cover the ground); *Light for Listeners* (too cheaply journalistic); *Concert Training* (one of the better suggestions, since it does indicate the goal fairly well); *Creative Insight* (nothing about music in this name); *Critical Listening* (too philosophical, however accurately it may describe our aim); *Recreative Listening* (gives the idea that the appreciation class is a mere playground).

Those, I think, are all the suggestions I received. There are just one or two that offer alternatives to the present term such as would be worth consideration if we were back in 1908, but after twenty-five years' use of a term, on both sides of the Atlantic, we should certainly not succeed in displacing it by another term a mere trifle better. However, though there is here, as I feel, no term worthy of being put forward for universal acceptance, and though I myself have never succeeded in inventing one, there are several which individual teachers or schools might prefer to adopt for their own use with their pupils. It would probably be just as attractive to call a class in the subject "a *Musical Culture Class*" (though this sounds "high-brow") or a *Musical Initiation Class,* or a *Musical Listening Class* (better, perhaps, *Music-Listening Class*), or a *Concert-Training Class,* as to call it a Musical Appreciation Class.

I can quite imagine some enterprising schoolmaster interesting a class of boys in a *Radio Class* (designed to prepare them to get value from their radio set), and, indeed, I can also imagine a successful weekly *Phonograph Hour,* or (where the teacher happened to be a fine pianist) a weekly *Piano Recital.* The less, perhaps, we use the rather unattractive term "Musical Appreciation" on class-schedules or when talking to children the better. But the training remains in principle the same whatever you call it, and it *is* Musical Appreciation teaching.

But after all, names do not matter so much as we may be thinking. The class will make its way in the affections of the pupils if the work be tactfully adjusted to their needs and carried through ingeniously, freshly, and with variety; and then whatever name is used will come to bear the right color in their minds. There are people with the most absurd and ugly patronymics who are beloved by all who know them and others with musical sounding and aristocratic names whom everybody shuns.

PART II

THE ALLEGED CASE AGAINST MUSICAL APPRECIATION

CONTENTS OF PART II

WHY AN APPRECIATION MOVEMENT?

WHEN there is any attempt at a change in the conditions of life, or work, or art we have a right to ask *"Why?"* But often the question receives its best response in another one— *"Why not?"*

So it is here. It is the former state of things, not the present attempt to change them, that should first be questioned. Since the tenth century music has increasingly ceased to be unilinear, until now it is taken as a matter of course that a musical performance implies either a combination of performers, or, if only a single performer, his use of a keyboard or other instrument capable of the production of many notes at one time and of interwoven melodies. Can that old system of musical education be defended, then, which throughout the whole school life limited the attention of its millions of potential future music-lovers to the single line of notes that their own voices could carry?

Take another point. During the same long period ceaseless experiment has been going on in the construction of musical instruments, and, since about the end of the sixteenth century, a growing sensitiveness to qualities of tone has led to ever-renewed attempts to combine them in more and more effective ways. As a result one of the outstanding phenomena of present-day musical life is the ubiquity of the orchestra, which, with its kaleidoscopic varieties of tone-quality, is in one form or another heard everywhere, not merely in the concert hall and opera house but in the place of light amusement and the restaurant, and which is electrically transmitted every evening into the home. This being so, is there any good reason why the class teaching of music to the rank and file of the scholars should confine all its attention, so far as tone-qualities are concerned, to the tone of the voice?

The complexity and variety of present-day musical effect being what they are, "Why" (if we are "Why-ing" at all) should the

37

school admit the importance of only one kind of tone, and that (in many schools) predominantly in a one-line treatment? Is it, or is it not, the intention that school training shall have some relation to the demands of after-school life?

What narrow conceptions of a great art are revealed in the fact that during the last half of the nineteenth century so many private teachers of music in Britain inscribed on their door-plate "Teacher of Singing and Music" (so implying that singing is no music at all), while the public educational authorities, paradoxically, recognized in their class-schedules the subject of "Music," meaning by that word nothing beyond singing! Cannot we now get away from all such "music-governess" and "school-marm" narrowness, looking beyond the walls of the teaching-room to the world outside, considering what musical employments and enjoyments are open to the emerging pupil, and preparing him for as many of them as possible?

But if we attempt to do this, and include in our curriculum the most widespread musical activity of all, that of the Listener, many professional musicians become excited and ask us *"Why?"* To which, as I have hinted, our best reply is probably *"Why not?"*, so putting the onus of reply on them and saving a good deal of time which we can devote to more practical matters.

In justice to the public at large, and to the general educationist, it may be added that, though they are often indifferent, it is not from them that comes the *"Why?"* but only from the professional musician and the music critic. And in justice to the professional musician and music critic it may be said that it is only from their British coteries (rarely or never the American) that we hear the chanted *"Why?"* and that, even so, the chant weakens in volume year by year.

But though it weakens it does not die away—in Britain, at all events; and though, as I have just said, we are entitled to counter the *"Why?"* with a *"Why not?"*, yet in view of the fact that the *"Why?"* is still parroted and the *"Why not?"* so often left unanswered, I feel I must do a little in the way of talking back to the critics—and of trying thus to throw a subduing cloth over the parrot cage.

It may be convenient to do this straight away—to take some of the stock objections and give them very brief but sufficient answers before entering upon the definitely practical part of the book.

"MUSIC IS NOT A THING TO BE TALKED ABOUT"

This argument is very often to be heard—if it can be called an argument in the face of the fact that it looks very like a mere assertion. It often crops up incidentally, as a dogmatic statement, but I have never happened to see it exhibited in whatever bearings it may have as a debatable proposition capable of being defended.

A typical introduction of the statement is that which occurs in an address by Professor Archibald T. Davison, of Harvard University (printed in full in the *Musical Courier* of New York, 13 December 1930). The title of the Address is "Music Deficiencies among the Average College Students" (any italics are mine).

"The question of the efficacy of good music is a subject on which I cannot be refuted. I have had active experience with good music, and I have never yet known it to fail. Good music in itself contains such vitality that you can't kill it if you leave it alone. I have always made it a principle to stand behind good music, and *to talk about it just as little as possible.* I believe that is the way to teach music appreciation. I think mere participation is the most effective way to develop music appreciation. I know that from my own experience. . . ."

"*In all the twenty years that I have had the Harvard Glee Club and the Radcliffe Choral Society, I don't think I have ever explained a piece of music.* I have allowed the students to have it and sing and sing it. After two years of that you will find they have an extraordinary taste which somehow just grows. . . ."

"I gave out the Brahms *Requiem* and felt that if I were not extremely careful I should kill the thing. We sang and sang the tenor and bass parts over and over, and when I got through they all clapped their hands and wanted to go over it again. When I run up against things like that, you simply cannot persuade me that if you handle good music properly it cannot be made to go. *And re-*

*member that all this takes place without interpretative comment of
any kind."*

It is difficult to see why this eminent musician should consider
that there is actual virtue in never "explaining," in refraining
from "interpretative comment of any kind." Some other choral
conductor who gets equally fine results would probably tell us
that on the introduction of a work of a new composer, or of
one in a style new to his singers, he invariably says a word or
two to awaken sympathy, and, perhaps, sits down at the piano,
plays a few phrases and lays bare the general plan of the
composition, and that by doing this he feels he gains an initial
advantage of importance. I myself, in youth, as a member of a
choral society, was thrilled by Hans Richter's suddenly breaking
off the rehearsal of the Beethoven Mass in D (in the "Agnus
Dei", where the key signature changes to two flats) and, in his
broken English, saying such words as to the inner meaning of the
music as thrilled every member of that great Yorkshire chorus.
Taking down my copy of the music I see that I promptly
recorded his thoughts on that page and others of the Mass, and,
with youthful enthusiasm, altered the title-page so that it reads
*Missa Solennis in D composed by L. van Beethoven, with a
few Remarks by Hans Richter.*

Of course, if Richter had been what we may call a "gassing
conductor" his poetry (for it was that) would have made less
effect on our minds. We were there that evening to sing, not to
have an Appreciation Lesson, but my point here is that the practice of one of the greatest conductors of the world was opposed
to the nowadays-so-common, highbrow, cast-iron theory as to the
sinfulness of "interpretative comment."

It is difficult to believe that there can be positive virtue in
such a negative policy as "never explaining," or that anything
is gained by making an absolute rule of eschewing all comment.
The impression I get is that Dr. Davison is getting fine results
from his singers as most who get such results do—by technical
skill as a choral trainer, an infectious enthusiasm, and that
inexplicable quality of "personality", and is then doing what

such people also often do—putting down his success to the practice of a few personal notions that have little or nothing to do with it all, though it may be interesting to hear of them.

It is curious, too, to notice that in the same address Professor Davison spoke of Appreciation as a necessary subject in secondary schools. (He is alluding to the subject of Harmony, which he wishes to exclude because "there is sufficient to be done in secondary schools by way of appreciation and ear-training.") Now Appreciation, as a curriculum subject, necessarily involves a certain amount of "talking about" music—cannot, indeed, be carried on without it. Yet a little later he not only hopefully discusses a certain proposed means of elimination "drivel courses in music appreciation" (would that there were means of eliminating drivel courses in *all* subjects!), but adds that if his idea were put into operation, "There wouldn't be much time to talk about music."

Reading this I turn to *Music Education in America, What is wrong with it? What shall we do about it? by Archibald T. Davison* (1926), and find the value of the Appreciation Lesson fully recognized and approval expressed for (at the right school age) "dilation on reiterated motives and rhythmic figures, on inversions and augmentations, on form and content," for "instruction in the simpler forms, some treatment of the structure of music . . . historical and aesthetic comparison of styles" (pp. 70 and 88). One is compelled to conclude that this very able musician, like a good many others, has not quite co-ordinated his ideas.

It may also be pointed out that Professor Davison's choral society consists of people with instinctive musical leanings, self-selected from the general mass, and that either (1) they have evolved appreciation for themselves (in which case they do not enter the present question), or (2) they have at some earlier stage been taught to appreciate music (in which case they are a shining example of the value of Appreciation Lessons).

The Appreciation of Music is surely on all fours with that of the Appreciation of Literature. There are hundreds of courses in the latter subject, all over the world. Where the teacher conducting the course offers not "drivel" but what we may fairly call "illuminating comment" he is greatly contributing to his students' interest and understanding. There is, then, no reason on earth why a teacher should make a point of merely bringing the students into contact with masterpieces and then trusting to their unaided perceptions. If he cannot, by judicious "pointers", call their attention to features of interest and value that they would without this have overlooked, either they are geniuses and need no teacher, or else they are unfortunate, for they have none.

Is it common sense to admit that progress in the arts of Composing and Performing may be forwarded by a teacher's comment but to maintain that progress in the art of Listening demands a holy silence? If it is, then let us do away with all Annotated Programs, all books on the lines of Groves' *Beethoven and his Nine Symphonies*, with Wagner's "Programmatische Erläuterungen" on works of Beethoven and other composers, and a pile of further very respectable writings.

It is my impression that if I were to send for the syllabus of the Harvard musical courses, or to discuss them with a musical Harvard student, I should find that a good deal of talking about the masterpieces is done by Dr. Davison, and indeed to talk about a work of art one loves seems to me to be almost a human necessity.

Let us now balance the stern American critic of "talk" with a British one:

"Talking about music always seems to me like keeping small boys outside a sweet shop explaining to them how the sweets are made. Let the small boy eat his sweets—let the public listen to music. Generally speaking, I view the modern teaching of musical appreciation with great distrust, and as I replied to a lady who asked me to express on a post card my views upon it: 'Appreciation in music is like modesty in life—both are indispensable, but there is no need to mention either.' Listening to music is the appreciation of an art, the direct impulse from one mind to another. And if it is true that this appreciation of art is creative in itself, the method which would teach the listener to understand music through the mind of someone else stands condemned."

That comes from the *British Music Bulletin* (organ of the British Music Society). It is signed "G. T. Holst," whom the Bulletin describes as "now one of the most successful *teachers and writers* on music in London."

That dates it, of course! I think about 1920. It will be seen that Holst was then considered a successful "writer on music." What *is* the difference, by the way, between writing about music and talking about it?

Anyhow, Holst used to talk about it, too. What about his Alsop lectureship at Liverpool and his temporary post at Harvard? And what about his occasional lectures on Byrd and Purcell? All these anti-talkers talk. And a good thing, too!

Then there is Vaughan Williams, who, as reported in the London *Observer* lately, said:

"My advice to all who want to attend a lecture on music is 'Don't; go to a concert instead!' "

Yet he himself had a highly successful career as a Cambridge University Extension Lecturer. Of course, this recent pronouncement may mean repentance, but those members of his audiences up and down the country who got their first knowledge of English Folk Song at his courses feel the need of none.

And, too, there is Archibald Grosvenor, the "Idyllic Poet" of *Patience*:

GROSVENOR. "Here is a decalet—a pure and simple thing, a very daisy—a babe might understand it. To appreciate it, it is not necessary to think of anything at all."
THE LADY ANGELA. *Let us think of nothing at all!*

"EITHER A MAN IS MUSICAL OR HE IS NOT"

This principle is, of course, equally applicable to any attempt to interest people in painting or in literature. *The Times Literary Supplement* lately, in reviewing *The Appreciation of Art*, by Eugen Neuhaus, spoke as follows:

"Somehow the very notion of a deliberately cultivated 'appreciation' of art excites hostility. In spite of the undoubted fact that people have been helped in such appreciation the stubborn conviction remains that if a man does not appreciate art as naturally as he does his dinner he had better leave it alone."

The reply to this "stubborn conviction" can be taken from a London evening paper of a few years earlier. A Royal Commission had just recommended that English literature (instead of the Latin and Greek classics) should be made the basis of culture in English schools and a writer in *Blackwood's Magazine* had protested against this. The *Pall Mall* settled him as follows:

"The objection he offers is that those who are fit to appreciate literary beauty will seek and find it for themselves, while those without such perceptions will only be stimulated in the class-room to 'false admiration and insincere criticism'.

"Upon this fatalistic reasoning no kind of teaching that is not strictly utilitarian would be worth giving—and, of course, the objection to English would apply with redoubled force to the classics themselves."

(Substitute at the beginning of the passage "musical" for "literary" and, at the end of it, alter as follows: "and, of course, the objection to Musical Appreciation would apply with redoubled force to Singing Class work." Then the objection is adapted to our purposes and so is the reply to it.)

The fatalistic objection often comes from professional musicians. The following, by Mr. Alex Cohen, M.A., a violinist and chamber music player of high artistic and professional standing in the English midlands, is an example. He is (in *The Radio Times,* May 1933) opposing radio attempts to prepare listeners for the music they are going to hear:

"We all either have something already within us to respond to the first intelligent reading we hear of a work or we have not; and if we lack this essential neither cold print nor warmer *viva voce* commentaries will of themselves supply the deficiency or enlarge our spiritual boundaries."

I venture to offer here some evidence from my own early life. It so happened that Mr. Cohen and I attended the same school— a school which at that date was newly founded, prided itself on its wide curriculum and was announced by a great educational authority of the day (Lord Playfair), after an inspection of schools all over Europe, to be the best equipped he had ever seen. Lord Playfair was an eminent scientist (in his earlier days he was Professor of Chemistry at Edinburgh University) and a practical man, and was doubtless impressed by our laboratories, workshops, gymnasium, &c., all of which were bigger and better than any at that time existing in a secondary school.

Looking back at my school experience I find that I got from it a sort of spiritual awakening—late in school life, when I was, perhaps, fifteen. The laboratories had done nothing whatever for me (I lay the stress on "me", of course); the workshops had done more. But I got most from a series of three yellow-covered books whose very name I have forgotten (though I remember that they were published by Longmans), but which offered what may be fairly called an Appreciation Course in English Literature. They gave me well-selected extracts from all the great writers, with a few biographical and critical notes (which notes I eagerly read), and set me searching the second-hand bookshops for volumes of "Cassell's National Library" (the 3d. paper-backed edition, sold second-hand at 2d. or, if very dirty, 1d.; the 6d. cloth-backed edition at 4d. or 3d.). I accumulated a library of my own and reveled in it. I began to appreciate literature as distinct from mere recreative reading. I rarely had a lesson out of those text-books, because the over-worked master took the period when they were in use as an opportunity to correct exercises, leaving the class to do its own study: I can now see that a little sympathetic and understanding direction from the master would have been an advantage, but there being no examination in this subject he felt he could reserve his energies, and so I got the "cold print" of which Mr. Cohen speaks, but not many of the "viva voce commentaries".

Later a clerical uncle, seeing the taste that had been awakened in me, gave me his copy of Gosse's *History of Eighteenth-Century Literature;* then I bought Stopford Brooke's little primer of English Literature. Leaving school I got a position as Assistant Librarian in the University of which Mr. Cohen a little later became an undergraduate. Daily seeing the late Professor Ransome and being attracted to his personality I read his *Studies of Shakespeare's Plots,* and was introduced to a new and very human kind of appreciation study.

And so I went on. I have never become a "literary character", but it is largely a taste for literature that has made my life a happy one, and, so far as I can see, I owe it to the accident of "The Doctor" (a headmaster of scientific attainments, rather than literary, but a lover of all good things) including Literary Appreciation (not under that name, of course) in the curriculum of the upper classes of his school and making a happy choice of a text-book.

Whatever Mr. Cohen may say, "cold print" *did* "enlarge my spiritual boundaries"—and if only there had been in the school some "cold print" and "warmer *viva voce* commentaries" on the subject of pictures and music I should guess that those boundaries would then sooner have been "enlarged" in other directions.

Personal experience counts more than theory in the building up of our convictions, and nothing can now shake my view that school life should offer youth the incentive to experiment in as many directions as possible, so that he may discover where his natural tastes lie.

And I would not limit the bounds of "youth" too strictly. When in the earlier days of Radio I was for five years Music Critic of the British Broadcasting Corporation, I received (literally) thousands of letters from listeners many of whom, in their twenties, thirties, and forties, were, for the first time in their lives, discovering that they were endowed with a taste for an art that they had never previously thought worth their attention.

At what age the human mind closes its lid and locks it I do not know. Does anybody?

"SOME PEOPLE ARE HOPELESS"

The argument is often advanced that as some pupils have no musical sense class teaching of musical appreciation is largely wasted.

It is curious that one never or rarely sees this argument applied to the class teaching of Singing. It is almost always Musical Appreciation that is singled out to receive the blinding blow of this fatalistic argument. However, the two passages I am going to choose for quotation do seem to show a little wariness on that point, for, though chiefly directed against Musical Appreciation for the Masses, as we may call it, they speak in fairly general terms, and so imply an application to all forms of musical instruction.

The first passage comes from an article in *The Times*, by Dr. H. C. Colles, its chief music critic (8 July, 1922):

"It is the fashion just now among certain musicians to proclaim loudly that everyone has some musical susceptibility, capable of development if it is caught young enough and treated rightly. 'Aural training', class singing, and listening to gramophones have been impartially acclaimed as infallible recipes for the creation of a musical nation. In so far as this means the realization that a great deal of musical capacity has been allowed to run to waste in the past, and a determination to conserve and foster it by every conceivable means in the future, such pronouncements have their value. But experienced teachers know that the general proposition is untrue. Every school will show a certain proportion of children who make no response whatever to any kind of musical stimulus."[1]

A more violent pronouncement on the same subject is this, by the musical writer of the *Belfast Telegraph* ("Rathcol"). It is part of a long Commination Service in which there is expressed some sympathy with the intentions, however mistaken, of the sinners of Musical Appreciation, all this effectively offset

[1] A Scottish logician who has happened to stroll in as I was correcting my typescript of this passage, grumbles at me as follows: "I think you treat the Colles extract with too much respect, and do not come down heavily enough upon its unfair controversial method. Of his five sentences, the second is a frank parody of the appreciation case used for rhetorical purposes. Sentence 3 states the appreciation case with a certain approval but then, in sentence 4, he refers to his own parody as 'the general proposition' in order to destroy it, whereas he has stated and approved of the general proposition in his sentence 3. In sentence 5 he has to hedge behind the words 'a *certain* proportion'." Perhaps the reader may care to pencil in the numbers of the five sentences and then follow the logician through his analysis. P. A. S.

again, however, by the round statement that *"music for the million is a blatant hypocrisy."*

"The craze for using music as a subject of 'general culture' and forcing it upon young people whom the Creator did not endow with any special aptitude for music has done, and will do if it be pursued, more harm than good to the cause of art. That it may add to that vague equipment called general culture, I admit; but general culture (in 99 out of every 100 only a smattering of ill-digested knowledge) is a species of education for which I have no use.

"When I myself gave weekly Appreciation lectures in a public school in this city I felt myself, more and more each week, to be one of the hypocrites. If I could have taken out about half-a-dozen musical and deeply interested boys from the forty or fifty I addressed, I would have been perfectly happy, and so would the half-dozen, I believe. As it was I could not help feeling sorry for many poor fellows who were, no doubt, yearning to be away at an easel or at the 'lab.' or the carpentry room."

In reply to these two typical expressions of this common objection it may be said:

1. It is admittedly almost true that "every school will show a certain proportion of children who make no response whatever to any kind of musical stimulus", but, as no educationist who has investigated the phenomenon puts the number of such deficients above 2 per cent., that fact is, in itself, of little administrative importance. There is probably quite a 2 per cent. average of mathematical deficiency, yet classes in mathematics have to be carried on and the whole body of children must pass through them.

2. Even the unmusical 2 per cent. are not necessarily forever [1] hopeless. Every teacher of class singing in an infant school can tell of "drones"—children whose attempts to join with the others result in a mere monotone—though they apparently imagine that they are, like their companions, faithfully following the curves of a tune. The remedy (generally, I am told, effectual) is to put the "drones" at the

---

[1] The American reader is advised to refer now to p. 277 for information on the organization of English schools. W. E.

front of the class and induce them for a time to listen carefully instead of actively singing.[1-2] When in classes of older children one finds such deficients they have probably not had the advantage of sympathetic and understanding treatment at an earlier stage.

It is possible that some musical deficients are only so through not having *heard* much music around them. Radio is probably everywhere reducing this factor in deficiency, yet it was as recently as 1930 that Professor Charles A. Fullerton, who has devoted himself generously to the special problems of the thousands of isolated rural schools in the United States, recorded that half the children above the third grade in the schools of Iowa could not sing the tune of *America* correctly.[3] (*America* is our *God save the King,* and is as current in the United States as in the British Empire—with other words, of course.)

It is very easy to be misled into thinking hopeless an individual who is not really so. When I was a school music master I had a case of a boy who was not merely a monotone but under my testing could not even tell me whether a passage I played on the piano went "up" or "down". It then occurred to me that his

[1] The late Edith M. G. Reed, Editor of *Music and Youth,* who had enjoyed great experience with classes of young children, told me that she sometimes found the defect to be one of voice production, and remediable when treated as such. Probably other thoughtful teachers could tell the same tale. P. A. S.

[2] In the United States the majority of teachers believe that the monotone ("drone") is vocally awkward, not aurally defective, and consequently they teach him to sing correctly, not to remain silent. W. E.

[3] Feeling sure that some unreliable report, though certainly one that must have appeared trustworthy, had fallen under Dr. Scholes's observation, the American editor submitted the above statement to Mr. Fullerton. The paragraph in his reply that relates to the point in question is as follows: "I am glad you wrote me, for the statement in Dr. Scholes's book would be very misleading. I do not remember of ever having said this, but one of my assistants who spent some time in the Extension Division of the Teachers College in teaching music in the rural schools collected some statistics from the schools that had not had any contact with our choir plan of teaching singing from the phonograph. I found that in all the *one-room rural schools* examined [my italics] there were only 64% of the children above the third grade that could sing America accurately, and when I included the first three grades also in the examination there were only 50% of them that could sing America accurately. Let it be understood that these were all rural schools that had not been touched yet by our choir plan. Judging from my experience in rural schools beginning twenty-three years ago, I think that it would be a fairly accurate statement of the conditions at that time." W. E.

answers were too invariably wrong to comply with the Law of Averages, and on carefully observing his case I found that he was, in this very elementary test, *not* always wrong, but, actually, always right! He had never grasped our conventional application to music of the ideas, "up" and "down" and "high" and "low", which he applied in the reverse way. This boy was, however, not merely a monotone in music but a dunce in every subject, and I abandoned him; in the light of what I now know I believe something might have been done with him.

Apart from these occasional "monotones" one has in any class a gamut of musical perceptions and powers varying from the very slightly musical to the very highly so. In this the music teacher is in exactly the same position as the class teacher of every other subject in the school's curriculum.

The difficulty of teaching sight-singing to a mixed class is extreme, and is one of the causes of the usual high percentage of failure. Few teachers, in my experience, have sufficiently worked out and practiced methods by which pupils of quick "ear" and high musical intelligence may be enabled to retain and even increase their interest while the less gifted are being helped onward; and fewer still have found means of avoiding the ever-present danger of the less musical or less conscientious pupils taking every note of a sight-singing exercise from the more musical or more conscientious and joining in it instanter instead of singing it "on their own", right or wrong. When I was engaged in inspecting music in schools (as for some years I frequently was on behalf of London University and, for a period, our national Board of Education) it was a constant experience with me to hear a singing teacher get very admirable singing of reasonably difficult sight-reading tests, and then by looking for and eliminating the one or two "leaders" unkindly to reveal to that teacher the disturbing fact that many members of his class were habitually doing no reading at all. Nothing but continual individual testing will check this commonest of all singing-class faults.

Problems of this sort happily do not occur with anything like the same acuteness in the Musical Appreciation Class, where exact measures of ability are impossible or at least undesirable (as creating the wrong "atmosphere"), but, of course, there exists the same variety. So, too, in any big concert room audience there are probably heard a thousand different versions of a symphony. A few keen-eared natural or trained musicians present perhaps hear all the composer meant them to hear. The rest hear, some of them one detail and some another, or perhaps we should say get one general impression or another; yet all, if they give their mind to the music, may get pleasure and mental and spiritual profit from the performance. So it is in the Appreciation classroom.

So it is in church when the sermon is preached, so it is in Parliament when some orator holds forth, so it is with the readers of a volume of poetry, so it is with the readers of the present book. All this is quite normal, and there is in it nothing to worry about.

I need hardly add that, given this varying capacity on the part of the members of his class, the Appreciation teacher must be on the alert to keep the keen interest of all those members, so that, although their capacity thus varies, effort to listen keenly may not do so. It is in his ability to "carry with him" all these different grades of musical intelligence that the good teacher reveals himself. In that he is little different from the good teacher of the French language, English Literature, Physics, or Mathematics. None of these subjects is by any school principal restricted to pupils of what the *Belfast Telegraph* writer calls "special aptitude", and every teacher of these subjects has probably at times longed, like him, to pick out the "half-dozen" from the "forty or fifty." If there is teaching in Heaven no doubt it will be under such conditions—St. Cecilia in cap and gown instructing "Rathcol" and myself and a carefully selected group of a few other musical saints and angels.

It seems to me that *the test of teaching is not whether you have trained the child all you would like to train him, but whether you have trained him higher than he was.* In correspondence with a Perfectionist-Selectionist I once put the matter as follows (without, however, converting him):

"In any class of forty you will have (say) four who will listen keenly to the piece you perform to them, twenty who will listen moderately, with attention divided, and sixteen who will not trouble to listen at all. Surely that teacher is very lacking in technique who cannot by a few well-chosen words, and by playing the themes of a composition a few times, etc., manage to promote a few of the sixteen in the lowest grade to the middle grade and a few of the twenty in the middle grade to the top grade. My fear is that the whole conception of Musical Appreciation is going to be vitiated by a demand for impossible perfection. Let us be content if we can give some help to some pupils and in another sense never content until we can give more help to more."

Is "General Culture" quite so despicable a possession as "Rath-col" and some others think? I recall a young relative of mine who had taken at an American university a cultural course of so varied a character that any British university official would dismiss it with a sneer. My relative, however, defended it. He had been shown what the various sciences and arts "were like", he said, and so had had avenues opened in many directions for his future choice. His life work declared itself to him by the finding of his major interest.[1] His business success and the steady recreation he has found in various branches of literature, music, and painting have, I consider, justified his education. But here we approach the deep places of educational theory, and I will not wade further in.

Nothing that I have written here or elsewhere is to be taken to mean that I myself believe that by Musical Appreciation classes you can make every child in a school "musical", or give every one of them the blessing of a listener's interest in music as a hobby for after life. There must inevitably be a percentage of failure in teaching this subject as in teaching any other. The trouble is that there is no real ascertainable certainty as to where in the class the failure will occur, for any youthful mind may be closed to a particular interest at one age and then, miraculously,

[1] Incidentally he then felt impelled to come to England, go through a specialized course in the branch that had so interested him, and take another degree. P. A. S.

open to it at another. We have got to pursue a "hit-or-miss" policy; no help for it!

I have seen the percentage of failure to evoke an interest in music held up to derision, with the proverbial tag: *"You can take a horse to the water but you cannot make him drink";* but I see in this no argument against taking horses to water. The time may come when by psychological tests, scientifically applied, every pupil's full potentialities can be discovered and recorded at the outset, and individual curricula framed accordingly. Meantime if we are to consider the pupil a horse and the arts as water our motto must be *"Take all the horses to the water and some of them will drink."*

In approaching the close of this section may I return to the subject of mistaken diagnosis?

A correspondent who is music master of a boys' public school in England writes to me: "In the junior school there is a boy, aged twelve, who was considered unmusical until, as a result of the Appreciation Class, he went home and sang the principal themes of the Fifth Symphony and asked his mother to buy the records with his accumulated arrears of pocket money." So you never know!

If Beethoven had been a schoolboy under me and I had found (what was the fact) that he could never dance in time, I might have dismissed *him* as fundamentally unmusical. Descending somewhat from the Beethoven level I will now for the first time reveal to the world at large what just possibly some one of my old schoolfellows may recall—that I myself, although I have since earned my living by music, was at school excluded from the singing class as having "no ear". The explanation is simple. When I entered that school I found the sight-singing and ear-training conducted on the Tonic Sol-fa method, which was totally new to me. My first teacher in this new school noted my inability to make anything of his *Doh-ray-me's* and *tafatefe's,* and told me to sit at the back of the class and do any other work I liked. What boy would refuse such an offer? I profited by the opportunity to begin an intensive study of the fiction of foreign adventure, and when at the end of each year promotion came, informed the next teacher "Please Sir, I've no ear; I never sing." Thus did I go through school, and the only profit that came to me from the singing-class work was that when, as a temporary Government Inspector, I found in a secondary school in South London sixteen boys out of a class of thirty-five sitting at the back of the room and reading books on the plea of "no ear", I was able to utter an enlightening word to the innocent music-master.

You, perhaps, who read this will smile and say that you, as a teacher, would never be taken in as I with Beethoven or my teacher with me. No, but you may make your mistake in some other way. Experience shows that it is almost impossible to "spot" the child who is utterly incapable of music.

Remember Beethoven and me!

Addendum

On the general subject of this section I have later consulted that very experienced practical teacher, Miss Mabel Chamberlain, of London. She writes to me as follows:

"1. I have come to the conclusion from my own personal experience that the number of children totally unable to benefit from musical training is no more than 1 per cent. But with these conditions: the training must be begun at 3 or 4 years of age and be continuous and properly graded. I would not exclude anyone from music lessons at least up to the end of the junior school (11 years of age), because it would not be safe to say definitely before then that a child would not benefit from training. Indeed, I have one case in mind of a girl (on the border line of mental deficiency) who had not responded to music and who was surprisingly and definitely awakened by rhythmic movements at the age of 13 years, when she came into contact with music expressed through movement. (She had missed it earlier, unfortunately.) *All* her work improved and she moved off the border-line of sub-normality.

"After 11 years, if children have had *proper* training and are still unresponsive, I might approve of their withdrawal from the music course. This proportion need be no more than the 1 per cent., I should say.

"2. When we come to the remaining 99 per cent. I am not able to say that, in my opinion, these can *all* be brought to an appreciation of a Beethoven symphony, even though their training may have been ideal. For this reason. The appreciation of a Beethoven symphony requires more than a knowledge of music as a language. It demands a certain stage of evolution, and all have not yet reached that stage. . . . You will probably appreciate my point when I draw an analogy from a spoken language, English, for instance. You may train every child in a school to read and write English, but when adult life is reached the various individuals will find their level of reading. For a few, a *very* few, I am afraid, it will be Shakespeare (comparable with the Beethoven symphony), with a large number it will be the typical popular novel (comparable with the bright, tuneful music of the obvious type which is broadcast in large quantities), and for a small number it will be the tuppeny novelette, *Tit-bits,* etc. (comparable with, and often not so vital as, jazz and low comedy).

"I know you feel that with training all can be brought to an appreciation of a symphony [*I don't!* P.A.S.] but I, with my philosophy and noting other people's reaction to other phases of life, cannot feel that this is possible within the span of one short earth life.

"This does not preclude the duty of a country to provide a *liberal* and *broad* education for all its young people. Given this, every individual can benefit as far as he is able. Offer to the pupil all degrees up to the symphony, and he will find his level. We must not be disappointed if many are unable to appreciate fully the highest, but we must offer the wide range because of the widely different degrees of development in human beings."

To this I add for the reader's consideration, some opinions of one who does not claim to be a musician, but has a great experience in education, Mr. A. B. Ramsay, now Master of Magdalene College, Cambridge, but at the time he uttered them Master of the Lower School of Eton College. (His reference to "public schools" must not be misunderstood by any American reader. In English usage this term means the large schools, generally boarding schools, for the children of the upper middle and upper classes, to which they go at the age of about fourteen.) This is what he says:

"Perhaps I may be allowed to state, with all deference, an opinion drawn from the humdrum study of boys' natures and from the few facts of my own experience as boy and tutor. I believe that the natal endowment, the mysterious, particular, physical arrangement of the brain cells, is necessary in the first instance. So far I agree with the Philistines—'*Nascitur non fit*'. But the next moment I am at war with them. For I am convinced that the native instinct exists in infancy in thousands of cases where it has never been suspected. It is the good gift of God, falling by the wayside, unrecognised and left to perish, or choked by the thorns of busy and quarrelsome homes. As with every other divine talent, the buried capital is not enough, the interest must be made by human care and industry. The flame must be fed; when once it is extinguished it cannot be rekindled. Therefore the responsibility lies with the parents in the first instance; and I fear that the words *nascitur non fit* may be given another meaning which truly represents the condition of many children naturally endowed. The material is there, but nothing is done with it. The genius is born, but, too truly, is not made.

"By the time the boys come to a public school their musical destiny is almost determined. They may be classified under four heads:

I. The boy with no natural talent. He comes to us in the same condition, whatever pains have been taken to make him learn. And I cannot help thinking that he will remain in that condition and that time and trouble are often wasted upon him.

II. The boy with a natural talent which has been entirely neglected. Can it be recovered at such a late date? I don't know enough about this even to venture an answer; but it would be interesting to hear the opinion of those who have tried.

III. The boy with a natural talent which has been neglected, but not entirely. I have a fervent belief that this boy should be rescued at all cost. I have many friends in this class who express undying gratitude to those who encouraged or compelled them to stick to music at school. "We were all the while behind", they say, "and could never hope for brilliant achievement; but we learnt enough to make music a beloved companion to us in after life, a source of perpetual enjoyment."

IV. The genius who has not been neglected at all. Simply from the argument of probability I conclude that the *rarity* of this bird is an absurd thing. It cannot be that, if all children were given the same chance, the number of talented boy performers would be so small. But here, as in Class II, I am out of my depth, and will leave the question to those who are better qualified to consider it."

"THE APPRECIATION TEACHER DEALS IN NOTHING BUT AIRY FANTASY"

This allegation is almost as prevalent as that of the "drunk and disorderly" in a London police court charge-sheet. Here is an example, quoted from Mr. Fox-Strangways by Mr. A. K. Holland in the *Liverpool Post* (14 November, 1927):

"A tentative hand went up and a diffident voice said 'Waves'. 'No,' said the teacher, 'the wind—the zephyr that blows over the Atlantic, across the Gulf Stream, through the Devon combes, that comes to us full of birds' cries, that, &c., &c.' And the diffident mind sank abashed; the opening heart knew that the path of music was closed for ever, if it could mistake waves for wind." [1]

To me, frankly, that case, exactly as reported, is incredible, though something remotely like it *may* have occurred, for not all the fools among teachers are occupied with mathematics, history, classics, and modern languages and literature. Mr. Holland evidently gives it credence; indeed, he goes further:

"I could quote scores of instances, in my own experience, of an even more disastrous nature, cases where the child's mind has been filled with these phantoms of a crude 'poetising' instinct, not *after,* but *before* the music itself was allowed to be heard."

I do not in the least like doubting the word of a friend, but I cannot but think that there is a little exaggeration here. "*I*

---

[1] I see that Mr. Holland quoted the story from *Music and Letters,* October 1927, and find that Mr. Fox-Strangways begins the anecdote "A man who knows tells me what once happened in a National School. The teacher played a piece of music and asked what it suggested." A similar, yet substantially different version was given in *The Musical Times* of December 1926, in the summary of a lecture by Geoffrey Shaw at Grantham; the title of the lecture was "First Steps in Musical Appreciation." (Compare report of another lecture, quoted on p. 71 of the present work.) P. A. S.

could quote scores of instances." I wish I had, at the time, and while Mr. Holland's memory was thus overcharged, relieved it by asking him to quote, say, just two or three score—with names, dates, and places.

And anyhow, *that* is not "Appreciation". If some butter merchant has been palming off on you margarine for best butter you do not write to the papers to say "Butter's no good!" However, I can perhaps hardly charge Mr. Holland with quite all this illogicality, for he assures us that he has "never abused the thing itself but only its methods". As I understand Mr. Holland's attitude it really amounts to something subtle like this:

"I don't object to butter if it's good butter, but it never is."

On a previous occasion this same writer had said in reviewing a book, "It is not a course in 'musical appreciation', as generally understood, for it is an outline not of fantasy but of fact." There is an example of libel by allusion!

"THE APPRECIATION TEACHER DEALS IN NOTHING BUT HARD FACT"

Plenty of examples of this charge can be found, as for instance the following:

"The most successful people in spreading musical culture are those who talk least about 'appreciation', a term which might well be regarded with suspicion whenever it threatens to roll off the end of one's tongue. Moreover, it has never been demonstrated to our satisfaction that that kind of analysis which tells that, after so many bars, we come to the first subject, and so forth, serves any useful purpose to the casual listener. After all, if one is interested in Mathematics, the Differential Calculus is vastly more entertaining."

It is fair to add that before and since June 1926, *The Music Teacher,* which so pronounced on that date, has carried courses of articles on Musical Appreciation. This was a momentary aberration; probably the summer of 1926 was a hot one.

The following is by Edwin Evans, and appeared in the New York *Musical Courier* of 20th December, 1920—a long time ago;

we may assume that the writer now knows better, but the expressions used give a hint of the opposition against which the Appreciation movement has had to fight in Britain:

"In the nineteenth century music completed its cycle by reverting to the stage when its mysteries were jealously guarded by the medicine man, who, for all we know, gathered round him a select company of adepts. If society were still at that primitive stage there would be a penalty inflicted upon those who dared to intrude at a concert unless they could give the pass-word proving that they had been duly initiated into the mysteries of sonata form."

Baldly and formally analytical Appreciation Lessons, we may suppose, have sometimes been given; since baldly analytical Annotated Programs are unfortunately pretty common. Here, for instance, is something printed as first aid to the public in a London program of a few years ago:

"The principal theme (a) on which the whole poem is built is given out in the Introduction, first on muted Horns, then on the Clarinet. This is followed by a small but important motif (b), played by 'Cello solo and answered by the Violas. A condensed form of theme (a), worked in with (b) during accelerando, brings us to the Allegro. The motif of the Allegro (c) is founded on the principal theme (a). This motif, or slight variations of it, brings us to the Andante, which is formed on the theme (b) and is given out by the Clarinet. At the end of the Andante the themes (c) and (b) form the development, and theme (a) is also heard on Strings. A descending motif (d) from the Allegro is used for the climax, which is quickly followed by a recapitulation of the Allegro very much condensed. The Andante motif is this time played by the Strings and accompanied by Trombones, and, later, triplets played by Horns form an important counterpoint. A motif (e) is formed from end of the Andante and given out by Wood-wind. This works up to a Stretto, which, gradually quickening, prepares entrance of chief theme given out by six Horns in unison. A further Stretto brings us to Finale, giving forth theme (e) by Horns and Trumpets in Octaves."

I could readily produce dozens of program notes pretty much on these lines, and have only picked this one because it happens to be written and signed *by the composer himself!* I am not, however, going to generalize a condemnation of Annotated Programs because they are sometimes foolishly factual, nor should any one condemn Appreciation Lessons on those grounds.

Very many examples of this kind of objection to Musical Appreciation work might be given. Often they come from critics who, like Mr. Evans, are adepts at the art of writing that kind of musical analysis which in the shape of "Annotated Program" notes helps an audience to listen to a piece of music with more comprehension than they could otherwise have done. Such notes are merely printed Appreciation Lessons adapted to the adult intelligence, and as every reader of this book may be supposed to approve of them (when drafted with an intelligent grasp of the psychology of the listener, as Mr. Evans's certainly are), there is no need to discuss the objection further.

There is, I suggest, something a little offensive in such expressions as we often read from the pen of music critics who do not happen to be in sympathy with the Musical Appreciation movement. As an example I offer the following, dragged by the hair of its head into an article on Alban Berg's *Wozzeck* (Mr. M. D. Calvocoressi in *The Listener,* 8 March, 1933). It will be remembered that Berg claims to have based his various movements on distinct musical forms, but so elusively that though their use can be substantiated they are not perceived by the listener:

"Here not even the most specious of 'Musical Appreciation' experts could tell the listeners 'what to listen for'."

"MUSICAL APPRECIATION MEANS TECHNICAL TERMS"

This absurd charge is sometimes seen, as, for instance, in an article by "A Musician" in the *Daily Mail* (5 July, 1927):

"There are well-meaning people who profess to teach 'musical appreciation' by explaining these technical terms. They seem to imply that if more people could talk about the 'inversion of the second subject' England would be more musical! It is as if familiarity with the language of the cookery-book would better one's appreciation of good food. It is the palate that needs attention, not the vocabulary."

All that, of course, is nonsense. Musical Appreciation is concerned with the living facts of music, not the names for those facts—except so far as names are necessary handles by which to take hold of facts.

(The general question of terminology receives attention elsewhere in this book.)

"APPRECIATION MAKES THINGS EASY"

This argument is at the date of writing still commonly used. It is based on a charge which takes two shapes. Sometimes it is stated that the protagonists of Musical Appreciation delude innocence by pretending that to appreciate music is an "easy job" (whereas it is difficult), and sometimes it is stated that they make it an easy job (whereas it should be difficult).

For example, Dr. Harvey Grace, in *The Listener* (21 December, 1932), discussing Fétis's *Music Explained* (see p. 4) says:

"*Music Explained* has at least one merit that is not common to its modern successors: it makes no pretense that the understanding of music is an easy job. Fétis is all for knowledge as the basis of enjoyment, whereas, according to some present-day appreciators, the listener need do little more than turn on the wireless or gramophone, fold his hands, and sit rapt in a sea of sound."

So also Dr. W. G. Whittaker (*Musical Times,* September 1932):

"This lamentable condition of affairs has been made worse by continual preaching that music can be easily understood."

These are instances of the first shape of the charge—that the Appreciationist deludes the tyro into believing that musical appreciation is easy. That shape of the charge which alleges that he *makes* music too easy generally amounts to an assertion that to learn to perform music is the only way to learn to appreciate it. Examples of this are given on a later page.

The first shape of this charge is easily answered. *The whole Musical Appreciation movement has actually originated in the observation of too easy-going an attitude on the part of the public.* People listen to (say) a Beethoven string quartet with half an ear, fail to grasp what is going on, feel bored, and then declare either that they do not care for Beethoven or that they do not care for Chamber Music. The injustice done to the more modern (and particularly contemporary) composers by this hearing that is not listening is particularly regrettable. If a piece of new music fails to run in the old familiar channels, and thus demands effort on the part of the audience, it is, by many people, at once condemned.

The Appreciation movement exists to remedy this. It shows those who come under its influence that music is full of detail which is lost unless *Attention* is given ("Attention!" might, indeed, be called the very motto of the movement).

It also shows that no amount of previous knowledge and experience is too great if one is to get pleasure out of the more complex sorts of music.

It aims at inducing people to work for their pleasures. It tells them that you cannot bring water from the well unless you possess a bucket in which to draw and carry it, and it urges them to provide themselves with the bucket—which will necessarily be at first a little one but which will, miraculously, grow bigger as they use it.

The allegation that *"according to some present-day appreciators the listener need do little more than turn on the wireless or gramophone, fold his hands, and sit rapt in a sea of sound",* is on the face of it absurd. There may be some mad athletic coaches and authors of books on athletics, but none so mad as to open their instructions with *"All the would-be athlete needs to do is to lie on a soft sofa."* What would be the purpose of training athletes or writing on athletics if there were "no more to it" than that? The book that began like that would be a small one, for it would obviously be complete in the one sentence! We have some neat little guides to Musical Appreciation, but none so miniature as that! Musical Appreciation must, of course, have some foolish teachers (every subject has), but none so foolish as to expect to make a living out of telling people "You don't need me!"

This curious error has, I think, originated in a natural way— though one that is not open to any very acceptable apology on the part of those who have made it. Musical Appreciationists do undoubtedly (and properly) speak encouraging words to their pupils. They do not say *"Listening to music is easy"*, but they do say, *"Work, and listening will become easier."*

But then they add, *"What baffles you now need not always baffle you."* They continually cry, *"The summit of the mountain is worth the climb"*, and they even say *"The effort of climbing will itself be found enjoyable."*

Taking up that mountain metaphor, not only do they cry *"The mountain is worth the climb"*, but they try to find the easiest paths. This is apparently an affront to some advanced musicians. As Mr. W. R. Anderson has wisely said (*Musical Times,* June 1931), "The man who has had to make his way without much help is sometimes apt to be a little severe. 'I had to find out for myself; let them do the same.' " He adds, "It is the philosophy of discipline and sound at bottom."

At bottom it *is* sound, but some very unsound superstructures are reared upon it. Obviously, in the teaching of any subject, there is a proper mean between doing everything for the pupil and doing nothing for him.

If you mean to do nothing for him you are, of course, no teacher, and the idea of the anti-appreciationists seems to be that, in the matter of listening, no teacher is the best teacher. ("I had to find out for myself; let them do the same!")

If this No-Teacher policy is to be applied at all let us honestly apply it all round. On the face of it there seems no more valid reason why youth should be left to struggle unaided towards an appreciative understanding of Music than toward an appreciative understanding of English Literature (and every school tries to help its pupils along that road).

And, turning to musical subjects, is there more reason why one pupil should be willingly helped to produce counterpoint or orchestration than that another, who has no creative bent, should be helped to "follow" them when they are produced?

Nobody complains of the professional student of music being asked to attend a class in the History of Music in the college of which he is a member, but, apparently, to hold listeners' classes in the history of music (and a suitable treatment of history forms a definite part of every Appreciation Course) is dangerous, and, indeed, immoral.

This idea that it is immoral, or at best weakening, to help students along their difficult track has really nothing in it. *Every teacher of every subject makes that subject as easy as he possibly can to every pupil.* He does not work the pupil's sums for him, but he shows him how to work them, and then gives him plenty to work so that he may exercise himself. And he makes the "showing how to work" as simple and lucid as he can (in other words as *easy* as possible), knowing that thereby he saves time and enables the pupil to get deeper into his mathematical studies. This is exactly what the teacher of Musical Appreciation does.

To *awaken an interest* in the various subjects, and then *to make their study easy* are aims of our whole educational system. The more interest you awaken and the easier you make the course the farther the student will travel. Save him effort that is needless and he has the more energy left for that which is needful, and can do his work more thoroughly and carry it to a higher point.

The argument about "making music easy" has, then, no validity—in either of its shapes.

It sometimes comes from keen teachers of piano and organ. Do they not make things easy? Of course they do. They teach and the pupil practices. The same division obtains in Musical Appreciation. It must; there is no other way!

In their objection to ease, the writers just alluded to remind one of Mr. Dooley's dictum that "It doesn't matter what you teach children so long as it's hard enough", and of the view of the good seventeenth-century Puritan, Dean Owen, that the Holy Spirit had arranged variations between the manuscripts of Scripture in order to encourage diligence in Scripture Study. And we may exclaim, as did the Quaker Penn on reading the Dean's idea, *"Whence came this whiffle and whimzy within the circumference of thy figmentitious fancy?"*

"APPRECIATION MAKES THINGS DIFFICULT"

This objection is less often heard, or we might take it and the last as mathematically canceling out, or as resembling the two mutually and equally destructive Kilkenny cats, whose strife left not a shred of either in existence.

It will be best to define this complaint by a quotation from an able article in the London *Musical Times* (August 1931), by Professor Howard D. McKinney, of Rutgers College, New Jersey. He is not unsympathetic with the ideals of Musical Appreciation but criticizes the methods:

"Take up a book on musical appreciation and note the method of its procedure: it is that of the teacher mind. Music is presented from the very first as a mental discipline to be gained through an intellectual process. Emphasis is laid on the necessity for recognizing phrases, themes, rhythms, details of instrumentation, &c. The whole thing is made difficult, and we take the attitude of priests of a sacred cult rather reluctant to admit neophytes into our order, and then only after initiation into the meaning of certain rites. Even so good an educationist as Mr. Grace bemoans the fact that the study of Appreciation has become so easy. We have forgotten, or perhaps never understood the fact that making it hard will never accomplish anything, that the learning of musical enjoyment is not a disciplinary process, is not even an intellectual one; that, on the contrary, music's prime function, even more than is the case with any of the other arts, is to give pleasure. I read recently a professional dictum which represents the attitude of most of us: 'Until we shake ourselves free of the accepted convention that music is primarily concerned with entertainment, we shall never enter into the full conception of her an an art'. Stuff and nonsense! Of course music is primarily concerned with entertainment, the finest entertainment in the world, in the broadest sense of the word, as something from which pleasure may be gained".

I will only add to this that the opponents of Musical Appreciation cannot have it both ways, and that if Professor McKinney's description of text-books of the subject is admitted to be accurate (a point that will be discussed later), then I am compelled to admit some force in his objection.

With his description of music as "entertainment, the finest entertainment in the world", would many of us quarrel? I cannot imagine any Appreciationist doing so.

"APPRECIATIONISTS TELL PUPILS WHAT IS 'GOOD MUSIC'"

This charge has often been made—always, I think, by the music critics of newspapers. Here are some examples from Mr. Ernest Newman, who in *The Sunday Times* has for some years interjected occasional gibes on the point. I have before me at the moment several relevant cuttings from his articles in that paper, dated from 1927 onwards.

"The writers of musical appreciation courses have done their best —though perhaps, when all is said, their best does not amount to much, for all this baby-talk about fugue and sonata form and structure and design and all the rest of it throws practically no light on the real Bach or Beethoven—to show us just why good music is good." (6 March, 1932.)

"Form really explains next to nothing in musical aesthetic; formally a canon or a fugue by Klengel or Kiel is the same as one by Bach, but as *music* the two inhabit quite different worlds. In what, then, does this difference reside? Has any exponent of 'musical appreciation' ever made it clear?" (2 July, 1933.)

To this last rhetorical question we will give a categorical answer. No "exponent of musical appreciation", as such, has ever concerned himself with this aesthetic problem, which is not his business but that of the critic.

The said "exponent" may discuss form, but this is merely to remove an obstacle to appreciation—in the sense of sensitivity. Obviously the listener who does not know in the least what the word "fugue" or "sonata" implies is at a disadvantage when he

hears one.   More obviously still, if it has never occurred to him
to listen to middle and under strands in the music, as well as to
the topmost one, he is, again, at a great disadvantage.   If his
observation has not been trained to recognize the difference
between the tone of an oboe and that of a viola he loses a great
deal of orchestral color.   And, similarly, if he has not the
remotest idea of the relative periods and the differing styles of
Bach and Beethoven, he is likely to remain partially deaf to their
music.

It is with those practical things that the "exponent of 'musical
appreciation' " concerns himself.

Mr. Newman maintains that "principles of form do not guarantee good taste."   This dictum has the approval of us all.
To train taste is difficult, and the "appreciationists' " general
attitude to the problem is that all they can usually do about it is
to ensure the child hearing plenty of good music, and being
put in the way of hearing it intelligently—after which they must,
perforce, trust to the gradual natural growth of powers of
discrimination.

How do Mr. Newman and others get hold of this wrong idea
of what Musical Appreciation means?   The suggestion I receive
is that the ambiguity of a word has misled them.   One of the
dictionary meanings of "appreciation" is "estimation, judgment"
(*Concise Oxford Dictionary*); but go on with the dictionary entry
and you come to "perception, adequate recognition"—and those
are the senses in which the word is used by musical educationists.[1]

It is regrettable, perhaps, that a word with a variety of meanings should have been adopted as the label for a useful type of
educational work, but it is still more so that after a quarter of a
century of such work, and the publication of a large number of
books upon it, the nature of the work should not have been
grasped by certain eminent writers upon music.

[1] In a rough-and-ready way it may be said that the verb "to appreciate" includes the two ideas of "to esteem" and "to estimate" and that in the term
"Musical Appreciation" the idea intended is, widely, "to esteem" and not at all
"to estimate."   P. A. S.

(The big general question of the training of taste is further discussed elsewhere in the present work; the question of the use of the word "Appreciation" has been discussed in an earlier section.)

"APPRECIATION TEACHERS OVERRATE MECHANICAL MEANS"

Here is an example of this allegation (Francis Toye in the *Morning Post,* 18 November, 1926):

"An enormous new public has undoubtedly come into music, but it is not approaching music in the old way. It is a very cheap, and, aesthetically, insensitive public, which seems quite content to eschew concerts, and to take its music from the gramophone and radio.

"In the main it believes that these useful contrivances provide music which, if not absolutely ideal, is satisfactory enough for all practical purposes. Even (perhaps especially) the more earnest portion of our new musical democracy is convinced of this. Have not those dangerous heretics, the 'appreciation'-mongers and the education-fanatics, been encouraging such a point of view for years?"

This criticism seems, unfortunately, to reflect the so-frequent music-critic view that only direct hearing in concert hall and opera house provides any musical sustenance worth absorbing. To any musical enthusiast not tainted with professional and "high-brow" narrowness it must be a source of high satisfaction to run through the correspondence columns of the British journal, *The Gramophone,* or its one or two American counterparts, or of *The Radio Times* and *The Listener,* and to realize what an enormous new public is now interested in the classics of music or the efforts of contemporary composers, and considers them matters worth thinking and arguing about. The impression one gets is certainly not that of "a very cheap, and aesthetically, insensitive public", but of a public that is increasingly using its ears and its judgment, forming its own opinions and fighting for them, and we may as well frankly admit that "appreciation-mongers and education-fanatics" think that far more good than harm has come out of the invention of means of taking fine music into the homes of those who never did go to concerts and probably never would have done so.

If the opponents of "mechanical" music would examine their souls (with a microscope if necessary) they would find that at the back of all their criticism is some lack of sympathy with their fellows, and if they would then turn to the Parliamentary debates at the time when it was proposed to introduce universal elementary education (1870), they would get further light on the question. It is an aristocratic bias that here disturbs social understanding. These people want to maintain an "aristocracy of art." Some of them actually use this immoral phrase.

"APPRECIATION IS NOT SO GOOD AS THEORY"

This curious statement has been met with.

"We hear a lot about aural training, and about 'musical appreciation', and without disparaging the importance of these, and the more especially of the former, elementary theoretical knowledge takes us further ultimately." (H. V. Jervis-Read, A.R.A.M., in the *Music Journal* of the Incorporated Society of Musicians, May 1931.)

This manner of setting up one study against another is indeed curious. It is rather difficult to see what would be a near parallel of it in (say) the study of English Literature. Perhaps the following:

"We hear a lot about bringing the pupil into contact with the masterpieces of prose and poetry, and trying to awaken his interest in them, but without disparaging the importance of this, spelling and grammar take us further ultimately."

I can only say that I fail to see any logical basis for such statements. Spelling and grammar, necessary as they may be for the writer and speaker, have little bearing on literary appreciation, and the "elements" of music, however necessary they may be for the composer and performer, have equally little on musical appreciation: the one type of work cannot then be a substitution for the other, though it may be a useful complement.

This statement looks merely like another unprovoked slap or

pinch for Appreciation, offering no basis for any discussion, and we can thus dismiss it.[1]

"APPRECIATION IS OPPOSED TO TECHNICAL PROFICIENCY"

This allegation is only occasionally heard, but it is best to include it in our survey.

"Some of the professors of the mysterious new subject called Musical Appreciation appeared to foster the notion that technical proficiency was not only unnecessary but even to be looked upon with suspicion. One frequently heard it at Competitive Festivals —which were, in his opinion, pernicious institutions—and it did incredible harm."

The association of Musical Appreciation and Competitive Festivals here is curious, and can presumably be ignored, as merely a side hit.

In reply to the charge against the "professors of the mysterious new subject" (the address in which the passage occurs was delivered in 1930, but the subject was, in this quarter, still regarded as "new and mysterious") it will be sufficient to say that a request for the names of one or two of the "professors" whose lack of wisdom formed the basis of the charge evoked no response. The whole statement is erroneous, and it is pleasing to note that the gentleman who made it (in a very public way at the 1930 Conference of the Incorporated Society of Musicians) has since introduced Musical Appreciation lectures into the curriculum of the institution of which he is the distinguished head. He must know more about the ideals of the movement now, and that is why I have suppressed his name. But the allegation he made was widely reported, may still linger in the minds of some, to the unfair discredit of the Musical Appreciation movement, and hence is properly mentioned here.

It is safe to say that *no* teacher of Musical Appreciation has *ever* declared or believed that technical proficiency is to be

---

[1] It is fair to the writer quoted to make it clear that he is not alone in his views. See remarks in M. D. Calvocoressi's *Musical Taste and how to Form it* (pp. 10 and 18). P. A. S.

"looked on with suspicion." All the Musical Appreciation teacher does is to point out that "technical proficiency" has its place not only in the arts of Composing and Performing but also in that of Listening.

"MUSICAL APPRECIATION IS BADLY TAUGHT"

So it doubtless often is. So is Sight-Singing. So is every subject. If we are to remove from the national educational curriculum the subjects that are somewhere or other badly taught that curriculum will suddenly become a blank.

That effort should be unceasingly made to secure better teaching of Musical Appreciation is of course evident. It can never be well enough taught until the world produces more fine musicians who happen to be also born teachers—which, of course, is equally true of such subjects as piano and sight-singing.

There is rarely seen any direct charge that Musical Appreciation is the worst-taught subject in music, but that impression is certainly given by the curious way in which musical and other journals select any reference to bad Appreciation teaching that may be made by any lecturer or speaker at an educational conference, and give it prominence, denuded of its context.

So a lecture by Dr. Geoffrey Shaw, H.M. Inspector of Music in Schools, given at the Oxford Summer Course in Music Teaching, August 1932, was thus reported in the *Morning Post, The Music Lover,* and other journals [1] (what follows is the whole report):

"The eleventh Summer Course in Music Teaching at Oxford has given Mr. Geoffrey Shaw, H.M. Inspector of Music, the opportunity for some cogent remarks. On Wednesday of last week he said: 'Many women sit down at a piano, usually a very bad one, and play not very well a piece of music, not a very interesting piece, to a class of children who are not at all interested. Then they ask them what the music represents, and after several guesses one child may hit

[1] I think that what happens on these occasions is that a local reporter, hearing a bright bit in a lecture, sends it out all over the country, so drawing his "penny a line" from a great many papers simultaneously. Whenever Dr. Shaw gives that lecture this is the bit the reporter picks. See footnote on p. 47. P. A. S.

on a likely suggestion. It is just a game with all the little shibboleths of a game. Can you imagine a more woolly-minded way of doing things?' "

Now Dr. Shaw is a known supporter of the Musical Appreciation movement, and we may be sure that in alluding to Musical Appreciation he said about it some very different things from that.

And when he asked *"Can you imagine a more woolly-minded way of doing things?"* he could not have resented it if some members of the audience had got up, told him of experiences in singing classes and piano lessons, and put the same question to him. Some of the greatest stupidity with which I myself have ever met has been in the teaching of those subjects, but I would not have anybody believe that on that account I condemn the country's teachers of sight-singing and piano, and still less would I have them believe that I think these subjects not worthy of a place in the educational system.

It is not unfair to say that, in Britain, Musical Appreciation has from its introduction been exposed to a steady process of denigration on the part of musical journalists (with, of course, a few splendid exceptions), and such reports as that just quoted seem to be designed to make it an object of ridicule. Some writers on music are made this way. If they hear of a single instance where musical appreciation teaching has come into the hands of a fool they are shocked and feel the necessity to tell the world, but if we call their attention to the fact that there must be over 20,000 schools in the British Isles through which the pupils pass without hearing the name of Bach or Beethoven or making acquaintance with any music but the simple unilinear music produced by their own voices they do not turn a hair.

So perverse is Human Nature!

"MUSICAL APPRECIATION ENDANGERS THE SINGING CLASS"

This fear is sometimes expressed. It has not appeared a great deal in the press, perhaps, but I get it sometimes in private letters and I gather that it lies at the background of a great deal of the opposition to Musical Appreciation. Here is an extract from a letter received:

"I cannot agree that time should be stolen from the Singing Class for anything concerned with mechanized music. It is always the Singing Class which is robbed for every conceivable subject, and it is the most musical hour in the school curriculum."

Where a separate school period can be secured for Musical Appreciation of course every one interested in that subject would prefer this. Where this is not possible (or stated by the school principal not to be possible—which amounts to the same thing), surely the claims of the Singing Class might yield a little, either one lesson in four being given to Musical Appreciation, or fifteen minutes of each lesson period, whichever the teacher finds most appropriate to his particular way of treating the subject.

Can it not be that the widening of the pupils' idea of music by taking it momentarily out of the unilinear aspect, by bringing to their ears various types of instrumental tone (instead of confining them to vocal tone), and also by introducing historical and biographical interest, may have a very favorable reaction on the definitely singing-class work?

Moreover, is not the view I have quoted (which comes from a much respected leader in musical education and one very far from antagonistic to the Appreciation ideals) wrongly oriented? He loves children's singing, sees in it a valuable social and artistic influence, and so, apparently, School Music is for him primarily Singing—with a willingness to admit other branches when that has been amply provided for. Would it not be more truly educational to look upon school music *as* Music; as the opportunity of bringing into the child's life a branch of art of the highest value, and then to consider what time can be secured for Music, what various approaches to Music are possible in school life, and how the time can be best shared among these? Perhaps some approaches must be reluctantly put aside for want of time, but at any rate *Music qua Music* should be the basis of consideration and not *Music qua Singing,* with other branches as mere after-thoughts.

I cannot but think that there is in some educationists' minds an unperceived "hang-over" from the old days when musical instruments were not to be found in schools, the Phonograph was not invented, Radio not dreamed of, and "music" in the British Educational Code meant, perforce, singing and such theory as lies at the back of vocal sight-reading. When Matthew Arnold was Government Inspector of Schools he always used "Music" in that way, e.g. speaking of an inspectoral visit to a London training college in 1861, and discussing "Music", he says:

"The students receive one lesson in the theory and one in the practice of singing from notes." [1]

Right into the twentieth century that particular official use of the word "Music" persisted and that view of school music— and apparently this condition has still not quite disappeared. Singing-Class work is looked upon as the necessity, and all other treatment of music as, at the best, a desirable luxury.

The "Appreciationist" does not wish to abolish or in any way weaken the Singing-Class work of the school. He regards Class Singing and Class Appreciation as complementary, representing as they do the dual position of the ideally-situated human being towards the art of music—his position as performer and listener.

If the element of composition can be brought in (as, indeed, it can by means of simple efforts at "melody making") all the better! Then the Music of the school represents, in its elementary way, the threefold activity of the human being in music— as *creator, executant,* and *receiver* of musical expression.

That would seem to be the ideal, and probably represents the proper starting point in planning a course.

Returning to the extract from a letter given above: the so-common use of phrases like "anything concerned with mechanized music" seems rather regrettable. This is argument by epithet. The writer of this letter is known to have no antipathy to

[1] *Reports on Elementary Schools, 1852–82,* by Matthew Arnold. Published by His Majesty's Stationery Office, 1910. P. A. S.

"mechanized music" as such, yet when engaged in friendly debate he unthinkingly weighs his side of the balance by a prejudice-creating phrase. So do many.

Suppose we rewrite the sentence for him:

"I cannot agree that time should be stolen from the class in which the children use their own voices for the use of their ears in listening to the string quartet, the orchestra, madrigal choirs, examples of music through the ages, and the like."

Does the view now look quite as reasonable?

I would like to add that I have seen this teacher's singing-class work and can testify that so far as such work can be made the basis of musical culture his was. But even under the direction of the best teachers of the world (of which I frankly consider him one) such work can only go a certain distance.

The "Singing Class" is an admirable and indispensable institution—but it is incomplete. Music, not Singing, is the thing!

"THE OTHER ARTS DON'T HAVE 'APPRECIATION' "

Music is the only Art in which Appreciation teaching is considered necessary. This statement is constantly repeated. For instance, the very well-known English writer on music who for a while assumed the pen-name of "Matthew Quinney", said in *The Radio Times* (14 February, 1930):

"*The large crowd of us who are fond of books . . . do not therefore start Book Appreciation Classes, or demand of the B.B.C. weekly talks on books and the Ordinary Reader.*"

As another instance of the same idea I quote Mr. A. H. Fox-Strangways, in *Music and Letters*, October 1927.

"Everyone wants nowadays to 'appreciate' music or to induce others to appreciate. That sounds kind and thoughtful, and two questions naturally occur. *Why is it done with regard to music only? And why was it not done before?*"

Take any syllabus of lectures for the general public, such as the Extension Lectures of Oxford, Cambridge, London, and

Manchester Universities, and there will be found a provision of far more courses of lectures upon the appreciative side of Painting, Literature, and Architecture than of Music. I have been one of the Extension Lecturers in Music of all those Universities, and we were always far outnumbered by the Extension Lecturers who were giving similar courses in Painting and Literature.

Take the syllabuses of such organizations as the Evening Institutes of the London County Council, and the same will be found.

Examine book publishers' catalogues. There is an easy way of doing this. Every five years the whole of the catalogues of the British book publishers are bound into two great volumes, each almost a foot thick, and are provided with an index volume of 1,600 pages of the smallest type, the whole costing £2 10s. 0d. It is a fascinating possession, and its Author Index and Title Index enable one to find particulars of any book that is in print. It can be seen at all the bigger public libraries.

I lift down from my shelves the massive Index Volume and turn to the Title section under "Appreciation." Here are books not only on music, but also some with such titles as *The Appreciation of Architecture, The Appreciation of Art, The Appreciation of English, The Appreciation of English Literature, The Appreciation of Poetry,* and *The Lesson in Appreciation* (this last covering all the arts).

But if you really want to find helpful books of that kind you should turn to the entries beginning "How to". British publishers, at the present moment, have on sale over 350 books with titles beginning like that. You can be told "How to" do anything you want to do—*How to Abolish Slums, to Appeal against Rates, to Apply for a Situation, to Argue Successfully, to Avoid all Diseases, to Become a Convincing Speaker, to Become an Auctioneer, to Buy a Car, to Bring Men to Christ, to Catch Coarse Fish, to Compose a Song, to Pray* (there are separate volumes on "How to Pray Well", "How to Pray Always"), *to Make a Fortune, to Secure a Good Job, to Select the Laying Hen, to Sing, to Stay Married, to Vamp* (dangerously ambiguous, this!), *to Use a Banking Account, to Use an Aneroid Barometer, to Use a Microscope, to Use your Mind, to Read the*

Gospel, to Turn People into Gold, to Succeed in the Christian Life—in Exams.—On the Stage.

I call particular attention to this list, because the world and its inhabitants are always experiencing troubles of one kind or another and in view of the low price of most of these 350 books the continuance of any perplexity as to how to get rid of them is clearly unnecessary. The most helpless individuals are considered in the provision offered, as will be seen when I mention that the list even includes *How to be Happy in Switzerland.*

Amongst those world troubles, of course, is the excessive leisure (sought or forced) and the tendency to employ it for the less worthy distractions. The "How to's" provide for all that, however. We find not only a *How to Enjoy Music* but also a *How to Enjoy Prints, How to Enjoy Pictures, How to Enjoy the Bible, How to Enjoy the Old Masters.* We find not only a *How to Listen to Music,* but also a *How to Look at Old Churches* and a *How to Look at Pictures* and a *How to Observe in Archaeology.*

And so on, and so on, and so on. There is to-day endless provision of books, classes, lectures on the appreciative side of all the arts; officially conducted tours of art galleries, with historical and elucidatory comment are now a happy commonplace of city life; yet, again and again, we see music critics and the more conservative sort of professional musicians coming out with this thoughtless statement—*Music is the only art in which Appreciative teaching is considered necessary.*

It will have been noted that one of the writers just quoted, writing in the British Broadcasting Corporation's official weekly organ, was allowed by its editor to make the astonishing suggestion that the B.B.C. did not attempt Appreciation work in Literature. It has always done so. The Corporation is kind enough regularly to supply me with all its syllabuses, &c., and as they appear I file them. Taking up casually one or two of them of dates previous to "Matthew Quinney's" article I find courses of "Talks" on *Poetry and the Ordinary Reader; Six Tragedies of Shakespeare: an Introduction for the Plain Man; The Bible as Literature,* and so forth. These are strictly comparable with

the Corporation's course on *Music and the Ordinary Listener*
and the like, and represent the exact parallel of normal Musical
Appreciation courses. So does such a course as that on *The
Meaning of Pictures,* also anterior to this writer's article. Shortly
after his article appeared there opened a fine course by J. C.
Squire on *The Enjoyment of Literary Forms,* the first talk being
devoted to "How to Appreciate Poetry", so that here we meet
the dreadful word itself—without protest from any literary highbrows, I think.

If objectors to Musical Appreciation would only inquire a
little they would find that some of the finest critical minds in
Painting, Architecture, and Literature are constantly busy in
Appreciation teaching, by mouth or pen. This is especially true
of literature. There must be hundreds, if not thousands, of
books about books, designed to help the thoughtful reader to the
appreciation of the poetry and prose of various periods, the
writers often being authorities of very high eminence. And
these books exist not merely in English but in all languages.

On the face of it there seems no good reason why music
should not be similarly treated. The population at large finds
it easier to appreciate a book than a string quartet.

It is curious that no objections are ever raised to Appreciation
work except when it is done in connection with Music. What
watch-dog has barked over this announcement which appears
regularly in the London *Times?*

"The Courtauld Institute, a department of the University of London, has been founded to provide teaching in the History of Art as a
means of education, and as a basis of appreciation. . . ."

"One man may steal a horse when another must not look over
the fence", and the painters, sculptors, architects, and literary
men are daily doing Appreciation work not only without raising any protest but, apparently, without a good many of our
musical writers so much as noticing what is going on.

"CONTINENTAL NATIONS DO NOT GO IN FOR MUSICAL APPRECIATION"

This statement is sometimes made. So far as I know, my friend, Mr. W. H. Kerridge, then Secretary of the British Music Society, first set the ball rolling, and another of my friends, Mr. W. R. Anderson, kept it on the roll by an article in the Journal of that Society in which he said:

"What is the answer to the conundrum which Mr. Kerridge propounded with such disarming modesty; how is it that in Germany, which seems to have nothing corresponding to our treatment of 'appreciation' as a speciality, they seem to have been tolerably musical for quite a long time?"

Among others the Editor of the *Musical Mirror* (March 1933) then took a kick at the ball:

"One would like to know the reason why this 'educational' palaver as applied to music is so necessary in England and America and presumably unnecessary in Germany, France, Austria, and other leading European countries."

And so it goes on—with the result that there is growing up a legend that Britain and the United States are the only countries in which any one thinks of teaching music from any point of view except that of the performer and composer.

It is to me inconceivable that educationists in other countries than those should overlook the fact that the education of children's ears for listening is as nationally important as the education of their throats for singing or their fingers for playing, but to put the matter definitely beyond dispute I applied to Professor Dr. Hans Mersmann, formerly Assistant Professor of Musicology at the University of Berlin, Professor of the Stern Conservatory, Professor of the Berlin Hochschule, Director of the Prussian Commission for the Collection and Publication of Folk Tunes, author of *Applied Musical Aesthetics, The Study of the Phenomena of Music, A History of Musical Culture by means of Examples* (4 vols. to date), *Modern Music since the*

Romantic Period, The Idioms of Modern Music, &c., Editor of *Melos.*

He writes to me as follows (April 1933):

"In reply to this question, I would say that Education for Listening to Music unequivocally pervades our present-day school musical activity, though to varying degrees. The reform in school music of the last decade, which has replaced the earlier *Singing* teaching with *Music* teaching, centres itself definitely upon the understanding of masterpieces, (*rückt gerade das Kunstwerk und die Vorbereitung zu seinem Verständnis stark in den Mittelpunkt*).

"Naturally the question of method is a more difficult one than that of aim. Generally speaking it can be said that the poetical explanation of music, formerly common, is to-day in a great measure superseded by more objective methods.

"Attention is given both to the association of such work with the actual making of music, not overlooking instrumental music, and to the preparation by means of Phonograph Records for the receiving of the proper impressions from masterpieces. The school radio apparatus also plays its role—though that has not yet been fully developed.

"With all these matters the official Ministries of Art of the various German States have been intensively occupied during the past ten years.

"Personally I have concerned myself particularly with methods of musical analysis and of a type of musical education resting upon this—one which shall seek to base itself not merely upon knowledge but, above all, build itself up in a practical way upon experience of the Art. This policy has been carried out not only in the Training School preparation of the Music Teacher (who ought to be capable not only of teaching his pupils to perform but also of teaching them to listen), but also among the general public, to whom I have addressed myself by means of Broadcasting."

It will be clearly seen from the above that German educationists, quite independently of any influence of reformers among their British and American colleagues (for such influence is, we may say, non-existent), have adopted much the same view as these as to the necessity of radically adapting music teaching to modern conditions.

If inquiries be made in other European countries it will, I believe, be found that the Musical Appreciation idea has sprung up independently in many of them. I happen to live in Switzerland, and the music master of the Collège (secondary school) in the neighboring town has several times been to me for phonograph records which he can use in Appreciation work in his school (he does not use the word "Appreciation", but, as I gather, he is doing work to which we should decidedly apply this name). My friend Mr. Wouter Hutschenruyter, formerly Director of the Conservatory of Music at Rotterdam, tells me that in Holland there is a good deal of what he calls "Education to the Enjoyment of Music" and describes to me the curriculum of a secondary school in Amsterdam, equipped with electrical phonographs and a large library of disks, including the *Columbia History of Music*.[1] Professor Adolf Cmíral, of the State Musical Conservatory, Prague, sends me interesting details of the use of the phonograph in "receptive training" in music in some of the Prague schools.

In the Instructions as to Secondary Education of the French Ministry of Public Instruction, published 2nd September, 1925 (Vuibert, Boulevard Saint-Germain, Paris, frs. 6.50), will be found a section devoted to *Instructions relatives à l'explication des chefs-d'œuvre de l'art*. Up to that date, it appears, the study of the masterpieces of art had figured merely as a part of the study of general history (which is more than it has ever done with us!):

"Mais cette fois on le dégage de cette histoire générale, afin de l'étudier en lui-même, comme on fait pour la littérature et les sciences. . . . C'est donc un enseignement de culture, non un nouveau chapitre d'histoire, qu'apportent les présents programmes."

This is the Appreciation attitude.

The "Instructions" proceed to explain the basis of the study. The study of Literature, they say, does not have as its end the

[1] It is worthy of mention, perhaps, that all the albums of this phonograph history (with their booklets translated) were published in Tokio immediately after their appearance in Europe. We may guess, then, that the Appreciation idea is gaining some hold in Japan. P. A. S.

training of professional literary men; the whole aim is to enlarge
and strengthen youthful minds by contact with the genius of the
great writers. And they continue, "it is difficult to see any reason
why the monuments of art should not be accepted on the same
footing as those of literature."

The method to be applied, we are told, is the same as that
used by the teacher of literature in the explanation of the great
poets or prose writers. Technicalities are to be avoided—one
does not need to be a practicing artist to understand art; good
sense and observation are the requirement. This principle is
then illustrated by a consideration of achitecture and painting,
and it is laid down that not merely photographs and lantern
slides shall be freely used, but that the fine buildings of the
locality, as well as any picture galleries, shall be made an object
of study. The History of Art and the biography of artists are
to be used as preparatory to the examination of actual works
of art. The teacher is not to do all the talking, but is to encourage his pupils to offer their remarks.

And so on, through eight pages of eloquently expressed common sense on the pedagogy of the Appreciation of Art, after
which follow eight more entirely devoted to a discussion of the
best way of treating Music in this scheme.

Here, however, a very curious lacuna occurs. The phonograph is forgotten, and thus a needless difficulty is raised—that
of finding a teacher of the subject who is a fine pianist or of
providing the teacher with such a pianist colleague. The difficulty is not a great one, perhaps, as most people otherwise qualified to teach the subject can play the piano, but the demand that
he shall be "un artiste d'une certaine virtuosité" may in some
places prove to be a rather high one to meet, and it is curious
that it should be assumed that orchestral works can only be presented to the class in transcriptions for piano solo or (what is
specially recommended) piano duet. Here the Instructions fall
a good decade behind their date. The occasional collaboration
of string players and vocalists is mentioned as desirable.

The works studied are to be related as much as possible to
their historic period and social environment; however, not his-

tory (the Instructions repeat), but *intimacy with actual musical works themselves,* is to be the main aim of the class; the works are to be analyzed and commented upon, and thematic quotation at the piano is to be a feature.

The subject is to be an optional one, and the course laid down covers fourteen class meetings (which seems too little) of eighty minutes each (surely twenty-eight lessons of forty minutes would be better). If pupils desire to bring with them (note this!) members of their family or friends it is suggested that they should be allowed to do so.

The teacher is given liberty to draft his course in his own way, but a detailed scheme is set out as a suggestion; it is arranged on an historical framework and runs from Lulli and Rameau (a preliminary treatment of the earlier music, is, however, recommended) through Bach and Handel, the French "Opéra Comique", Gluck, Haydn, and Mozart, Beethoven, Weber, Schubert, &c., Schumann, Liszt, Brahms, Wagner, the Italian nineteenth-century opera composers, Franck and Debussy (I have naturally omitted many names, yet even so those I have given look to me far too many for less than nineteen hours of class time).

There are full suggestions as to works to be performed, and it is agreed that a library of music and books on music shall be brought into existence for the use of pupils.

The whole aim of the course is cultural. Its weaknesses are those I have mentioned; it is really rather ridiculous to discuss such a subject as "The Orchestra of Berlioz" without any orchestral tone being heard, and the ground obviously cannot be covered in the time: however, we may suppose that the music teachers of the Lycées of France are quite aware of the existence of the phonograph and also that they will use the liberty the Minister of Public Instruction gives them and cut a good deal out of the course. That the time factor has not been sufficiently considered we see by examining any one of the fourteen lessons in the syllabus.

The scheme is not a perfect one (who was the Minister's musi-

cal adviser?)—but it *is* a scheme of "Appreciation" training. It
has as its aim the building up of interest, attention, and taste.
As is stated at the outset and several times repeated, the cultural
study of Literature is the model.

Since I wrote the above I have happened to meet at a literary
dinner in France the principal of a Lycée in an important university city. He tells me that the course is in successful operation
in his institution and that *the phonograph is being used.* I have
also come across a cultured Frenchwoman who described to me
with enthusiasm the benefit her son had received from one of
these courses in another French city. The scheme seems, then,
to be in full working order.

In order to remove the impression held by many British music
critics and others that the literature of Musical Appreciation is
a purely British-American article of commerce, it occurs to me to
give here the names of just a few books for the German amateur
that I happen to have on my shelves. I am sure that there are
many others like them.

Hermann Unger. *Musikalischer Laienbrevier—ein Spaziergang
durch die Musikgeschichte für Musikliebhaber.* (Munich, Drei
Masken Verlag, 1921.)

Walter Möller. *Musik-Verständnis für Jedermann.* (Wilhelm
Möller, Oranienburg.)

Carl M. Weber. *Wie wird man musikalisch? Eine Anleitung
sich musikalische Verständnis anzueignen und über Musik rich-
tig zu urteilen ohne Musik studiert zu haben.* (Leipzig, Glock-
ner.)

Dr. Max Burkhardt. *Führer durch die Konzertmusik: volkstüm-
liche und allgemeinverständliche Ausführungen über ca. 1500
Werke von 114 Komponisten.*

Hermann Kretschmar. *Führer durch den Konzertsaal.* (Several
large volumes describing an enormous number of pieces.
Leipzig, Breitkopf & Härtel.)

The *Konzertführer* ("Concert Guide") class of literature, with
its explanations of the compositions to be found in programs,
is, of course, common.

"MUSIC IS FOR THE ELECT"

There is a gang of cultured bandits in our country that wishes to keep music as its own private preserve. Innocent by nature, I first realized the existence of this astonishing narrowness only in 1926, when (of all people!) the Editor of the *Music Bulletin* of the British Music Society came out on the front page of his journal with the following amazing claim:

"The truth is that music—like all the arts—is essentially an aristocratic culture, and the present movement towards its democratization is fundamentally erroneous."

As we had all of us, from the foundation of the British Music Society, understood that it existed for the very purpose of widening to the utmost the interest of the British people in music this seemed to me to come upon the Society like an unexpected sentence of death.

The Editor's attention was called to the apparent conflict between his personal views and the declared aims of the Society he represented, and he replied in a couple of closely argued pages—the best he could do, and no man in that rather awkward position could have done much better.

The Society, he admitted, in one part of his article, had as one declared object the bringing of pressure to bear on educational authorities in the effort to secure music a larger place in the curriculum, but, said he:

"Music as a force in education is a very different thing from music as a force in life, and we were thinking of the latter aspect in declaring music to be essentially an aristocratic culture. That is to say that whereas music can be appreciated by countless numbers of people because of incidental qualities (qualities that are conditioned by the laws of association, and sometimes can be definitely recognized as non-musical), yet the purely musical appeal of music can only be made to the purely musical state of mind, a condition which almost by definition exists but rarely in a single being. . . .

"There is no reason to be found why music should not be a force in education. Perhaps, of all the arts, music is the best for the equal development and co-ordination of the intellect, the intelligence, and the emotions. The other subjects in the educational curriculum are applied to each of these things severally. For this reason alone, it is no tax on one's mental and moral honesty to subscribe to this important object. But when we are questioned as to what will be the result of this application of music to education, we may beg leave to differ, either totally or to an extent, with our associates. Because we vote—and even strive a little—for a millennium, we do not of a necessity believe that a millennium will ever come to pass. Every day we perform little acts and give little pledges of implicit good-will towards society in general, which do not in the least represent the nature of our faith. A man may stop his car behind the outstretched arm of a policeman, and yet disbelieve heartily in the reality of the State. In the same way, we may throw in our lot with the cause of music in education, and still be in doubt when we are told that the second or third generation from now will be musical in the fullest and highest sense. The attempt, and not the deed, engages us. The eternal causes are the lost causes; they are eternal because in a sense they are unattainable; they represent something which humanity might, yet never will, grasp. They furnish life with hope and the illusion of progress."

This has to me the appearance of the merest circumlocutory talk and, having quoted the original peccant passage, I have merely quoted this subsequent defense of it in the attempt to be fair. If any of us believed, with the writer, that the present movement towards the democratization of music is "fundamentally erroneous", we would surely apply our energies to some more promising scheme for the betterment of human life. Who told him, by the way, that the workers in the movement had expectations that "the second or third generation from now will be musical *in the highest sense"*? Surely we are content if we can make each generation a little more musical than the last, in the sense of giving it a greater pleasure in music, which, without using any mere cant terms, we may surely call a humanizing influence and one of the refinements of social life. If, as that writer tells us, "Of all the arts music is the best for the equal development and co-ordination of the intellect, the intelligence, and the emotions" that is surely enough justification for our expenditure of energy, and we will push on with its "democratization", leaving to a responsible Providence the question of the proportion of people whom we can succeed in making *"musical in the highest sense"*. In all this we merely share the privileges and disappointments of all who labor at any task of "democratization" of art, of literature, of religion. *"Behold a sower went forth to sow. . . ."*

This ridiculous incident illustrates the narrow-minded opposition which has in Britain confronted the Musical Appreciation movement—an opposition springing from a dual defect in the minds of some of our writers on music, an equal lack of logic and of social sympathy.

The year 1926 seems to have been a bad year. Perhaps because broadcasting was now showing its possibilities writers of limited human sympathies ran amuck. Here is another saddening exhibition of the same year (editorial in *Musical News,* 6th November):

"The great danger of throwing open the arts to the enjoyment of the people cannot be fully realized by those who glory in the facile achievement. It does not yet seem to have occurred to them that in publicly revealing the secrets of art and publishing a full catalogue of culture, they have surrendered the onus of selection and yielded the control of taste to a body that is not equipped, and cannot readily become equipped, to assimilate such highly seasoned pleasures. The public, wide-eyed in the possession of so much treasure, is at a loss to know how to select with a connoisseur's discretion, and abandons itself to a taste that is decidedly open to the stigma of unintelligence.

"Well, it has been done, and the doors of culture have been thrown open to the masses. We have all connived at it, trade, profession, teachers, and appreciationists, and if we are now beginning to discover that what was precious is becoming considerably less so since we have elected to let everybody handle it, it is our own fault. The most that we can now do is to save what we can and carry it out of the clutches of the crowd."

When in that organ of musical popularization, *The Gramophone* (July 1933), we find one of the most able writers of its staff declaring that "the mob, flattered to the top of its bent, is spoiling music", we see the same ugly narrowness of view, and realize with a shock that small-mindedness is to be met with everywhere.

We even see it, for once, in an American journal (*The Music Lover's Guide*) in these words:

"Certain works and certain composers will always be restricted in their appeal *and fortunately so* [my italics]. There is music one would not like to see become popularized, toughened and smothered by excessive performance and unappreciated hearing."

We see it again when Canon Hannay, otherwise "George A. Birmingham", at a Library Association Conference (August 1931) declares that Blake's *Jerusalem* has been "completely defiled since it was put to Parry's setting and sung all over the place by women's institute choirs and school children at speech-days" and begs his audience to "keep beauty safe from the ruin of popularity."

Whether the speaker made this pronouncement in his capacity of Christian Minister or Irish Humorist is perhaps not quite clear. Assuming that his oratory was delivered in the former capacity, he had his reply from the music critic of the *Liverpool Post* (10 September, 1931). "Keep beauty safe from the ruin of popularity" said the Priest-Canon, and the Music Critic asked:

"But who is going to keep art and beauty safe from the snobbery of coterie-worship? Is it the case that people who think art is for their own particular set only are afraid that if it gets outside their charmed circle it will not be art any longer, and that they will cease to admire what is admired by the populace? Blake's *Jerusalem* is a doubly unfortunate example, for according to Canon Hannay, Blake ought not to have wanted to build Jerusalem in 'England's green and pleasant land', but in the drawing rooms of Mayfair and the rectory gardens of leisurely ecclesiastics."

Does it not seem a little regrettable that an aristocratic view of privilege should (even if in jest) come to us from an official of a church whose founder left him marching orders to "go out into all the world and preach the gospel to every creature"?

The thought behind all these expressions seems to be that of the (alleged) hymn of the Calvinistic predestinarians, the believers in an "elected" few and a lost many irrevocably condemned even before birth:

> We are the sweet elected few,
> Let all the rest be damned.
> There's room enough in Hell for you,
> We won't have Heaven crammed.

At the risk of being called all manner of bad names, I make my personal expression of faith as follows: *Music is the widest of all the arts. It has something for everybody. And upon those who, by natural endowment, social privilege, or educational advantage find in it the greatest enjoyment there is imposed the duty of helping others to such enjoyment.*

A TRADE OBJECTION TO MUSICAL APPRECIATION

The most honest (and perhaps the best founded objection to Musical Appreciation) that I have ever seen is one printed in the *Journal of the British Federation of Music Industries* in October 1925.

The Federation had sent a traveling representative to various firms up and down the country to ask them their reason for not joining the Federation, and got replies such as *"We do not like your Journal"* and *"We do not agree with your handling of labor matters."*

One reply received referred to the work of the Federation in employing a permanent staff lecturer on Musical Appreciation, and stands as follows:

"'Musical Appreciation' does not interest us. If our customers 'appreciated' music they would not buy our pianos."

(It is just possible that we have here some obscure reference to the strange idea that personal performance and "Appreciation" are in some mysterious way in antagonism. But perhaps this is too subtle an interpretation and it gives me more pleasure to accept the statement without gloss. It is very satisfying as it stands.)

"APPRECIATION HAS FAILED"

This charge, occasionally heard, is typically exemplified in the following, by my friend, Mr. Ralph Hill, in *The Chesterian* (July–August 1930):

"It is now nearly twenty years since the 'Musical Appreciation' movement began its work to bring about, in the words of Mr. Stewart Macpherson, 'the one great objective . . . to get the general level of popular interest and understanding nearer to that of the artist, to show the plain man that a great art is worthy of his regard, and—once that is admitted—to prove to him that such an art deserves a little trouble on his part to understand and appreciate it.' . . .

"One would certainly expect that in view of the increased facilities of musical education and the united efforts 'to show the plain man that a great art is worthy of his regard', appreciable results would now be in evidence even to the casual observer. Considering the high aims of the musical appreciation movement the results obtained are decidedly poor: concerts devoted to the performance of the best music are still only patronized by Arnold Bennett's 'passionate few' —the sale of sheet music of the best kind, apart from that published for educational purposes, is, if anything, declining; a fact which goes to prove that amateur performance is losing attraction."

This criticism seems to me to be wholly unscientific. (*a*) Twenty years is a short period in the history of educational endeavor; (*b*) the number of schools in Britain even now including Musical Appreciation in their curriculum is, unfortunately, fractional; moreover, the work is still largely in the experimental stage and is, admittedly, not always well done, since the training of teachers has not yet proceeded far; (*c*) concert attendance is an extraordinarily poor test; it is common for music critics (whose life is lived in concert halls) to take concert attendance as a criterion of musical progress, but during the twenty years in question the Phonograph and its Records have been enormously improved and the Radio has made it possible for people to hear abundance of fine music without stirring from their hearth; (*d*) the enormous competition of the automobile has been a very disturbing factor; so has the increasing tendency to live out of town; and there are other social changes.

It seems to me that before we could accept this writer's gloomy view we should have to sit down to the very careful sifting of a lot of evidence. We should need, firstly, to examine the suggestion that the musical activities this writer mentions have actually remained stationary or declined; secondly, to consider the social changes that, largely as a result of the Great War, have so evidently come about; thirdly, to discover roughly what amount of Musical Appreciation teaching has gone on during that period and what has been its quality in general, . . . and so on!

When we come to call witnesses, the music publishers, with one voice, would put down the decline in their sales to the Radio, which, they would tell us, has tended to rob indifferent performance of all its attractions and so has put out of action thousands of amateur singers and players who formerly were among their customers.

We should then take the evidence of school principals and others on the impression they have obtained as to the success of Appreciation Classes in awakening an interest in music. . . . And thus, at length, we should form an opinion.

It is my expectation that if ever such an inquiry is carried out the report will be that in the measure that Musical Appreciation training has been introduced into the schools of the country and intelligently and enthusiastically carried out it has had a great effect in providing an interested public for music.

Certainly I, for one, have not the slightest inclination to be despondent as to the results of Musical Appreciation. I think that the movement has probably been one of the factors in enabling music to "stand up to" a very disturbing set of new conditions, and also that, if the campaign had opened twenty years earlier, and had not been consistently crabbed by the leading music critics and unsympathetically viewed by so many professional musicians, it would have been able to set up an even more effective defense against the inroads of the many new competing interests that have come into social life.

NONSENSE ARGUMENTS

In addition to all the arguments against Musical Appreciation set forth above, there are heard from time to time some that may be promptly dismissed as too foolish to justify the expenditure of breath or ink. I give the following as an example. It is by the Poet-Playwright-Music-Critic, W. J. Turner, author of books on Beethoven and Wagner, &c.—a writer on music apparently taken quite seriously by a good many British music-lovers.

"I am not anxious to see England become a musical nation in the sense that everybody should be educated to appreciate music. In the first place, it is not possible, for such wholesale appreciation can only be a sham; and, in the second place, in a truly enlightened and highly developed society every person's appreciation would be individual in kind, scope and degree. Appreciation can never be taught, and all attempts to teach it are injurious. The young should be trained in a practical discipline of mind and body directed towards simplicity and correctness. I would have every child taught either to sing or play some musical instrument up to the age of eighteen, merely as a technique like mathematics or swimming. At the age of eighteen all teaching should stop, and those who have any power of understanding the art of music should be left to find it out for themselves. This would involve no playing of the great masters to or by students. Up to the age of eighteen nobody should hear any music by Bach, Beethoven, Mozart, Schubert, Handel, or Haydn, and no operas by Verdi, Purcell, Monteverde, Rossini, Scarlatti—in fact, no music by any old master. Nothing could be more ridiculous, for example, than giving Mozart's sonatas to schoolchildren, or allowing anybody under the age of eighteen to read a line by Shakespeare, Milton, or any great poet of the past."

It would be very interesting (but purely as a study of Mr. Turner's mind) if we might have some explanation of the method by which the young people fortunate enough to be reared under his régime are to be kept at their studies.

PART III

THE TRUE PHILOSOPHY OF APPRECIATIVE TEACHING

CONTENTS OF PART III

REMOVING OBSTACLES

"Let a man and a beast look out at the same window, the same door, the same casement, yet the one will see like a man and the other like a beast." BUNYAN.[1]

WHAT should be the Appreciation Teacher's general attitude? He is often reproached for that attitude. He is told he is sentimental and fanciful, academic and dryasdust, patronizing and opinionated. None of these charges can be laid against him if he will assume the attitude I suggest—a negative attitude rather than a positive one. *He should look upon himself not as a doer but as an undoer.*

This is what I mean. Nature and chance and the perversity of humanity have placed in the path of the would-be appreciator of music certain obstacles. It is the Appreciation Teacher's business to remove these—nothing more.

One advantage of the attitude I suggest is that it prevents the teacher doing too much ("putting himself between the composer and the listener" is one of the charges sometimes made against him). Another is that it keeps before him the fact that it is the listener himself who must do any work that falls to be done—that the teacher cannot do it for him. And there are other advantages, among them those of keeping him diligent (for there are sometimes formidable obstacles to remove) and of keeping him humble (for he is a mere road-clearer, not a musical preacher, or a musical theorist, or a music critic issuing opinions on matters of taste, but a mere remover of impediments in the path of his pupils).

The teacher who adopts this attitude will start out with few fixed notions as to what he is to do. He has to find what the obstructions are and remove them. They may not be all of the same kind and size for every listener, but in general the chief of them will be found to be as follows:

[1] From a posthumous work, *The House of the Forest of Lebanon, c.* 1690. P. A. S.

1. The obstacle of TEXTURE. The listener cannot hear so many things going on at one time. His ear tends to follow the upper thread of the texture and to neglect the rest.

2. The obstacle of FORM. The listener gets bewildered with any elaboration of formal arrangement, fails to recognize musical themes when they come round again, and after a few minutes finds himself "lost."

3. The obstacle of COLOR. For lack of a trained color-perception he fails to enjoy as he should many passages in which color beauties and contrasts are a predominant feature.

4. The obstacle of STYLE. The listener when he hears music of a period far earlier than his own finds it archaic; he fails to penetrate to the human feeling beneath the older forms and textures of his ancestors. Similarly, when any advanced contemporary music is put before him he finds himself unable to grasp it. So, too, with certain composers of marked individuality; their idiom is strange to him, and, because strange, repellent.

It is to remove these obstacles (and any others he may discover) that the musician accepts office as the Appreciation Teacher.

I have said that the teacher's role is a modest one. It is more modest even than I have indicated. To a large extent he cannot even remove the obstacles he finds, but can only advise his client how to remove them himself. Here is a letter from a satisfied client (not of myself, I think—of some other "Appreciationist"). I came across it the other day among some old papers. It dates from 1924, when Radio had barely begun and the Phonograph offered the big chance for acquaintance with music.

"Six years ago my wife and I attended a lecture on musical appreciation and it was such a revelation that since then nearly all our leisure time has been spent in further exploring.

"Our acquaintance with the classics has necessarily been through the medium of the gramophone [1] and literature, including various popular books and biographies of the composers.

---

[1] Older readers may recall the struggle between early manufacturers over use of the terms "phonograph" and "gramophone." The English finally adopted the latter term, the Americans the former. When the English term occurs in a quotation from an English source, as here, it is invariably retained. W. E.

"The study has been one of the best, if not the best investment I have made during my lifetime. Adequately to express my deep pleasure derived from the old masters' works I should have to do the business in music, for language would be too barren for the purpose.

"Anyone who has not done what we have done cannot realize what he is missing in neglecting twelve months' pleasant study of the simple rudiments of 'learning to listen.'

"I possess 9 complete Symphonies, several string quartets (complete), Beethoven's 'Emperor' and violin concertos, and a lot of chamber music, and the sense of appreciation obtained from following with miniature scores has been worth many times the cost of the records and time spent in studying them."

Every intelligent Appreciation Teacher who has had adults under his direction can produce testimonials like that. It is folly of the highbrow professionals and music critics to tell us there is nothing we can do.

We can remove obstacles—or, rather, set people removing their own.

REMOVING THE OBSTACLE OF TEXTURE

Nothing I could write on this subject could be more practically suggestive than an extract I am now going to give from an article by an able and popular writer. In *The Listener* of Christmas Eve, 1930, Dr. Harvey Grace wrote as follows:

"There is interpretation in listening, as in performing.

"But technique comes before interpretation; and just as one of the first difficulties to be overcome in the playing of a keyboard instrument is the performance of two or more simultaneous independent parts, so the technique of listening depends largely on the ability to hear and distinguish more than one part at a time. The natural tendency of untrained listeners is to be concerned only with the tune, or with the top part. Even a tune stands a poor chance with such listeners unless it is at the top; when it occurs in an inner part or in the bass it is apt to be missed unless it is made very prominent, or is kept free from distracting elements above or below.

"How is the listener to develop this faculty of part-listening? (We may call it so, for it is the analogy of part-playing.)

"Here are a few methods—many more will suggest themselves to the enterprising reader. If you have a capable pianist handy, get him to play, rather slowly for a start, such things as the Two-part Inventions of Bach, while you try to follow the progress of the two parts (or 'voices', as they are usually called in music of this kind). Or you may begin by concentrating on the lower part, in order to cure your natural inclination to think only of the top. Another helpful plan is to listen only for the appearances of the subject, which will be sometimes in the upper part and sometimes in the lower. . . . After working through the Two-part Inventions you may proceed to the Three-part, which will test you much more severely, for the addition of a single part more than doubles the complexity.

"Descants—i.e. counter-melodies written against hymn-tunes and folk-songs are just now very popular. You may obtain collections of them at a small cost (Novello's issue some particularly good examples of both hymn-tune and folk-song descants by Geoffrey Shaw). Ask your pianist friend to play (or better still persuade a couple of vocalists to sing) the tune and descant together; and after concentrating your ear on tune and descant separately, try to listen to the two together with equal receptiveness.

"Gramophone records of fugues from Bach's '48' are now obtainable. Use these as material, beginning by listening for the subject, afterwards for countersubject or any other regular features, such as the episodical matter that reappears from time to time. When a stretto occurs try to follow the subject as it enters in the various parts. A listener with an average-good ear, intelligence, and perseverance can soon make astonishing progress. In fact, thousands of ordinary listeners have almost unconsciously developed this faculty during recent years, thanks to the frequency with which they have been able to hear complicated orchestral music. Thus, for one person who ten years ago could spot and enjoy Wagner's simultaneous use of the three chief themes near the close of the 'Meistersinger' Overture, there are at least a hundred to-day. By the way, this is an instance of the increased pleasure we may derive from music through trained listening. The more you know about music, and the better trained your ear, the greater your enjoyment. When you can take in such a combination of themes as this of Wagner's you will receive an added thrill of pleasure every time you hear the Overture; whereas to the hearer who can follow the top part only this glorious passage will seem quite ordinary. So, as with 'Eyes' and 'No Eyes', the 'Ears' have a far better time than the 'No Ears.'"

About the same time as he said all this Dr. Grace also said (*Musical Times,* April 1931): "Even a modest degree of technical ability and the conscientious study of good music at first hand—that is, as a performer—increase the ability to understand and enjoy music far more than any amount of time spent in so-called 'musical appreciation.'" Yet above he appears as our Arch-appreciationist, for nothing could be more orthodox from the Appreciationists' point of view than the very practical advice he gives, which is exactly the kind of advice they frequently give, though they are not always so ready with workable expedients. The intelligent school-teacher of Appreciation should have very little difficulty in adapting these expedients to class use, and, inspired by them, he will doubtless invent others.

As perhaps the earliest possible introduction to this kind of work I suggest the use of my game of "Camouflaged Tunes", the only contribution to British Sport that I have ever made and hence a source of pride. The rules of this game and sixteen examples of material for playing it will be found in *The First and Second Books of the Great Musicians.*

Briefly described, the game consists of performing on the piano with the left hand the opening phrase of the melody of a well-known song or hymn tune, and with the right hand a counterpoint to it, the players in the game then competing to be the first to identify the left-hand tune. (Many adult music-lovers have failed at this.)

Children who know the hymn tune "Tallis's Canon" may be interested in the use of that as an exercise in listening. The tune occurs in both soprano and tenor, with a measure's overlap, and the exercise (which calls for a high degree of concentration) is to listen first to the tenor, and then, when that has become easy, to the tenor "with the left ear" and, at the same time, the soprano with the right. There are some passages in Sullivan's tune to *Onward, Christian Soldiers* that can be similarly used.

The class use of James Easson's *Book of the Great Music* (mentioned elsewhere in the present book) must necessarily tend towards the removal of the obstacle of Texture.

Having worked at texture problems for a time (and with tact on the part of the teacher such work will be much enjoyed), some bright pupil may be disposed to ask the question, "Can even the composers themselves hear *everything* they write?" To this I guess the answer to be, frankly, "No." With all reverence and awe I modestly state my doubt whether even John Sebastian Bach himself could follow the windings of every bit of every thread in every one of his five-part fugues and eight-part choruses.

I may be wrong about this, the capacities of exceptional minds being to ordinary people incredible. But at any rate a reasonable view as to five-part fugues and similarly high-powered pieces of counterpoint is this: To get great enjoyment from them you *do* need to follow the entries and motions of the "parts" or "voices" that are for the moment carrying the principal theme or themes, and, after that, the more you can hear of the other parts (which we may call the "momentarily accompanying parts") the keener your enjoyment.

REMOVING THE OBSTACLE OF FORM

Nothing has brought the Musical Appreciationist greater obloquy than the fact that he dares to teach people something of the forms of music. I could, if I went through my files, quote a great many pieces of choice Billingsgate shouted at Appreciationists by musical highbrows (generally young and sentimental) who look upon the mention of "subjects" and "developments" as profanation. Here, however, is the view of a famous conductor, who discusses the probable results of the fact that "the great public schools have placed Musical Appreciation on their curricula":

"Now it is incontestable that the ability to enjoy music increases in proportion to the hearer's knowledge of it. The man who understands musical form has very much more pleasure in listening to a good performance of a fine work than he who hears only a vague disorder of meaningless, if sometimes pleasing sounds. The direct consequence of the energy now given to the intelligent teaching of music to the young should, therefore, be a large intelligent demand for good music." (Sir Henry Wood, in the London *Evening News*, 1 January, 1928.)

Composers, in my experience, endorse this view. In my years as music critic of the London *Observer* I was frequently honored with the visits of composers who were kindly willing to give me the opportunity of going through some new orchestral or chamber work with them at the piano before I was faced with the duty of forming an opinion of it in its complete orchestral form. Their usual procedure, I noted, was to go through it first in skeleton, showing me the themes out of which a movement grew and the way they had treated these, and then playing the movement as a whole. In other words they made the form clear to me—which, of course, is the method of the normal English annotated concert program and of such books as Grove's exciting *Beethoven and his Nine Symphonies* (still selling after nearly forty years). Ernest Newman, who in his articles gets in an occasional dig at Musical Appreciation, himself adopted the orthodox Appreciation methods when he used to write the program books for the Hallé Orchestra at Manchester, and in his little book on Elgar he describes the works in the way of formal analysis. Stravinsky once provided me with a formal analysis of some of his work so that I might print it on "Pianola" rolls, side by side with the perforations that produced the music. He wrote an introduction to one set of rolls, in which he said:

"It has my cordial approval. I have contributed with the liveliest satisfaction to this beneficent work of musical dissemination.

"I consider that to listen is not enough. It is further necessary for the listener to hear with understanding the music to which he listens. He cannot but derive more enjoyment from works by being enabled to enter more intimately into their contents and their components. It is not only the lay listener of whom I speak. I speak also for the initiate. Inspiration is a mystery to all; to unveil such part of it as may be unveiled cannot but be a useful task."

And so on! Everybody does it—including those who say it is sin (not that Stravinsky ever said so). And they are obliged to do it, for it is the only way of quickly bringing the listener to grips with a composition.

It will be seen that nobody really has any fear that study of the form of a piece will remove one from contact with its spirit. But very many *talk* as though they were obsessed with such a fear. The fact is that good music is tougher than is sometimes pretended.

If the Appreciation teacher feels that he needs to have in his pocket a *laissez passer* to present to any who try to stand in his way as he goes about his lawful occasions, he might take this one, signed by Schumann—*"Only when the form becomes clear will the spirit become clear also."*

Surely we have all found that true. A work unfamiliar to us has proved a mere quarter of an hour of confusion, relieved by passing moments of clarity when some straightforward theme has happily appeared, or perhaps of excitement when a climax has been built up. On a second and third hearing we have grasped all the themes, have gone some way towards observing their treatment, and have begun to feel that we are coming into touch with the composer and can already tentatively decide whether his work is going to be food for us or not. The idea of the composers I have mentioned as calling on me in London with their scores under their arms was that they could expedite this process by making me somewhat acquainted with the material and form of their music before they gave me a performance of it as a whole—and I always found they were right.

Of course they were at one and the same time removing obstacles both as to form and as to texture, and, indeed, the two aspects are necessarily closely connected.

The Musical Appreciation teacher's treatment of this subject of Form falls into two departments, which we may call that of Form and that of Forms, i.e. that of the principles of arrangement in music (based on fundamental psychological fact) and that of the rather surprisingly limited number of definite schemes of arrangement that have, in practice, been based on these principles.

The principles of arrangement may be taken to begin with the placing of phrase against phrase and the building up of sentences. There can be great interest to children in observing this; I recall that years before I heard the word "phrase" and "sentence" applied to music I relieved many tedious hours in church by analyzing the hymn tunes and chants and speculating as to whether the music itself, apart from the words, was not *saying something* (something rather argumentative, it appeared), and following some principle of logic that I tried vainly to seize.

With this aspect of musical structure is bound up the punctuation by the various more or less definite types of cadences (corresponding to commas, full stops, &c.), and the introduction of simple effects of variety by modulation. I, personally, have the feeling that (from an Appreciation point of view) the conscious and planned study of these simple phenomena is sometimes overdone—that a good deal of subconscious or semi-conscious observation of these phenomena is normally carried on by all of us, and that we acquire perhaps an almost sufficient measure of skill in the mental analysis of these smaller features of musical form by dint of merely hearing the quantities of hymn tunes, waltzes, marches, &c., that every child does hear.

The extent to which it is necessary for a teacher to labor to make a pupil conscious of what he already sub-consciously possesses is a pedagogical question that each must answer for himself. It seems to me chiefly a question of time available. Where a teacher has the advantage of first meeting his pupils in their infant years he (or more likely she) will naturally deal very largely in small change, since the bigger sums will be beyond the pupils' grasp. The methods of interesting little children in music and leading them to *live* it as it proceeds have been very fully worked out by many experienced teachers (mostly women) and need not be entered into here, except to say that they are properly largely based on physical activity of some kind or other. (The greatest of all such methods is that of my friend Jaques-

Dalcroze—which, of course, is carried far beyond the small-child stage.)

With older children the music can be better taken in larger mouthfuls. Instead of considering music minutely, phrase by phrase, they would rather spend their time in considering whole "subjects" and their contrast and repetition. To note what a composer does with a subject in a development section of a sonata or symphony can be for them a fascinating piece of detective research.

The study of the various Forms should be as unconstrained as possible. There can be no objection to a free-and-easy and un-text-booky treatment of such a matter as the so-called "Sonata-form". We have all been young and should remember it. I found the following description of the typical eighteenth- and early nineteenth-century Sonata-form in an article by a musician of ninety-five (Francesco Berger, 1834–1933, wrote this article for the *Monthly Musical Record* in 1929):

EXPOSITION

A. First subject: It is a fine day.
B. Second subject: I hope you are well.

REPEAT

A. It is a fine day.
B. I hope you are well.

DEVELOPMENT, OR FREE FANTASIA

A. The fine day we are now having is very agreeable after what we have been experiencing lately. It is also very healthy, and allows us to, &c., &c.
B. In hoping that you are well I am also hoping that you are able to continue working at that book which we all, &c., &c.

RECAPITULATION

A. It is a fine day.
B. I hope you are well.

CODA (*if any*)

P.S.—I forgot to mention that so-and-so has happened. Believe me, very truly yours, N.N.

If a class of boys of twelve or thirteen had that before them on the blackboard they would be prepared to listen attentively to a good many first movements of Sonatas, Symphonies, and String Quartets by Haydn and Mozart and to exercise their wits in applying the Berger Formula to the music. And in so doing they would be engaged in something far more important than "learning the ropes" of Sonata-form, since they would be acquiring the habit of concentrating on music, of "focusing".

And that bit of listening practice accomplished they would be prepared to go on to Beethoven first movements and others of a somewhat less elementary lay-out than those of Haydn and Mozart.[1]

There may be "highbrows" reading this chapter who will be shocked at the flippancy of such an educational procedure. We will not argue with them but insult them to their faces and pass on. *They* are not young.

I have spoken above of the comparatively small number of forms in music. One might imagine that the number of ways of combining thematic material would be unlimited but, as a matter of fact, only about six distinct forms have ever been invented and accepted:

1. A two-section form, SIMPLE BINARY.
2. A three-section form, SIMPLE TERNARY.
2. A form derived from the first, COMPOUND BINARY (also called, "First Movement Form" and "Sonata Form").
4. An elaboration of the second, the RONDO.
5. The AIR WITH VARIATIONS.
6. The FUGUE.

Perhaps for completeness it should be added that there are a certain number of short pieces running on perfectly continuously, without any divisions such as would enable us to define the form (e.g. the first Prelude of Bach's "48"); probably "Unitary Form" would be the best label for these.

Of course elaborations of these six forms occur. There exist combinations of Fugue and Compound Binary, of Rondo and

[1] The fact that Mr. Berger allowed for some new matter in the Coda suggests that he may have had Beethoven in mind. P. A. S.

Compound Binary, and so forth. And in many modern compositions the internal dividing partitions of a composition become very thin, so that the clear and unmistakable lay-out of the older music is lost. Nevertheless this scheme of six forms may be held fairly to cover the whole ground of instrumental music (and most vocal music too).

The teacher should realize this because confusion is often imported into the study of the subject by an unnecessary multiplication of forms. For example, the movements of the Bach-Handel Suite are spoken of as though each were a form. As a matter of fact, Allemande, Sarabande, Courante, Gigue, and all the rest are merely different rhythms and styles applied to the same Simple Binary form—a form which completely satisfied the composers, performers, and audience of those days, and was used thousands of times over.

It is very desirable, of course, that children should learn to recognize those different classical rhythm-styles, and there is little difficulty about this. If they can recognize a Waltz or a March when they hear it they can recognize a Minuet or a Gavotte or a Sarabande. A game or competition can be made by playing to them a string of half a dozen or a dozen opening phrases of pieces of this type and asking them to note on paper the rhythm-style (i.e. dance title) description of each.

I myself, strangely, went through school without ever being told or finding out what a sonnet was. I had read sonnets, and had accepted the vague impression that they were short continuous poems, generally of a reflective kind, and that they managed, if good, to convey an astonishing amount of thought and emotion set to a very attractive rhyme-and-rhythm music. But it was only in after-school conversation with a retired sergeant-major (of all people) that I learned incidentally that a sonnet necessarily possesses fourteen lines, and was led to inquire further (I never revealed my ignorance to the sergeant-major), and to discover that, as the *Concise Oxford Dictionary* tells us, they "usually rhyme thus: *pig-bat-cat-wig-jig-hat-rat-fig; lie-red-sob-die-bed-rob,* or *lie-red-die-bed-pie-wed*—or otherwise."

They might just as well have told us that at school. Not every boy in the class would have been interested, but I would.[1]   And, similarly, school pupils may just as well be told (or led to find out for themselves and to make a note of—for that is the proper way!) the characteristics of the different types of musical composition.

Reverting to the parenthesis of that last sentence, while we need not make an iron rule of telling the class nothing (all iron rules are a mistake), the less we tell the class and the more it tells us the better.[2]

I close this chapter with a little special attention to the Variation Form—in its different guises of simple variation, ground bass, passacaglia, &c. This form may possibly be found to be the very best means of accustoming children to "focus". A simple example like the so-called *Harmonious Blacksmith,* or some other set of variations by the fluent, melodious Handel, will

---

[1] It is not necessary to the enjoyment of a sonnet that this formula should be remembered. But it certainly must help any intelligent child of an age to read sonnets to have attention called to it, because ever after the subtle *enchaînements* (in the French sense of the word) become a source of pleasure. P. A. S.

[2] We should beware, however, of faddy extremes. Compare the section on Science in the National Board of Education *Report of the Consultative Committee on the Education of the Adolescent* (1926):

"The special equipment required for the teaching of science hardly exists in many schools at the present time. This lack of equipment is largely due to the peculiar history of science teaching in elementary schools during the last five decades. When in the early seventies a systematic attempt was first made to introduce the study of science into elementary schools, the teaching largely took the form of 'object' and observation lessons, designed to link up certain scientific truths with everyday life. Courses in physiography, or the science of every-day life, were much in vogue, and experimental demonstrations were frequently given in the class-room. Later, from 1887 onwards, the theory was developed that no science was worth teaching unless it were based on the student's own experimental work, and demonstration was regarded as positively harmful. As, however, the method of experimental demonstration was the only way in which science could satisfactorily be taught in most primary schools, the science lessons gradually disappeared or were replaced by lessons on nature study, which were supposed to lend themselves to heuristic teaching. Unfortunately, during this period, any science apparatus that had been provided in these schools was gradually broken up and not replaced."

The above will illustrate the stupidity of attaching ourselves to a swinging pendulum instead of deciding for ourselves where the true path of progress lies. (There is, by the way, some little analogy between the agitation of 1887 and onwards as to the proper method for getting the pupil to think scientifically and the present-day agitation in favor of musical performance as the *only way* of learning to think musically, i.e. by the pupil's own "doing".) P. A. S.

make a good start. It could be performed to the children as a basis for the GAME OF MUSIC CRITIC. Each child imagines himself a newspaper critic charged with the duty of listening to a new piece of music and giving an interested public a description of it, section by section. The general character of the Air should be described and then what is done with it in each variation. Not merely formal analysis but a little emotional analysis also will be in place, the variations being described as "peaceful", "exciting", and so forth. The child can make brief notes as each variation is heard (an intermission being made after each variation for the purpose) and then, on occasion, at any rate, can be allowed to write up the notes into a continuous and essay-like description, adding any more truly critical thoughts that occur to him as demanding expression (but no sentimental nonsense—see the schoolgirl essay I have given on another page).

One or two selected children can then read their critical description, section by section, the teacher illustrating by repeating the performance of the Variation in question, or of some part of it, so that the class can check the description's accuracy.

The wide range of variation music, from the English Elizabethans to Brahms and Elgar, gives immense scope for the application of this idea at intervals over the whole school life from the age of about ten (or less) onwards.

I have never tried this Game of Music Critic, since my own school-teaching days were over before it occurred to me (indeed, I only thought of it five minutes ago), but it looks to be one which an ingenious teacher could develop usefully in various ways.

In the work of training Musical Appreciation there must be no settling into a rut. The teacher should constantly produce some novel device, and (usually) the more he can destroy the idea of Musical Appreciation being a "lesson" the better.

Boy-Scouting and Girl-Guiding teach their practitioners a great deal, but their spirit is not that of the schoolroom. The schoolroom spirit has its place, of course, but when art is the subject of study that place is not the front one.

REMOVING THE OBSTACLE OF COLOR

For a London journal I once wrote over two hundred consecutive weekly-column articles on music, and I believe the most popular to have been one in which I tried to help the ordinary concert-goer to overcome the Obstacle of Color—or, more accurately, the obstacles in the way of the perception of color.

The article took a phonograph record, then recently issued, of *Siegfried's Funeral March,* and analyzed its color effects in such a way that any one possessing a phonograph and this record could go through the music, passage by passage, and exercise his recognition of the tone-colors of the various instruments and combinations. I will reproduce the analysis here, as an example of "what the public like" in the way of guidance in Musical Appreciation. The figures indicate the measures.[1]

1 and 2 KETTLEDRUMS alone.

    3 VIOLAS and 'CELLOS enter with a low chromatic wail.

4–7 HORNS and TUBAS alone in unisons and octaves.

    8 KETTLEDRUMS and chromatic wail again.

9–12 Similar unison and octave passages to 4–7, but given to BASSOONS, CLARINET, and BASS CLARINET.

12–14 KETTLEDRUMS.

14–15 LOWER STRINGS, *Staccato.*

16–18 Loud, detached barks on LOWER BRASS, with KETTLEDRUMS, while WOODWIND hold long chords; LOWER STRINGS have their chromatic wail.

19–22 The four TUBAS and BASS TUBA, beginning softly and working up to the most thrilling *fortissimo,* cry out a wonderful passage of intense grief. At the climax TROMBONES and HORNS join in.

23–25 Similar to 16–18.

26–30 TRUMPETS, BASS TRUMPET, and TUBAS, with a background of tremolo chords on the lower STRINGS.

30–36 A little bit of plaintive melody is taken up in turn by (1) COR ANGLAIS, (2) CLARINET, and (3) OBOE doubled by HORN.

---

[1] At the opening the speed is so slow that a measure lasts a long time. From bar 16 onwards, a steady march rhythm begins. P. A. S.

At 34 the HARP has a soft *arpeggio*, followed by a *pianissimo* chord.

36–40 Need not be particularly described.

41–44 A swelling, piercing tune on TRUMPET, with nearly full Orchestra accompanying.

(Here this side of the Record ends.)

45–47 FULL ORCHESTRA, *fortissimo*, yet dominated by the smallest instrument of all—the PICCOLO.

48–51 BASS TRUMPET tune, doubled by HORNS.

51–53 Similar to 45–47.

54–60 Similar in orchestration and material to previous passages.

61–62 A noble passage for full BRASS (easily recognized by its characteristic triplets).

63–64 Full ORCHESTRA.

64–71 A melody on CLARINETS doubled by COR ANGLAIS. Touches of HARP can be heard, as also the chromatic LOWER-STRING wail.

71–72 WOODWIND chords, with the wail continuing.

73–75 BASS TRUMPET melody again.

75–77 A tune in four part harmony on the HORNS.

79–83 The piece dies away to its conclusion—the wail on the STRINGS and soft-toned chords on TROMBONES and TUBAS.

Though this description gives measure-numbers it will be seen that the passages can, by any intelligent person, be identified without the use of the score, and, of course, very many of my newspaper readers would know themselves to be incapable of reading an elaborate orchestral score if they got it. Despite these facts the publishers reported that they sold over sixty copies of the score during the following three days, which, with the large number of letters I received from readers, is my reason for thinking this article my most popular one. It showed me that many people are worried at the feeling that a great deal of color effect passes them by unnoticed, and are quite willing to do a little intensive work to overcome this obstacle to full appreciation of orchestral music.

The Phonograph offers clearly the only practical means of getting to grips with the problem of the recognition of orchestral color and its combinations. The fact that passages can be repeated as often as desired places this medium far above any other available.

That special records exist with the various instruments separately heard is known to all teachers. Games can be devised by the use of these and then of appropriate records of the simpler orchestral music—the game of Spotting the Oboe, and the like. With very young children something might perhaps be done in the way of their making the motions of playing some particular instrument when it appears. To listen for the kettledrum (which in its softer entries is often overlooked by listeners) and to imitate its player when he comes into action, might have attractions (any child would love to make a *crescendo* up to *fortissimo*). A class might even be divided into (say) trumpeters and drummers, flutists and oboists, and the like, records of suitable compositions being chosen for the purpose.

A class with a little working acquaintance with the staff notation could make good use of certain pages of James Easson's *The Book of the Great Music,* as a companion to one or two of their orchestral phonograph records. I give here a page from his treatment of Mozart's Symphony in G minor:

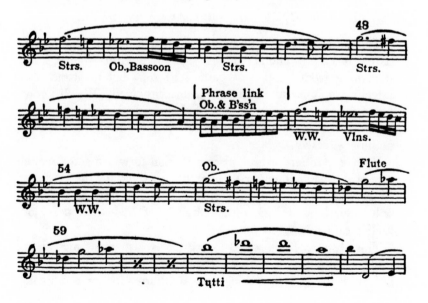

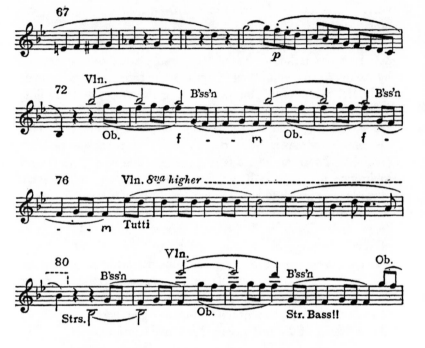

REMOVING THE OBSTACLE OF STYLE

This obstacle usually disappears with familiarity. A piece of sixteenth-century choral music (say an English Madrigal or something from a Mass of Palestrina) may fail to attract the listener simply because its idiom is unaccustomed. We all know how violently some of our grandfathers kicked at Wagner and how a program of his music nowadays fills the concert hall as nothing else will.

If a composition or type of composition to which some members of the class are rather recalcitrant be treated for the Obstacle of Texture, the Obstacle of Form, or the Obstacle of Color it will often be found that the Obstacle of Style disappears of itself meanwhile.

This obstacle, if suspected to exist, may also sometimes be at least partially disposed of by preparing the mind of the class. A little judiciously chosen biographical information or a suitable anecdote may predispose them to patience. In some cases it may be tactful to make a frank introduction on these lines: "Next week we will listen to a rather stiff bit of Sibelius. Some people find it bare and austere but others say that once you get to know it, it is full of feeling. We will just see how it affects *us*. This Sibelius, by the way, is a Finnish composer. Some of you know his *Valse Triste,* which is played in all the cafés and cinemas. Come to think of it, perhaps we had better have the *Valse Triste* or his *Finlandia* next week and the other thing the week after" . . . and so forth!

We need a collection of evidence as to what styles most immediately attract and most immediately repel children of various ages, by the way. If musical-educational papers would take up points like this and get together the experience of readers, they would be doing a useful work.

What I have written in Part IV of this book under the heading of "The History of Music" has, of course, necessarily a great bearing on this problem of the Obstacle of Style, and some readers may care to turn to it straight away.

PART IV

SOME DETAILS OF PRINCIPLE AND
PROCEDURE

CONTENTS OF PART IV

ATTENTION

IT cannot be too strongly emphasized that the teacher's main lever in lifting out of the way the obstacles just referred to is the cultivation of the habit of Attention.

Most of us only give half our attention to a musical composition when it is being performed, the other half being given, by fits and starts, to the people around us, the gestures and antics of the conductor, some domestic or business difficulty that happens to cross our mind, plans for the morrow's doings, or what not. It may be supposed that few members of an audience give their close undivided attention to a symphony from its first note to its last.

How much we lose in this way is constantly brought home to me by observation of people's varying attention to landscape. I happen to live (or rather I happen to have been able to decide to live, for volition decidedly comes into it) in such a position that from my window I am able to enjoy one of the finest views in the world—in the foreground forests and vineyards and two beautiful old castles, then a lake and, beyond its five-mile breadth, mountains rising almost sheer from the water. People come from all over the world to enjoy our scenery, and many settle for life—as I hope I have done.

If you live in a place of popular holiday resort like that you are not altogether cut off from your friends: we have frequent callers. All, on being taken on to the balcony or into the grounds, exclaim *How beautiful!* Not one yet has failed to pay this expected tribute.

But what a difference in the degree to which different individuals enjoy the beauty! Some take a comprehensive sweeping view, utter their sincere *How beautiful!* and turn to other subjects. Others examine the landscape, item by item, remark on this mountain or that, on this village or that, on this building or that, on the varying colorings of purple and green and blue, on the trees and the vines and the boats.

I feel that it is these last who get their money's worth for the journey they have undertaken and who are genuinely repaid for the fatigues of travel. They see a hundred times more than the others.

So it is with a picture or a poem. By mere dint of attention one man will get much more out of it than another. There are all grades of picture-lovers; the lowest being represented by the lady who once said to my wife in a picture-gallery—*"Do come on, dear. Why can't you learn how to take them in at a glance as I do?"* So, too, there are all grades of poetry-lovers. To make a confession, I myself have fallen several grades since I was a boy. Working under pressure most of my time, I find that when I try to relax from business over a book of poetry, and to concentrate in another and more pleasurable way, I can only with effort do so. I find myself passing impatiently from poem to poem, "taking them in at a glance" instead of focusing, concentrating, giving *attention.* I need a course of Poetry Appreciation lessons to pull me back to my old habit of attention. I am quite sure that some who read this will admit to themselves that they have fallen into the same need. Modern life is too relentless; it makes for divided interests and dissipated attention, and from this, undoubtedly, music suffers.

It is quite certain that thousands who call themselves music-lovers have never begun to realize this necessity for Attention, and those writers who have told us, and are forever telling us, that Appreciation makes music "too easy" ought to realize how foolish a remark they have been making when we assure them that the prime object of the Appreciationist is to bring about THE HABIT OF ATTENTION.

There is a very real sense in which it may be said that Appreciation makes listening not more but less "easy". It makes listening *not more easy but more pleasurable.*

We are, I suppose, all of us, good enough philosophers to avoid confusion between pleasure and ease.

"PRESENTATION"

I have found that many of my American friends use, almost as a daily technical term, a word that is not, I think, so much used, or used in just that way, in Britain—the word "Presentation" (which they pronounce with a long "e" in the first syllable).[1]

The authority for the use of the word with just the sense in which they use it is ancient. The *Shorter Oxford English Dictionary* gives 1597 as the earliest date known for the use of the word in the sense of "A setting forth, a statement".

I will give an example. On one occasion in America when, lecturing to an audience of 1,500 high school boys and girls, I had the happiness to please an educationist friend who was present, he came to me with a compliment I much valued— "Say! that was a bully preezentation. That rang the bell!" Whether this commendation was deserved or not is irrelevant to the point at which I am driving, which is that in American educational circles method and manner do count.

The impression I have received in the course of years (though I may be quite wrong about this) is that American teachers are more interested in the elementation of "Presentation" than are British. It has seemed to me that the way in which a teacher or lecturer "lays out" his material receives more notice among the Americans than among us. I believe that a British teacher listening to a lecture may be paying quite as much attention as would an American teacher to *what the lecturer says,* but that he or she is probably paying rather less attention to *the way he says it.*

Now the way a thing is said is of high importance. Heaven knows how many prophets, philosophers and poets the world has had within it without learning anything from them, merely because they were not, in their "Presentation", systematic, logical, coherent, and intelligible—to say nothing, for the moment, of being humanly sympathetic and hence initially interesting.

---

[1] Some American must have mispronounced this word in conversation with Dr. Scholes. All good Americans use it generously, but with a *short* "e" in the first syllable. W. E.

It should be noted, however, that some of the greatest thinkers have been the best talkers, that great learning and deep thought have often been accompanied by great ability in "Presentation". Take up Darwin's *Origin of Species* and you will see that he has this ability. Faraday, decidedly, had it, and was a past master in the art of expounding the principles of electricity to audiences of children.[1] Sir Oliver Lodge has it. When he gives a broadcast talk on some phase of science thousands listen who up to recently never took any interest in the subject, and at the end of the talk they have definitely gained something—which last cannot be said of all attractive lecturers, for (as with the preachers) there are some who can enthrall an audience, flatter them by the suggestion that they are learning, and yet leave in their minds practically no deposit of fresh thought.

For an example of defective "Presentation" in musical literature, take up one of Parry's very valuable books—say his *Bach*. For an example of good "Presentation" take up any book by Hadow. Parry's book, by the value of its ideas, compels one to travel to the end, but the journey is not easy: one has constantly to turn back and examine afresh the ground one has passed over, and even so one is worried by the thought that one is missing features of the landscape.

We have many an example of unpractical presentation in the series of popular treatises that from time to time appear. A publisher organizes a series covering all the subjects in science, art, and literature, and commissions well-known specialists to write the volumes on their particular subjects. In any such series it is common to find that among a number of finely practical volumes are scattered a number of others that are nearly valueless to the public—the authors not having gauged the minds of their readers. To those who have studied the subject already these volumes are of no interest, being somewhat too elementary *réchauffés* of what they already know, while to those who do not know it (those for whom they are really in-

[1] See Tyndall's account in the *Dictionary of National Biography*. It seems, however, that Faraday sometimes overestimated the previous knowledge of the members of an adult audience. P. A. S.

tended) they are unintelligible because of the technicalities they introduce. If we could imagine a person who knows all the terms of a particular art or science without knowing its principles then perhaps we could imagine the person for whom some of those manuals are suitable—but human imagination has its limits!

The many articles on music in the latest edition of the *Encyclopaedia Britannica* have, at the time of writing, been before the musical world for four years; I have never seen them reviewed in any musical periodical, despite the fact that they contain some of the sanest and most erudite writing on music in the language. But are sanity and erudition the only requirements? I, as a musician, if I want to know about Biology, ought to be able to turn to the *Encyclopaedia* and, being an ordinary, fairly educated man, understand what I find. So, too, any biologist wishing to know about music should be able to turn to Professor Tovey's articles in the *Encyclopaedia* and get what he wants from them. Can he? I doubt it. Take the article on "Sonata Form" as a test case. It is admirable, but is it suited to the needs of the general reader?

A very great proportion of the musical literature issued suffers in just this way: it is unintelligible or almost so to the very people who need it and for whom it is written—crowded with detail perhaps, instead of drawing the necessary few clear lines, or, like some of these *Encyclopaedia* articles, reflecting over facts unknown to the general reader or principles he has not grasped.

Here is an example of something deliberately drafted to help the "lay reader" (and how pleasant it is to find that admirable unpaid ecclesiastical official remembered!). It occurs in a most excellently thought out and generally well-expressed article on "The Sport of the Age" in *The Fortnightly Review* (December 1930):

"Let me here explain, *for the benefit of the lay reader* [my italics], that the two crucial divisions of the scale in the older system are at the fifth and the fourth. These divisions determine tonic, dominant, and sub-dominant harmony, and therefore, of course, all the chromatic subtilizations of these. Abolish this traditional division of the language of music into three main tonal relations—those of tonic, dominant, and sub-dominant—and the fabric already begins to crumble. The whole-tone scale does abolish this distinction, for now the octave is not made up of five full-tone intervals plus two half-tones (E to F, and B to C), but simply of six full tones, the scale now being C, D, E, F sharp, G sharp, A sharp, C. The old harmonic society, that was based on the clearly-defined relations of a king-chord, two prime-minister chords, and some dependent people-chords, has thus been undermined. The next step was inevitable. Kingship and aristocracy went by the board; the scale was completely democratized; each note was declared to be as good as any other note, to be as capable of performing the same functions; the old tonality had given place to atonality."

Can the "lay reader" understand that passage? I should say that he will stumble at the outset over the terms "tonic, dominant, and sub-dominant" and their "chromatic subtilizations", and having thus stumbled, never catch up again. Just an extra six lines at that point, a statement as to what notes constitute these three chords in the key of C major, a reference to vamping, to the concertina as commonly played, to the harmonies of Sankey and Moody, to the waltzes of commerce, to anything that would make him recognize the chords that are being talked of, and he would have continued happily to the end. That passage as it stands would have been perfectly in place in the *Musical Times,* but in the general press it needs a little simplification. I offer this suggestion with deference and merely as my personal opinion, for the article is by the most-read music critic of the British Isles, Ernest Newman: he has thousands of "lay readers", for whom, on occasion, he provides suitable nourishment without in so doing losing his hold on the vicars and deans and bishops who also sit under him.

It is, too, really amazing how confused is much of the actual writing in books of music. Look at this from a well-known *Dictionary of Musical Terms* on sale everywhere in the English-speaking world. It is from a definition of "Trio", and attempts to make clear the reason why we speak of Minuet and *Trio.*

"The curious appellation is thus accounted for. When in times long gone by, to the first minuet (consisting of two parts) a second (likewise of two parts) was added, the latter was for variety's sake written in three parts, the former being generally in two parts only."

We who know music can see what he means. But what will the person who needs the definition make of it? It will merely leave him dizzy! I see no harm in giving the name of the author of this definition, much as I respect his memory, for his writing was generally so perspicuous that his failure has thus become a warning to the best of us—the late Professor Frederick Niecks.

I once by chance came on a highly technical article that any one can read and I put it forward as a model. Turning to *Chambers' Encyclopaedia* for some date or name concerning *Oratorio,* my eye was caught, as it often is in a book of reference, by a neighbor article, in this case one on *Orchard.* It struck me as a bit of the clearest expository English I had ever read, and referring to the table of contents to discover who wrote it I found, to my surprise, the name of R. D. Blackmore (of *Lorna Doone*). That man could write, and he visualized his readers. Any English gardener who is not quite illiterate can grasp that article at a first reading, any cultured Englishman can read and re-read it for the perfection of its style, and any teacher can admire it as a model of "Presentation".

I suggest that this matter of "Presentation" is worth a very great deal more attention than musicians have usually given it, and that a higher general standard would be possible if in discussing books on musical subjects reviewers would apply as much discriminating judgment to manner as they do to matter.

Exposition is an art, and there is no reason why we should not feel the same thrill in its able practice as we do in the able practice of any other art.

But able practice comes to few of us by nature. It is only after effort that intelligibility is attained. Can you, a teacher, describe clearly and interestingly any incident that happened within your notice as you went to school yesterday morning? If you had the luck as you went along to see an interesting murder committed could you give the jury a clear idea of just what happened? Can you explain to a reasonably intelligent stranger the half-mile route to the railway station? Can you sum up the gist of a speech or sermon you have heard, in such a way as to convey a clear and correct impression to your listener? Can you give a friend an impromptu ten minutes' sketch of Beethoven's or Bach's or Wagner's position in musical art? Can you sketch out an imaginary lecture on the orchestra or a course of six lectures on *The Growth of Music* or *The Story of British Music?* Can you plan and deliver a lesson to the third form on *Haydn,* or to the sixth [1] on *Wagner and the Opera,* or *Elgar,* or *British Composers of To-day?* Can you take any subject which you already know, as a subject, and lay out, in your mind or on paper, a suitable term's course of instruction in it for pupils of a given age?

Do you really prepare your lessons in Musical Appreciation or do you just walk into the classroom with a couple of phonograph records in your hand and a couple of vague ideas in your head? Having planned your lesson to the last little point, do you find yourself adaptable enough to deviate suitably from the plan when you realize that some of what you had intended to say is above the heads of a part of the class? Do you take steps to find out how far your instruction is "going home", and after every discovered failure think out its nature and grasp how you can avoid its repetition?

Do you find your ready-to-hand vocabulary adequate? If not, are you taking steps to improve it by exercising yourself in producing apt adjectives to characterize all sorts of situations that occur, the people you meet, the music you hear, and so forth? Nobody can be a good teacher who talks confusedly

---

[1] Six "forms" ("grade" divisions) have been established in English schools since the 16th century. As the six forms include pupils from the ages of eight or nine years (First Form) to the ages of sixteen or eighteen years (Sixth Form) it is obvious that a "form" exceeds the span of a year which is allotted to a "grade" in the United States. However, subdivisions of later date exist, such as Lower Fourth, Upper Fourth, "Remove" (between Fourth and Fifth Forms) and some form between the Fifth and Sixth, and these allow for more precise grading. W. E.

every day; do you, then, take pains to make yourself clear in general conversation?

In other words, are you just content to know *your subject,* or do you take pleasure in acquiring *the art of its "Presentation"?*

ON THE ART OF DEFINITION—WITH FUGUE AS AN EXAMPLE

Obviously the knack of framing a simple, precise definition is an essential part of the technique of the real teacher, whatever his subject.

An apt definition in Musical Appreciation teaching brings to a point and summarizes what the pupils should, in most cases, have already been led to observe.

For in general the pupils' observation must come first and the teacher's definition last. One dare not lay down an absolute rule on this or any other point in teaching practice, but the common order will certainly be (1) Observation, (2) Definition.

Take Fugue for an example. The teacher feels that the moment has arrived to introduce the class to this type of composition. Having excited their interest in any way that appears suitable he performs a fugue (preferably a lively one) and invites them to notice as closely as they can its characteristics. With luck one or another member of the class will mention to him all the outstanding characteristics such as:

1. That the piece played is not in "lumps" (or chords) so much as in interwoven melodies (a class that has been previously trained to observe should certainly make this remark at once).
2. That at the opening the piece begins with only one "line of notes", others then being added one by one.
3. That all these "lines of notes" begin with the same little tune.
4. That this little tune often recurs subsequently throughout the composition—pervades it, in fact.

Doubtless some members of the class will also call attention to points of minor importance, some of them peculiar to the particular composition played, and these can be quietly put on one side for later consideration, and the main points above first crystallized by the class or the teacher into a precise definition. This may take the following form:

DEFINITION—*1st Draft*

A Fugue is a composition in a certain number of "lines of notes", which enter one by one at the opening. Each line of notes begins with the same little tune and this tune becomes the main material of the whole piece.

The teacher recasts this into the conventional shape, introducing to the class the necessary technical terms:

DEFINITION—*2nd Draft*

A Fugue is a *Contrapuntal* composition in a fixed number of VOICES (or "Parts"). At the opening the Voices enter one by one with the SUBJECT, out of which the whole Fugue then grows.

That, though incomplete, is a fairly adequate working definition from a listener's point of view. There are thousands of people who never trouble to listen to a Fugue because they have not been led to observe these simple laws of its being, and consequently do not gather what the composer is doing. Any teacher who, in a first lesson, draws the class to that point, keeping their interest throughout, has done a good piece of work, and quite enough for one day. Indeed, once that point has been reached it may be felt good business to go no further for a little time with anything like "teaching", but, for a week or two perhaps, to take opportunities of performing and re-performing to the class (mingled with recapitulatory performance of compositions of a different type already known) a selection of three or four Fugues of a nature as immediately attractive as possible and well contrasted as to speed, mood, character of subject, &c.

Perhaps some of these Fugues, having become familiar, may then be examined in detail and various other features elicited, e.g.

1. Many members of the class will by now have been struck by the fact that the second voice to enter does so in a different key from the first voice, and so the idea of ANSWER is intro-

duced. But note that it is not good to explain anything as though it were a mere arbitrary fact. The origin of the Fugue is *choral singing* and the phenomenon we have just noticed obviously arises, in the first instance, from this fact. We see in Subject and Answer a reminder of the difference in pitch between treble and alto voices and between tenor and bass (roughly a difference of a fifth—with the other difference of pitch between the treble and tenor and between alto and bass, i.e. about an octave). To this may be added, as another part of the explanation, the fact that *change of key* in music is welcomed by the mind of the listener, as offering relief and variety, that (as the pupils have observed previously in simpler forms) the relation of Tonic-Dominant is the most natural one, giving such relief with the least possible "wrench". In this way the phenomenon of Subject-Answer is rationalized, and a glimpse afforded of the part played by historical circumstance and aesthetic principle in the bringing into existence of musical conventions.

It may here be remarked that to the listener the difference between "real" and "tonal" Answers has little or no importance. It is not noticed by the normal ear, and there is no reason why it should be noticed, since it is merely a composer's device—a makeshift to avoid a certain inconvenience. A student of composition needs to know all about it; a listener need know nothing. And as for describing compositions as "Tonal Fugues" or "Real Fugues" just because of the appearance or non-appearance of that detail of construction (often only in the Exposition), that is an antiquated academic absurdity.

We can now add a detail to the definition already accepted, so that it will run as follows:

DEFINITION—*3rd Draft*

A Fugue is a *Contrapuntal* composition in a fixed number of "VOICES" (or "Parts"). At the opening the Voices enter one by one with the SUBJECT, out of which the whole Fugue then grows.

The successive appearance of the voices at the opening of the Fugue (called the "EXPOSITION", or "Enunciation"), is alternately in the Tonic and Dominant keys; the voices which give it out in the

Dominant are considered to respond to those that give it out in the Tonic, and so to their introductions of the subject the term ANSWER is applied.

We have now a definition that covers practically every composition to which any musician would think of attaching the description "Fugue". If a piece of music conforms to that definition it is a Fugue, and if it does not it is not a Fugue. Obviously, then, it is the only universally acceptable definition of a Fugue.

We can now, however, proceed to collect from the pupils any other characteristics of their little selected and varied batch of Fugues, and as they do so we shall probably accumulate the following list of devices, none of them essential but all of them frequent:

1. Countersubject.
2. Episode.
3. Pedal.
4. Stretto.

Very many text-book definitions of Fugue exist which include all these. But properly they are no part of a definition, for look into Bach's "48" (which we all accept as the most typical and standard collection of fugues in existence) and you will find:

1. COUNTERSUBJECT. Fourteen of the "48" have none whatever, and in some of the others the use of the Countersubject is very slight or non-existent once the Enunciation is closed. Evidently, then, the presence of a Countersubject is not essential to Fugue.[1]

2. EPISODE. The very first Fugue in the "48" has no Episode whatever—yet we all accept it as a Fugue! It "feels" thoroughly like a Fugue (which is the only reliable test) and doubtless hundreds of musicians the first time they heard it did not notice the absence of Episodes. Evidently, then, the presence of Episode, however usual, is not essential to Fugue.

[1] At the entrance of the second voice the first voice must accompany it with *something*. By the degree of persistency with which this something recurs in the Fugue as an accompaniment to the Subject (if it does recur at all) it sets up a claim to be called a Countersubject. Just what degree of persistency is necessary to the claim is a matter on which no authoritative and agreed decision appears to exist, but there are very many cases where nobody would ever think of asserting such a claim. P. A. S.

3. PEDAL. Twenty-eight of the "48" have no Pedal whatever. This, then, is also quite clearly one of the non-essentials.

4. STRETTO. Twenty-nine of the "48" have no Stretto. The same remark, then, applies.

Sometimes we see not only all the four devices included in a definition of Fugue, as though they were essentials, but also that of Codetta. From a listener's point of view the Codetta (often a mere few notes in length) is perhaps generally of rather slight importance. If there is anything in a Fugue that the class can be pardoned for overlooking it is a Codetta.

Anyhow, eleven of the "48" have no Codetta, so that to include that feature is merely to load up the definition unnecessarily—to say the least.

(Here, in discreet parenthesis and a subdued voice, I would add that in many Fugues the class can be generously excused if they fail to notice the Countersubject. Hidden as it is, from its second appearance, in the web of melodic threads, it often takes a pretty good musician to pick it out. Let us bachelors and doctors of music be honest with ourselves; how often after hearing a Fugue for the first time has it occurred to us that it has or has not a Countersubject? On a microscopic consideration of intentions, the composer's use of a Countersubject has its artistic justification, in many instances, in a negative rather than a positive advantage; he has, by uniformly using one and the same secondary theme as the accompaniment of his primary theme avoided introducing a lot of new and varying melodic matter in his Enunciation and has thus prevented a slight element of disunity. From a listener's point of view, then, Countersubject is often relatively unimportant—and this heresy is uttered with confidence!)

We can now add to our definition, so that it appears as follows:

DEFINITION—4th Draft

A Fugue is a *Contrapuntal* composition in a fixed number of "VOICES" (or "Parts"). At the opening the Voices enter one by one with the SUBJECT, out of which the whole Fugue then grows.

The successive appearance of the Voices at the opening of the

Fugue (called the "EXPOSITION", or "Enunciation"), is alternately in the Tonic and Dominant keys; the voices which give it out in the Dominant are considered to respond to those that give it out in the Tonic, and so to their introductions of the subject the term ANSWER is applied.

In some Fugues the following additional characteristics occur: (*a*) Each of the voices that has entered with Subject or Answer may, throughout the Exposition (and possibly elsewhere in the Fugue) continue with one and the same definite melodic phrase, called the COUNTERSUBJECT. (*b*) The various groups of entries of the Subject matter of the Fugue throughout its course may be separated from one another by passages (usually of a "development" nature) called EPISODES. (*c*) At some point (generally towards the end) the bass voice may for a time remain stationary on the Tonic or Dominant note, thus producing the effect called PEDAL. (*d*) In one or more such groups voices may enter with Subject, or with Subject and Answer, in an overlapping called STRETTO.

Of course nobody could be expected to learn this definition by heart but the class should know its substance, and if it has built up the definition clause by clause in the manner shown it will have little difficulty in doing so.

We now come to the question of the general "form" of Fugue. By the time a class has reached the point where it is to make acquaintance with Fugue it has probably heard a good deal of varied music and has learned that very much of it falls into a three-division shape. Ternary, or "Aria Form", of course does this in a very simple way, and "Sonata Form" (though for historical reasons often labeled "binary") does so in a more elaborate way.

Writers often, with that passion for classification that leads musicians to wish to thrust every piece of music into either the "binary" or the "ternary" pigeon-hole, speak of Fugue as ternary. Practically all the authors of text-books on composition do so, and so, too, the writers of text-books of Appreciation. To the present writer this seems to be one of the most lamentable exhibitions of the academic mentality. How very, very few Fugues *feel* to be ternary, as you listen to them—and music being written for the ear, not the eye, the effect on the ear is necessarily the criterion of form.

Compare a piece in "Aria Form", or in classical "Sonata Form". Here the three divisions are quite unmistakable. A child can be told to hold up its hand when the first section returns as the third section and, if at all musically intelligent and a little experienced, will do so with almost infallible correctness. Rarely is any exercise of that sort possible in Fugue, the very object of the composer being, indeed, to *avoid* throughout his work noticeably clear divisions of every kind.

The remark of Professor Donald Tovey in the *Encyclopaedia Britannica* that "Fugue is a texture the rules of which do not suffice to determine the shape of the composition as a whole" is obviously sound. The "rules" of Fugue are indeed very slight, and so far as its "form" is concerned practically amount to nothing more than the simple universal rule that into whatever keys it may stray in its middle portion it shall end in the key in which it began.[1]

This return to the tonic key, in order to end, is clearly not enough to constitute a ternary form, otherwise practically all compositions would have to be considered ternary—including all Bach's dance pieces, almost all of which we all of us treat as simple binary.

Now look through Bach's "48" (using the eye this time, instead of the ear). Where is there one that has a return of the Exposition? In every case, indeed, the most striking feature of the Exposition (the feature that most catches the ear) is entirely absent—i.e. the appearance of the voices one by one. And in few cases has the final portion of the Fugue any resemblance to the first portion beyond that of being based on the same subject matter (as nearly all the Fugue is) and that of being in the same key. In a great many cases there is room for doubt as to

---

[1] The suggestion has been made (I think also by Professor Tovey somewhere) that it is, strictly, incorrect to speak of "*a* Fugue", and that we should rather describe a composition as written "*in* Fugue". Here again the idea is that Fugue is a definable style rather than a definable form. (See Vaughan William's article on Fugue in Grove's *Dictionary*.) P. A. S.

where the final section begins, and text-books which analyze Bach's "48" will often be found to differ on this point.

Then the final portion is usually a good deal shorter than the first portion which it is supposed to *repeat* (for "Recapitulation" is the habitual text-book term for this portion).

I have had the curiosity to look into this last point a little nicely. I will accept the analysis in that standard text-book on the "48" by the late Dr. Iliffe. It sets out every Fugue in a ternary tabulation accounting for every measure of it under the head of "Enunciation Section", "Modulatory Section" or "Recapitulation Section", and the disparity between the first and last of these is striking. You will find an Enunciation of 12 measures and a Recapitulation of 3 (Fugue 7), an Enunciation of 22 and a Recapitulation of 5 (Fugue 12), an Enunciation of 70 measures and a Recapitulation of 18 (Fugue 36), an Enunciation of 24 measures and a Recapitulation of 2 (Fugue 24). Dr. Iliffe shows indeed, four Fugues possessing only 2 measures of "Recapitulatory Section", three possessing only 3 measures, five showing only 4—and so on. The so-called "Recapitulation" is, then, in many cases most perfunctory, considered as such.

Obviously Bach did not have the recapitulatory object in mind. He wanted to wind up his Fugue in the tonic key, and he did so —*voilà tout!* There are even two instances where Dr. Iliffe himself is baffled in the attempt to find a "Recapitulatory Section" (Fugues 19 and 20): in these he gives merely an "Enunciation Section" and a "Modulatory Section", showing the latter as ending with a "Coda".

In only three of the "48" are the so-called "Recapitulatory Sections" as long as the "Enunciation Sections" and if all the "Recapitulatory Sections" are added together they amount to only 376 measures as against 921 in the "Enunciation Sections".

Surely the time has come to abandon this text-book fiction of Fugue as a ternary form! [1]

---

[1] Among well-known writers on Fugue who unhesitatingly adopt the ternary "fiction" (as I venture to call it) are Iliffe, Prout, and Riemann. On the other hand, Stewart Macpherson (*Form in Music*, p. 205) says bluntly; "A fugue is frequently divided, for the purposes of analysis, into three parts, viz. (1) the Enunciation (or Exposition); (ii) the Middle (or modulatory) section; and (iii)

I would suggest that a fugue with many entries separated by episodes suggests to the ear rather the Rondo type of composition than the simple ternary.

There seems to be something about Fugue that sends even the best-balanced analysts off their heads, and the amazing attempt to cram it into a ternary strait-jacket illustrates this. When we come to lesser theorists we find the area of muddle extending far and wide until it covers the whole area of Fugue.

One piece of folly committed by some of them is to stigmatize the Fugue as a purely intellectual exercise.

"Inspiration, as we understand it in these days, there is none; neither to the heart nor to the senses does the fugue address itself but to the mind only, by the ingenuity of its procedures and the inexhaustible variety of its combinations.

"A fine fugue can certainly, it is true, evoke an idea of the grand, the monumental, by its strong construction, its unity, and the harmonious proportions of its lines.[1] Another fugue will appear subtle and ingenious, by the pertinency, or by the unexpectedness, presiding over the working up of its various artifices. But no other emotions are to be sought from it; the pleasure which it offers is purely intellectual, unimpassioned and without enthusiasm." (Lavignac,

the Final section. It must be said, though, that this division of the latter part of a fugue into Middle and Final sections is in many cases entirely impossible, as there is often little or nothing that in any way indicates such a separation of its parts as is implied thereby. In many of the fugues of Bach this is notably the case." P. A. S.

[1] There seems to be some very poor psychological and aesthetic thinking back of such statements as these. "Inspiration" appears to be confused with "emotion" (presumably, the same emotion that is to be expressed in an ensuing composition) and unless a composition throbs with that kind of expressive emotion it is apparently considered as devoid of any and every kind of feeling, even of "enthusiasm". On the psychological side, then, the author quoted has apparently never discovered "feeling" and "affective coloring" as contrasted with "emotion". As to aesthetics, the belief upheld by so many aestheticians, to the effect that art is always more truly *impressive* than *expressive*—and, indeed, even those terms themselves and the thought they connote—would appear similarly never to have entered the writer's horizon. And since the author is the eminent Lavignac, one wonders whether for once he failed to express his precise meaning, or whether it could be that the distinguished translator failed to translate Lavignac's thought exactly. However, the explicit statement by an American, a little further on, is open to no such conjectures. It all seems to prove that musicians themselves cannot be relied upon to give us a clear understanding of what music is and what psychological factors are engaged in its reception. W. E.

Music and Musicians. "Sixteenth Printing" of the American Edition, being the 4th Edition of it, "Revised and Edited" by no less an authority than H. E. Krehbiel. Still on sale.)

Now surely, to any man or woman with ears and heart, the existence of the "48" with its wide range of emotional expression (from playful to profound), or of Bach's organ fugues, with their even wider range, is enough to condemn such a statement as that (and the harm it must do in a book for young students is appalling!). Yet we find such statements again and again. Here is a parallel passage from another author. Lavignac was Professor of the Paris Conservatoire for over forty years, the writer of what follows was for some time on the staff of one of the admirable women's colleges of the United States:

"It is in some respects unfortunate that chronological order requires one to begin with the driest and most difficult of instrumental forms, the Fugue, which represents the highest development of counterpoint. Opinions differ as to whether emotion is ever found in a fugue, or whether works in this form are purely intellectual exercises." (Grace Gridley Wilm, *The Appreciation of Music,* 1928.)

Akin to this heresy is the one that Fugue is bound by "strict rules", whereas it is, in fact, subject to absolutely no rules whatever except those mentioned in the very simple definition given above. Once the Exposition is over we may say that Fugue is one of the freest of all forms (indeed so free that, as I have hinted, it is rather a style than a form). If any reader who has been brought up in the "strict rule" heresy will take the trouble to analyze Bach's "48", their infinite variety of plan will show him its folly.

Here are some examples of statements of the heresy. The authoress just quoted makes the following perfectly amazing assertion:

"There cannot be much room for play of imagination in a fugue written in strict form. The subject once chosen, the composer of a strict fugue is hampered by rules almost as exact as a formula in engineering."

The following comes from *Music, What it Means and How to Understand It,* by Leigh Henry (who, it will be seen, treats Fugue as a thing of the past):

"The Fugue was one of the strictest musical forms; the rules for composing it were very fixed" (page 129).

The number of authors who have perpetrated thus blunder is very great, though not all are quite such whole-hoggers as the two just quoted, who, it may be guessed, think of Canon and Fugue in one mental breath—the strictest and one of the freest of musical styles. One guesses that thousands of young people in Musical Appreciation classes must have been told this stupid tale about the machine-like "strictness" of Fugue—with what result one can imagine. One would like to give them all a rousing performance of Bach's *Fuga alla Giga* on a big organ, and tell them to forget all they have ever been told on the subject. The teachers who do this sort of damage to musical minds are the brothers and sisters of those who spoil for life so many young people's enjoyment of Shakespeare.

I now propose to offer just one or two of what I consider "bad shots" at a definition of Fugue—all of them from well-known and widely sold books.

The following comes in the glossary at the end of Kinscella's *Music and Romance for Youth*:

"A composition in which two or more independent voices or parts combine at regular intervals to state, contrast, and develop the characteristic features of a single theme."

Now even if it be admitted that this is correct, *does it mean anything* to the person who, not knowing what Fugue is, turns to the glossary? Moreover, the term "regular intervals" is ambiguous; if it applies to intervals of pitch, that only refers to the "stating" or Exposition section, not, as is implied, to the whole. If it applies to intervals of time it is untrue. And the words "contrast and develop" are vague. No! That will hardly do. It is a definition that does not define.

Here is another attempt, from *A Gateway to Music,* by Blancke and Speck:

"The most intricate and highly developed form of polyphonic composition. A fugue of the simplest type consists of a theme or subject stated by one voice or part and answered in the dominant by another voice; the development then follows. The details of fugue composition are involved and technical."

Put yourself in the position of a person who does not know. He is given the impression, surely, that only two voices are involved. And, apart from that, the definition is exasperatingly vague. (The word "development", by the way, is not included in the glossary, and the words "the development then follows" are left for him to guess about.)

And here is a "bloomer" from Florence Jubb's *The Rudiments of Music for Piano Students*:

"The subject is heard in one voice part and then a second enters with the answer in the dominant—the COUNTERSUBJECT."

Is there any such enormous difficulty in briefly defining Fugue? If the definitions already given in this chapter be too long for a mere glossary, how would one of the following serve?

A. A composition either choral or, if (as very often) instrumental, yet in choral style to the extent of being a woven texture of a fixed number of melodic lines, each with an independent existence like that of a voice part in a choral work. Its main material is a brief thread of melody, called the "Subject", with which all the parts in succession enter at the opening and which thereafter constantly re-appears in one part after another.

B. A composition made up by the interweaving of a fixed number of separate "voices" or "parts", independent like those of a chorus. A brief snatch of melody serves as its "Subject", re-appearing continually throughout the course of the music. At the outset the "voices" enter one by one, and with this "Subject" (alternately in the keys of Tonic and Dominant).

Surely dozens of brief definitions like that are possible, varying slightly in their wording, but always bringing in the three cardinal features of Fugue: (*a*) its polyphonic nature, (*b*) its development from a "Subject", and (*c*) the one-by-one entry of its voices at the outset. Where these authors seem to me to fail is in not *themselves* having a clear idea of what are the distinguishing features of a Fugue.

I have felt a little compunction in selecting these passages for quotation as they are no feebler than a great many other textbook attempts at definition of the Fugue. What follows, however, can fairly be quoted as possessing exceptional qualities. It occurs in a chapter, "Polyphonic Forms", in Dr. Sigmund Spaeth's *The Art of Enjoying Music* (1933). After a quotation from Milton and some remarks on this, we come to actual definition as follows:

"It is horizontal music of the highest type. A single theme is introduced, without accompaniment of any kind. It must be short enough to be easily retained in the memory, yet long enough to have a definite melodic outline. Usually a few measures are sufficient. This theme, or subject, is immediately answered, often by its own imitation in a different key, sometimes by a second subject of independent character, although it should properly grow out of the first subject in some way. There may be a third and even a fourth subject. After they are all introduced in an exposition similar to that of sonata form, there is a definite development, and again the formula of statement, contrast, and reminder asserts itself."

I hope I am not being unfair to Dr. Spaeth when I say that all this, unless it is interpreted in the light of some personal idea in his mind but unknown to us (or possibly based on some special fugue of which he is thinking as he writes), is merely a confusion. It is incredible that Dr. Spaeth is describing, as a normal type, that rarity, the Fugue with two, three, or four subjects.

An example which he gives in music type, a little later in the chapter, may possibly throw a little light: it is the No. 21 in B flat, from the "48", which, it will be remembered, is in three voices and possesses from the outset two countersubjects, regularly used throughout the Fugue (of the "48" there are seven or less on these lines). If we read that definition again with that particular (exceptional) fugue in mind we can perhaps get an inkling of what Dr. Spaeth is driving at, but even so we must still, surely, remain baffled at the notion of the subject being immediately answered ". . . by a second subject of independent character", and so on. I give it up! This definition is too rich in opportunities for conjecture. The book is described as one which "can be used by any teacher who has a real enthusiasm for music, not necessarily a technical knowledge". Perhaps my own modicum of technical knowledge is getting in my way. At all events I confess myself baffled!

Really this question of clear, precise definition is worth every teacher's attention. Can you, on the spur of the moment, offer in the fewest possible and the simplest words a definition of any of the common phenomena of music? If not you are not prepared for your task, for it is evident that the subject you are supposed to teach to others is not clear in your own mind.

"ACADEMIC"

The history of Education is the history of constantly revived attempts to rescue various subjects from the academics. Musical Appreciation is one of those attempts at rescue; yet, in the course of nature, music will sooner or later need rescuing from this also—if we don't look out!

How academicism can ruin an enthralling subject of study we see if we take up a school edition of Shakespeare of twenty-five to forty years ago—preferably the famous Clarendon Press edition, or the Pitt Press Shakespeare for Schools, one of which was used in every better kind of secondary school and both of which were excellent in their way but that not in the very least the way of youth.

I find on my shelves a play in each of these editions and observe that in the Oxford production (issued 1891) the late Professor W. Aldis Wright supplies 122 pages of Introduction and Notes to 74 pages of Shakespeare, and that in the Cambridge one (issued 1900) Mr. A. W. Verity offers 181 pages of Introduction and Notes to 110 of Shakespeare.[1] As in both cases the

---

[1] In the United States an edition of Shakespeare's *Merchant of Venice* (issued 1916) contained 94 pages of Shakespeare to 73 pages of Notes. A later edition

notes are in small type and the play in large the disproportion is terrifying—"But one halfpennyworth of bread to this intolerable deal of sack". (However, nobody got drunk on it!)

Consider the impression this abundance of apparatus must make on the mind of a schoolchild—THE TERRIFYING DIFFICULTY OF UNDERSTANDING SHAKESPEARE!

As a schoolboy I was more fortunate than some. We used "Hunter's Annotated Shakespeare", which had merely three or four pages of introduction, few notes except those few absolutely necessary to the modern reader faced with occasional archaic expressions, and these notes at the bottom of the pages, instead of at the end of the book (the incessant turning backwards in the other two editions must have been the very devil! What was the point of it? Why is French literature edited for British school use still usually annotated in this thread-breaking fashion?).

Twenty years ago there was issued the S. P. B. Mais edition, with the notes still further reduced (but, again, placed at the end—which is wrong), and these including many skilful pointers to dramatic intention and significant detail. Other editions, of course, abound, with varying good and bad qualities. But all nowadays, I think, tend to economy in notes and introductions.

The issue that is raised in my mind as I examine the four editions I have chosen for mention is this: *Is the object of our Shakespeare lesson to give the pupils enjoyment of Shakespeare, or is it to teach them English grammar, etymology, history, &c., using Shakespeare as our means of doing so?*

We frequently see letters like this in the papers:

"Many people put Shakespeare behind them for ever when they leave school because they were forced to study him when they were there. If his works were never treated as a school subject many would turn to them in later life through curiosity, and enjoy them as a discovery of their own." (*Times*, 10 August, 1931.)

As I myself was happy enough to be brought up on the modest Rev. John Hunter's edition, and by masters who had the sense

of the same play (issued 1929) had 103 pages of Shakespeare to 17 pages of notes: and the tendency so manifested continues. W. E.

to allot roles to members of the class and have Shakespeare read as dramatically as possible, I should probably not be able to understand these complaints but for recollecting seeing an elder sister grapple nightly with the Clarendon Press edition and afterwards finding the Pitt Press edition in use (for examination preparation) in two schools where I became music master.

Despite these letters, there is nothing wrong with Shakespeare as a school subject; nor is there anything wrong with Scott as such. Says Mr. J. B. Priestley (interview in *Teacher's World*, 23 July, 1920): "It is extraordinary how few young men read Scott. They were made to read him at school and found him dull, and now they do not read him for themselves." Sir J. C. Squire says the same thing; in reviewing a volume of Scott's letters he exclaims: "What a pity it is that one of the most enchanting characters in our annals is so inadequately appreciated simply because the young are made to read his novels and poems at school!"

Now, so far as I know, there are no heavily annotated school editions of Scott. Even his own absurdly weighty baggage of antiquarian annotations is nowadays often discarded. Mr. Priestley says that the trouble is the choice of the wrong works for the purpose: not *Ivanhoe,* he declares, is the right meat for babes, but *Rob Roy.* Without altogether realizing what is wrong with *Ivanhoe* I should personally agree that the vigorous and swift-moving *Rob Roy* is indeed as good a beginning as could be made. Anyhow, this choice of suitable works for school reading is one on which too much care cannot be taken. My schoolboy experience leads me to think that the common notion that the fanciful "pastoral plays" of Shakespeare are the right food for youth is all wrong. We liked life and action, and the historical plays pleased us best of all. Our minds had not developed to the point where they could relish delicate fantasy. We did not want the light and airy, but vigorous action and the rumbustious.

The main thought I have in writing this section is that we musicians should take warning from our colleagues on the literary side of education. When we find Quiller-Couch in his

The Art of Reading saying, "As Greek is commonly taught, I regret to say, whether they have learnt it or not makes a distressingly small difference to most boys' appreciation of Homer", we should pause a moment and reflect. He is concerned with the Appreciation of Homer and we with the Appreciation of Music. After reading his cheerless statement we should never see a Classical Master without it flashing into our mind—"There, but for the grace of God, goes——!"

Necessary warnings are then, (*a*) that the choice of the right masterpieces for study is a vital factor for success and that the very works that seem to us just the thing for the young may not be much relished by them, and (*b*) that the plan of heavy annotation (of unnecessary annotation, and annotation not *strictly relevant to the matter in hand*) is fatal.

An eternally sound maxim is that whatever dissipates "atmosphere" kills interest.

Aldis Wright was doubtless a man full of the minutest and most accurate learning, and, moreover, of the finest literary perception, but he did not understand the young, and I have some fear that in time to come some of the very best of the musicians who come to be engaged in Musical Appreciation may be the ones to bring it into discredit. It is common to hear fears expressed of Appreciation work falling into the hands of teachers who are not good enough musicians; I have just as much fear of its falling into the hands of musicians who are not good enough teachers.

The following I take from a letter written by Ernest Newman in commendation of certain apparatus intended for the teaching of Musical Appreciation: [1]

"If anything could reconcile me to the idea of being a child again and going once more through the awful round of pains and penalties and repressions and inhibitions peculiar to childhood, it would be the prospect of being able to learn music by a method such as this.

"The thesis might almost be maintained that if any of us still love art and literature after we have grown up, it is not because, but in spite of, our education in these matters. I myself can still re-

[1] The "Audiographic" Pianola Rolls of the Aeolian Company. P. A. S.

member how cordially I detested Shakespeare at one period of my school days, because Shakespeare, as we were taught him, was not a great imaginative poet but merely a pretext for certain exercises in parsing and analysis, and unusual grammatical constructions, and the lore of obsolete words. I have often thought since that Shakespeare must be a pretty good poet to have stood up against the way we were 'taught' him. And Beethoven and Bach and the rest of them must be pretty good composers if we can still like them after the way they were drummed into us, and the forbidding atmosphere of theory in which they were wrapped."

Presumably that drumming was done and that "theory" administered by sound professional musicians.

It was the Local Examination system that produced those heavy editions and killed the love of Shakespeare. Let us watch the examination menace in music.

And now, to close, a skit by some hand unknown, on a certain Shakespeare authority (a good-humored skit not to be taken too seriously, for A. C. Bradley's *Shakespearean Tragedy* is a great work):

> I dreamed that William Shakespeare's ghost
> Sat for a Civil Service post.
> The English paper in that year
> Was on the subject of "King Lear".
> William answered rather badly—
> You see, he hadn't read his Bradley.

HEARING AND DOING

There is an amazing statement, made often by musicians of great eminence whom we all respect, to the effect that music is not primarily an art of the ears, but one of the voice and fingers.[1]

This is not their exact wording of the statement, but it is almost what the statement amounts to. I give a few examples.

Sir John B. McEwen, Principal of the Royal Academy of Music, was in December 1932 reported in very many papers as having thus addressed a London choral society:

[1] A discussion bearing on this point will be found in the *American Editor's Preface*. W. E.

"Just as watching a football match will not improve the wind or stamina of the onlooker, so passive surrender to the magic voices of mechanized music will bring no live musical experience to the hearer. Active participation in real music-making is the goal to which all initial experience should lead, and failing that there will eventually come satiety and disinterest, if not actual distaste."

If this statement is not what I have described at the opening of this chapter it is very near it. The following, at any rate, is a fair paraphrase: "The Ear and Mind are insufficient for the enjoyment of music; unless the Throat or Fingers are engaged our 'musical experience' is dead."

Read Sir John McEwen's dictum afresh. It bears terribly hardly on concert audiences. The floor of the Queen's Hall swarming with Promenade Concert enthusiasts, "all silent and all damned". Out of all that crowd in the hall only the hundred men on the platform enjoying any "live musical experience"— or, reading the allegation in another way (for, as reported, there are several ways of reading it), out of all that audience only those who are impelled by what they hear to become performers profiting by what they hear!

Can this be so! Why do these people come, pay their shillings and stand there night by night. They must *think* they are getting something "live". Yet, if we are to believe Sir John, they are experiencing *satiety and "disinterest", if not actual distaste!*

When the reader has got his breath again I offer him the following, by Dr. H. C. Colles, chief music critic of the London *Times,* and of all our musicians one of the most genuinely desirous of our musical welfare; it comes from an introduction he very kindly wrote to the prospectus of a valuable "National Conference to discuss the Future of Amateur Music-Making", held under the auspices of the British Federation of Musical Competition Festivals, on 10th June, 1933:

"Concerts, festivals and competitions are all very delightful and useful things in their way but they are not musical life . . .

"A musical life is led by one to whom the making of music himself is an essential interest. . . .

"Can anything be done to start young people in real musical life, to rope them in to some form of corporate music-making. . . ?"

Those passages are taken from the beginning, middle, and end of Mr. Colles's page article. I have omitted many wise remarks, tending to encourage people to learn to sing and play and, this done, to set to work to sing and play together (which we all wish them to do), but I have certainly not by my omissions given any wrong impression of this very eminent music critic's view— musical *life* to him means self-performance.

Compare his address to Scottish students and teachers connected with the examinations of the "Associated Board", reported in *Musical Opinion,* November 1930: "Mr. Colles emphasized the clamant need, in these days of intensive mechanical music, to make music for themselves. *No full understanding and appreciation of music was possible without it.*"

This able writer has long held these extreme views. In the London *Times* of 1923 he went so far as to say: "It is better to make music badly than to listen to it well, *and the best that good listening can do for us* [my italics] is to send us back to enlarge our own achievement."

There is, surely, real contempt for listening here. A Busoni's chief end in life to send us to our own pianos? Surely not!

Concerts, &c., are, Mr. Colles adds, "chiefly delightful and useful". . . . How? Not as concerts; not as opportunities of hearing fine music—"*Such events are indeed chiefly delightful and useful as indexes of the life that engendered them*" (this seems to mean that their chief delight and use is to the performers, the delight and use to the audience being quite secondary). It is all very puzzling, especially as coming from a man whose business in life is to frequent the London concert halls and discuss what he *hears*.

Personally I consider all such striking pronouncements as rough-and-ready oratory uttered with a good practical purpose. They cannot have been thought out. If you reflect a moment you will see that they are only made possible, even as oratorical flights, by the circumstance that music happens to demand the participation of three parties, composer, performer, listener, whereas most of the other arts only require the participation of two, for instance the painter and the picture-lover, the poet and the reader.

The Principal of the Royal College of Art would not be able to address a body of picture-lovers as the Principal of the Royal Academy of Music addressed that body of music-lovers. There is no comparable middle activity for them to practice. Yet without any such middle activity there are thousands of keen picture-buyers and haunters of picture-galleries, and we must concede that they are enjoying an artistic life. The painter paints the picture and they enjoy it. Nobody says to them "How unfortunate! Painting has no essential *middle activity*. We must invent one, or 'there will eventually come satiety and *disinterest* if not actual distaste'. Set to work and COPY PICTURES! Copy them well, copy them badly; copying and only copying is artistic life."

Returning to Music: surely the composer creates not for the performer but for the listener. The performer's intervention is necessary, of course, and, by applying his intelligence and musical feeling to the interpretation of the composer's imperfect notation he even becomes a bit of the composer himself. But, with all his importance, the performer is really only the servant of the composer and the listener. *Music is composed to be heard and the performer is the means of its being heard.* Music is an ear-art, not a finger-and-voice art, though it calls for fingers and voices to give it utterance. So I see the matter! [1]

Of course performers enjoy their job, and hence it is good to encourage people to become performers. Of course constant performance of other people's music often teaches them a good deal, and may naturally be expected to tend towards equipping them for more efficiency in the role of listener, when they transfer to this role. But this idea that you *must* perform or you cannot be said to "live" is decidedly nonsense. Beethoven wrote to express himself and to convey his feelings to *us,* and the necessary middleman is his and our very obedient servant. The

[1] Again the reader is referred to the *Preface* by the American Editor. W. E.

better the middlemen the better the music, and the more justice to Beethoven and to our reasonable claims as his clients.

The habitual dragging in of denigratory expressions like "mechanized music" is unfair and confuses the issue. If two "middle-men" intervene in the shape of a live one and a circular sheet of vulcanite, it does not affect the principle: we may get a somewhat less perfect service, as we do when several greengrocer middle-men come between us and the growers of our vegetables, with the result that the products are not quite so fresh when they reach us, but even so I should guess, from all I have read of the standard of orchestral playing in Beethoven's day and his own practices as a conductor, that we often enjoy a better effect than he himself ever did (certainly we, as hearers, get more of Bach than his singers did). Anyhow, I myself claim that I have enjoyed live musical experiences from a phonograph record, and nothing that even the Royal Academy of Music and *The Times* can say can rob me of that experience.

I cannot believe that Bach and Beethoven labored to provide what we may call mere "fiddler-fodder": they wrote with an audience in their mind's eye and whoever despises that audience slights them and their efforts.

There is, of course, a lamentable begging of the question in such an expression as "passive surrender". Strictly speaking "passive surrender" and "active participation" (the terms used by Sir John McEwen) are not proper alternatives. Between "passive surrender" and "active participation in music-making" (in the sense of performance) there is a middle course that has been entirely overlooked by the speaker (if he is reported correctly) and that is "active surrender" or "passive participation", or (since neither of these is a quite happy term) "active participation as *listener*".

It is with this middle course that Musical Appreciation concerns itself. The teacher of Performance attends to the preparation for *active participation in music-making,* and the teacher of Appreciation to that for *active participation in music-listening.*

There is a sense in which any "participation" in music always means creation. The composer, obviously, creates. The performer tries to grasp the composer's thought and to re-create it in the way the composer would wish. The listener, on his part, has to re-create what the performer is putting before him. His participation is, then, active enough!

The composer's work, as he leaves it, is a mass of indications for sounds, phrases, sections, balanced stresses, and contrasted tone-colors, all in some subtle relation and proportion to one another.

The performer has to seize all these details in their relation and proportion and re-create them in tone. He may fail or succeed.

The listener has again to seize them in their relation and proportion, and re-create them in his mind. He also may fail or succeed, and that he shall succeed is the preoccupation of the Appreciation teacher.

Lowering our voice and speaking confidentially, does any listener ever *quite* fully re-create the whole of an elaborate new orchestral work?

Surely not! At the first hearing a great deal is lost; at the second hearing (if it follows quickly) less, and so on. The more sensitive the musical perceptive faculties the less the loss, and it is to train and exercise those faculties that the Appreciation teacher chiefly labors.

Doubtless the listener who has himself been a performer hears (or "re-creates") some details that he might otherwise have missed. It is to be doubted, however, whether the actual performers of the moment hear as much as the well-equipped and sensitive listener sitting in front of them and at a proper distance. I have had intense pleasure from listening to some of Sir John McEwen's delicate and thoughtful chamber music; would I have had as much if I had been playing (say) viola? Perhaps I would, but it would not have been the same kind of pleasure; it would have been largely Player's Pleasure, not Listener's Pleasure. "The looker-on sees most of the game", and the listener hears most of the music. Obviously the performer in concerted music of any kind could not do his duty to his own vocal or instrumental line if he were listening to all the lines on equal terms. He enjoys the gains and suffers the losses of a specialist; the listener, as a general practitioner, on the other hand loses the thrill of specialist action but gains the advantage of an all-round grasp.

On this subject of Hearing and Doing the falsest of false analogies are constantly perpetrated by many of the keenest and most valuable workers in the fields of musical education and criticism. So we find one of His Majesty's Inspectors of Schools, Mr. Cyril Winn, reported as having said:

"No teacher of English would dare maintain that real appreciation of literature could come by reading only without any constructive effort and few mathematicians are there who would agree that their skill could be acquired merely by following their demonstrations. That which consists solely in observing and analyzing the works of others is educationally barren, and the most desirable form of musical appreciation emerges from realization through effort." (Quoted in *Musical Opinion,* November 1931.)

Surely there are muddled thoughts here. First about English literature. So far as I see, by "constructive effort" Mr. Winn can only mean the writing of English by the English literature class. Doubtless it helps. But I suggest that there are many people with a keen appreciation of English literature who have done very little writing, and certainly there are thousands of poetry-lovers who have never written (or possibly even recited) a poem.

As for mathematics, here the whole argument goes to the winds. Mathematical ability is the ability to do. The "appreciation" of mathematics cannot be said to exist. To follow a mathematical demonstration one must be a mathematician, whereas to follow a symphonic performance one certainly does not require to be a composer. It is no good trying to compare mathematical understanding with the "appreciation" of any art. (But we cannot all think of the best illustration every time we get on our feet to speak, nor can it be claimed that we are always exactly reported!)

What is more worthy of serious criticism is the second half of the above quotation, which consists of a statement for which I should guess Mr. Winn to be actually responsible and which I should deny *in toto.*

Just read the passage again, and ask yourselves whether it be true that the observation and analysis of the "works of others" is so "entirely barren." I suggest that there are some thousands of broadcasting listeners who would smile at the allegation that because they do not perform (for that is what I take "effort" to mean here) their devotion has been "barren". Among them are probably some who have become, by dint of listening, more genuinely musical than many a professional pianist, violinist, or vocalist.

However, I may have misunderstood Mr. Winn: and it is just possible that he is not putting forward the old worn-out idea of playing and singing being *the* thing, and listening merely of secondary value. That is a cliché all the more to be condemned since any observant person with inside knowledge of any choral society can find in that society a fair number of really keen choralists who rarely take the trouble to go to any concerts, except those at which they themselves sing. And so, too, with amateur orchestras. If the instrumentalists and vocalists of London (the very people who ought to show the effects of "realization through effort") really cared devotedly for music, would our ancient Philharmonic Society have so long been in a distressing financial condition?

Those who talk lightly of the small need of Musical Appreciation work and stress the value of performance might ponder the fact that the "doers" of music (in the sense in which they use the word) sometimes show little interest in any form of musical activity except "doing" (again in that sense). It is surely common knowledge that the members of choirs and choral societies (in the mass; of course there are many exceptions) do not support chamber concerts and piano recitals. They are satisfied with "doing", and if you test their knowledge of, and interest in, music of the kind they themselves are not accustomed to "do" you will often find them lamentably deficient. *The singer's interest is often not music but his own act of singing; the player's not music but his own act of playing.* I once met an organist friend on the top of a bus near the Queen's Hall during the "Prom." season, and to my surprise he told me that though he had for years frequently passed the Queen's Hall during the "Prom." season he had never once had the curiosity to be present at a "Prom." concert. I once took a professor of the piano at one of our great colleges of music (a man of high and deserved fame in his calling) to a concert at the Aeolian Hall, London; for over a decade that hall had been one of the most active centres in London for chamber music, vocal and piano recitals, &c., and throughout that decade he had lived within a mile of it, yet on our entering he looked round curiously and remarked that he had never been in it before. I was once a member of a very enthusiastic church choir of which I am sure not two members besides myself ever went to concerts. At the same time I was member of a famous North of England choral society of 200 members, of whom I do not believe more than twenty ever turned out to hear our local string quartet, which was a good one, giving a fine series of monthly concerts every winter.

I could multiply instances of this kind, and so, I am sure, could many of my readers. So far from its being possible to assume that an enthusiastic performer of music is a real supporter of musical enterprises and a keen enjoyer of music in general, the contrary is, very unfortunately, rather the case. The keen supporters are often no performers at all, though, of course, some of them *have* done more or less performance in their time, and if they have it enormously helps them.[1]

To say the least, if "doing" (in the narrow sense) and listening are complementary, and so I regard them, it is quite as often the "doers" who should be told to develop their listening as the listener who should be told to set to work at some form of "doing".

---

[1] I venture to quote a pertinent remark from a letter that has reached me from a well-known and admirable musician who has particularly developed choral and orchestral activities in the boys' public school over whose musical activities he presides. He points to the danger of a false diagnosis, in these words—"Fine team-work, in conjunction with decent music, is so exhilarating that it often passes as real aesthetic experience." P. A. S.

My friend Professor Howard D. McKinney, of Rutger's College, New Jersey, made some plain-spoken remarks on this subject of doing and listening in the London *Musical Times* of August 1931:

"I am willing to grant that participation in music gives a kind of interest that can come in no other way, the interest of the doer; also that it gives a certain admiration for and understanding of the skill of the composer who wrote the music, which can hardly be gained through hearing alone. But I wish that I possessed the assurance that the best method of approach to musical appreciation for the average person was through performance. My observations certainly do not confirm such a sweeping statement; indeed I have often found the opposite to be true. The very process of acquiring mental and physical dexterity and power of co-ordination sufficient to perform music with any degree of facility sometimes destroys the love of music: witness the thousands of pianoforte pupils who give up the ghost, and usually any further interest in music *per se,* each year. What is more, this facility, once acquired, often occupies the interest and attention of the player and singer to the exclusion of any attention to what they are playing or singing. It is suggested that choirs and amateur orchestras are the best musical appreciation classes. I wonder! It seems that if this were true, choir singers and directors—and I am not referring to village choirs alone—should be more interested in better music than they are. Singers of my acquaintance do not seem to have developed great avidity for acquiring musical intelligence, and if amateur orchestral players have much interest outside their own particular part, I seem to have missed noting the fact. The mere ability to perform music does not give an *open sesame* to its beauties or a necessary understanding of its message. If cultivated properly performance may be a stimulating and fructifying influence; but we must avoid confusing the issue here. An ability to perform music, and a love of music coupled with a real knowledge of it, are individual attainments, the second by no means the corollary of the first."

In the main, it will be seen, Professor McKinney takes the same view as I. Yet I am sure that neither of us underrates performance. We merely suggest that others overrate it. We would have as many performers as possible. But we would not

have those who train them suppose that in teaching them to play
or sing they are doing the whole of their duty.

Without going so far as Dr. Johnson and declaring that "Playing music is a method of employing the mind without the labor
of thinking, and with some applause from a man's self", I would
assert that a great deal of playing may on occasion be carried
on without the player acquiring that kind of concentration, of
acute perception, that is required for sensitive listening.[1]

How much playing is possible with how little listening is
evident to us all again and again in the way piano pupils, and
sometimes even virtuoso pianists of the highest eminence (and
the highest fees), hold down the sustaining pedal through clash-
ing harmonies. As an adjudicator at British Competition Festivals I have sometimes, in a junior class, writhed as competitor
after competitor held that pedal down (without *once* raising it)
throughout a whole composition. Dr. Henry Ley, in his Presi-
dential Address to the Royal College of Organists in 1933, said
of organ-playing:

"I have known pupils hold down a pedal point on the wrong note
for two lines and be quite unconscious of it, which proves that they
are using their eyes when playing, and not their ears, and therefore
cannot be said to be in a fit state to make the organ sound in any
way a musical instrument."

These were certainly players within Dr. Johnson's definition
(of doubtful psychology, perhaps, but we know what he meant)
—"employing the mind without the labor of thinking". To
enable them to defy that definition what they needed was a
course of good Appreciation lessons.

We often find otherwise sane and sensible people writing
slightingly of "mere listening"—even my revered old friend,
Tobias Matthay:

"Self-expression, however tentative and inadequate [note the
width of this charity] is a vastly greater influence, aesthetically, edu-

[1] Perhaps the player needs, at least in some cases, not a different "kind of
concentration" but a different *direction of attention*. He probably listens less
comprehensively when he plays than when he does not play; but he could overcome that habit in some measure, by trying. W. E.

cationally and morally [note the width of this claim], than ever can be *mere listening."* [1]

Really the performer is nowadays taking too much on himself. We must put him back in his place. Let us remind him that in the great days of seventeenth- and eighteenth-century instrumental music (the days which brought into existence the symphony and the string quartet), composers were writing for the "passive" enjoyment of princes and their courts, certainly not for the "active" enjoyment of performers. The performers, indeed, were the composer's official underlings; they ranked among the domestic servants of the court and wore the livery thereof. Haydn's earlier orchestral works were composed for a listening Esterhazy; his later for a London audience. Nowadays writers and speakers are beginning to tell us he wrote them for the blowers of horns and oboes and the tappers of drums.

I close this section with a quotation from Pepys (12 February, 1667):

"T. Killigrew and I to talk. . . . He tells me he hath gone several times, eight or ten times, he tells me, hence to Rome to hear good musique; so much he loves it, though he never did sing or play a note."

Poor Tom Killigrew. Think of what it meant to make eight or ten journeys from London to Rome in those days. *And he never knew that, with all that effort, fatigue, and expense, he was not enjoying a "musical life".*

HEARING AND SEEING

Efforts to popularize music are met by all possible kinds of opposition. Every discouragement is (deliberately or thoughtlessly) placed both in the way of the musician who wishes to help others to share the joy that means so much in his own life,

---

[1] Lurking under this statement is, again, the assumption that the performer deals with ideated music and that the listener never does. The facts hardly sustain the belief. So little do players and singers deal in reflection with the music they perform that a new commandment, indeed, seems needed and is hereby proposed: *Thou shalt not commit unpremeditated music.* W. E.

and also in that of the member of the general public who has awakened to the fact that such a joy exists and begins to find it becoming his. And his discouragement often comes from those very leaders of opinion who, when they happen to be in another frame of mind, do much to awaken enthusiasm and to spread enlightenment. I offer the following as a striking example:

"Any one who listens to the wireless and the gramophone should make a habit of doing so as often as possible with a score, preferably a full score. Miniature scores of hundreds of works can be obtained easily nowadays, and many of them, in fact all the classics, are quite cheap. The reading of a full score, as distinct from conducting or playing from it, is not very difficult. A beginning may be made with string quartets, from which it is easy enough to go on to moderately scored classical symphonies and thence to more and more complex works. There are listeners, of course, who may say that they cannot read music at all. The answer to them is that they are not listeners in any proper sense until they have mastered this modest attainment and that one can hardly be an intelligent lover of music any more than a performer without being able to follow the notes. Inability to read music will do as little for the listener as illiteracy for a lover of books and plays. Nobody would pretend to know Shakespeare merely from stage performances; nobody may claim to know any music as it should be known only from a hearing of it, especially an indirect hearing." (E. B. in *The Birmingham Post*, 11 July, 1932.)

The general advice to the hearer to become a reader also is, doubtless, good. But can we accept all those downright assertions? *"They are not listeners in any proper sense until they have mastered this modest attainment"; "One can hardly be an intelligent lover of music . . . without being able to follow the notes"; "Inability to read music will do as little for the listener as illiteracy for a lover of books and plays";* and, strongest of all, *"Nobody may claim to know any music as it should be known only from a hearing of it".*[1]

The last statement I have quoted sums up the others and it

---

[1] In justice to Mr. Blom I quote some support for him from a high quarter. Sir Henry Hadow, addressing the members of the Staff Sight-Singing College, some years ago, said, "No one really understands music who appreciates it through the ear." P. A. S.

will be sufficient to consider it. Let us look at a little list of just a few of those whom it condemns:

1. All those who in the age of Byrd and Palestrina revelled in the enjoyment of their works. There were then practically no written or printed scores in circulation (music was almost entirely in single "parts", one in the hands of each performer of the choral or instrumental body).

2. All those royal and noble patrons of music to whose support of the art we may be said almost to owe the treasures of eighteenth-century chamber music, orchestral music, opera, and oratorio. They listened to music nightly, but how often did they look into a score?

3. All the many keen lovers of Bach's organ music (unless they are themselves organists), for it is certain that precious few of them possess the printed organ works of Bach.

4. All blind musicians, many of them, as we know, very gifted. The number of scores of orchestral or chamber music (for instance) available in Braille is relatively few. A blind concert-goer may become closely intimate with the popular things of our concert repertory, but apparently he can never attain to really "knowing."

5. Most of those eager young people who throng the Promenade Concerts in London every autumn, stand (after a day's work in offices and shops) throughout a two-hour program, applaud and discuss the items they have come to love by repeated hearings—but, apparently, do not really "know" them! [1]

6. The writer of that article himself—as concerns the very considerable body of more recent music which, though often performed, has not been made available in published scores.

Is not this rather absurd? Is music an art of the eye or of the ear?

Venturing on a protest against this pronouncement of my friend's I was gratified with a column of defense of it (*Birming-*

[1] We have even had one music critic, and one widely respected for his artistic enthusiasm and his judgment, who, as was revealed after his death, could not read a score—Mr. A. J. Sheldon, successor of Mr. Newman and predecessor of Mr. Blom himself as critic of the *Birmingham Post*. This, of course, is exceptional, but it is some testimony in favor of the view I am now advancing. P. A. S.

ham Post, 23 July, 1932). As, however, it took the shape of merely an able advocacy of the admirable practice of studying scores, it did not touch the point—which is the lack of tact, propriety, humanity, or justice of publicly excommunicating nine-tenths of the members of the musical church.

To the list of the excommunicate given above I might have added other categories. I will just add one more, making seven. This category will generously rope us all in. There are some scores nowadays that are practically unreadable. All of us who confess ourselves baffled by them are, then, however many times we may hear these works, still numbered amongst those who do not "know the music as it should be known".

"Of a certain modern work two eminent conductors have said to me that it would be impossible to conduct it without knowing it by heart, so many signs are there for them to follow in the quickly moving procession of sound. The mere number of lines to be read simultaneously, the space to be covered by the eye in a moment of time, the continuity of the horizontal phrases in their vertical combination, plead one and all that the sounds that the composer intends . . ." and so on. (Hubert J. Foss in *The Monthly Musical Record,* July-August, 1933.)

We most of us think that we can appreciate the relatively simple music of a military band. Can we?

"The *reductio ad absurdum* of the academic tradition is the brass band score and its slightly less difficult companion, the military band score. The admirable *Downland Suite* of John Ireland is literally a closed book to the majority of readers and even for a trained score-reader needs the utmost care and slowness in deciphering . . . it remains the exclusive property of bandmasters until it is played to the public." (Hubert J. Foss in the same article.)

The plain fact of the matter (and we may as well be honest and confess it) is that scores are every year becoming less and less valuable to the listener because they take more and more time to understand.

"For the first time in history music has, for (at the least) 99 per cent. of musicians, passed the limits of mental readableness. Take, for example, Schönberg's monodrama *Erwartung* for soprano and orchestra, for the very fine performance of which the other day we are duly grateful to our uncommercially-minded B.B.C. Could any one of us lay his hand on his heart and say that, after any amount of laborious spelling-out of the huge score, he could, *at the proper pace,* at all adequately realize all this seething diversity of harmony and color? . . . However much we extend the musical vocabulary graspable by the ear as words, not as letters, the eye has more rigorous limits." (Dr. Ernest Walker in *The Monthly Musical Record*, April, 1933.)

Coupled with the strange claim against which I am now inveighing is another one, a close relation of it. Certain writers actually allege that more can be got out of the score of a work than out of a hearing of it.

"The mere reading of music is, then, a necessity to the student of musical history. But it is more than a necessity: it is a keen pleasure, and, for me, a keener pleasure, in nine cases out of ten, than that of concert-going. I have never committed myself to what would be the nonsensical statement that the eye can do the work of the ear so well that there is no need ever to *hear* music. All I have claimed is that—for me, at least—a reading of a piece of music gives me so much more pleasure than the average performance that I would not go to more than ten or twenty concerts in the year of my own free choice. The performances that give me the greatest pleasure do not throw the slightest new light *on the work* for me: it is the performer who thrills me. I see no more in a Schubert song after Elena Gerhardt has sung it than I did before: what has made the experience worth having is the beauty of her voice and the perfection of her style." (Ernest Newman in *The Sunday Times*, 22 November, 1923.)

Mr. Newman has often made assertions like this, but let us consider to what they amount. In order to perform that Schubert song with genuine artistry, Gerhardt has had to give it weeks or years of study, applying to it all the experience of a lifelong specialist. It is logical, then, to say that if the musician "sees no more" in it after her singing than he did after his own reading, that reading has also been spread over some weeks or years and has brought to bear upon the interpretation of the composer's notation an equal degree of experience in vocal interpretation. (Of course, in Mr. Newman's case this condition may be met. I believe that in the Birmingham School of Music, years ago, he specialized in teaching Lieder interpretation.)

Consider the position of a conductor. A new symphony appears and he decides to give it a public performance. He must study it daily, soak in it, master its "subjects" and their treatment, weigh in the balance the relative values of simultaneous instrumental strands so that he may give each its proper measure of prominence in performance, debate with himself innumerable questions of speed, of *accelerando* and *rallentando* and *tempo rubato*—come in fact to *live* the music. If he does not take all this care even able critics may be misled as to the value of the music. For how many of us who are not professional orchestral conductors can bring to a score the necessary experience, or give it the time required, to produce in our minds as we read the effect of a fine performance? If Mr. Newman can do this we must envy him, but I frankly suggest that there have been one or two occasions upon which that eminent critic himself has praised a new work, after the study of its score, which he did not feel so much inclined to praise when it came to performance (I have the impression that I could recall a case or two if called upon).

And this is no discredit to Mr. Newman since the ablest and most experienced orchestral conductors sometimes fail in the same way. We may take it that nobody in England can read an orchestral score more fluently than Sir Henry Wood, yet we have occasionally seen him put into his program some new work that at once revealed itself as a comparative "failure", and that, therefore, we could hardly believe he had fully grasped when, the composer's manuscript submitted to him, he was compelled to "hear with the eye". Every conductor in the world would admit that he had sometimes committed errors of this sort. Occasional false judgments are, indeed, unavoidable, and there are just as many experienced critics who would admit with Professor Shera (*Sheffield Telegraph,* 1 July, 1933, referring to Strauss's *Intermezzo*), "it would be unfair to judge only from a reading of the score", as would say, as Mr. Newman sometimes does after a first performance of some particular work, that "without the score it is not yet possible properly to judge its value".

How many of us dare claim to be cleverer at score-reading than Von Bülow?—

"If any one pretends that he can realize a score by reading it silently, then he is simply talking nonsense. I personally cannot do it. I must first glance it through (*einer Ueberblick gewinnen*), then read the lines separately, then study the harmonies, and do it over and over until I almost know the score by heart. And then, when I conduct it, I invariably discover beauties or faults which my spiritual ear has been unable to detect." (Lecture to students and conductors, quoted by Dr. G. A. Pfister in *Musical News,* 13 October, 1923.)

It need hardly be said that nothing in this chapter is intended to discourage teachers from urging pupils to learn to read music. It is an accomplishment of very high value, and more might well be done by teachers of Musical Appreciation to train the eye along with the ear. A notable experiment in this direction has been made by Mr. James Easson in his "Junior Score Reader" called *The Book of the Great Music* (Oxford University Press, 2s. 6d.). This is intended as a companion to my own *Book of the Great Musicians* and embodies a principle I should have been proud to adopt in that book if I had been smart enough to think of it first. (See p. 111.)

The plan is to give in notation just such essentials of a score as a class of school pupils can be expected to follow when these essentials are detached from their entanglements, and in this way to lead on to the ability to follow scores (vocal, piano, chamber music, and orchestral) when listening to music. The music represented includes a Wilbye madrigal, Purcell, Handel and Bach harpsichord suites, a Bach fugue, Haydn and Beethoven piano sonata movements, a Haydn string quartet movement, shorter piano pieces by Chopin, Schumann, and Macdowell, a movement of Elgar's Organ Sonata in G, Mozart's Symphony in G minor, and Grieg's *Death of Ase*—all but one or two of which are obtainable in phonograph record form. An example from the Mozart "junior score", reproduced on p. 111, will illustrate the method.

Putting the complication of scores aside for the moment, I should like to point out that to the average school pupil mental hearing of a mere single line of music is much more difficult than many musicians imagine. An error arises on this point from the extraordinary and psychologically inexplicable faculty some musicians have possessed from early childhood of immediately imagining in sound anything they see in musical notation. Strange as it may appear, there are children who for English reading only require to be taught the alphabet, upon which they immediately set to work ("on their own") to practice reading, and in a very short time become proficient; similarly there are children who in music only require to be taught the notation, after which they can in a short time sing at sight anything within their vocal range.

Such gifted individuals as these (endowed usually, I think, with the sense of absolute pitch) do not understand that to the normal person the learning of the notation of music is only a very small step towards the ability to read vocal music at sight. Thousands know G by sight and name who cannot sing G—an item of the fabric of music which to those not possessing absolute pitch takes on a different color in every key in which it appears—which color has to be recognized before it can be framed in the mind and then reproduced by the voice.

The notation of music is easily and quickly learned, the mental effects the notation is intended to convey can only be acquired by most of us after a minutely graded course of instruction and abundant practice. When Mr. H. J. Foss says (*Monthly Musical Record*, July–August, 1933): "It is easily demonstrated that the ordinary notation of music can be assimilated into the mental system of the ordinary man with little more difficulty than the alphabet of his own language and less than the alphabet of other languages", he is boldly exaggerating (for while any child can learn the French alphabet in an hour or so, the multitudinous signs of music cannot be acquired in anything like that time). But even if we accepted his statement we should still have to remark that it has no practical bearing on the question he is discussing. He is clearly one of those lucky instinctive sight-readers and has no conception of the mental processes by which the rank and file of us read music.

Many other good musicians have talked in much the same way, and Mr. Foss would probably find no difficulty, if he walked round his library, in putting before us confirmatory statements from some very eminent hands.[1]

There is a really well-written *Introduction to Music* (1926) which, so far as I have examined it, is in general extremely accurate and practical, but which breaks down, as I feel, quite completely at one point. The author's intention, as explained in his preface, is to supplement the appreciation books by providing the "theory" that an intelligent non-performer requires in order to read scores. So far as I know the book is alone in this particular aim, and it is interesting to see how it is carried out.

After two chapters devoted chiefly to tune and rhythm (I should say fairly successfully, given an intelligent adult reader) we come to several devoted to aspects of pitch. A number of elaborate exercises are provided for the reader to "hum through". But beyond adding the names of the notes, here is the only help the book supplies (p. 38):

[1] Here is an extract from Sir Henry Hadow's *Music*, in the "Home University Library", that, as I feel, illustrates the over-sanguine expectation of the gifted musician when advising the normal man: "Last, and most important, the listener should if possible learn to read music; by which I mean not to sing or play at sight, but to read silently as one reads a novel. This, except in the case of complex modern scores, is easy to acquire with a little patience. Begin by recalling from the page some simple music (e.g. a hymn tune) which you know by heart: proceed to others which are less familiar: memorize compositions and try to realize them away from the instrument: follow symphonies or quartets with the score in your hand and read them over again afterwards while the recollection is still fresh. In no long time you will find the notes on the page as significant as words, and when you have done so you will have added a new language and a new literature to your possessions. We are not treating music fairly if we restrict our knowledge of it to the concert room; it is when we can read a Beethoven quartet 'with our feet on the hob' that we have really won its friendship." P. A. S.

"This is the sort of training you must undertake for yourself; strike on the pianoforte C, or hum any convenient note and think of it as middle C; the note on the second space is A, or *la;* hum it. Then go through the same process mentally, thinking of the two sounds in succession. Gradually the process will get to be automatic, so that you pass from note to sound without consciously thinking of the name of the note at all. This is the first stage in reading music. Below will be found typical exercises for humming. Not many people have the gift of "absolute pitch", that is, of carrying about in their heads the standard middle C. It is sufficient in these exercises to pitch on any convenient sound and call it C. Of course, broken male voices will sing notes an octave lower than those written. The exercises may, if desired, be played on any instrument."

Thus, in a few lines, does the innocent author (using not absolute pitch but a new variety of relative pitch, apparently) attempt to do what any teacher of sight-singing considers to require at least two or three years of systematic and graded ear-training.

And this author has had experience as a music master in English public schools (the only possible explanation of his retaining this delusion, for it is such, being, it seems to me, that in his classes he has, like so many singing teachers, left undetected that absolute-pitch-boy who leads the others).

The methods to be adopted (laborious but dependable) can be realized by the study of any of the works of the late John Curwen or Dr. W. G. McNaught, or Professor W. G. Whittaker's *Class Singing* (Oxford University Press), or a multitude of other books by practical teachers who, however musically gifted, did not happen to be born with the silver spoon of "absolute pitch".[1] Teachers who were born with it inevitably find it extremely difficult to teach sight-singing to a class of normal

---

[1] That extraordinary ability in learning to read music is due to the reader's possession of "absolute pitch", or is even correlated with such possession, is a belief that would bear scientific investigation. Many teachers in the United States must have made observations that parallel those of our distinguished American psychologist of music, Dr. Carl Seashore. In an address delivered to teachers of music Dr. Seashore once said that in his long experience many persons had come into his laboratory with absolute pitch—but few had left with it! W. E.

children. The organist of a famous Cambridge college told me recently that, being an "absolute pitcher", he found it impossible, to train his boys in sight-reading, so, wisely, left this branch of their instruction to the master in charge of the boy's ordinary education, who fortunately happens to be also a musical enthusiast.

Occasionally one comes across musicians who cherish the idea that one learns singing by singing—that a child whom one accustoms to looking at the book as he sings by ear will unconsciously pick up the association between sight and sound. This is true of a very few children (probably mostly "absolute pitchers"), but if one reflects a moment upon the extraordinary way in which the staff notation falsifies distances (the interval of a major third from C to E for instance being the same size on paper as that from the minor third D to F, which has a totally different mental effect—and this is merely a simple and obvious example), it will be realized that to the bulk of a class or a choir the process is impossible.[1] The explanation of its apparent success (of which its protagonists assure us) is for the most part the one suggested earlier—the gifted individuals are leading the crowd, which picks up each note with so much rapidity as to create the impression of spontaneity. A test of the class, individual by individual, would quickly reveal the futility of this method (if the word "method" can be applied).

In conclusion I would sum up as follows: (1) Children should be taught to read vocal music; (2) from that (a necessary beginning) it is desirable that they should be led on step by step to read piano music, chamber music, orchestral music, involving among other things the recognition of the sound-values of chords (aural harmony-teaching, in fact) and the recollection of the timbres of instruments; (3) but the available time will certainly not suffice to give all members of an average class great proficiency in such an attainment; (4) even without this, however, they can get great pleasure from listening to music, and, indeed,

[1] Do "absolute pitchers", one wonders, always bear in mind the signature sharps and flats, and the accidentals that have appeared in the first part of a measure, to the end that they think E♭ and not E, or F♯, not F? W. E.

even the born blind can come to love Beethoven's *Eroica* Symphony—and have done so scores of times.

"EAR-TRAINING" VERSUS "MUSICAL APPRECIATION"

It is not my idea to put those two into opposition. Others do so, however.

As long ago as 1921, Dr. John E. Borland, then Chief Music Inspector to the London County Council, was complaining of "the enthusiast for the appreciation of music, who thinks that all definite ear-training and sight-singing should go by the board" (interview in the *Daily News,* May, 1921).

I never met an enthusiast of that stamp, but if my friend says he exists I must accept the fact.

Another kind of enthusiast of whose existence I *have* had frequent proof, is the enthusiast for Ear-Training as against Musical Appreciation.

It was a group of enthusiasts of that kind who recently, at a Conference on Musical Education, passed a resolution embodying these clauses:

"The aims of the study of musical appreciation, as we understand it, are (*a*) the development of a high degree of sensitiveness to the art. . . ." [1]

"In our opinion the development of a high degree of sensitiveness to the medium of the art represents the scope of the aural training class. . . ." [2]

Now Music being, as I have just maintained, an ear-art, it is certain that every bit of Aural Training that a human being is willing to undergo will in some measure help him to its intelligent enjoyment. There is a great deal of Aural Training demanded as the necessary basis for Sight-Singing, and hence class work in Sight-Singing can help greatly towards Musical

---

[1] There was, of course, a (*b*), but this was declared entirely "unsuitable as a subject of elementary education", so I have omitted it here. In justice to the drafters of this Resolution I give it in full in an Appendix. P. A. S.

[2] See the *American Editor's Preface* for a discussion that bears on this point. W. E.

Appreciation, if the pupil be shown how to apply it and if it be properly supplemented.

Yet when this is admitted, Sight-Singing with *its* Aural Training is a separate thing from Musical Listening and *its* Aural Training, and very good listening can be and is done by people who have never passed through the Aural Training of the schools.

Even Messrs. Macpherson and Read, in their remarkable synthesis of Sight-Singing, Aural Training, and Appreciation, *Aural Culture based upon Musical Appreciation,* recognize this to some extent by treating Appreciation (in their second and third volumes at any rate) in a distinct section, headed "Appreciation of Character, Form, Style, and Period in Musical Composition". While cleverly basing their Aural Training on Appreciation (the use of attractive extracts from actual compositions to illustrate every point) they do not go so far with their synthesis as to base their Appreciation, point by point, on their Aural Training.

There is so much that can be perfectly well grasped in listening, if one has only learned *observation,* and to which it is not necessary to put a name as one has to do in Sight-Singing and Aural Training work. Intervals, harmonies, and rhythms that could only enter at an advanced stage in a systematic Aural Training course are easily noticed and remembered in listening. A child can go away from the concert hall humming many a melody of which he could not identify the notes by either their *do-mi-so* or their alphabetical names, and of which he could not notate the rhythms. So far as the listener is concerned I see little need to know anything about "feminine endings" and the actual names of cadences, and the details of modulations, and the like. The listener takes all these things in his stride; they flash past and are gone and he has perceived them subconsciously.

In planning Appreciation work, then, surely it is best largely to ignore the Aural Training syllabus, to spread over the school life the hearing of a series of compositions, carefully chosen as being of interest to pupils of the varying ages in question, and gradually to draw out of the class, by its own observation, as chance offers, the recognition of such phenomena of Music as concern a listener to it.

I would sometimes devote a term's work to the study of a period, or to the compositions of a particular composer—which would tend to a more humane interest and which would be more easily carried out in a course not tied to a graded system of Aural Training. Messrs. Macpherson and Read are not opposed to this, but I feel that their definite Appreciation Scheme is a little hampered by the attempt to keep it in as close connection as may be with their Aural Training scheme.

Obviously there is room here for debate and for experiment. I have no wish to be dogmatic. It is perhaps merely personal to me to feel that too perfect a system of correlation would, in any case, be fatal to what I may call "humane interest."

Every teacher must decide on his own policy and the frankly free-and-easy one would be mine, but even to a teacher who agreed with me I would recommend a detailed study of what is certainly one of the most carefully worked-out musical-pedagogical schemes ever published, that of Messrs. Macpherson and Read. (It is fair to the authors to add that they themselves say: "This book is intended purely as a *guide* to the teacher and it is not the wish of the authors that it should be regarded as setting forth any rigid, prescribed system of teaching.")

Coming back to the Resolution I have quoted: It was strenuously defended in the press for some months by certain fine musicians and keen teachers, who quoted the Macpherson and Read book I have mentioned but really went beyond its teachings. Such expressions as the following seem to me to bring Musical Appreciation into an unnecessarily close relation with the minutely graded work of the Sight-Singing-cum-Aural-Training class:

1. "The bulk of the time would be spent on real aural training, based on concentrated listening with its complementary sight-singing and dictation."
2. "How can you take in music seriously unless your ear has been trained and your musical memory improved by progressive

steps? . . . Frankly we cannot conceive any serious work without this thoroughness in foundation-laying."

3. "Musical appreciation is the logical development of ear-training. On what other basis is appreciation possible?"

4. "The most effective way to appreciate music is to go through the mill, to learn to sing, read and write music, to train the ear to distinguish one sound from another."

5. "The only sound bases for real appreciation are graded aural training and self-performance."

6. "It is a thousand pities that the idea has got abroad that appreciation is possible without the mental training which the term 'Aural Culture' implies."

On a careless reading of such expressions as those (and they received a good deal of careless reading) one is inclined to think that they amount to a mere plea for thoroughness. But they are far more than that. They represent a movement to tie up Appreciation to formal ear-training, as one might tie up the study of English Literature to English Grammar.

In the study of English Grammar the scientific spirit should be in the forefront; in the study of English Literature, the artistic spirit.[1] And the same applies with Aural Training and Appreciation.

Thousands of people who could not work a paper on English Grammar (who perhaps could not tell you the difference between an adjective and an adverb or a preposition and a conjunction) have an instinct for English Literature. A teacher or lecturer desirous of helping this to develop would not begin by giving them a course in Grammar. If in announcing his class he said (paraphrasing the first of the extracts I have just given): *"The bulk of the time will be spent on real grammatical training, based on concentrated examination of passages of English, with its complementary reading and dictation"*, he would not get many students. Indeed the person of genuine literary taste is the very one he would drive away by such an announcement.

[1] The danger, in America at least, and probably not less in England, is that the "scientific spirit" will be carried into the artistic field. There is little chance, on the other hand, that "artistic spirit" will be employed to solve the problems that arise in the factual field. W. E.

The man who is eager to know more about literature wishes to go direct to literature. For his purposes Grammar is very little necessary, since he has picked up enough Grammar by ear. We all talk Grammar as M. Jourdain talked prose, and an occasional error that we may be in the habit of making has little bearing on Literary Appreciation.

So it is with Musical Appreciation. Even if we have never learned the name of an interval or a rhythm we have from our cradles had music all around us. We have subconsciously become accustomed to every one of the general conventions of melodic shape and harmonic combination, and take all these things as matters of course. If we wish to perform we must delve down into grammatical detail, but if we are only concerned with listening such detail is unimportant.

Nothing could be more erroneous than the following confident dictum:

"Music deals with logical ideas for the building up of which we have no inborn capacity and for which the tools are not from birth put into our hands as are the tools of speech."

The author is discussing listening (his title, indeed, is *Appreciation is Vexation*), and he has gone quite wrong at the outset! The listening tools *are* "from birth put into our hands", *exactly* "as are the tools of speech". Nowadays, at any rate, from the cradle to the grave we hear not only speech but music around us. The two are very nearly on all fours. By hearing speech we get the meaning of speech; by hearing music we get the meaning of music. Ordinary use of speech and ordinary conventional music (in both cases if free from complexity), offer no difficulties of "appreciation" to any of us.

It is when speech is put together in a *literary way,* treated as an art, and used for the expression of elaborate chains of ideas that are novel to us, that our need of guidance begins. And in music we can all enjoy the main features of an ordinary march or waltz, though thousands of us are lost when the first movement of a symphony has been going on for three minutes.

When an English poem baffles us or fails to attract us it is not because we know too little English Grammar. We can have our difficulties removed by a wise teacher, and then become enthusiastic about the poem, but the help he gives us will not be grammatical. The pundit who scoffed at the idea of Appreciation without preliminary "definite ear-training and sight-singing" and said "We might as well try to catch the appreciation of Shakespeare before teaching English" did not reflect. English Grammar is a relatively recent subject in the English school curriculum and there was plenty of appreciation of Shakespeare among English people before it was introduced.

There is a book by Dr. P. B. Ballard, on *Teaching the Mother Tongue*. Dr. Ballard was for a quarter of a century Inspector of the London County Council Education Department, and here are some of the conclusions at which he has arrived. He tells us that English Grammar, as an educational subject, has severe limitations:

"I always mean grammar in the narrow sense, the grammar that begins with the picking out of nouns and verbs, and ends with the parsing and analysis of a complex sentence; all the intermediate stages leading up to, and being determined by, the final flower of a perfect piece of parsing. This is what grammar meant to all teachers in the 19th century; this is what it means to most teachers to-day. It was the grammar that was prescribed by the Board of Education under the old system of payment by results; it was the grammar of the text-books that flourished under that system. . . . The tale of its downfall is told in full, lest we forget; and forgetting, wish to return to those lean and lenten days when grammar took all the joy and gusto out of the English lesson and gave no nurture in return." . . .

"English grammar is of little use in learning English; French grammar is of more use in learning French; Latin grammar is of more use still in learning Latin; but the usefulness of grammar is in every case limited by the fact that *it requires a more mature intelligence to grasp the grammar than to learn the language itself* [my italics], and that for the young mind, instead of making the difficult easy, it makes the easy difficult."

We are not compelled to go quite all the way with Dr. Ballard, still less to apply to Aural Training every strong expression he uses about English Grammar. But we can take a hint. When a symphony movement bothers the inexperienced listener a course in Aural Training, though good in itself, would directly help him very little. What he needs is to be enabled to pick out the musical themes and to find what the composer does with them, to be enabled to watch the play of orchestral color, to have his attention drawn to inner and lower melodies which he was in danger of missing . . . and so forth. All that is a sort of Aural Training, if you like, but it is not the kind taught in the Aural Training Class, which, quite properly, has other aims.

The foundational character of the work of the Aural Training Class is, of course, tremendously valuable in its general results. Any sharpening of the ears helps any musical work. But there is so little *direct* connection between Aural Training (in the scholastic sense of the term) and Musical Appreciation, that to harp upon Aural Training as the indispensable basis of Appreciation is merely pedantry.

As a corrective, see Sir Hugh Allen's address to the students of his Royal College of Music in 1920. The kind of listening he is so anxious they should cultivate is a kind open to all of us, whether we have "studied music" or not:

"It is astonishing to find out what can be done by concentrated listening among a lot of sounds heard simultaneously. . . . If you were brought into this Hall blindfold to hear a work for strings, could you determine without previous knowledge how many strings it was written for—and that, at the moment when all were playing? Could you differentiate between a quartet and a quintet of strings? Under similar circumstances, could you tell whether an orchestra contained four horns and three trumpets; or, on hearing the full orchestra, say of what instruments it was composed?

"In a choral work, could you tell if a chorus was written for two sopranos, alto, two tenors, and two basses, and not for two sopranos, alto, tenor, and bass? Can you fix your attention on the viola part of a string quartet, and really hear it? Can you hear the inner workings in a Bach fugue of three or more parts? . . . Can you keep your mind so free from disturbances that you can placidly and reasonably follow the intricacies of a work as it is unfolded in performance, and enjoy the beauty of its themes, the wealth of its colorings, the logic of its design, and out of it all carry away with you something really worth having—not merely a hazy memory of a fine performance, but a fairly clear idea of what it is all about, or how it hangs together?"

A man can belong to that type of fine-eared Listening-Musician without being able to tell you the names of the notes. Thousands lovingly observe flowers who know no botany and thousands understand and enjoy a good performance of Beethoven who do not "know B from a bull's foot".

Here I thought I had finished this section of my book, but on reflection I have decided to add something from our great British pioneer of both Appreciation and Aural Training—something that must, I think, carry weight with even the pedants. The School Music Section of the Incorporated Society of Musicians' Conference in December 1932 debated this question:

"Can the use of the term 'Musical Appreciation' be discontinued and all that it connotes be understood to come within the scope of 'Aural Training'?"

After a "lively discussion" it was decided "to make no recommendation with regard to this particular suggestion" (*The Music Teacher*, February 1933). The Society's Journal (March 1933) printed a brief paper submitted by Mr. Macpherson to this Conference, which must surely have weighed heavily with the members in voting as they did. It includes this passage:

"I want first to give, as briefly as possible, my own reasons (which are set out in full in my book *The Appreciation Class*) for thinking that what the expression Musical Appreciation really stands for cannot without definite loss be covered comprehensively by the term Aural Training.

"1. Without some kind of qualification which shall connote an aesthetic (i.e. a definitely musical) basis, as well as a technical one, the danger at once arises that Aural Training will tend—as, in some places, it *is* tending—to revert to the old-fashioned 'time and tune' tests, and the dull sight-singing and dictation of an earlier day. There *are* people to-day who apparently see in the possession of the power to read a single vocal line at sight the musical salvation of the multitude. The advocates of this view evidently find it difficult to realize that, immensely important and necessary as such sight-reading power is, its acquirement is purely a technical matter, and not *of necessity* an awakening of the musical faculty, unless it is linked up with certain other things. Because the teaching of ear-training and sight-singing has so often been divorced from the thought of real, living music, and has degenerated into a mere imposition of 'tests', it has times out of number become an ordinance which has bored the pupil to tears. . . .

"2. It *is* of the utmost importance, as I see the matter, that the regular Aural training lessons should be supplemented from time to time—say two or three times a term [1]—by a 'Listening' lesson, 'Appreciation' lesson, or whatever it may be called, in which the most technical *minutiae* of Aural training may take their place in the subconscious region of the pupil's mind, while attention is given to the music in its broader outlines. But, mark you, this lesson is not (as some people seem to take a delight in thinking) one in which he may merely 'loaf', while the teacher plays to him, but one whose aim is to make him definitely *attend* to the music, and to encourage him to form a habit which shall prove to be an antidote to the aimless hearing so often fostered by an unintelligent and indiscriminate use of wireless, and the like.

"Moreover, we must not, surely, forget that a very real approach to music may be made in this broader way, perhaps by some whose ability on the more technical side of Aural training may not be very great. 'The wind bloweth where it listeth', and many an otherwise unresponsive child has been first brought within the magic circle by this very means.

"It is, then, the desire to rescue Aural training work from the clutches of the humdrum, unmusical and uninspiring type of teacher (who, it is true, *may* know the facts he has to teach, but who nevertheless ought never to be allowed to teach them!) that makes me wishful for such work to be linked up with that *something* which

---

[1] I personally think this too little, because I look upon "Musical Appreciation" as partly a matter of the building up of a "Listening Repertory". P. A. S.

the term Musical Appreciation was meant to stand for. Get a better term, if you will and if you can; but, whatever is done, don't let us abandon the idea at the back of the term, nor scrap the expression itself unless and until we can substitute something really better."

Reading through what I have written in this section of my book as well as what I have quoted from Mr. Macpherson I would summarize my own position in this way:

1. Aural Training is a valuable basis for Appreciation.
2. But it is evidently not an indispensable basis, since thousands of people have achieved a very real appreciation of the best music without it.
3. Further, any adequate training in "Appreciation" includes the giving of historical and biographical teaching that can in no sense of the words form a part of "Aural Training."
4. The two things are then, though related, distinct, and, in any case, the *spirit* in which the one kind of training is conducted is essentially different from that in which the other should be conducted, the one being technical and the other aesthetic.
5. No good can, therefore, come by the confusion of the one thing with the other. It is for the teachers to work out for themselves suitable proportions in the allocation of lesson time and to settle the relation of the one subject to the other, but they should occupy distinct places in the minds of both teacher and the pupils—some aroma of *romance* being preserved as a feature of the appreciation technique.

THE HISTORY OF MUSIC

(A good deal of the discussion in this section assumes the favorable conditions of the Secondary School; in the Elementary School, with its shorter school life, less can be done than is here sometimes assumed.)

Probably the historical approach to Musical Appreciation is one of the very best approaches. And it is one of the most important. It has a great practical bearing on the problem of the Obstacle of Style, already discussed. Moreover, properly presented, it gives the pupil the view of the Art of Music in its proper status—as one of the means of human expression through the ages.

There is the more need for the music teacher to include the History of Music in his curriculum since general history books still usually neglect it: the school pupil in his lesson on English History, for instance, learns of the great writers of the reign of Queen Elizabeth but not of the great composers, and a few weeks later he is hearing something of Dryden without a word of Purcell.

It is, however, not a bit of good to teach the History of Music merely as names and facts; just as it would be not a bit of good to teach the History of Painting in that way. Unless the teaching of the History of Painting is grouped around examples of the pictures of the different periods it will be unintelligible; and so will the History of Music unless it is grouped around the hearing of examples of music.

The examination schemes for school-leaving certificates [1] are still often very defective in this way; they can be crammed for by pupils who do not know the music about which they are talking. (To devise examination schemes which shall completely avoid this evil is, admittedly, difficult; but it can be done.)

Another fault of some examination schemes is the concentration on some one period to the exclusion of all other periods. A school-leaving examination, if it touches the History of Music at all, should ensure that the candidate has a general grasp of the development of European Music from, say, A.D. 900 (about which time harmonized choral music began) to the present day. The system on which the brood of candidates one year is expected to know all about the Palestrina period and the brood the next year all about the Beethoven period is thoughtlessly stupid; the *young person leaving school should know at least something of the history of the Art of Music in the whole period from which comes the music he will hear in concert rooms or by the Radio*—and that means Byrd to Bartòk or thereabouts. Then to understand how Byrd's music and that of his contem-

[1] See p. 302 for explanation of these examinations.

poraries came to exist means pushing back 600 years, which takes us to the tenth century (the work of these 600 years, however, need not entail much expenditure of time, as a school-child study of them would be purely a preparation for the music to which their experimentation and effort led).

Of the teaching of English History at a certain institution Matthew Arnold over sixty years ago complained:

"Another class took the period from Caesar's landing to the reign of Egbert, and knew the history of this period, or what passes for its history, minutely; but only one of them had heard of the Battle of Waterloo."

Narrow period concentration in teaching is, then, one fault we have to avoid and it can be avoided if examination boards will cease to promote it and *if teachers will themselves really get a grasp of the main lines of the history of music as an evolutionary art,* instead of knowing only, as some of them do, a few historical facts and some biography.

It may be added here that a sound elementary general knowledge of the History of Europe is indispensable to the teacher of the History of Music. The History of Music is so interwoven with social history that it cannot be disengaged from it without falsification. Such factors as the break-up of the Holy Roman Empire into a multitude of little states, each with its monarch and its court, the Reformation, the Renaissance (to mention only three) are vital in the History of Music, and the teacher of pupils approaching the school-leaving certificate age should certainly understand them in their main bearings.

If the teacher, in addition to studying the History of Europe and the History of Music will study either the History of Painting or that of Architecture (with, perhaps, a preference for the latter) he will find, by analogy, a great light shed on the evolutionary principle in the History of Music. There are plenty of simple books.

A framework of dates is indispensable. Speaking of the teaching of History in general the Board of Education's report on *The Education of the Adolescent* (1926) said:

"Whatever historical details are selected to form the various sections of the scheme, it should, in its entirety, form a coherent whole with a definite framework of knowledge in chronological sequence. Of this framework much will be forgotten in later life; a few vital dates and facts should, therefore, be driven home at every opportunity—preferably by use of a time chart."

So it should be with the History of Music.[1]

Few or none of the pupils intend to become professional musicians; their minds will be occupied with all manner of subjects other than Music; but they should be sent out with, at any rate, a "framework", with "a few vital dates and facts."

Every teacher is at liberty to decide for himself what those dates should be. I suggest the following as a minimum:

A.D.

900. The Beginnings of Experiment in "woven music" (unisonal vocal music continuing, however, to our own day in the two forms of Christian plainsong, Jewish synagogue song, &c., and of folksong).

1625. The culmination of "woven music" in PALESTRINA, BYRD, &c. (Palestrina died 1594, and Byrd and Gibbons 1623 and 1625, but it is not necessary to know exact dates).

1625. The great advance in Keyboard Music during the same period. The Englishman, BULL, might be taken as the type, and his date of death remembered as about the same as those of Byrd and Gibbons (1628—marking the virtual end of the madrigalists and of the keyboard pioneers).

1600. The beginning of Opera and Oratorio and all that this means. Associate with opera the names of PERI, CACCINI, and MONTEVERDE, and with oratorio the name of the priest, St. Philip Neri (d. 1595).

1650–1750. Now we come to a few cases where exact dates may as well be learned, though they are not essential. It is easy to associate PURCELL, BACH, and HANDEL in this period of a century and to remember that Purcell's birth date is probably 1658

---

[1] Time-charts of the History of Music are to be had. There are one or two sectional ones in my *Listener's History of Music* and a comprehensive one in *The Good Musician* by Easson, McCrore, and Chamberlain (Novello & H. W. Gray & Co.).

A.D.

and that of Bach and Handel (reversing the last two figures) 1685. Get an association established between Purcell and the Restoration, and Handel and Queen Anne and the first two Georges.

The birth and death dates of these three are Purcell 1658–95; Bach 1685–1750; Handel 1685–1759. The fact that Domenico Scarlatti's dates are 1685–1757 makes it very easy to "throw him in".

1730. We now come to HAYDN and MOZART, the latter's birth and death dates well within those of the former—1732–1809, and 1756–91. (Get Haydn's old age associated with Napoleon's army in Vienna in 1809, which is easily done by means of several Haydn anecdotes, and then even if the actual dates are forgotten the essential will remain.)

1770. BEETHOVEN (1770–1827), SCHUBERT (1797–1828). Note that these two great Viennese composers died almost together, the one, however, much younger than the other (roughly, as though they were father and son: the story of Schubert's being a torch-bearer at Beethoven's funeral comes in here; his own funeral followed next year).

1810. MENDELSSOHN, SCHUMANN, and CHOPIN. The three great "romantic" composers who were to a large extent mutual admirers and friends. The pupil will probably think of them as a group of piano composers, and this is not altogether wrong. He can call them "the 1810 Romantics". The full dates are Mendelssohn 1809–47; Schumann 1810–56, Chopin 1810–49, so they were all born at the end of the first decade of the nineteenth century and passed approximately as the century reached its half-way. WAGNER was born at almost the same time (1813–83).

1830. BRAHMS (1833–97). Remember him as a young protégé of Schumann and as dying just before the nineteenth century ended, and that places him.

1840. The Nationalists, DVOŘÁK (1841–1904), GRIEG (1843–1907), MUSSORGSKY (1839–81), and RIMSKY-KORSAKOFF (1844–1908), can be taken as typical and they were all born about the same time—1840 in round figures and near enough.

1860. The great British composer ELGAR 1857–1934.
The French impressionist, DEBUSSY (1862–1918).

That, I suggest, can be taken as the irreducible minimum of dates. Birth dates of living composers I have not included, because the pupil, in his Appreciation course, has gathered that they are alive and has, perhaps, formed some sufficient general impression as to their age, and that is enough when we are compiling a mere rough-basis list like the present.

If the pupil has been led to take an interest in the biographical and historical side of the Appreciation work he has a number of other names of composers in his mind and has them roughly placed in relation to the composers included in this list, or, if he has a good memory for dates, has them more exactly arranged in his mind. Moreover, as in after life he meets with other composers he will create more or less precise period associations for them by means of this list. A list like this is really a set of pegs on which to hang a lot of facts as they come to hand. It offers the very smallest number of pegs that will do the work, and so the more happily placed teachers will, I hope, be dissatisfied with it and extend it.

Is there any virtue in what is claimed as such in a recent small book on the History of Music—the fact that it "does not contain a single date"? The principle of speaking in broad terms in a small general book may be good; "middle of the nineteenth century" and "in the dawn of the new century" and terms like that often satisfy the need, but while there is a very good reason for not overburdening with actual dates the general reader or the school pupil to whom music is only one subject among many, the attempt to avoid them entirely becomes artificial. The proper principle (for our school purposes, at all events) is rather the one just suggested—to settle upon a small series of key dates, to insist on that being known, and to relate events and composers to it, by associative ideas of the one kind or another.

The same book (Prof. Percy Buck's *History of Music,* in Benn's Sixpenny Library) offers us another experiment. It begins with "Music at the Present Time" and works back in its last chapter to "The Infancy of Music". The scheme has its attractions. We do not begin with the archaic, and undoubtedly the general reader who starts upon the normal History of Music

often puts it down discouraged before he has got rid of the
Greeks and Egyptians. The principle laid down by the author
of the little book now under discussion is that "understanding
should proceed from the known to the unknown" and it is a
sound enough principle in general. But it does not work here—
if "the known" is taken as the music of our own day. The first
chapter on "Music at the Present Time" is compelled to go back
to the period when "the musical arena of Europe had been dominated by the personalities of Brahms and Wagner" and to describe the ideals of these composers, so that the significance of
"the Debussy period" and of the work of Delius, Elgar, Ravel,
Sibelius, Strauss, and others can be appreciated, and then in the
next chapter Wagner and Brahms appear again in their proper
place.[1] This defect (the defect of every chapter having to
reach out its hand and borrow from the following chapter in
order to get a basis for itself) necessarily obtains throughout the
book, which is skilfully and interestingly written but, being
arranged as it is, should be read from back to front if it is to
be understood by the type of reader for whom it is intended.

[1] The troublesome question is whether the kind of understanding of music
sought through study of its historical development can be attained except by
regarding the music of any period in the light of what preceded, what followed,
and what was contemporaneous—all three! Appreciation, in the sense of an
aesthetic response, may, as Calvocoressi claims on p. 183, need no such integrat-
ing thought—may need only the music of one composer at a time, considered
in comparative isolation—but nice discrimination and appraisal of qualities can
rest only on a large view drawn in perspective. The present, if that be true,
can be known only in the light of the past; but the past, similarly, can be
known only in the light of the present. The best argument, then, for beginning with the music of early times would be that a basis for orientation would
be afforded by the general acquaintance possessed by pupils with the music of
to-day, and that this acquantance could (and necessarily would) be drawn upon
constantly when attention was turned upon the "different" music of earlier
centuries.
But in that light, the teacher might begin almost anywhere, the attractive-
ness of the music to pupils of the ages represented being paramount to considerations of historical chronology. A class seldom maintains a fixed personnel
anyway throughout the entire unwinding of the complete historical scroll; and
experience has shown that new entrants who fall into the middle of developments soon acquire perspective from *their* vantage point—always assuming that
the teacher is one who loses no opportunity to extend lines of illuminating
thought to the hazy backgrounds by which the central figures acquire meaning.
That, indeed, is the indispensable condition: a teacher who has wide perspective and who knows how to use it. With these conclusions Dr. Scholes, as may
be seen on the next page, is in substantial agreement. W. E.

As it stands it is a valuable recapitulatory sketch for readers who *already know* their history, but must be a puzzle to others.

The lesson from this seems to be that the "known to the un-known" principle must be applied with a good deal of thought. The sensible plan in class teaching, I suggest, is to begin *at the earliest period of which the students have come to know and love any of the music* (i.e. the Palestrina-Byrd-Bull period), to study this, and to work forward from that to the present day. It will be a simple thing then to turn back and complete the scheme by showing how the Elizabethan period's conceptions and ideals of music evolved from the earlier conceptions and ideals.

This is practical pedagogy, which the other scheme certainly is not.

At what stage in the school's Musical Appreciation course should the History of Music be introduced? The reply to this is probably as follows: From the outset perform hardly any piece of music without some little incidental biographical or historical information—often thrown in casually but neverthe-less likely to stick. Then, as the repertory of music heard and remembered begins to increase to a point where comparisons as to style and method are possible, introduce such comparisons briefly, so preparing the mind for the evolutionary conception. The pieces earliest heard will probably be chosen for their sim-plicity and attractive qualities, but after a time a composer-interest may be introduced by devoting two or three consecutive lessons to the same composer, including the biographical aspect (which always involves the mention of other composers of the period and so establishes associations).

At a suitable point in the course embark upon a definite his-torical study, (of, say, a couple of terms) covering the whole period of 1,000 years from A.D. 900 to 1900 and bringing into proper relation all that has been previously picked up by the way.

A scheme I personally like even better than this is the one laid down in my three *Books of the Great Musicians,* which from the outset base lessons largely on biography and in the earlier treatments dwell rather particularly on the childhood of the composers.[1] I think this is a *human* scheme, and that is important. After seeing the work through many editions I still feel its plan to be one I personally could not better with pupils who were to be in my care from the age of about ten to twelve onwards, but in the last years of school life (in a secondary school) I should want to follow it up with a short systematic historical course, co-ordinating all the varied knowledge that had been acquired and introducing the pupils to some rather more serious work, comparable to what they would then be doing in literature.

Such a course might be based upon the *Columbia History of Music through Eye and Ear,* a set of Albums of Phonograph Records with accompanying booklets, or (in the case of a group of serious-minded pupils) upon *The Listener's History of Music.* This last (intended for the use of intelligent adults), rather to my surprise, I have found in use as a text-book in a New York school—under a teacher, however, of somewhat exceptional skill as pianist and expositor.

I have sometimes found Dr. Colles's *Growth of Music* (3 vols.) in use in the upper classes of the secondary schools, and where the pupils are keen and the teacher able the work may be found an admirable one for the purpose.

Cram books of all sorts should be avoided. There are books on sale for school use which include composers whose names, I could wager, their authors themselves never met with until they set to work to compile the books. There is one now on sale, and already in its second edition, that tells its young readers of Schenck and Kauer and others of that ilk. (Kauer is not even in Grove's *Dictionary* and probably not one professional music critic in ten could tell you who he is. Do not mention any Kauers to your pupils; Johnson, alluding to the boredom of acquiring *remote* fact, said, "You teach your daughters the diameters of the planets, and wonder when you have done that they do not delight in your company.")

If you wish to know whether the author of a History of Music

[1] The three books assume about three years' growth of the reader while engaged on them. P. A. S.

for young people knows his business see whether you can understand his account of the Modes. If you readily can, try the passage on an intelligent elder pupil who as yet possesses no knowledge of the subject. If the author passes this test it may be taken that he has the gift of exposition. Then turn and see what is said about the Fugue. If it is spoken of as a "strict form" the author knows nothing about Fugue (beyond the rules for the exposition), and is merely passing off crude, popular superstitions about it. If he treats it as a ternary form he is academically minded and distant from actualities. If he says (probably copying Professor Tovey in the *Encyclopaedia Britannica*) that Fugue is texture rather than a form, and if he then proceeds accordingly, give him good marks and examine him further.

Try him on the Gavotte, for some reference to this is likely to come into a history. If he says (as many do) that "A Gavotte is a stately dance beginning on the third beat of the measure" and goes on to say that the Bourrée is another "beginning on the fourth beat of the measure", strike him off your list, as a writer who creates puzzles for his readers instead of solving them. (I as a child was much worried by that statement that the mere opening notes of a piece decided its classification.)

Check him then on the steps by which the Opera developed; see if he has a clear idea of the relations of literature, painting, and music in the Romantic Period. Open his book here and there and see if his literary style attracts you. If he does not pass all these tests and a few others you will devise, discard him.

There are so many bad books on the History of Music now on the market, and they may have so disastrous an effect in killing your pupil's interest, that it is worth a good deal of trouble to avoid them.

A little book that thrilled me as a boy and that I read over and over again is Davey's *History of Music* (Curwen); it is now rather out of date but is nevertheless worth putting in the school library as supplementary reading.

Parry's *Studies of Great Composers* was written for young people, but is just a little too solid for them. Nevertheless it, too, should be available—for the more ardent members of the senior Musical Appreciation Class.

At the end of this section I return to the beginning, which referred to a grasp of the History of Music as a lever for the removal of the Obstacle of Style. The only suggestion I have ever seen that this is not so is the following from M. D. Calvocoressi's *Musical Taste and How to Form It:*

"It is often said that musical works are better appreciated when 'seen in their historical perspective'; that is, considered with reference to the conditions under which they came into being. The truth is that knowledge of this kind is satisfying and desirable, all knowledge is—but has no bearing whatever on musical enjoyment."

I venture to guess that no writer upon painting, architecture, literature, or any other art has ever penned such a sentence as that. My friend "Calvo" evidently does not analyze his own mental processes. Full to the brim as he is of the finest historical knowledge, he does not realize how much it contributes to his artistic pleasures.

As an Appendix to this chapter I give an extract from an article by Professor W. G. Whittaker, on "The Teaching of Musical History." Any readers who have the issue of *The Music Teacher* for December 1932 on their files should turn to it, as it is full of good ordinary common sense. With the following passage, however, I do not entirely agree, and I put it forward here for the teacher's own consideration.

Here is a syllabus suggested by a writer for a year's course for a senior class of children:

"A brief survey of (1) The characteristics of madrigals; (2) the polyphonic school, illustrated by music of Bach and Handel; (3) the classical school, illustrated by music of Mozart, Haydn, and Beethoven; (4) the romantic school, illustrated by Schubert's songs, Wagner's operas, Chopin's and Schumann's pianoforte works and Berlioz's symphonic poems; (5) the more modern school, illustrated by Stravinsky's 'Fire Bird', Debussy's 'Arabesque', Elgar's Cockaigne Overture and various songs and pianoforte works.[1]

---

[1] Incidentally, why call Bach and Handel "the polyphonic school"? Were the Madrigalists not also polyphonists? This illustrates the misleading character of

"Could any group of young people, or of adults, digest such a Brobdingnagian meal? The only result would be acute musical indigestion and a confused brain. Any one of the five sections would suffice for an entire session. No doubt a teacher is anxious that his charges should know something about the general history of music from 1500 to to-day, but enthusiasm must needs be tempered with discretion if the best results are to be obtained. After all, history courses only serve to *introduce* the hearer to the subject, to set him on the path of quest, and it is better that a little should be done well than that a great deal should be done indifferently. One or two general talks as an introduction to the period under survey and, at the conclusion, a succinct linking up of the period with what followed, are certainly useful. The student learns something about one period thoroughly, and so gets to know how to study other periods for himself. If he knows one period well, he is sure to wish to know in the same thorough manner what led up to it and what followed it. The true object of education is to induce people to study for themselves, and to give them ideas which will guide them in the future. . . . It is a question whether any adult·taken through such a lightning-conductor course as the above would have any clear idea of any single period or would have gleaned anything but a few vague and confused generalities."

Professor Whittaker's comment expressed in the footnote needs, of course, no endorsement: the syllabus has, indeed, a very amateurish appearance.

But is Professor Whittaker right in considering that "any group of young people or of adults" would find the course "a Brobdingnagian meal?" The meal is to be a "cut and come again" one of at least thirty sittings. Is it so impossible in that time to absorb the items of that menu? I should say,.Not at all.

The teacher who could not in thirty periods give a class of "any group of young people or of adults" a pretty good notion of the general course of development of the art of Music during the whole of the period of three centuries represented in that syllabus is, in my opinion, no teacher at all.

labels. Are not Bach and Handel as "classic" as Haydn and Mozart? Did Berlioz write any symphonic poems? Do Stravinsky, Debussy, and Elgar constitute a "school"? Are Debussy's Arabesques adequate examples of modern tendencies? W. G. W.

If the history study is to last only one year, a general course like that (only better laid out, of course) is exactly what I would recommend. If the history study is to last more than one year, then I would recommend such a general course as that for the first year, and more intensive study of selected periods for the second year, such as:

First Term.   The Music of Queen Elizabeth's Day.
Second Term.   Purcell, Bach, and Handel.
Third Term.   Haydn, Mozart, Beethoven.

or

First Term.   Woven music—Byrd to Bach.
Second Term.   Sonatas and Symphonies—Haydn to Brahms.
Third Term.   Opera from its beginnings to Wagner.

Or something like that.[1]

The question I here introduce is eminently one for debate among practical teachers and is very important, especially since, as I have said above, the make-up of the syllabus for school-leaving examination is involved—and once the school-leaving examination is passed most of the pupils are out of the teacher's influence for ever.

Personally I am all against specialization before general study. I think that a boy or girl leaving school, if he has any musical interests at all, has a right to complain if he or she has not been given a survey of the whole field of music, as represented in the concert room and radio program.

I should like to see this question submitted to any body of teachers of English History or of English Literature.

Or I would like to call up Matthew Arnold (see reference to him above) and ask him to arbitrate.

I think there is a serious fallacy concealed in the statement: "The student learns something about one period thoroughly, and so gets to know how to study other periods for himself. If he knows one period well, he is sure to wish to know in the same thorough manner what led up to it and what followed it." Few

[1] This catholicity of mind (shared by all good teachers of Musical Appreciation) with respect to the proper form for a course, suggests that just as fugue is a "texture" not a form, so is Appreciation a mode, not a form. W. E.

ordinary school pupils are going to be inspired (or, indeed, to be able), on leaving school, to tackle the periods of Musical History that were left out of their school course, and to apply to each of these periods the energy and time equivalent to a thirty-lesson course under a skilled teacher. The suggestion is too sanguine and only takes account of the few very keenest musical spirits of the class. The study of the History of Music and the acquirement of a deeper appreciation of it, once school is left behind, are usually going to be done (where they are done at all) in the haphazard manner in which we all educate ourselves once we have turned our back on places of education. As interest is aroused in one composer or another by such accidents as meeting in programs with works that attract one, coming across interesting new books, and so forth, we may do a little intensive work, and for this a *general* course is the best preparation, because wherever we want to start business we have a little capital in hand.

There is another point. Some minds are more attracted to the music of one period than another. I know fine musicians, including one of our greatest choral conductors, who have never been able to feel enthusiasm for the English madrigalists, and at least one or two whose perceptions are closed (apparently by nature) to Bach and all he represents; these are extreme cases, but it is a recognized fact that at a given age a particular individual feels far more drawn in one direction than another. A general course is, then, the only one which is fair to all the members of a class, as offering them all the means of finding their affinities, temporary or permanent.

Much as I approve of thoroughness I believe that in educational procedure errors may be committed in its name. A phrase like "it is better that a little should be done well than that a great deal should be done indifferently", with which we all immediately and mechanically assent, may be very misleading. It could be used as a plea for early specialization in any subject whatever.

This whole question of generalization *v.* specialization is, however, as I admit, one that wants talking out—with, as the background for the talk, the desire to be *practical*.

BIOGRAPHY AND ANECDOTE

Inseparably tied up with History is Biography.

As men made the History so the lives of men are the basis for historical study. This obvious fact is worth repeating because there are nowadays so many scoffs at Appreciation teaching on account of its often carrying a biographical flavor.

The scoffers are sometimes professional music critics—the very race that provides most of our learned volumes on "Whether Wagner was a Jew and If not Why not?" and "Who was Beethoven's Unsterbliche Geliebte?" These writers are like the author of the opening pages of the *Spectator,* who, commenting a little sarcastically on the fact that "a Reader seldom peruses a Book with Pleasure till he knows whether the Writer of it be a black or a fair Man, of a mild or cholerick Disposition, Married or a Bachelor, with other particulars of a like nature that conduce very much to the right understanding of an Author", at once proceeds to give just such particulars about the Author to whom he was now introducing them—himself.

What, after all, is wrong with the supplying of such particulars? It may be illogical of mankind to want them, but mankind *does* so want them—I think because it gives the feeling of having met the other man. When we have met a man we want to know his work. I met a great Italian author the other day and then, for the first time, bought one of his books.

With children, especially, this principle holds good. They love to meet human beings, and after a story or two about Beethoven are far more ready to give attention to any of his music that may come their way. After all, the securing of *attention* for a work of art is the first requirement of any scheme of appreciation training in that art; you cannot appreciate without attention, and so stories of Beethoven are, as lesson material, not so contemptible as we are always being told. Many professional musicians are too "superior." One would think they had been born at the age of thirty.

Let us boldly tackle that question of anecdotes. It is always cropping up. Some Doctor of Music is invited to visit an Elementary School, finds a young girl telling a class of eight-year-olds about the footsore boy Bach finding coins in herring heads, and writes to the musical press to say "Musical Appreciation is Mere Anecdote". ("A string of gramophone records with no more illumination than a few picturesque and apocryphal anecdotes about the composer concerned" was one Doctor of Music's description of some lesson he had heard.)

Next time an educational conference of musicians is held the distressed doctor gets up and tells his tale—"Musical Appreciation is Mere Anecdote"—and every one murmurs "How Dreadful", and holds up his hand for a resolution that Musical Appreciation *should be* "Aural Training", or *should be* Instrumental Study, or *should be*—anything else that it is alleged it isn't.

Surely there is nothing wrong with Anecdote. "I love anecdotes", said Dr. Johnson, and he spoke for all of us. From childhood to the end of life we are in our anecdotage.

Suppose instead of taking the opinion of these Doctors of Music and Music Critics we take that of a Professor of History—one of the most eminent; one to whom History is History and not a mere subject in the school curriculum; one to whom a proper understanding of the history of mankind is the basis for mankind's direction of its future. He does not agree in the very least with our Musical Doctors and Critics. He goes farther than I myself, with all my heresy would, without him, have dared to go. *He would tell children anecdotes even if "apocryphal".*

"I think that children should be made familiar with the fictions of history—I am inclined to think that a child is not properly educated unless it knows such amusing stories as that of Alfred and the Cakes, Canute and the Waves (which is even more ridiculous), and William Tell and the Apple, and so on. I don't suggest they should be taught as the truth. To save his face, of course, the teacher, since he doesn't want to be considered a downright liar, must tell his pupils that they are most probably not true. But for history teaching they rouse interest and perhaps have an imaginative value. *The purpose of history teaching is not to give children an encyclopedic knowledge of events, but to arouse their interest in the past of their own country or of the world. . . ."*

The italics as the end of that passage are my own. The passage itself comes from a *Teacher's World* interview (29 October, 1929) with Professor G. M. Trevelyan, O.M., C.B.E., F.B.A., D.C.L, LL.D. Litt.D., &c., Regius Professor of Modern History in the University of Cambridge, and one of our foremost historical authors. Nobody in England stands higher as a historian than Professor Trevelyan, yet he "is inclined to think a child is not properly educated unless it knows such amusing stories as . . ."

What are we to make of it? Who is right? Here are Musical Doctors and Critics who sneer at the anecdotal side of biography (and even, sometimes, it seems, at biography itself), and there is a Regius Professor applauding even the *non vero* if *ben trovato.*

If any of the Doctors and Critics have read thus far I know what they will begin to do. They will begin to hedge and to say that they only objected to "meaningless" anecdotes. (They didn't—not always, at any rate. But let that pass.)

Anyhow the reply must be. *"Such as . . .?"* and a pause for further information.

I take up a Musical Appreciation book for children, open it anywhere and turn over the pages. Here are anecdotes galore:

The child Handel practicing the harpsichord in the garret.
    "   " running behind the coach and so getting taken to the court of the Duke.
    "   " composing a weekly motet for his master.
The child Bach surreptitiously getting hold of his big brother's music book and copying it by moonlight.
    "   " trudging to Hamburg to hear music (the herrings' heads incident).
The child Haydn cutting off his brother choirboy's pigtail in church.

The aged Haydn carried in his armchair to hear the great performance of *The Creation*.
The child Mozart playing the violin to the customs officers.
    "   "   saying he would marry Marie Antoinette.
    "   "   playing to George III.

And so on . . . and so on . . . and so on: there must be hundreds of anecdotes in that book and I cannot see that one of
them is "meaningless". Every one of them "means" something
—to a child, at any rate; it means *humanity* as distinct from a
name on the front page of a piece of music, or on a phonograph
record label or in a radio program.

And every one of those anecdotes conveys some idea of social
conditions and musical life at the time the music of those composers was written—cannot fail to do so.

If those tales of girl school-teachers reeling off "a string of
gramophone records" with mere "picturesque anecdotes" are true
it is regrettable. They are probably doing the best they can,
but they should learn how to do better. But even so I would
not say that their so-called Appreciation teaching is worthless. I
would rather a child of mine had that sort of training than none.
To tell anecdotes of Bach (so awaking interest and securing
attention) and then to set going a record of *My heart ever faith-
ful* may be to give an experience that will be remembered to
the end of the child's life, and to lay the foundation of a lasting
and intelligent interest in Bach.

"Musical Biography is not Appreciation" we are told. Who
ever said it was? All the sensible Musical Appreciationist
claims is that Musical Biography is one of the greatest interest-
arousers in his whole bag of tools.

And can you educate without interest?

ON "GOOD" AND "BAD" IN MUSIC

What is "Good Music"? Nobody can say. Yet we all know
compositions we are *sure* are good, compositions we are sure are
bad, and compositions about the value of which we are not sure

at all, feeling that we need further intimacy before we can know our minds.

So far, then, there is no quarrel among us. We are all agreed that "bad" and "good" are terms that can be applied to music as they can be applied to pictures or literature or houses or food.

But to define "bad" and "good" in clear, unmistakable terms baffles us. If any one asks us whether a particular composition is "bad" or "good" we can give a pretty decided opinion, but if he asks us our reason we shall have to think a bit, and if he asks us for a criterion he can apply to the world's music in general we begin to "hum and haw", and in the end probably tell him there is no rule. Then, if he is a very patient man, and we have an hour or two before us, we can go on to discuss particular compositions and find out their characteristics. But it will be noticeable that in general we shall make up our minds first as to whether a composition is bad or good and then justify it by analysis after, which practice may, to our questioner, look like putting the cart before the horse, but yet can be justified on sound psychological grounds.

Suppose we put before that man two fugues, one of J. S. Bach and one of P. A. Scholes, who in his student period used to write one a day for a time and could, perhaps, find a relic or two of that period somewhere in his lumber-room.

At a first playing through of the two fugues we decide that one is good and the other pretty bad, I will not say which. Perhaps the subject of the one is stronger. But as soon as we use that word the inquirer, if he is as maliciously determined as I have imagined him, begins to ask what we mean by "stronger." And then we point to the respective curves of the two subjects, and show how one of them flabbily hangs about certain notes while the other goes straight to a mark—probably reaching its highest or climactic note only once and then descending from it and hence not cheapening its effect.

And we analyze the respective rhythms of the two subjects, and find that in its couple of bars or so one of them has by subtle refinements acquired about twice as much rhythmic interest as the other.

And then, playing a passage or two here and there, we show that the part-writing of the one is freer, less constrained, than the part-writing of the other. The three or four or five parts seem just to go their own way, yet to fit together perfectly all the time, whereas in the other one, though the parts do fit together, they have plainly had to be cajoled into doing so.

Then the key contrasts are better managed in the one than the other.

Then again, just as in the subject itself there was one high spot, so in the fugue as a whole (the good one) there is probably one high spot—a point of real climax somewhere near the end, after which the fugue declines in force, but not in workmanship, and sinks at last to a dignified end.

About the good fugue there is a perfect logical sense. Everything seems to follow what has gone before, as one phrase of a well-thought-out argument follows another. And, indeed, skill in logic is half the art of composition. Beethoven sometimes throws logic to the winds. For a moment he is deliberately illogical. He is engaged in a steady argument, and suddenly leaps out of it into an unrelated digression. But we feel purpose in this, and purposeful repudiation of logic is a sort of logic in itself.

So here are some of the characteristics of good music—strong material, a sense of climax, unity, variety, progression from point to point, all those things which we can describe as music's logic. And if a composition has got those qualities we generally, as I hinted, *feel* them first and *find* them after.

Now much bad music is deficient in logic. It may not be definitely lacking in a sense of forward progression, in variety yet unity of material, and so forth, but it does not make its points strongly. A lot of schoolroom music (I mean music written specially for the schoolroom) is like that—a very flabby sort of self-expression, and more "put together" than "grown"; mechanical rather than organic. Much of this music has passages that could be cut out without being missed or in any way weakening the composition. Such music is poor music.

A masterpiece is always concise. Where it is not, it is so much the less a masterpiece. In second-rate music the pointless introduction of passages that have no special meaning and the useless repetition of passages are common weaknesses.

I think one's sense of what is good and bad in music can be enormously strengthened by a very detailed analysis of a large number of compositions that all the world has long accepted as good. If we try to see *why* a fine composer has written a certain effective passage in a certain way, we shall learn to detect passages that are not written in the way they should be. I once spent two years in making a close analysis of various compositions for the Audiographic Series of the Aeolian Company (a series that promised to be useful but then, after the expenditure of many thousands of pounds, had to be abandoned in the great economic stress of the early 'thirties), and was astonished to find in how many cases a composition that had maintained its popularity over a long course of years had evidently done so largely by its close economy and relentless logic. It is almost impossible to find a long-lived piece that is not closely logical. The hearers have not realized, or even thought about, that quality, but it is nevertheless largely the basis of their continued enjoyment of the composition. Much bad music is like rhetoric without common-sense—a mere flux of uncontrolled feeling. So what I call the logical sense is a definite feature in good music.

And another feature (perhaps it ought to have come first, and I did just allude to it) is strong subject-matter. If we play merely the opening measures of Beethoven's thirty-two Pianoforte Sonatas, without going farther, we feel that a master is beginning to speak. Every note has purpose. The introduction plunges us right into the depths, head over heels.

Compare Bacon's essays. They do the same. Every one of them *grips* us with its very first words. For instance, the essay called "Of Truth": "'*What is truth?' said jesting Pilate, and would not stay for an answer.*" Or the essay, "Of Marriage and Single Life"; "*He that hath wife and children hath given hostages to fortune; for they are impediments to great enterprises, either of virtue or mischief.*" Or the essay, "Of Empire"; "*It is*

*a miserable state of mind to have few things to desire and many
things to fear. And yet that commonly is the case with kings."*

And so on. At the very outset of a sonata of Beethoven's or
an essay of Bacon's we realize that the man is going to talk
strong sense and not to mumble platitudes. The very opening
assures us of a coming logical treatment. Something is propounded, and so forcefully that we feel confident that it will be
sensibly discussed.

Now those qualities of strength, logic, common sense are vital
to music. I could for a long time go on instancing other qualities of good music. I should like, in particular, to try to define
beauty (I could not succeed, but it is good fun to try). I should
like to talk of a composition as the expression of emotion, and to
talk of worthy and less worthy emotions and manners of expressing emotion.

But if I went on all day I could not completely and satisfactorily define goodness in music—nor could you.

CAN WE TRAIN TASTE?

In the last section I tried to uncover some of the criteria of
good music—criteria that, so far as I can see, are based on psychological principles and must therefore last as long as the mind
of man, and that also, one may remark, have their obvious counterparts in the other arts.

I believe that with an intelligent adult class (say at one of our
great schools of music) a great deal could be done in the way of
testing all sorts of music by the help of such touchstones as I
have mentioned.[1] I think that the result of this would be to
awaken a critical sense in the student, such as he could apply
throughout his life—sharpening it all the time by dint of use.

I am very far from saying that by the application of any criteria ever discovered all the good music can be stored into barn
and all the bad given over for burning, or composers driven into
two pens as sheep and as goats—such dichotomy being executed

[1] The teachers of composition are, of course, constantly using just such touchstones in discussing their pupils' efforts. P. A. S.

with infallible exactitude. Even the literary critic, who has a much more tangible art with which to deal, cannot quite boast of attaining that measure of certainty. Still *something* can be done, and that particular London music critic who is always looking to a future when the men of his craft will work by rule and not by instinct may make a start whenever he wishes, for I make him a present of the above criteria. Indeed he is applying such criteria all the time, and when he offers a reason for his preferences or his antipathies (as he often does) I believe it will generally be found to be classifiable under one of those heads. In effect, what I did in my last section was to dissect out a few of the principles upon which our subconscious acts; and I am assuredly not the first to do that. The subconscious does not usually tell us why it is acting as it does, but we can often discover this if we reflect, and that is all I have done.

In order that the subconscious shall learn to act promptly and decidedly we need to hear much music. Not merely the conscious, but also the subconscious (*much more* the subconscious, I think) can acquire a standard, a basis of comparison.

And anybody's subconscious will act properly if given abundant time. In a few months the café and cinema public gets tired of compositions it at first took to wildly, though there are certain tunes of Schubert, Schumann, Dvořák and others of which it never tires. This shows a critical sense, though a somewhat slow-acting one.

I do not say that all people, even those who hear much music of all sorts, acquire an ability promptly to distinguish good from bad. There are incapables in all walks of life, and in the days when the London Promenade Concerts had a first part devoted to the best music in the world and a second part devoted to some of the worst there were people who clapped the Fifth Symphony and then did not go home with the judicious at 9.30 but lingered through the interval and clapped *Roses in Your Garden* just as heartily.

In the main, however, it may be said that by hearing much music a standard *is* acquired and that the individual who has heard enough good music will not care for the bad—will quickly "see through it", will find it obnoxious, will turn off his switch and write to the *Radio Times* about it.

Bernard Shaw once told a London audience how he came to possess a taste for the better music. It was a struggling music-teacher who gave him the chance of hearing regular and frequent rehearsal and performance of symphonies, operas, and oratorios:

"I was brought up in a town where there were no official or commercial opportunities of hearing music, nevertheless before I was ten years old I was so accustomed to good music that I had to struggle with a strong repugnance to what is called popular music. Strauss's waltzes, which were rampant at that time, positively annoyed me. This familiarity with serious music I owed altogether to a man who, like most musicians, had no private resources, and made his living by giving lessons in singing and playing the piano. But this did not satisfy him. He walked through the streets of the city; and whenever in passing a house he heard some person scraping a violoncello inside, he knocked at the door and said to the servant: 'I want to see the gentleman who is playing the big fiddle.' He did the same when he heard a flute, when he heard a violin, when he heard any instrument whatsoever—simply knocked at the door and insisted on seeing the poor terrified amateur, to whom he said: 'I am forming an orchestra; you must come and play in it.' And being a determined person he usually had his way."

The allusion to the Strauss waltzes there is interesting. At the present moment we are getting a few of them back and welcoming them. But then we have just gone through twenty years of Jazz and the Waltzes come fresh to us, whereas in Shaw's youth they were heard to boredom. I should say they are good stuff in their way, but not so good as to stand endless repetition.

Anyhow, the point of my quoting Shaw is that by the lucky chance of hearing plenty of music he came to *know his mind,* and like most others who enjoy a like chance, and profit by it, his mind settled on the side of what we call "good".

Ruskin never had this chance, and so when he had chagrined Hallé by preferring Thalberg's *Home Sweet Home* (which some

schoolgirls had persuaded him to play) to a Beethoven sonata
(letter of 3 December, 1864), he wrote to apologize:

"My 'children' tell me you were sorry because I liked that 'Home,
S.H.' better than Beethoven—having expected better sympathy from
me. But how could you—with all your knowledge of your art, and
of men's minds? Believe me, you *cannot* have sympathy from any
untaught person, respecting the higher noblenesses of composition.
If I were with you a year, you could make me feel them—I am quite
capable of doing so, were I taught—but the utmost you ought *ever*
to hope from a musically-illiterate person is honesty and modesty.
I do not—should not—expect you to sympathize with *me* about a
bit of Titian, but I know that you would, if I had a year's teaching
of you, and I know that you would never tell me that you liked it,
or *fancy* you liked it, to please me. . . . You must not therefore
think I only cared for the bad music—but it is quite true that I
don't understand Beethoven, and I fear I shall never have time to
do so."

There you find Ruskin what he always was, a protagonist of
"Appreciation." He feels he could remove obstacles out of
Hallé's route to Titian and that Hallé could remove obstacles
out of his to Beethoven, but the point of my quoting the letter
here is not this but that for want of *experience* (such as Shaw
had) he was taken in by a shallow piece of music that was the
antithesis of everything he loved in those arts of which he had
experience.

Imagine Ruskin before a piece of architecture on the Thalberg
level! Yet that architecture would probably have delighted
Hallé. I believe that where an individual is in any degree a
thinker, with standards in any department of life and work, he
will, *with sufficient experience,* come to see through the preten-
tious and the shoddy. He may not always admire the fine things
of the bigger and more complex sort; obstacles may remain, and
so they may seem to him dull and uninteresting. But he will
not be bamboozled by the cheap-jack merchant.

All this points the way of the school Appreciation teacher.
Boys and girls of eight to fifteen are, as I think, too young to

be bothered with criteria such as I have offered.[1] It would only waste their time to put such in their hands—as well as tending to make them self-consciously critical and even perhaps priggish. Personally I should not think of occupying their minds with any considerations of quality in music, but should multiply as much as possible their opportunities of hearing the best, under favorable conditions, and trustfully leave the rest to Providence.

So far as I am aware this is the general practice among Appreciation teachers. They would not refuse to discuss the subject if a pupil raised it, but they do not think it worth while to raise it themselves. Dr. Cyril Norwood, President of St. John's College, Oxford, in 1923 (when he was Headmaster of Marlborough) addressed a gathering of musicians in these terms (see *The Music Teacher* for October of that year):

"Since a child is usually surrounded by bad and vulgar music from early years, his master should try to instil at school a sense of the difference between good and bad, and to give simple explanations why one type of music is good, and the other is bad."

All I can say is that it is my conviction that the scheme "would not work." I rather doubt if any "Art" Master or teacher of English Literature concerns himself with the bad—at all events as regards the rank and file of his pupils, and I see that Mr. W. B. Maxwell, Chairman of the National Book Council, said (Annual Meeting, 1933): "I think we should remember that love of literature and literary taste are not quite the same thing. It is the first that we want to cultivate, and the second may take care of itself." (He then goes on to draw lessons from some experiences of the Headmaster of Eton, so that I take him to be alluding, as I am, to the proper policy for those entrusted with the education of youth.) I do not wish to be dogmatic, however. I

[1] Criteria and attempts at judgments are hardly appropriate to children of the ages mentioned, but joyful conscious recognition of factors that subconsciously have given rise to musical pleasure can be elicited by a discerning teacher in connection with simple music at a very early age. See the testimony on p. 260, and that on p. 298 as suggestive. Dr. Scholes also gives admirable suggestions in his *Listener's Guide to Music*. In America such attempts to "step down" factors of musical interest to their lowest terms, for recognition by little children, have been carried quite far, and detailed printed suggestions have appeared. W. E.

myself just once in my life tried to demonstrate, by examples, the difference between good and bad music. This was in certain American schools where I was pressed to try the experiment. I felt that I failed—but then I never expected to succeed. If others have attempted such a task and come out triumphant, let us hear about it!

What I do think quite in order and well worth doing is, when performing a piece of fine music, to express any enthusiasm one generally feels at any of its details. I see little value in performing a piece of bad music in order to be able to say "Aren't those dull harmonies", "Just listen to that shapeless melody", "What a vulgar rhythm"!—the features in question being perhaps the very ones that have most attracted and fascinated some of your pupils in their inexperience. But I do see value in such expressions of wonder and delight as honest George Grove utters on so many pages of his book on the Beethoven Symphonies; only we must not be so lavish with praise as he was, or our sometimes perverse modern youth will perhaps react in a way we do not want!

Our real duty, as I think, is the one I have already laid down—the removal of obstacles. I agree with Mr. S. C. Kaines Smith, Director of the Birmingham Art Gallery, formerly Lecturer at the National Gallery, and author of a useful popular book, Looking at Pictures, as well as many books of learning and research. Addressing the Parents' Educational Union in 1928, on Can Appreciation of Art be Taught?, he said:

"It is no good trying to make a child enjoy beauty to order. We must teach the child to see, and it will learn the result of seeing for itself."

That, with the necessary change of two words might be the Musical Appreciation teacher's motto. He should teach the child to hear and leave the result of hearing to itself.

In closing this section I should like to introduce the idea of a definite Listening Repertory. Just as every performer possesses a repertory of compositions which he really knows and to which he can do justice if called upon (a large and varied repertory if he is not merely a performer but an artist), so should every listener possess a repertory of compositions which he knows and to which he can, without undue effort, listen with understanding when they crop up in concert or radio program, &c. The teacher of Musical Appreciation might well give serious thought to the compilation of a minimum list of the finest and most typical madrigals, fugues, sonatas, symphonies, string quartets, waltzes, nocturnes, &c., (two or three of each, representative of different periods and of all the greater composers), with which he intends that every pupil who passes through his hands shall, in the course of his school life, make an intimate acquaintance. This list he will then, throughout his teaching career, amend as the result of ever-growing acquaintance with both music and the youthful mind.

If every music-loving boy and girl went out into the world unconsciously equipped with a touchstone of excellence in each of the principal forms and styles of music, the problem of public taste would be largely solved.

ON STOOPING DOWN TO THE CHILD

Here is an important point of practice on which teachers must make up their own minds—provided only they do not make them up too quickly and without a sufficient basis of experiment.

Should we, in the choice of music, carefully stoop down to the level of the child mind or expect the child mind to rise up to something nearer our own level?

The first view is thus expressed in a reasoned article by Mr. E. G. Porter in *The Musical Times* in September 1931; he is discussing both appreciation class work and children's concerts:

"One of the several factors that must practically annul the value of presenting great musical works to the average child, and one which seems to be almost tacitly ignored, is that masterpieces are the outcome of some great adult experience that children cannot appreciate. It is thus as futile to play, say, the *Coriolan* Overture to a youngster as it is to show a baby in arms one of Turner's pictures;

for just as the latter can appreciate the colors but not their meaning, so the former can appreciate the melodies but not their intellectual justification.

"Such a large number of great works ought to be barred on this ground that there seems very little left. Even such small forms as the Chopin Mazurkas have such a large adult emotional content that to make children listen to them, let alone play them, is liable to train them to concentrate on the outward signs rather than the inward graces of music."

The second view appears in the following extract from an article by Professor F. H. Shera (then Director of Music at an English public school) in an article in *The Journal of Education* in June 1920:

"There is no reason for invariably putting before a boy music which he can fully comprehend at the outset. We do not expect him to realize at school the full meaning of the Psalms, of Shakespeare, of Aeschylus. Why should we do the like in music? Great art becomes greater and truer with the growth of experience; and just as we introduce the boy at school to great literature, so we ought to introduce him to great music." [1]

I do not wish to decide dogmatically between these views, but I incline to the latter. I remember a remark which I came across in a school pupil's report of (I think) a lecture given in a High School in an American city. It ran: *"It rose above the heads of our students, but things are only gained when one reaches above."*

If that spirit of readiness to reach up can be inculcated, of course, the teacher need not in his programs reach down— or not so far, for with the best will in the world there are limits, of course, to the upward reach at any age.

Is it not the fact that the *spirit* of great art can sometimes penetrate, despite the fact that its *body* has not been fully understood?

[1] The reader may care to glance at a discussion that bears on this point in the *American Editor's Preface*. Certainly it would be a pity—and monstrously inhibitive of growth—if a child were never permitted any experiences save such as were within his complete comprehension. Even adult life would shrink pitifully if such a pedantic principle were imposed! W. E.

If it comes to that, how many of us really fully understand any great masterpiece?

I have the impression that there are appreciation classes being happily and usefully entertained with little minuets and gavottes that might, on occasion, get a great thrill and the glimpse of a big conception from an experience of something with more depth and height and light and shade and color and complexity.

PICTURES AND STORIES IN MUSIC

The question of "Program Music", eagerly debated up to the early years of the present century, is now no longer much discussed. This is just as well. It is a very vexed one.

From the earliest days of instrumental music, composers have tried on occasion to use it to paint a picture or to tell a story; in the Romantic period of the nineteenth century there was a great extension of the practice, and it is only in the post-war days that the practice has tended to disappear—except in the matter of children's piano music, which is still largely narrative, pictorial, or at least "suggestive" (as Macdowell would say) of some happening or scene alluded to in the title.

As I shall have occasion in this section to say about program music one or two things that are opposed to a considerable body of opinion, I think it well to define my personal attitude to it.

It is, to me, in general inferior. The composer who is working to an extra-musical scheme is hampered: he cannot allow his musical themes to develop themselves in just the way that, if he had left himself quite free, he would consider the very best. Moreover, his primary musical material is likely to be second-rate, for if it serves his literary or pictorial purpose his musical judgment is apt to be complaisant.[1]

And not only is the composer hampered but often also, the listener, because instead of being able to listen to the music purely as music he is driven to fit the bits of the "program" to the bits of the music, and this means finding himself wrong and

[1] There are, of course, abundant cases where there is no inferiority; we have the signal example of a composer, Wagner, who practically never conceived music without an external stimulus. P. A. S.

getting right again and being in doubt and being in certainty and doubt again—not the best state of mind for a listener.

What I have just said applies obviously not to a composition of a vaguely "descriptive" character (A "Lake", a "Fairy Dance", and the like) but (say) to a tone poem of the Liszt or post-Liszt period. Elgar's *Falstaff* is by some considered one of his greatest works. It is not so to me. It attempts to follow out a "program" that brings frequent interruptions and changes into the flow of the music, and that, printed and distributed to the audience, merely baffles them, so full is it of detail. Probably there have been few members of any audience with that "program" in their hands who have reached the end of the "program" exactly as the orchestra reached the end of the music—unless they have managed to make adjustments as the music went on.

There are highbrow musicians who say: *"The Music's the thing; hang the program! I never worry about that."* This attitude is in such flat contradiction to the composer's intentions that it does not seem to need condemnation. The composer is, *almost as in opera,* producing a sort of combination art. Elgar's *Falstaff* is not literature or music but a blending of both—like Verdi's *Falstaff,* only with the literature not uttered aloud. Part of the failure to appreciate some of Berlioz's orchestral music comes from people listening to it too much *as Music.* It will not always stand this. It must be listened to as what it is—a combination.

My position, then, as to program music is that, from the nature of the case, it ought not to be listened to simply as music (and by music here I mean the one art that is capable of expressing strong emotion direct, without the use of "ideas"), but to be listened to as a combination-art, as a sort of music-drama or music-picture—and combination-arts I personally do not quite thoroughly enjoy. This is not a full statement of my views, but it is near enough for present purposes.[1]

Having shown that I am not a great lover of program music I shall not be so likely to be misinterpreted when I say that I

[1] The aesthetic problem is well treated in Santayana's *The Sense of Beauty* and in Louis Arnaud Reid's *A Study in Aesthetics.* Aesthetic and pedagogical aspects together are discussed in Earhart's *The Meaning and Teaching of Music.* W. E.

do not altogether agree with the musicians who are always wanting to hang, draw, and quarter young Appreciation teachers whom they have caught in the act of attaching pictorial and literary ideas to a piece of music issued by its composer without such. This device for securing children's attention and interest can, of course, be enormously overdone, until the children are given the impression that music is simply one pleasant but puzzling means of telling stories and painting pictures—that every musical composition "means" something outside itself. But to speak as though every piece of "pure" music is so "pure" that to attempt to interest a child by fitting to it a few literary or pictorial ideas is a desecration seems to me excessive.

We understand that Schumann's *Album for the Young* pieces were written as "absolute" music and then, as each was finished, the composer found a literary or pictorial idea that fitted it and chose a title accordingly. Suppose he had not added the title to a particular one of the pieces and some teacher playing it to a class of children had found an appropriate title and used it, would it really have been such a crime?

On the other hand, we are told that Chopin often wrote his pieces to a literary or pictorial idea and then adopted a colorless general title, such as Nocturne or Polonaise. If a teacher playing one of these pieces to a class of children attempts to find the literary or pictorial idea in order to interest them in the music, does it greatly matter?

There are plenty of compositions of Mendelssohn to which a literary or pictorial idea can be attached such as will express the spirit of the music, and if to attach these ideas will grip the attention of a child I do not see that there is any objection to using them. The music is still fine music and felt as such, and even if the literary or pictorial ideas remain for the whole life of the child attached to the music (as some fear they may do), no world-disaster is thereby involved. Mendelssohn would probably approve. He loved children and they loved him, and though a man of fine taste he was not one of an impossible severity.

The real cheapening of music comes when the ideas adopted are weakly sentimental or in other ways foolish.

I have before me the report of a piano recital given by a well-known pianist to 2,000 school-children. A prize was offered by a local musical society for the best essays upon the various items of the program and the essay of the prize-winner is printed. As all this was ten years ago the dear child I am going to quote is now in her twenties and will have sense enough to smile if this page unfortunately comes under her eye. (Still I hope it will not do so.)

She wrote an essay on each of the chief pieces in the program. Her first is as follows:

"The Moonlight Sonata

"I am conscious of a sea of upturned faces, full of expectation of something uncommon and beautiful.

"Then following the burst of clapping, a silence so intense that one might have heard a pin drop. But what is that which interrupts my thoughts? A sound so sweet that I, as if in a dream, am borne down a stream past snow-capped mountains, which, as the moon casts its rays to light my path, turned to glittering gold. But my thoughts were not upon these things, but on a far more beautiful scene; for I sailed on a carpet of stars mixed with colors whose shades are known to nature only. The reflection of a sky so wonderful that pen and ink cannot describe it; and, content, sank deeper and deeper into the land of dreams.

"But what is this which disturbs my slumber? A breath of air? Impossible! Rain? Incredible! True, nevertheless. My boat was now swaying. The waves were higher. But oh! even worse, the moon has disappeared and I am left alone in the gathering gloom.

"The wind is rising now, I am tossed here and there, but no one comes: and still the storm rises. The shriek of the tempest rises higher, the streaks of lightning give a more terrifying aspect.

"For over an hour the tempest raged. I no longer thought of home or loved ones far away, hope had departed from my breast and I lay like a corpse at the base of the boat.

"Fate would never desert me and it was not her wish that I should perish. The storm abated, and hope rose again within me.

"I awoke from my reverie, and found the subject of my dream to be a beautiful melody, played by a master hand."

I offer that as an example of the silly stuff that girls will write if their teachers encourage them. I cannot defend it, and indeed, I think the practice of asking children to write essays on music on the whole a rather dangerous one. Here I blame not the child but the promoters of the competition who rewarded her.

But that is not to say that I agree with the heavy academics who entirely condemn the occasional practice of using pictorial or literary ideas. If I did I should have to condemn Beethoven himself, who towards the end of his life actually had the intention of bringing out a new edition of the Piano Sonatas, because he had the desire to indicate the poetic ideas on which many of these were based, and thus to facilitate comprehension and determine the interpretation of them (see Niecks's *Programme Music*).

The plain fact of the matter is that a phrase of music expresses an emotion, that sometimes a word or a thought can express the same emotion, and that by uttering the word or the thought we may make the emotional significance of the phrase clear to a child who, perhaps, listening half-heartedly, was going to miss it.

It is going a little farther than to add pictorial illustrations to a book of children's poems, but not so much farther that it need be made the continual subject of acrimonious complaint.

The first condition we have to meet is to interest the children in music. Do let us be reasonable!

As I have found myself, rather unexpectedly, launched into the subject of musical essay-writing by children I push out a bit farther. Here is an essay, translated from the French, which contrasts healthily with the one just reproduced. It is by a boy of fourteen, written after a Children's Concert at Geneva conducted by Weingartner. If you can get your pupils, say once a year, to write in this frank and objective spirit, you can learn something from them that may guide you valuably in your work.

Mr. Weingartner thought well to describe to us in full detail the whole orchestra, from the harmonics of the violin to the baying of the trombone. . . . At last, after he had made us wait almost half an hour while these explanations were given, the *Mastersingers*

Overture rang out. It is a horrible din, but there are people who think it beautiful. For myself I cannot understand Wagner; he deafens me. However, warm applause was heard.

Next Mr. Weingartner let us hear one of the movements of Mozart's magnificent Jupiter Symphony. Now Mozart I love. *That* is something truly beautiful. Here is melody—to say the least. When this piece ended I expected applause that would bring the house down. . . . Nothing of the sort! I was astonished, thought there must be some mistake and ventured on a few hand claps that were swallowed up in the silence of the hall.

It turned out that they had now got in store for us the best movement (the 3rd) of Tchaikovsky's Pathetic Symphony. What *must* the others be like? It is pathetically detestable—and, above all, interminable. When it finished I had again to put up with five minutes of frantic applause. It appeared that the audience liked it, if I did not, and the applause seemed to me all the more out of place since it did not come when I expected it, after the Mozart symphony.

I left feeling crushed by Wagner, Tchaikovsky and Beethoven but with pleasant memories of the beautiful Mozart Symphony.

(Recorded by Aloys Mooser, in the article "Musical Impressions of Geneva Schoolchildren", in *Dissonances,* March 1931.)

ON USING THE PHONOGRAPH IN CLASS

There is a complaint that begins to crop up now to the effect that the Phonograph no longer holds the attention of a class. I will give two examples of this complaint.

A highly respected leader in musical education writes to me in defense of the Singing Class (of which he regards me as an enemy because I have protested against school music so often being *all* Singing Class and have pleaded for a little of the time to be given to listening to fine music). He says:

"Things are different from our younger days. Children are *bored* now with wireless and phonograph. They must be taught to do things for themselves."

Then, too, Mr. A. Forbes Milne, Professor of the Royal Academy of Music and the very able Director of Music at Berkhamsted School, writes in the *Music Journal* of the Incorporated Society of Musicians (July 1932):

"The phonograph is of the utmost value to the teacher who knows how to use it wisely, but if it is in constant use, children soon become quite blasé."

It seems to me that there is a fallacy here. Both these writers seem to have at the back of their minds (the back of our minds being the place where we keep things we do not know we possess) some idea that the Phonograph should be *an attraction in itself*. In the early 1920's it still certainly was; by the early 1930's it was fast ceasing to be so. The Phonograph, as such, no longer grips attention; the music must do it and the teacher must so present the music that it *does* do it. We do not complain that the blackboard has now lost its novelty attraction—though the first blackboards ever seen may have had it.

It is up to the teacher, not the apparatus, to maintain interest, and as the first friend I have quoted is decidedly able to maintain interest in a singing lesson he is able to maintain it also in an Appreciation lesson. How? By seeing to it that the pupils "do things for themselves" as much in the one lesson as the other—the art of Listening being, as I have pointed out, like singing, a form of *doing*.

I see that Mr. Milne goes on to say:

"Personally I use the Phonograph more often with senior pupils than with junior, and I find that this has decided advantages."

So I should expect. His senior pupils have been longer under his excellent influence, and are more ready to settle down to a job of real listening. He does not know it but he is paying himself a handsome and well-deserved compliment. With some teachers it would be the other way; the youngsters' interest, such as it was, would be gradually waning and by the time they entered the stylish life of the fifth and sixth forms [1] they would be calling music "all rot", or would, at any rate, be mildly bored with it.

The matter just discussed can be summarized thus: The teacher who expects Phonograph music to supply a tonic for the attention of his class will find the "kick" it gives soon lost; it is so with all tonics. He must expect the Phonograph to

[1] See footnote, p. 124.

supply not a tonic but food, and treat it accordingly. He is the
cook and it falls to him to arrange some attractive menus, and
so to maintain the appetite. It must be wholesome food, too,
so that his charges will feel they are being fed and rejoice therein.

He may find one or two spoiled (*blasés*) individuals turn
against their food and he cannot altogether help that; he is
supplying not *à la carte* but *table d'hôte,* and he must go on the
principle of the greatest good to the greatest number, as all good
hotel cooks do.

Leaving all metaphors (and that one worked nicely for quite
a long time!), a teacher who *is* a teacher, with sufficient well-
chosen records of chamber music, orchestral music (lighter and
heavier), vocal, choral, solo, violin, organ music, &c., extracts
from operas and extracts from oratorios, can surely keep interest
alive.

All the same if he has a piano and a decent one, and can
really play it, he should use that too, and develop as much of a
Corney Grain or Walford Davies pith and point in speaking
from a piano stool as he possibly can.

At this point in my chapter I turn to my files to see what
others have written on the subject, and I decide boldly to steal
great slices from an article by a teacher whose practical experience
and common sense are evident—Mr. William W. Johnson, Music
Master of the County School for Boys, Gillingham, Kent. His
article appeared in *The Music Teacher* (June 1929):[1]

"Compiling a library of records suitable for class use is an interesting problem. With a small terminal grant from the School Fund I
am able to supply immediate needs—or rather, the needs of my
pupils. Generally speaking, I seldom buy album works outright,
but choose movements here and there from the complete quartets,
symphonies, and concertos to suit my purpose. I think it a mistake
to secure records of works not in their original form: there seems
little point in presenting, say, a 'cello rendering of Schubert's *Moment
Musical* No. 3, or a piano arrangement of Saint-Saëns *Le Cygne.*
Music that can seldom be heard in the class room I greatly favor,
while pianoforte and vocal music forms but a small corner of my

[1] More of Mr. Johnson's experiences will be found in Part V. P. A. S.

library. My collection therefore contains for the main part instrumental solos, chamber music, and orchestral works. I am always on the look-out for records of the less familiar orchestral instruments: a single disc of Mozart's *Horn Concerto,* or, his *Bassoon Concerto* makes excellent teaching material. It is notable, too, how much children like the works of modern composers. Movements from Holst's *The Planets* (especially No. 1, *Mars*), Ravel's *Jeux d'eau,* and extracts from *Petrouchka* I have found give great delight.

"Young children love to listen to the various tone qualities of orchestral instruments, to music about things and people, to music that tells stories, and to music that moves in different ways. Some of my most effective material for such lessons has been chosen from Dukas' *L'Apprenti Sorcier,* Saint-Saëns' *Danse Macabre,* Ravel's *Ma Mere l'Oye,* and a host of good Marches and Dances. Obviously it is the program in these works that attracts, but it is remarkable how very keenly quite young pupils will follow the music. Give boys but a rough idea of the story of *The Ring,* and they will be entranced by the galloping rhythms of the *Ride of the Valkyries* and the steady ring of the hammer in *The Forging Song.*. Quilter's *Children's Overture* brings back happy memories of kindergarten tunes, while the *Nutcracker Suite* demands attention by virtue of its clever combinations of orchestral instruments. The hackneyed *Hear my Prayer* has a special charm for boys, not so much as an anthem, but as the performance of a talented chorister.

"Older pupils are more interested in the growth of music, in the way woven melodies were made, in the rise of pattern music, its development into romantic, program, and impressionist styles, and in the way operas and ballets changed through the centuries. Teaching material for this work is limitless: I have used records of a Palestrina Mass, Elizabethan madrigals, choruses from the *Messiah,* the *New World* Symphony, Mendelssohn's Violin Concerto, Debussy's *Poissons d'Or,* and so on. . . .

"Growth, progress and logical sequence mean little or nothing to small pupils, who lack what is known as the 'time sense'. Therefore it is wiser to frame their lessons around the landmarks in musical history, leaving chronological study until later.[1] . . .

"Schemes such as these may look very well on paper, yet if they

[1] I call particular attention to this wise remark, which will, I hope, be read in conjunction with some of my observations elsewhere in this book, on the teaching of the History of Music. P. A. S.

turn out to be mere lectures or recitals, and not lessons in intelligent listening, they will have missed their mark. After all, the abuse of the phonograph in the classroom is a very easy matter. The last hour of a long day's work may be very comfortably spent if the music is 'turned on' and the pupils told to listen; but very little permanent good will have been done if the tired teacher resorts to such a method. The phonograph is an aid in so far as it is used pointedly, sparingly, and effectively. To imagine that a class of children will listen to a whole symphony, or the three or four movements of a string quartet at one sitting is to show a lack of knowledge of the child mind. The prolonged interest and continuity of thought of the trained teacher will never be instilled into the growing pupil, who will have done well if he concentrates for the length of a single movement.

"The phonograph is especially valuable in that the same motif, phrase, or sentence may be played over several times at will—and this is necessary if we wish to foster intelligent listening. Sir Arthur Somervell has told music teachers innumerable that 'the first time nobody hears it, the second time just a few, and the third time the majority hear it!'—and even hearing does not imply understanding. Constant repetition of important phrases is essential, even though it may spell the ruination of a much-treasured record. . . .

"Except in the Matriculation Class,[1] where a systematic course of musical history is being followed, it is rarely wise to expect children to listen to more than one single side of a record without interruption. To give examples, it would be far better to play over the first section of the Scherzo of Beethoven's Second Symphony two or three times to show how a composer pits one group of the orchestra against another (in this case the wood-wind against the strings) than to cause a possible confusion of thought by playing the whole movement once through without comment. Or again, the *Gypsy Rondo* from Haydn's G major Trio is adequate material for one lesson on musical pattern. Let the children listen hard during the first two renderings to get a general impression, and then bid them write down (in any symbols they wish) during the third and fourth renderings their suggestions of the scheme they think the composer employs. Then play them (on the piano if possible) the rondo movement from Beethoven's *Sonata Pathétique*—and let them com-

[1] See p. 302.

pare notes with the previous exercise. In this way a knowledge of the structure of the rondo will be impressed for all time. . . .

"Quite a number of lessons may be given on the instruments of the orchestra with the aid of the phonograph. The recent re-recordings of these instruments are excellent, and come through most faithfully on a good machine. Where it is impossible for the pupils to examine the actual instruments, drawings or photographs may be exhibited during these talks. Silas Birch, Ltd., issue some very clear diagrams for class use, or cuttings from an instrumental catalogue should suffice. Where a band is contemplated, or in being (and this should be in every school nowadays), I am convinced such lessons awaken an interest and a real desire to learn to play some of these rarer instruments. . . .

"Besides a study of the orchestra, an examination of the artistic devices of pattern (phrasing, balance, repetition, &c.), and a consideration of the various styles of music through the ages, the phonograph may be used to develop keen listening for contrapuntal writing. Trios and quartets are admirable for this work. One may lead from the variations, say, of the *Emperor* Quartet to a simple fugue of Bach or Handel, *via* a chorus from *Messiah*. It is not expected that the plan of the Fugue will be thoroughly explained, but the fact that there are three or four independent strands of melody to be heard at the same time should be impressed. Children love to count the number of entries of the subject, but they find it easier as a rule to identify vocal entries at different pitches than entries of parts on a single instruments. The piano, of course, should always be used in conjunction with the phonograph, and nowhere is it more useful than here, when one voice or part is played alone, then the others added one by one until all four are going at the same time. The class might also sing the subjects in parts. With younger children, use should be made of Percy Scholes's 'camouflaged tunes' in the introductory lessons. . . .

"I believe that the vocal record also has a place in the appreciation lesson. Occasionally I like to play a record of a familiar song really well sung, and indicate the fine points of technique, phrasing, and nuances of expression which make for artistic singing, and yet which are most difficult to describe in words or achieve by practice.

"At the end of the term I make a habit of holding a recital of the more popular works that have been already studied. The program is compiled by the children themselves, who enjoy voting for their

favorite pieces. I invariably add one or two 'surprise items'—
new records that I know will be appreciated.

"The school phonograph should always be at the disposal of the
Musical Society—an activity that should be in every school. While
talks on composers with illustrations of their works at the piano are
not recommended as subjects for class lessons,[1] chiefly because such
lessons seldom demand concentrated listening, it is good to allow the
more talented pupils to give short lectures on such subjects."

I close this discussion with a reference to a truly practical point.
Teachers and lecturers often wonder how they can mark records
in order to be able to find given passages. Here is the method
recommended to me by Dr. Frances Clarke, of the Victor
Company, U.S.A.:

Dip a very tiny soft brush in white ink, play the record to the
beginning of the desired passage (perhaps replay a few grooves to
get the exact spot) and drop the little brush ahead of the needle for
one line. It makes a very clearly observable place and does not harm
the record.

MUSICAL INTELLIGENCE COMPETITIONS

There are many devices in education that are useful as tonics
though not as foods. Could we in class make good use of the
competition idea in connection with Musical Appreciation—say
once a term or once a year?

Would it do a class any harm to have its sporting spirit applied to its music listening—occasionally? Might it not drive
home the idea of keen listening as a factor in musical enjoyment? Might it not reveal to a few who believed that they
had been listening for years the fact that they had been not
listening but only hearing?

I am not *sure* that I favor public competition of this sort. If
any one dares to propose such a thing he will certainly be
dropped on by all the pundits, who will charge him with dese-
crating music. Perhaps it would be desecration to carry out a
public competition in the ability to hear music, but I suspect

[1] I personally think this statement goes rather too far. P. A. S.

that it is only our conservative prejudices that tell us so, since we cannot seriously allege that there is desecration in competition in hearing whilst we go on approving of competition in performance, the latter, of course, now one of the regular and most respectable features in British and American musical life.

As a suggestion (and without endorsing every detail) I reproduce particulars of a "Music Appreciation Contest" held at Tulsa, Oklahoma, in 1927. I take it from the Proceedings of the Music Supervisors' National Conference for the latter year. It will be seen by the announcement of the awards at the end that the competitors came as teams representing schools from various places. The contest was staged by the Southwest Music Supervisors' Conference.

I do not personally like the term "Music Appreciation Contest", but think "Musical Intelligence Contest" would be unobjectionable.

MUSIC APPRECIATION CONTEST

Directed by MARGARET LOWRY, *Kansas City, Missouri, Chairman of the Music Appreciation Committee.*

Program played by KANSAS CITY LITTLE SYMPHONY ORCHESTRA, N. DE RUBERTIS, *Conductor.*

1*a*. The orchestra will play for four marches, one of each type listed, but not in the order listed. After listening, number them in the order in which you think they are played.
Toy March . . . . . .
Soldiers' March . . . . . .
Processional . . . . . .
Funeral March . . . . . .

b. The orchestra will play six folk melodies. Write in the correct space the name of each song and the name of the country to which it belongs.
1. . . . . . .
2. . . . . . .
3. . . . . . .
4. . . . . . .
5. . . . . . .
6. . . . . . .

2. You will hear five dances, each of which is a waltz, minuet, or
   gavotte.   Write the name of each dance in the correct space.
       1. . . . . . .
       2. . . . . . .
       3. . . . . . .
       4. . . . . . .
       5. . . . . . .
3a. *Ländler,* by Mozart.   You have discovered that in many composi-
    tions tones are grouped into musical sentences.   As you listen
    to *Ländler,* by Mozart, put a cross on your paper each time you
    hear the end of a sentence.   At the end of the composition give
    the total number of sentences which you have heard. . . . . .
 b. *Gypsy Rondo,* by Haydn.   In any composition which is called
    a Rondo you may always expect to find one most important
    tune which appears several times.   As you listen to the Gypsy
    Rondo count the number of times you hear the tune which
    Haydn has used most frequently. . . . . . .
4. From behind the stage you will hear several short pieces played
   by different instruments.   Write down the name of the instrument which is playing, the family to which it belongs, and the
   name of the composition.
       1. . . . . . .
       2. . . . . . .
       3. . . . . . .
       4. . . . . . .
       5. . . . . . .
       6. . . . . . .
       7. . . . . . .
       8. . . . . . .
       9 & 10. . . . .
5. The orchestra will play two pieces of descriptive music.   After
   listening carefully to the first number, write the name which you
   think best suits this music, and give briefly your reasons for
   selecting this name.   Do the same with the second number.
6. The orchestra will play the *Spanish Rhapsody,* by Chabrier, for
   your enjoyment; this is not a contest number.

Comments and Answers to Questions

1a. The marches were played in the following order:
    1. Grand March from *Aida,* Processional.

    2. Funeral March, by Chopin.

    3. Toy March.

    4. Soldiers' March from *Faust*.

b. Ten representative folk tunes had been prepared for the contest, of which six were used. A memory contest. The songs were:

    1. Song of the Volga Boatmen.

    2. Irish Tune from County Derry.

    3. Santa Lucia.

    4. Sweden, Distant Sweden.

    5. All through the Night.

    6. Nobody Knows the Trouble I've Seen.

2. The children were asked to identify merely the dance type, not the composition or the composer. The following numbers were used:

    1. Gavotte, Bach.

    2. Minuet, Haydn.

    3. Minuet, Bach.

    4. Gavotte, Beethoven.

    5. Waltz of the Flowers, Tchaikowsky.

3*a. Ländler,* by Mozart. This composition contains twelve sentences, the coda being omitted.

  b. Gypsy Rondo, by Haydn. The first violin section played this theme four times before the test began. The theme appears eight times.

4. The entire orchestra left the stage: from behind the stage snatches were played by various instruments. Only the name of the instrument was taken into consideration in the grading, although the names of the families and of the compositions were to be given.

    1. French Horn—Brass—*Mignon.*

    2. Bassoon—Woodwind—In the Hall of the Mountain King.

    3. Clarinet—Woodwind—*Oberon* Overture.

    4. Flute—Woodwind—Dance of the Reed Pipes.

    5. Oboe—Woodwind—Finale, Fourth Symphony, Tchaikowsky.

    6. Cello—String—Unfinished Symphony.

    7. Trumpet—Brass—Triumphal March, Grieg.

    8. Trombone—Brass—Spanish Rhapsody, Chabrier.

    9 & 10. Viola and English Horn—String and Woodwind—In a Village.

5*a*. MacDowell's "To the Sea" was played. The best names given this number in the contest were: "The Coming of the King of Thunder"; "The Sea"; "The Roaring Water"; "The Roaring Sea."

b. Debussy's "Golliwog's Cakewalk" was played. The best name given this number in the contest was: "Dance of the Unreal People": this comment was made: "It is too light for real people, too heavy for fairies, but mysterious."

The Individual prize, an Orthophonic Victrola given by the J. W. Jenkins Sons Music Co., was awarded to William Beams, Muskogee, Oklahoma.

The Elementary School Prize, a Cello given by the J. W. Jenkins Sons Music Co., was awarded to the Lincoln School, Oklahoma City.

The High School Prize, an Orthophonic Victrola, given by the T. E. Swann Co., was awarded to the Woodrow Wilson Junior High School, Tulsa.

Items 2 and 4 look to me the most valuable. I think item 6 a very capital one, as, the competition being over, it restores music to its normal place as artistic enjoyment.

For one reader who adopts a scheme like that lock, stock, and barrel, there will probably be ten who will take some ideas from it and develop them in their own way.

I can, for instance, imagine a teacher of smallish boys seizing on 3*b* and devising a game of "Musical Detectives", or "The Musical Sherlock Holmes" (for that great hero was, let us remember, a musical man—a skilled violinist and author of a monograph on *The Polyphonic Motets of Lassus*).[1]

---

[1] I offer a suggestion as a quotation to head the paper of instructions for the game of "The Musical Sherlock Holmes". It is a bit of dialogue from the short story, *A Scandal in Bohemia.*
WATSON. I believe my eyes are as good as yours.
HOLMES. Quite so. You see, but you do not observe. The distinction is clear. For example you have frequently seen the steps which lead up from the hall to this room.
WATSON. Frequently.
HOLMES. How often?
WATSON. Well, some hundreds of times.
HOLMES. Then how many are there?
WATSON. How many! I do not know.
HOLMES. Quite so! You have not observed. And yet you have seen. That is just my point. Now I know that there are seventeen *because I have both seen and observed.*

THE SEMINAR

How would an occasional attempt at the Seminar work? It seems to me that something might be done with it—at all events with elder pupils.

The *Shorter Oxford English Dictionary* gives this definition of Seminar:

"In German universities (hence in certain British and American universities) a select group of advanced students associated for advanced study and original research under the guidance of a professor."

The last words are the essential ones—a seminar is not a university lecture course; the students *themselves* carry on the "study and research", though under guidance.

I know of no musical seminar in any British university at present and only of one—in the United States—under my friend Professor Kinkeldey at Cornell University. When I was last at that university his seminar consisted of five or six men who, having taken their B.A., were preparing for their M.A., or having taken their M.A. were preparing for their Ph.D. He allotted each of them some task in musical research (mostly historical, I think), and they met weekly to report progress and to discuss with the Professor and one another what they had done and to receive hints as to further work.

Every novel procedure, if good in itself, is advantageous in music teaching, and so, especially, is any procedure which throws weight on the initiative of members of the class. Could we adopt the Seminar system in some such way as this (for use, say, once or twice in a term—more with a senior class, perhaps).

A group of three or four bright pupils might be allotted a composition for study. If the group includes a good pianist, it might be a piano piece. If not, it might be in the form of an orchestral or chamber music phonograph record and a miniature score.

The group would carry through an intensive study of the music, and would prepare a joint description of it in writing, and would then, on a given date, meet their teacher, in the presence of the class, and demonstrate to him and the class their analysis of the form, orchestration (if an orchestral piece), and so forth.

One member of the group (or possibly one member of the class at large) might come prepared with a ten-minute biographical essay on the composer, as an introduction to the subject of the meeting.

Obviously this general idea is capable of adaptation in many ways and I throw it out as merely suggestive.

The idea is to make members of the class *give themselves an Appreciation Lesson* occasionally, and, having done that, give one to the class.

Two or more groups could, if desired, be working simultaneously on different pieces. Indeed, comparison might be introduced. Suppose one group worked at a Handel fugue (or a Handel suite movement, or, in the case of an advanced class, a whole suite) and the other group at a similar composition by Bach. Then when the two were demonstrated, at the same meeting or consecutive meetings, the class might be asked to define its impressions of the two composers and their style.

Or one group (if intelligent) might be given both a Handel piece and a Bach piece and asked to produce and demonstrate a critical comparison.

The Seminar idea might, if preferred, be worked as a voluntary, regular after-school activity for a group of the musically élite.

It occurs to me that a reading of Caldwell Cook's *The Play Way; an Essay in Educational Method* (1917) might be useful to many teachers as suggesting unconventional ways of bringing pupils into the work of teaching themselves.

A fine teacher imbued with the Caldwell Cook spirit and ideas might, just possibly, find a way of carrying out *all* the work of an Appreciation Class on Seminar lines.

I have suggested above the use of a miniature score. Sometimes, however, the task should be to prepare as close a description as possible of a piece of music without seeing the score, and then, in class, to have it checked by the score. This would mean very intensive listening and would have high value.[1]

"LISTENERS' REHEARSALS"

"No one thinks it odd that the orchestra and chorus should be amply rehearsed for these occasions. But has anyone ever considered rehearsals for listeners?"

So writes C.E.M. of the *Birmingham Daily Mail* (15 February 1933), and his question surely suggests something that the Appreciation teacher can do.

The local choral society announces its annual performance of *Messiah*. The Appreciation teacher puts on a couple of Handel lessons with as many *Messiah* records as he can collect, or invites the voluntary attendance of any pupils interested (perhaps with their parents) to an after-school-hours "Listeners' Rehearsal" of *Messiah*.

The local orchestral society announces its annual concert, and he gives a lesson or two on the instruments of the orchestra.

An opera company is coming to town. He picks out of their advertised program the work with fewest murders and least adultery (provided that he can lay hands on phonograph records of parts of that particular work), and tells the story, interpolating his records at their appropriate places.

And so on. It becomes one of his normal interests to connect his work with the musical activities of the district, so diminishing the academic associations of that work and strengthening the realization of its practical value in increasing pleasure in some of the good things of daily life.

And of course he does not forget the Radio. He looks out for works of interest to be performed on Saturday or Sunday, when there is no homework to be done, and makes these the subjects of studies with his class.

The principle that lies behind such enterprises is that expressed

---

[1] The ideas set forth in this division are most attractive and stimulating. Doubtless some measure of the "seminar" plan has been tried at some time by one teacher or another, but a full exploration of its possibilities remains to be made. W. E.

centuries ago by William Byrd in the introduction to a volume of his works:

"A song that is well and artificially made cannot be well perceived nor understood at the first hearing, but the oftener you shall heare it the better cause of liking you will discover; and commonly that Song is best esteemed with which our eares are most acquainted."

It was with this aim, to make "eares acquainted", that a hundred years since (13 November, 1826), Moser, a Berlin concert manager, engaged the seventeen-year-old Mendelssohn to give a public piano performance of Beethoven's Ninth Symphony, in preparation for the first performance of that great work in that city a fortnight later. And with the same aim we have seen phonograph performances, with spoken elucidations, given in the Queen's Small Hall, London, preparatory to orchestral concerts in the greater Queen's Hall adjoining.

Do not let us forget this idea of "Listeners' Rehearsals." It is attractive and practical.

COMMON ERRORS IN HISTORY, FORM, ETC.

The Muddle of the Modes.

It is rarely that a book on Musical Appreciation, whether intended for teachers or for pupils, quite clearly explains the modes. Of course, in many classes of younger pupils it will be unnecessary to touch on them more than to say, when some old madrigal or similar work is performed: "If you find the music a little strange at first that will be because it is not entirely written in one of our major or minor scales of to-day, but has clinging about it the influence of one of the older scales called 'Modes'."

If, however, you want to go beyond this, get the facts correctly, and do not merely grasp them theoretically but understand the conception and motives that lie behind the modal system.

We may, for our purposes, cut out the Ancient Greeks, with the merest reference to the fact that they have some responsibility—the modal system with which we are concerned (that of the Christian Middle Ages) being supposed to carry on the Greek system and to some extent doing so.

The conception on which the Modes are based takes account of a much smaller number of musical notes than we have in use to-day. A piano without black notes would very fairly represent the material available at the period in question. It would have seven different notes, instead of our twelve, as keyed instruments at one time did have.

Obviously from each of these notes a scale might be started. Thus the Dorian ran from D to D, the Phrygian from E to E, and so forth.

A moment's experiment on the piano will show that the tones and semitones fall differently in these two modes. When we play the scale of D and the scale of E to-day we choose such white and black notes as give us the same order of tones and semitones for both scales. But if our keyboard had only white notes we could not do this, and the two scales would sound different from each other.

In every mode two notes were of special importance, the Dominant (generally the fifth note up of the mode) and the Final (its bottom and top note). A normal melody in the Dorian Mode would lie entirely or almost so between D and its octave, and would be likely to circle about and emphasize A, which would thus, in fact, dominate the melody and so be rightly considered the "Dominant." And it would close on the Final (D).

In intoning a passage of the liturgy a great part of the intonation would be on the Dominant of the mode in use at the moment, and at the end of the phrase the voice would drop or rise to the Final. The existence and functions of Dominant and Final are essential features of the modal system, and it is misleading to describe that system without explaining those functions, as is sometimes done. It may be pointed out to the class that to-day we still retain the conception of the 1st and 5th notes as specially important, and still call the 5th the Dominant.

Note that a melody in the Dorian Mode, if it lay too high for the singers, might be taken at a lower pitch, or if it lay too low at a higher pitch. The singers, once the starting note had been given them, would go ahead without being aware of any change. For it is not pitch that defines a mode (here is where many of the description in popular histories fail to make the facts clear), but the order of tones and semitones lying between Final and Final. A melody in the Dorian Mode would obviously sound the same at any pitch (the only difference being a greater or less brilliance according as it was higher or lower). But a melody in the Phrygian Mode would have a different *flavor* from one in the Dorian Mode.

We can understand this if we think of the only two of the Modes with which people in general are acquainted to-day, what we call the Major and Minor Modes, which are substantially the Ionian and Aeolian Modes of the Middle Ages. A melody in the Major Mode has just the same flavor at any pitch and one in the Minor Mode has the same flavor at any pitch, but a melody in the Major Mode has a very different *flavor* from one in the Minor Mode.

More than anything else, then the Modal System may be looked upon as supplying a variety of *flavors*—a greater variety than our normal system of to-day supplies. To the Medieval man those flavors were more or less familiar and were acceptable. To us to-day the flavors of only two of the Modes are really familiar (unless we happen to attend a church where the ancient music is used), and that accounts for the sensation of strangeness we experience when we hear a piece of plain-song in one of the other modes or a piece of harmonized music influenced by one of them and reproducing some of its characteristics.

But remember that the "Medieval man" has existed right down to our own day, though we personally may not have known him. Cecil Sharp, who died in 1924, collected among the peasants of England and those of the Appalachian range in the United States hundreds of modal folk-song melodies, which he then published and so preserved. They may sound strange to up-to-date town-bred people, or even to country people who have soaked in the music of the phonograph and radio, but to the old people who sang the songs to Sharp, and who had learned them from their parents, the modes represented in them sounded perfectly natural—as indeed they are.

The above account is not anything like complete. But it tells quite as much as any school class is likely to assimilate, and if more is told confusion will probably result and the whole be forgotten, except for the vaguest general impression. Moreover, it puts the subject in a form accessible to the youthful mind and leaves it a little of its human interest, instead of treating it entirely as a matter of musical theory and dry history.

Of course, other suitable treatments are possible, and in a school where much plain-song is sung a fuller explanation might indeed be given—at any rate to older pupils. Album I of *The Columbia History of Music* includes some examples of plain-song and early harmonized music. It also includes examples of sixteenth-century secular and sacred choral and instrumental music, in some of which the modal flavor can be felt.

Dance Definitions.

A very frequent piece of bad pedagogy is this kind of statement:

"The Gigue is a quick dance, generally in compound time, starting on an unaccented quaver." [1] (Home, *Short History of Music*.)

The Gavotte "begins on the 3rd crotchet [2] of the bar, while the Bourrée always starts on the 4th." (Grove's *Dictionary*, s.v. *Bourrée*.) I could quote definitions on these lines indefinitely; nearly all the dances are similarly defined in nearly all the books. Obviously the above definitions should run:

"The Gigue is a quick dance, generally in compound time, *each phrase of which* starts on an unaccented note."
"*The phrases of* the Gavotte begin on the 3rd beat of the bar, whilst those of the Bourrée begin on the 4th."

The point, of course, is that the definitions as originally drafted suggest that the position of the mere opening notes defines the character of the dance. You cannot expect a class of children,

[1] In the United States, an eighth note. W. E.
[2] In the United States, a quarter note. W. E.

or a member of the public referring to a work of reference, to reflect that in a dance tune the phrases are likely to fall alike as regards their position in the rhythmical scheme. Frame the definition accurately and you at once cut out a source of puzzlement and suggest the fact that I have just mentioned.

It is no good saying that pupils should not be puzzled by such a definition. They *will* be puzzled. I myself was, forty years ago.

Anyhow, why not define correctly?

Binary Form.

An error that is occasionally found is the following:

"Sonata form is the most elaborate and complicated of all, because it is developed from *two* principal subjects—for which reason it is called the *binary* form, *bi* meaning two. (Hannah Smith, *Founders of Music.*)

"Sonata Form—called also Binary Form (because based on *two* principal themes." (Dunstan, *Cyclopedic Dictionary of Music.*)

"Binary . . . either a form of composition divided into two contrasted sections (as in many dances) or one based upon two principal themes (as in sonata form). (Pratt—*New Encyclopedia of Music and Musicians.*)

The word "binary" has reference not to the presence of two subjects but to the division into two sections.[1] If the instrumental movements of the Purcell-Couperin-Scarlatti-Bach-Handel period be examined the great majority of them will be found to be laid out in this way:

Section I—closing with a Cadence in the Dominant (or Relative Major).
Section II—Leading back to the Tonic and closing in that key.

That is binary form—in its original state. The various movements in Bach's French and English Suites and Partitas are the examples of it best known to the rank-and-file pianist.

---

[1] It would be very absurd if "binary" referred to the number of *subjects* in a composition and its companion term, "ternary", to the number of *sections* (not but what musical terminology is sometimes absurd, of course!). P. A. S.

A little later, in the C. P. E. Bach-Haydn-Mozart period that immediately followed, we see the first section, which had formerly been more or less unified (often a treatment of one little motif), blossoming out. Instead of merely beginning in the tonic and working at the end to a dominant (or relative major) cadence, it now gradually becomes elaborated to the point of possessing a definite subject in the tonic and another in the dominant (or relative major).

Further, the second section now tends to "develop" these two subjects at greater or lesser lengths, and then to repeat (or "recapitulate") them, so really bringing into existence a very effective sort of ternary form.

But though the form is, by all ordinary tests of ear or eye, Ternary, its historical origin has been kept in mind by the application to it of the description "Compound Binary", a description the more plausible perhaps since the double-bar division (with its repeat mark) still appeared at the end of the first section, whilst no break of this sort was interpolated between the second and third sections, which had, then, still the appearance of being merely one continuous section. And in earlier specimens not only was the first section marked to be repeated, but also the dual, second-third section was marked to be repeated as a whole.

Note clearly, however, that the word "Binary" is here a survival, due to the original division into two simple sections and not an innovation due to the use of two subjects.

As a matter of fact none of the terms in use for this form is quite suitable.

1. "Compound Binary Form" is unsuitable because of the clear Ternary division.

2. "Sonata Form" is unsuitable because it suggests the form of sonata as a whole.

3. "First Movement Form" is unsuitable because a fair number of sonatas, &c., have first movements in some other form, and also because the form often occurs in later movements of sonatas.

Of these three terms the present writer thinks "First Movement Form" perhaps the least objectionable, but it is a moot point! [1]

Returning to the historical origin of the term "Compound Binary", the process whereby the Simple Binary evolved into the Compound Binary can be conveniently studied in (*a*) a few of Bach's Preludes in his "48"—especially in the second book; (*b*) the keyboard sonatas of C. P. E. Bach—many of them very interesting works, yet nowadays much neglected; (*c*) the keyboard sonatas of Haydn, or his earlier symphonies.

It is much to be desired that teachers of Musical Appreciation should now and then, for their personal improvement, undertake a little task of historical research such as is here suggested. It would give the historical attitude that is so much needed. The best guide to such a study is Hadow's *Sonata Form.*

Clavichord, Harpsichord, Virginals, Spinet.

Considerable confusion exists in the minds of some writers of popular musical literature as to the distinction between these instruments. It may therefore be desirable to state the facts succinctly.

The domestic keyboard stringed instruments up to the end of the eighteenth century fell into two distinct classes, as follows:

Class I. Clavichord.

Class II. Virginals, Spinet, Harpsichord.

The instruments of both these classes were like the modern Grand Piano in this respect—that the strings were placed horizontally and were operated upon from below.

The distinction between the two classes lies in the method of tone production, the strings in Class I being *struck* and the strings in Class II being *plucked*.

In Class I a piece of metal called a "tangent" sprang up and sounded the string, and in Class II a piece of wood equipped

---

[1] A friend upholds "first movement" as the least objectionable; for, he says, it means first movements of *sonatas,* and it is in their first acquaintance with sonatas (e.g. juvenile study of Clementi, Haydn, &c.) that most people make their first acquaintance with the form. P. A. S.

with a projecting quill did so, the quill twanging the string as it passed it.

The earliest and simplest member of Class II is the Virginals. It was (like the Clavichord in this) in the shape of a shallow box that could be laid on a table, the strings running in front of the performer (i.e. parallel to the keyboard). The Spinet, on the contrary, was of a sort of wing shape (like a very small grand piano), and the strings ran away from the performer (more or less at an angle of forty-five degrees to the keyboard). Both Virginals and Spinet were simple instruments with only one string to a note.

The Harpsichord was an elaborated Spinet. Its strings ran at right angles to the keyboard (like those of the grand piano of to-day); it had several strings to a note; it often had two keyboards, and stops and pedals controlling a number of mechanical devices for increasing or decreasing the amount of tone, and altering its timbre.

But the devices mentioned *were* mechanical, and as in all the instruments of Class II, the player's "touch" had little influence on the tone, whereas in the instrument of Class I, "touch" was an important factor, subtly expressive effects being obtainable through its control. (This explains Bach's preference for the Clavichord.)

The great period of popularity of the Virginals was that of the sixteenth and earlier seventeenth centuries. In the later seventeenth century the Spinet came in and drove the Virginals from the field. The Harpsichord enjoyed high favor also from the later seventeenth century, but on account of its greater cost never superseded the Spinet, the two existing side by side as grand and upright pianos have done.

The piano, invented in the early eighteenth century, began to compete seriously with the Clavichord, Spinet, and Harpsichord towards the end of that century and before the nineteenth century was far advanced reigned supreme. The tone-production of the piano, as everybody knows, is by felt-covered hammers.

The above is admittedly only a partial account of the instruments in question, but it is sufficient to prevent the confusion that so often exists.

The instruments sometimes sold by English old furniture dealers as Spinets will be found, on examination, to be merely examples of the early oblong piano.

Bach and Equal Temperament.

Such statements as the following (arising out of a discussion of Bach's "48") are extremely common:

"Bach boldly abandoned the old *true scale,* by which one could play in only a few keys on a given instrument, in favor of the tempered scale, in which the semitones are all relatively equal, thus making it possible to modulate from any key to any other whatsoever." (Hamilton—*Epochs in Musical Progress.*)

"Why did Bach call his work *Das Wohltemperirte Klavier* (the well-tempered Clavichord)?

"Because he wrote it for the Clavichord, an instrument somewhat similar to a Pianoforte and tuned in *tempered intervals,* in which case enharmonic notes are similar. Previously, such instruments as harpsichords, virginals, and spinets had been tuned rather in *just intervals,* in which case enharmonics were not available and only a few keys could be used." (Lowe, *Viva Voce: 250 Questions and Answers for Pianoforte Diploma Candidates.*)

The particular error here under discussion is the extremely prevalent one to the effect that the scale in use before Bach was a "true scale" or one in "just intervals."

An instrument tuned on such a scale as that would be capable of a satisfactory effect only in one key—the one to which the instrument was tuned. It is impossible to go fully into this subject here (too much acoustics and mathematics are involved), but at any rate it is a fact that the usual tuning in Bach's day was not "true" or "just" but on a compromise system—some sort of a "Mean Tone" system (see article "Temperament" in Grove's *Dictionary*), the exact sort probably varying slightly according to different musicians' ideas. Bach's organs were tuned on such a "mean tone" system and gave reasonably good effects in about six major and three minor keys, beyond which began to be noticeable an out-of-tuneness picturesquely called "the Wolf." When Bach tuned his domestic instruments to "Equal

Temperament" he substituted for a few big "Wolves" a greater number of little ones, whose fainter howling is hardly heard. (Some English cathedral organs were tuned on a "Mean Tone" system right down to the latter half of the nineteenth century, and must have thereby been very limited in their usefulness.)

The point is that what Bach did was not to introduce the spirit of compromise in tuning but to extend it—or rather to popularize its extension, for there are a few virginal and other compositions as far back as Queen Elizabeth's day that could, as it appears to us, only have been performed on an instrument tuned as Bach tuned his. (These occasional compositions may have been written in a spirit of experiment; with Bach the era of experiment was over.)

It will be noted that the second of the two quotations given above speaks (probably merely by oversight) as though there were some tuning distinction between instruments of the harpsichord class, on the one hand, and the clavichord on the other. I know of no evidence to this effect. And, of course, "Well-tempered Clavichord" is a mistranslation (see below).

Bach's "Well-Tempered" Instrument.

The title of Bach's "48" is not "Well-tempered Clavichord", as so often stated, but "Well-tempered Keyboard" (*Wohltemperirte Klavier*)—a much wider term.

The forty-eight pairs of compositions which it comprises were not all composed expressly for it. It includes some Preludes and Fugues written at various periods as independent compositions and later used in making up the two books of the "48": some of these were doubtless conceived for Clavichord and some for Harpsichord, and to any one who knows the capabilities of the two instruments it is not difficult to distinguish clear cases of each. Undoubtedly the first Prelude requires the Clavichord to make its greatest effect, but the third one suggests a two-manual Harpsichord, and the twentieth Fugue (A minor) calls for a Harpsichord with organ pedals (of which Bach certainly possessed a specimen). In a general way Bach evidently intended the work for any instrument the home possessed.

The Clavichord is known to have been Bach's favorite domestic keyboard instrument, and this (coupled with the resemblance of the general term "Clavier" or "Klavier" to the particular term "Clavichord") has doubtless led to the so common mistranslation of the title. There is a corresponding French mistranslation, "Clavecin Bien Temperé", i.e. "Well-tempered *Harpsichord.*" So the English popular error allots the work to one instrument and the French popular error to another—and it belongs to neither exclusively.

The best translation is probably *"Well-tempered Clavier"* (using "Clavier" in the sense of a keyboard instrument and not in the modern German sense of pianoforte),[1] but we can cut out all difficulties by calling it simply by its nickname, "Bach's 48."

"Classic" and *"Romantic"*

All sorts of muddles and misunderstandings are constantly occurring through the varying uses of these two chameleon words, so that it seems desirable to decide on the best manner of their application in a musical context, and to keep to it. I suggest the following view as the sound one.

Most (probably all) works of art make a double appeal to us —the appeal of *beauty* and the appeal of *emotion.*[2]

There are works of art that leave us relatively cold as to emotion but yet stir very strongly our sense of beauty.[3]

---

[1] "Pianoforte" is, properly, Hammerklavier, i.e. Hammer-keyboard (a very good term), but with the increasing rarity of domestic keyboard instruments other than the "hammer" variety the word came to be shortened. P. A. S.

[2] I am not, of course, professing to use strictly psychological language. The reader wi ll understand what I mean, and that is enough. P. A. S.

[3] That we can have emotions that are unconnected with any sense of beauty is obvious; but it is difficult to see how our sense of beauty can be strongly stirred without our being stirred emotionally. Clive Bell's terms (in his *Art*), "emotion of beauty", as contrasted to "emotions of life", would appear to be better; and Santayana's "principle of beauty", as contrasted to the "principle of interest", similarly expresses the thought without denying emotion to our sense of beauty. Santayana's terms also agree well with the terms "classic" and "romantic." And in this latter connection a distinction that some critic made in application to literature may help to clear up confusion. "The classicist," this critic said, "strives for the creation of ideal beauty; the romanticist writes of whatever is of interest to human kind." In this light the question becomes one, not of whether emotion is stirred or not, but of whether it is stirred by idealistic meanings or by human interests. W. E.

There are others that stir our emotion strongly, yet which do not strike us as extraordinarily beautiful.

There are still others that impress us strongly in both ways.

In fact, the balance may be tipped on one side or the other, or may be stabilized in the middle—may take any position.

In a good deal of Bach's work and a great deal of Mozart's and Haydn's the balance is down somewhat on the side of beauty. In much of the later Beethoven's, in Chopin's, Schumann's, and Wagner's it is down on the side of emotion; that is to say that, however great may be the "beauty-interest" in the work, the prime appeal to us is felt to be the emotional.

The "beauty music" we call "Classical" and the "emotion music" we call "Romantic."

Now from the opening of the nineteenth century in France, Germany, England, and elsewhere the Romantic element gained on the Classic element in literature and the pictorial arts: it was a period when artists in the different media felt much interest in one another and the literary men and painters greatly influenced one another and also the composers. This, then, is the true Romantic Period in music—the period in which came a *conscious striving* after the strong expression of emotion and, too, a conscious recognition of kinship with the artists in other media who had the same aim.

Weber, Berlioz, Schumann, Chopin, Mendelssohn, Wagner, Liszt, are some of the names that most prominently represent this Romantic Period. They all, in one way or another, experienced an impulse from Music's sister arts. They read Romantic Literature, studied Romantic Painting, and associated with the Romantic writers and painters.

By adopting this classification of the Romantics, we assimilate the Romantic School in Music to the similar schools in the other arts with which it was so closely connected. No one questions the nomenclature so far as these arts at that period are concerned, and we do well to apply it to the music of the same period so as to fall into line with those who teach or write about the other arts.

In doing this we do not deny the presence of the Romantic element in earlier music, indeed it is doubtful if any good music exists that is devoid of that element. We are simply reserving the title of "Romantic School" for *the group of composers who, of set purpose, sought romance and who formed part of a sort of international confrérie of artists of all kinds who were doing so.*

According to this classification we consider the pre-Beethoven composers Classics and the post-Beethoven Romantics, and label Beethoven and his contemporary, Schubert (for these looked both ways), as Classic-Romantic. Brahms, too, at a later date, can, if desired, be considered a Classic-Romantic, though personally I prefer to consider him a full member of the Romantic School and the qualities of his music seem to me to justify this.

The members of the Romantic School mentioned, being strongly connected by the Romantic principle and wishful to express their feelings as directly and strongly as possible, tended, on the whole, to pay less attention to the more or less set form of the sonata, symphony, and string quartet, &c., as it then existed. Some of them brought into existence and practiced the new free type of the Tone Poem and wrote a good deal of music with a "program" basis, often adopting as that basis some work of the contemporary Romantic School in poetry or painting.

This devotion to "Program Music" was, however, an effect of their Romantic aims, and it is those aims and not the writing of Program Music or any partial or complete abandonment of the Classical forms, that define them as the Romantic School. It seems rather misleading to say (as very many text-book writers do) that by "Classical School" we mean the composers who kept to the classical forms and by "Romantic School" those who, to some extent, abandoned them. To state the thing in this way is to put the cart before the horse.

The "Romantic Composers", then (I reiterate), were those composers who represented in their art the aims and feeling of the Romantic Period in art (and in life). Adopt this nomenclature and the music student can read the history of painting or of literature and can trace affiliations. He can read of Körner and associate him with Weber, of Hoffmann and of

Jean Paul and at once see the bearing of their conceptions on those of Schumann, of the novelists Dumas and Hugo and the painter Delacroix and grasp the fact that they had their musical counterpart in Berlioz, of the Polish poet Mickiewicz or the Parisian novelist Georges Sand and understand their influence on the sensibility of Chopin. And so on—these are but a few random examples.

This view accepted, it is best to regard the Nationalist School that followed as a branch or offshoot of the Romantic School, since the Nationalism that found violent expression in various parts of Europe in 1848 was certainly in great part an outcome of the Romantic feeling of the literature of the period. And so Smetana, Dvořák, Grieg, and others fall into their places, and the course of events is seen as logical.

The above is a very summary argument. In Volume II of *The Listener's History of Music* I have gone much more deeply into the whole subject, and there, if any one wishes to trace the relation of literature, the plastic arts, and music during the Romantic Period, he has, I think, the material.

From the definitions of "Romantic" that I see in school and college text-books of the history of music, &c., I have certainly the impression that a lack of understanding exists owing to a tendency to consider music as an art apart—which, once the nineteenth century is reached, it certainly was not. The article "Romantic" in the latest edition of Grove's *Dictionary of Music,* which totally ignores the other arts, shows how far the isolation can be carried and with what narrowing results to conceptions of the history of music.

The Puritans and Music in England.

In *Music* by Ursula Creighton (1928) the following occurs (page 73):

"It was the time of Puritan rule, and music, together with all other art, was regarded with suspicion. . . .

"English music did not become famous again until after the return of the Royalists."

The space above marked by dots is in the book itself occupied by a contradictory assertion that "the English people still loved music", with a correct allusion to the musical proclivities of Cromwell, Milton, and Bunyan. This writer is, then, aware of the truth as to Puritans and music yet cannot quite bring herself to acknowledge it. And her book has passed under the eye of our highly honored Professor of Music at Cambridge, who writes a Preface, in which he says he has read it "with much enjoyment."

Such statements as that above quoted can, of course, be found by the dozen, yet there is not so much as one word of truth in them. *English Puritanism had not the slightest objection to art in general, or music in particular, and the idea that it had such an objection is not to be found before well on in the eighteenth century.*

The Puritans objected to elaborate music (as to ritual and vestments) *in church,* and hence when in power they disbanded the choirs and removed the organs. But to base on that circumstance a theory that they objected to music, as such, would be as illogical as, three centuries hence, to base on the fact that we to-day do not admit dancing into religious worship a theory that we are opposed to dancing as such.

The publication of all kinds of music except church music was particularly heavy during the Puritan régime of the middle of the seventeenth century. Music-teaching was actively pursued, London abounding in fine teachers. Opera was first introduced into England during the period and had the definite backing of leading Puritan statesmen. Our concert system began at this time—in the taverns, apparently partly as a result of their buying organs from the churches. The Puritan government appointed a "Committee for the Welfare of Music."

The whole subject is discussed in detail in a monograph of my own, to which the reader may be referred for all details.

Mistakes About Various Composers and Compositions.

The popular violin composition, "L'ABEILLE" or "THE BEE", is, it is true, by "Franz Schubert", but to prevent the perpetuation of a widely accepted error it is desirable in programs to add after his name the dates (1808–78).

The popular song, "PASSING BY", is not correctly described as by Purcell." It is by Edward Purcell Cockram (died 1932), who, unfortunately, adopted the pen name of "Edward Purcell." It has frequently appeared under false colors in programs in Britain and America and has also been taken into at least one anthology of classical songs (with resulting legal trouble, by the way, since it is still copyright). The simplicity of the melody gives the song an old-world flavor and seems to encourage the error.

The poem of this song is always described as by Herrick. It first appeared in Thomas Ford's *Music of Sundry Kinds* in 1607, when Herrick was sixteen, and it is not known how in later times his name came to be attached to it.

The song, "THE LASS WITH THE DELICATE AIR" (properly "with *a* Delicate Air"), usually ascribed by the labels of Phonograph Records, by school song collections, &c., to "Arne", is not by *the* Arne (the composer of *Rule, Britannia, Where the Bee Sucks, Under the Greenwood Tree,* &c.) but by his son. To save confusion the name should be given in full, "Michael Arne."

"GOD SAVE THE KING" is not by Henry Carey. The statement that he wrote it first appears as late as 1796, when Carey's son tried to get a pension from the British Government on the strength of it.

Some (not all) of the known facts are (fairly correctly) stated in Grove's *Dictionary of Music* under *God save the King.*

Pending clearer knowledge it is best to attach no name to the tune, simply styling it "traditional English", or something like that.

A sad confusion occurs in a few books, and occasionally in programs, between LOEILLET and LULLY. There is an excuse for it, as will be seen.

Jean Baptiste Lully, the founder of French grand opera, was born at Florence in 1633 and died at Paris in 1687.

Jean Baptiste Loeillet, virtuoso flautist and also harpsichordist, was born at Ghent in 1653 and died at London in 1728. Unfortunately (perhaps in the attempt to get the English among whom he lived to pronounce his name something like correctly) he spelled his name "Lully" on certain of his published compositions.

The name of GLUCK is very often spelled Glück, probably because the latter word, as the German for "happiness", is so familiar. The error in spelling involves, of course, a corresponding error in pronunciation.

Handel's "THE HARMONIOUS BLACKSMITH" was not given this name by the composer, and the legend about the composer sheltering in a forge at Edgeware and hearing the tune there is now entirely discredited. This composition is a movement from the composer's Fifth Harpsichord Suite. Its first appearance under the popular title was in the early nineteenth century: a publisher (Lintern of Bath) had when young been a blacksmith and played this piece a great deal; hence he conceived the fancy title. The explanatory legend was invented later.

The statement sometimes seen that the air was taken by Handel from a composition by Wagenseil implies early development in the latter composer, who was only five years of age when the Suite was published.

HANDEL's "WATER MUSIC". The facts are *not* as stated in so many popular histories of music, biographies of the composer, and books on Musical Appreciation—i.e. it was *not* composed as a means of effecting a reconciliation between the composer and George I. So it is now said.

The water party on the Thames, to which legend assigned it, was in 1715, when the King and the Composer were decidedly on bad terms, so that the purpose attributed to the music had great plausibility.

It is now found, however, that the water party in question was one that took place in 1717, and by this date monarch and musician, it is stated, were already good friends again. (On the other hand, the late Mr. Barclay Squire, a good authority, did not entirely discard the notion that in 1717 there might have been some lingering discord that was resolved by the performance of this delightful music.)

There is not really very much involved here. Handel did write the music for performance before George I at a barge party on the Thames, and whether he thus healed the breach or had earlier been forgiven is the only point in dispute.

The story is naturally a favorite one with Musical Appreciation teachers, both because it is romantic and because it connects with the pupil's knowledge of English History. However, that connection still remains even if the reconciliation motif disappears.

The very popular story of PALESTRINA'S "SAVING OF CHURCH MUSIC" by the composition of three masses (of which one was the "Missa Papae Marcelli"), which is told in innumerable of the older histories of music, has now been shown to be without foundation, and should therefore be dropped. (See Zoe Kendrick Pyne's *Palestrina,* the latest edition of Grove's *Dictionary,* &c.)

The "BEE'S WEDDING" of Mendelssohn was not so called by him. He called it "Spinning Song," evidently intending to reproduce the continuous whir of the wheel. It seems a pity to abandon this perfectly adequate original title, which accurately reproduces the composer's descriptive intention, as the newer title does not.

The spelling of the Italian name for the Kettledrums is not "Tympani" but "Timpani" (indeed, the letter "y" does not exist in the Italian language—except for a few foreign words that have been imported).

COPING WITH THE HORRORS OF MUSICAL TERMINOLOGY

It is reasonable to expect that at the end of several years' school contact with the masterpieces of music, together with the incidental discussion of these, the average intelligent pupil shall go forth into the world equipped to read and understand the average annotated program or intelligible article on music.

It is to be doubted, however, whether this modest aim is commonly achieved. The fact is that the terminology of music is rather extensive and puzzling. How puzzling it can be to the layman will be realized if the reader will consider him as hearing at the same concert the following groups of pieces:

A Beethoven Piano Concerto (Orchestra with a Solo Instrument).

Bach's Sixth Brandenburg Concerto (String Orchestra with no solo Instrument).

Bach's Italian Concerto (a mere keyboard suite, with no orchestra at all).

It is quite clear that no definition of "Concerto" can be given in a few words, and that, indeed, to understand how the same term comes to be applied to so many widely differing types calls for considerable historical knowledge.

Following this, the layman may hear of "Sonata Form" and may ask somebody to tell him what it means. He will gather that it is a single-movement form, and will then be puzzled to find that most sonatas are in three or four movements. Somebody will then tell him that the first of these movements will commonly be in that sort of form, which takes its name from the fact. But the next Beethoven Piano Sonata he hears may chance to have no movement at all in that form. Before he recovers from his bewilderment at this fact somebody may play him Corelli's famous twelfth Violin and Keyboard Sonata, and he will find it to be merely an Air and Variations, or one of the Harpsichord Sonatas of Scarlatti, which he finds to be a single movement of another kind, or Purcell's "Golden Sonata", which he will find to have no movement in "Sonata Form" and, moreover, to be for four instruments, whereas he had been told that the word "Sonata" was only applied to compositions for one instrument or, at most, two. Here, again, only historical knowledge will reveal any logic in the nomenclature.

"Overture" may then begin to puzzle him. He hears a Handel Overture and thinks he understands what the word means, and then to his surprise finds Handel's contemporary, Bach, sticking a piece he calls by this name into the very middle of his Goldberg Variations for Harpsichord. He then finds certain Bach orchestral suites called by this name and immediately after meets with Mendelssohn's *Hebrides,* which is a single movement of such a nature that he wonders, perhaps, why it is not called a "Tone Poem" (if he has met with this term). Here again, a quite considerable degree of familiarity with the historical development of music is needed if the problem raised is to be solved.

As the layman proceeds he gets involved in all sorts of further little difficulties. He learns the degrees of the scale and supposes, as the Super-tonic is so called because it is immediately above the Tonic, the Sub-dominant is so called because it is below the Dominant, but then he reflects that the Sub-mediant is four notes above the Mediant, and wonders where he has got mixed.

And so one might go on! Dr. Harvey Grace in an interesting article in *The Listener* (22 October, 1930) on *What Ought Listeners to Know?* has, it seems to me, somewhat minimized the difficulties:

"Among the ways in which the layman expresses his indifference —sometimes even hostility—to musical knowledge is his objection to the professional's use of musical terminology. It is an odd thing that, although players of games, in discussing the technique of sport, may discharge a whole battery of queer terms, a musician who lets drop an occasional expression peculiar to his art is accused of 'jargon.' 'Why not talk plain English?' he is asked. . . . 'What do you mean by recapitulation, or development, or dominant? Why the dickens don't you use terms that are understood by the average intelligent person?' But an average intelligent person . . . doesn't boggle at the far more mysterious terms of games. . . . Moreover, practically all the terms most commonly used in music are drawn from the normal vocabulary. Recapitulation, development, dominant, for example, mean in music exactly what they mean in every other connection, whereas the majority of technical expressions in golf and other pursuits concerning which the average intelligent person grudges neither time, labor, nor money, have no general significance whatever."

The principle Dr. Grace lays down is sound enough. Every sport must have its own special vocabulary and music-listening is no exception. But it seems to me that the vocabulary of the informed music listener is not only more confusing than that of

the golfer, but is also many times more copious, and to test
its actual extent I have made an experiment. I have collected
the technical terms that occur in normal annotated concert
programs, and these I proposed to print at the end of the present
book, as constituting the requirements of the ordinary concert-
goer, and hence of the teacher of Musical Appreciation, and
(within the limits of their patience!) the classes he teaches.[1]

My process has been as follows. I have first taken all the
words from the "Concert-Goers' Glossary" in my *Listeners' Guide
to Music* (1919). These I collected, when I wrote that book,
by combing a series of about 330 annotated programs of the
Queen's Hall Promenade Concerts, and extracting any specialist
terms that occurred either in the titles of pieces, as set out in the
programs, or in the Annotations, and by adding to these specialist words found in the titles (only) of 800 concerts of the
Royal Philharmonic Society, covering a century's working of the
society, plus a number of terms found in programs of Chamber
Music concerts and Piano Recitals and Vocal Recitals. I have
now, further, gone completely through the four volumes of
Mrs. Rosa Newmarch's *Concert-Goers' Library of Descriptive
Notes* (1929–31), which partly, but only partly, duplicates the
Promenade Concert programs already examined; this work con-
tains detailed descriptions of nearly 300 of the standard works
in the repertory, consisting as it does of her notes written for the
Queen's Hall Orchestral Concerts, and other series at Glasgow,
Liverpool, Sheffield, and Norwich. In order to test whether
American practice included the use of words not found in
British practice (which it did not, to any extent) I then went
through Mr. Felix Borowski's annotations upon about 130 compositions performed by the Chicago Symphony Orchestra (all
the music heard during its thirty-first season). Finally I took
a complete volume of *The Radio Times,* containing the name
of every piece of music broadcast in England, Scotland, and
Wales during its considerable period, together with annotations
on many of the pieces, and many critical articles, and any additional terms I found here I added to my list.

[1] As to the method of publication of this list finally adopted, see Preface.
P. A. S.

It may fairly be supposed, then, that the list includes all the terms the ordinary concert-goer requires for his understanding of programs or his general reading. Most of the terms, I find, occur again and again. There were very few "freaks", or terms occurring just once or twice and not further.[1]

It will be possible for teachers to use this list as a test of their own teaching on the side of terminology—i.e. to look carefully through it and to gather whether they are, in their lessons, gradually bringing about familiarity with all the usual terms. The pupils of higher classes can use it as a means of revision and of filling any little gaps in their knowledge of the details of musical practice. Test papers can be compiled from it. And so on!

In order to make the list more useful I have gone to a little trouble to cast it into something of a system, terms in any way related in their significance being grouped together.

And finally, realizing the difficulty that we all find in framing concise and precise definitions, I have worked through the whole series of terms suggesting such definitions in the best way I could compass. The list of terms with their definitions has been published separately at a small price, as I think it likely that many teachers will find it a useful companion to Appreciation work, at any rate in the later years of their pupils' school life. There are, surely, many ways in which such a list could be made of service. For one thing, it is good that pupils should *see* the words and not merely hear them. Here are the names of some

---

[1] In November 1931 Henry M. Kraus and Henry Harap, of Western Reserve University, published in the *Journal of Educational Research* the results of an investigation into "the vocabulary necessary for an intelligent understanding of the musical content of magazines and newspapers." It was a very thorough investigation, of the genuine American type. The number of words the authors read in their musical articles amounted to 7,600,214 (there's exactitude!). The musical terms met with were 17,676 in number, or, eliminating duplication, 352; of these 214 occurred at least five times. The figure 352 is a lower figure than my own (over 600) due, doubtless, to the fact that I have included not only the terms found in articles but also those found in programs.

A table showing "Frequency of Musical Terms in Newspapers and Magazines" makes rather curious reading—saxophone 215 and oboe only 9; jazz 317 and sonata 15 (yet symphony 251: how can we account for this disparity?); syncopate 61 and counterpoint 9; ukulele 102 and violoncello 7; harmonica 67 and pianoforte 8 (the survey can surely not have taken in criticism of recitals). P. A. S.

instruments as they were written in an examination at an English public school—"Catarrh", "Violent Chellow", "Tuber", "Pickelow".

The student who leaves school knowing a reasonable portion of this list will be in a happy position. He will possess a dual advantage, something like that the celebrated Dean Gainsford is said to have promised his divinity students—"Gentlemen, a knowledge of Greek will enable you to read the oracles of God in the original and to look down from the heights of scholarship upon the vulgar herd."

When all is said, however, the most terminologically ardent musician can never compete with the biologist or the chemist in the attaining of heights from which to "look down upon the vulgar herd." Sir Henry Hadow in his lecture on *The Place of Music in Humane Letters,* urging that "at some stage in musical education in schools there should be some systematic drill in the elements of theory", points out that in the matter of technical terms the musician is in a position of ease compared with the scientist—"I have read a book on psychology", he says, "in which one of its most eminent professors is described as a hormic interactionist, and even this pales before 'strophanthinisized, phenyldiethylammonium iodide' and 'the morphology of the Telenephalon of Spinax.'" He then in a footnote adds two other examples of scientific terms which, he says, he was unable to mention in his lecture as he did not know how to pronounce them — "Hydroxyketomethyldihydropyridene-carboxylonitrile" and "Dicyanohydroxymethylcyclohexylethanedicarboxylicanalyde."

Such terms as these, he suggests, "must make the exchange of chemical repartee very difficult."

In closing this discussion I would plead for the use of Plain English in the titles of compositions. There is a snobbery that delights in the use of foreign languages and even in their misuse, for incorrect French or German seems often to be preferred to correct English.

In a French concert room or opera house the names of foreign compositions are, as a matter of course, given in French.

In an English one it is considered that there is virtue in retaining the original. So we get *"L'Après-midi d'un Faune"*, with the result that, as I have proved, a good many people think of "Fawn"; and *"Pavane pour une infante défunte"*, with the equally distressing result that many people think of "a dead child." Thus do Debussy and Ravel come to cross purposes with their listeners.

What does *Götterdämmerung* mean to the man in the street? In France it is always *La Crépuscule des Dieux* and with us it should be *The Dusk of the Gods*. (An English composer would more likely have called it *The End of the Gods*.) It sometimes looks to me as though those who organize music in our country try to erect around their activities a ring fence that will exclude the participation or interest of all but linguists. I think few people realize how the ordinary British citizen has half-consciously felt himself warned off the musical field by unfamiliarity with the languages in use on it.

"Then said they unto him, say now Shibboleth; and he said sibboleth: for he could not frame to pronounce it right. Then they took him, and slew him at the passage of Jordan: and there fell at that time of the Ephraimites forty and two thousand."

ARE ONLY PROFESSIONALS TO TEACH?

An opinion that has considerably astonished me is the following from Mr. Stewart Macpherson, in *The Music Teacher* a year or two since:

"With 'cultural' courses of lectures in music, whether for schoolteachers or the general public, one has every sympathy, and one would encourage them by every means in one's power. But to urge, or even to suggest in the remotest and most indirect way, that after one of such courses, a teacher (we will say) in a Primary, or even a Secondary, school, whose knowledge of music is usually limited to the comparatively small stock-in-trade essential for him to deal with an elementary singing-class, shall be given a free hand to present great works of art to his class, with his own comments thereon, is an outrage upon commonsense and educational decency.

"I readily acknowledge that here and there a choice spirit might be found with that unique gift of artistic insight which is most assuredly not the prerogative of the professional musician alone, and with the *personality* necessary to awaken that insight in others. But such a combination of qualities is to be discovered only on very rare occasions; and even then, to carry the matter any distance, some kind of specialized knowledge is soon found to be inevitable."

On reading that pronouncement one's first depressing thought is that all Musical Appreciation teaching is, by its terms, automatically excluded from the schools attended by the children of every class of society except the upper class and the upper middle class. Mr. Macpherson, a kindly man of genuine social sympathies, would be the last to urge class legislation in matters of art and education, yet what he here advances amounts to it. For we may fairly interpret his view in this way—*"No Appreciation teaching except by professional musicians."* Let us see what that means. The following small body of the nation's children is to be restricted to unilinear music of its own making and debarred from contact with all the masterpieces except such as it can perform out of its own throats.

Public Elementary Schools

England and Wales 20,730
Scotland 2,919

Public Secondary Schools

England and Wales 1,329
Scotland 252

_____

25,230 schools
Total number of pupils, between 7,000,000 and 8,000,000.

Practically none of these children, it appears, are to be allowed the benefit of an introduction to the great things of instrumental musical art. They will, on leaving school, know *something*, at any rate, of Shakespeare, Milton, Scott, and Dickens, but of Bach, Beethoven, and Elgar they will be entirely ignorant. Is it necessary? Is it fair?

It will be noted that Mr. Macpherson does, at any rate, remember the existence of the Primary and Secondary schools. Musicians often forget them. They were completely forgotten, apparently, by the members of the Musical Appreciation Section of the Lausanne Conference of 1931—see Appendix. And they were completely forgotten, apparently, during a discussion of the Music Masters' Section of the Incorporated Society of Musicians, held at Eton, a month earlier, for, from the report in *The Musical Times* (July 1931), I gather that a member made this preposterous assertion (without any one reproving him!):

"The education of the whole country fell into three tiers—universities at the top, public schools in the middle, and preparatory schools at the bottom!" [1]

Whole country, indeed! The children of not one taxpayer in a hundred are remembered in this neat summary of our educational organizations.

In frank opposition to an old and honored friend, and the Father of the Appreciation Movement in Britain, I would give it as my deliberate opinion that Mr. Macpherson is completely wrong in his low estimate of the powers of elementary and secondary school teachers and in his high estimate of the musical knowledge required to do reasonably good Appreciation work. Let us examine the qualifications of the type of Appreciation teacher he wishes to throw out of action:

1. He has in most cases been trained to teach; he is a disciplinarian; he understands class management.
2. He is described by Mr. Macpherson as equipped to teach a singing class.
3. He is imagined by Mr. Macpherson as having attended a "cultural course" in music.
4. He evidently has some keenness about music or he would not have troubled to attend the "cultural course."

[1] For the guidance of any American readers I will repeat that, by ancient practice, boys' boarding schools for the upper classes are called "Public" Schools and that "Preparatory" Schools are for younger boys of the same class, intending later to proceed to the "Public" Schools. What are described above as "Elementary" and "Secondary" schools correspond to the "Public" schools of the United States. Properly, of course, English "Public" schools are Secondary schools, and they are thus treated in some parts of the present book. P. A. S.

5. He may not be able to play the piano, and if he can do so, the instrument at his command may not be a very good one, but we can pretty safely assume that he has a phonograph at command with a sufficient library of Records. (Many Education authorities have now organized loan libraries of Records, on which the schools of the area can draw.)

On the other hand, he may be imagined as not enjoying a very wide musical culture; he probably does not know a great deal of music—at all events, in the intimate way in which Mr. Macpherson's former students of the Royal Academy know it. But if he is, as we have imagined he must be, somewhat "keen" on music he certainly possesses a Radio set, reads the articles in *The Radio Times* preparatory to any program that interests him, and week by week, imperceptibly widens his interests and knowledge. It is also not unlikely that he possesses a domestic phonograph, buys a few good records occasionally, and subscribes to the journal *The Gramophone*, which has many good articles descriptive of the music of the new records as they appear. (Of course, for "he" throughout, understand "he or she."

I submit that such a teacher as this (and there are some thousands of that type in the country) may achieve very efficient teaching in Musical Appreciation if he will take real trouble to hear and rehear the music he intends to introduce, and so to become really intimate with its spirit and thematic content, form, orchestration (if it is an orchestral piece), and style. Why not?

He will not be able to go so deeply into the structure of the music as a well-trained musician, or to discuss the place in history of its composer as cogently as a university professor of music, but the very fact that he is an amateur gives him a sympathetic understanding of his class, who are also amateurs, and his teaching experience and powers of easy discipline may easily bring it about that the net result of his lesson is greater than that of many a fine professional musician.

After all, it is as important to secure professional teaching as to have professional musicianship. Both, of course, if we can get them, but how often is that?

With all the emphasis I can command I wish to plead for a touch of statesmanship. Need musicians always take such small views? There is something almost morbid about the conviction musicians have that if any piece of musical work gets out of their own hands it will be badly done.

As for the frequent demand that every teacher of Musical Appreciation should be able to give a piano performance of the music required, it may be suggested that those who make it [1] completely lose sight of the problem before the country. "Whilst the grass is growing the steed is starving", and before we get good pianos and good pianists into all those 25,230 schools several school generations will have passed out of our influence for ever—to swell the number of those before whom the British Broadcasting Corporation inevitably, at present, casts its pearls.

What our country needs musically is the building up of a new branch of the musical profession, equipped with both musician-ship and educational skill, on the lines of the music supervisors' branch in the United States. Let professional musicians work for that, by all means; it would be found to be an enormously powerful lever for the raising of the general musical taste and skill of the country, and would also be the financial salvation of a profession very hardly hit by the combination of a period of bad trade and the ubiquity of the Radio. But while waiting for the bringing into existence of a regular army to fight our cam-paign let every well-disposed and intelligent volunteer be eagerly welcomed. It is not right that from either narrow-minded pro-fessional jealousy or a spirit of academic propriety, eight million children should have their contact with a great art limited.

THE "DAMAGED MUSIC" SCARE

I have just discussed a severe sentence of Mr. Macpherson on the Elementary or Secondary school teacher who dares to attempt

---

[1] e.g. Professor F. H. Shera, of Sheffield University, in the *Sheffield Daily Tele-graph* of 14th November 1932—"Nobody should be allowed to teach apprecia-tion who is incapable of giving such a performance." P. A. S.

appreciation teaching and I would like to carry the discussion further. We are told that for that teacher to be *"given a free hand to present great works of art to his class, with his own comments thereon, is an outrage upon commonsense and educational decency."*

Strong words! From others than Mr. Macpherson I have seen yet stronger.

The emphasis of that sentence, if its author were speaking instead of writing, would, I feel sure, be laid upon the words, "great works of art." At all events it is the people who, in their declamatory denunciations of the humbler Appreciation teachers, *do* lay the emphasis there to whom I am now venturing to address myself.

I suggest that there is a fallacy hidden away in this expression of concern for "great works of art."

It is so easy to let undetected fallacies pass us by.

I once knew a family of which the father began to develop a disturbing habit. Coming across an item of interest in his evening newspaper he would say, "Here's something interesting to all of you!" The family would then put down their own reading and dutifully listen. If a sigh or mild protest were heard, or the remark, "We can read it for ourselves later," it would be met with the explanation, "Well, if I read to you *all together* it saves time." This plausible explanation was accepted until one day the youngest child piped up, "Dad, *how* does it save time when you read to us all together?" And that fallacy of "sentences running concurrently" was exploded.

I knew of one who had a good tale which he told in various companies. It illustrated the power of "suggestion." A man had a horrible dream. He was to be executed; was led to the block; the ax descended. "And," said the narrator, "the dream was so vivid and the shock so great, that he died in his sleep." The people to whom this tale was told would say: "Yes, I can quite believe that! People *can* be killed by shock." At last he told the tale in a certain company and (this time) the eldest of the company, an old lady of over ninety, spoke out, "If that man died in his sleep," she questioned, "how does any one know he had the dream?"

We are most of us pretty unthinking, and readily pass the little fallacies of conversation. And so some of us have for years been accepting this objection to the spoiling of "great works of art." The phrase appeals to our emotions. Masterpieces are in danger. We feel as though we saw a maniac slashing the pictures in the National Gallery, or the Germans battering the cathedral of Rheims, or the speculative builder razing Nature's masterpieces from England's green and pleasant land.

We get the same sympathetic feeling, of course, when we find Canon Hannay troubled because Blake's *Jerusalem* is being "completely defiled," or that American writer worried because fine music is being "popularized, toughened, and smothered by excessive hearing." We feel that some dreadful deed is being perpetrated and begin to wonder whether we ought not to "do something"—perhaps found a "Society for the Prevention of Cruelty to Art."

And yet, when, for a moment, we put our head under the cold douche of reason, can we justify our concern? A dog suffers if I ill-treat it, but does a sonata?

So far as I know, a connoisseur can take up that sonata next day and never know I have been ill-treating it. There is, in fact, no such crime as cruelty to masterpieces. When they are incompetently performed or crudely explained there is only the crime of cruelty to *people.*

All this seems very obvious now, does it not? But was it obvious before? I am sure we have many of us, when we listened to a bad performance at a concert or heard of an ineffective or foolish Appreciation Lesson in a school, suffered from some sort of semiconscious and vaguely defined sympathy *with the music.* We need have none. Music can no more suffer than can the Equator, of which Sydney Smith complained that somebody spoke disrespectfully.

So far as the Appreciation Lesson is concerned, then, it comes to this—However badly it may be carried out, if one pupil has been interested there is at least that tiny gain, if ten pupils have been interested there is ten times the gain. The fact that the lesson has been imperfect does not matter to the masterpiece that formed its subject. The only possible harm is that, if the teacher is a fool, some wrong attitude towards a particular piece of music or to music in general may have been suggested to the class by the teacher, some misinformation imparted, or (in the most extreme instance imaginable) a distaste for music provoked by a dull and academic treatment.

Against the wrong attitude we can take our precautions: books and articles on Musical Appreciation can and do warn the teacher against the cheaply sentimental or over-pictorial view of music and the thoughtless idea that every piece of music tells a story.

Against the misinformation we can take similar precautions. There is obviously no more reason why misinformation should be imparted in the Musical Appreciation lesson than in the lesson in English Literature or that in English History—if the teacher will take the same pains over his preparation of the one as over his preparation of the other.

Against the danger of evoking a distaste for music we are less easily able to guard. It is largely a matter of the teacher's own degree of enthusiasm for the art, of his tact, and of his possession of an adequate teaching technique. I suppose I shall be regarded as an enemy to my own trades union if I say that when reflecting on this danger I find that I have more fear of my brother professional musicians, with their apparently almost inescapable tendency to an academic view of the art, than of the ordinary school teacher. The study of Shakespeare in our schools, as I have remarked elsewhere in the present book, was long turned by the pundits who wrote the text-books and the examination syllabuses, into a torture of etymology and literary dryasdust, and the appreciative study of music might, I admit, for a time suffer in a similar way.

The teaching of no subject can be made fool-proof, and if there are to be fools in appreciation teaching they are likely to be of two kinds, the shallow fools and the deep ones. I fear the deep ones the more; it is they, I feel, who might spread abroad that "distaste for music" to which I have candidly alluded as a possible danger.

But let us return to our First Subject. *There is in the calendar no such crime as Cruelty to Works of Art. There is a crime of Cruelty to Youth. This crime is committed whenever there occurs a case of Bad Teaching. But it is also committed in every place which provides No Teaching.*

And No Teaching (so far as the schools in which eight or nine millions of British children are concerned) is what our sentimentalists decree. "Spare, oh spare that Symphony!" they cry. And to the needs of the children (the citizens of a decade hence, in whose hands the destiny of culture in our land will rest) they turn their backs with indifference.

That is the way with sentimentalists. How they would have been shocked if they had seen the priest give to the starving David and his companions the shewbread of the altar!

But perhaps it is I who am now becoming sentimental!

PART V

ACTUAL EXPERIMENTS AND EXPERIENCES IN VARIOUS TYPES OF SCHOOL

CONTENTS OF PART V

[1] See pp. 277-8 for information on English schools. W. E.

(E) THE EXAMPLE OF A GREAT ENGLISH CITY

INFANT AND ELEMENTARY SCHOOLS, ETC.

I HAVE some expectation that the present section of my book (the part of which I am not the author) will be found by many readers to be the most useful. It consists of personal records of the experiments and experiences of a great number of practical teachers. These have come to me in response to the following letter, very kindly inserted by sympathetic editors in practically all the British educational and musical journals.

THE CHILD AND THE MASTERPIECE

There is at present a great need that teachers who have, perhaps for years, been working out a practical technique in what is called "Musical Appreciation" (by which I do not mean "Aural Training" or anything of that kind, but the actual bringing together of the child and the masterpiece) should pool their experiences.

In order to effect such a "pooling" I propose to include in a forthcoming book (probably to be called *Music—The Child and the Masterpiece*) relevant extracts from communications from teachers. It would be particularly useful to record:

1. Various teachers' experiences as to the best methods of gaining and retaining the interest of pupils of specified ages.
2. Their findings as to what type of music most interests children of specified ages (with any lists of compositions found attractive).
3. Instances of success and failure, with the suggested explanations.
4. The extent to which biographical information, on the one hand, and analytical exposition on the other have proved useful in securing attention for fine music.
5. Any experience bearing on the effective use of the Gramophone.
6. Any devices invented by the teacher, and found of service.

And so on. . . . I do not suggest that the communications need be based on the above list of heads; they are merely offered as examples.

It is important that various types of school should be represented —boys' and girls', elementary, secondary, "preparatory", and "public."

If any of your teacher readers care to co-operate in this effort I shall feel most grateful, and I am sure they will be doing good. We have had a good deal of theorizing about "Appreciation": now (after nearly a quarter of a century of increasing activity in this school subject) let us know just how it works in practice, and try to find ways of making it still better.

As will be seen, a number of very interesting replies were received. Almost all opened with some expression of the modest writer's doubts as to the value of what he was sending me, and this prelude I have ventured to suppress.

(A) INFANT AND ELEMENTARY SCHOOLS, ETC.

Some Infant School Experiments.

What can be done with the youngest children to be found in our schools in the way of direct introduction to masterpieces? Miss G. Rostron, of the Daisy Hill School, Westhoughton, Bolton, Lancashire, has tabulated here the methods and results of a few very carefully thought-out experiments. The average age of the children in question is six and a half years. Could a better beginning be made? Here is the *habit of listening* begun!

Gramophone Record	Preparation	Result
"Messiah"; *There were Shepherds*. (Columbia.)	The Bible Story was told several times as graphically as was in my power. No mention was made of a gramophone record. When the children knew the story thoroughly, the record was played without any previous description.	An instant success. Always treated with great awe.
Largo from *From the New World*. Hallé Orchestra. (Columbia.)	Words were put to this lovely melody and it was used as a school hymn. Then the record was introduced.	It was not long before some children heard this melody broadcast. It became a favorite with some older sisters.
Londonderry Air. Hallé Orchestra. (Columbia.)	Words were taught, and the song was sung fairly well for such young children.	It has been appreciated by each class to which I have taught it. Mr. Alfred Barker's solo violin seems to speak to them.

Gramophone Record	Preparation	Result
Ride of the Valkyries. Bayreuth Festival Orchestra. (Columbia.)	This took more preparation than any other. Hours and hours of search and research into the story until I had fitted the parts which were suitable for little children. The Valkyries became Warrior Maidens and the Gods became giants. The story was not changed, only cut.	I should like to go a little more into detail here, for the results were more definite than had been expected. When the record had been gone through once the children asked permission to let a favorite teacher hear it. They were left to do the honors themselves. I was very much surprised at the eager and intelligent way in which they asked her to listen to this, and that, and especially when one cried "Listen, that's Brünhilde asking her sisters to hide her." (The words on the record are German.)
Beethoven, Violin Concerto, Slow Movement. Kreisler. (H.M.V.)	The melody was used in a little Fairy Play and afterwards introduced on the Gramophone.	Interest at the time, but the record has not been used on any other class.
Horn's Cherry Ripe. (Columbia.)	The words are recited and explained and the melody is left to make its own appeal.	These records are always popular and after they have become well known they are asked for instead of Nursery Rhymes. In buying them we considered two things: 1. The melodies. 2. The excellent word production.
Arne's Where the Bee sucks. Sung by Elsie Suddaby. (H.M.V.)	This is treated in the same way.	
Schubert's Hark, Hark! the Lark. Sung by Master E. Lough. (H.M.V.)	This also needs very little explanation and preparation.	The children in this neighborhood speak a debased form of the Lancashire dialect and have very harsh voices, and we find the records very useful.

We have also in frequent use *Nursery Rhymes* and *Songs from "When We Were Very Young"*, but these are not part of the special training.

Breaking New Ground in Elementary Schools.

A music teacher in Elementary Schools in Leicester sends the following interesting account of an attempt to break up new ground—for the wider aspects of music study had been neglected in these schools until her work began, and, as I gather, her efforts formed part of a general forward movement in the district. While not forbidding me to mention her name she expresses some preference for modestly remaining anonymous.

Following the well-known educational maxim to proceed from the Known to the Unknown, I find it best with classes having definitely non-musical children in them to relate the music to other subjects in the curriculum, chiefly, of course, legend and literature, the social side of history, and occasionally art. . . . I give to the course a historical framework and begin with *"Sumer is i-cumen in"*, talking of the literary and historical associations, illustrating by record and the actual singing of the round. Next: *Tudor Music* and the instruments in use then—lute, harpsichord, viols, etc., etc. (I once spent a fortnight at the Dolmetsch Haslemere Festival): I have found all grades of children keenly interested in these. The *Columbia History* records have been my very good friends here. All this, too, links admirably with Tudor social history. *Purcell* comes next, teaching some of the songs and introducing to the Suite form of music.

To prepare the way for later composers comes next a series of talks on the instruments in a *Modern Orchestra,* with the help of Hawkes' admirable Charts, together with some hand leaflets which they also supply. For children who have knowledge of a Percussion Band this is an easy matter. Records of "Instruments of the Orchestra", which are always very popular with the children, and suitable solo records such as Saint-Saëns *Le Cygne* (for curves in music) and the Air on the G String (for sheer beauty of musical line) seem to cast a spell over even the youngest.

For familiarizing with Orchestra I have begun with Quilter's *Children's Overture,* first taking words with tunes on the piano, then by record. A very popular story suite is the *Casse Noisette.* An orchestrated *Londonderry Air* or any other familiar tune is a further step in musical apprehension.

I then take the great composers, with discrimination, using the pictorial chart, a copy of which I enclose. This, I may say, I prepared first in large wall-size for a music room (photographs on postcards) and it was published in this smaller form by Messrs. Evans in *The Music Teacher* (October, 1928) and republished last year in

The Music Student. The large sheet is of great use and interest in the music class-room.[1]

Biographical sketches of the composers have been very popular, especially the passages dealing with their childhood. The average small boy is far more interested in the little Handel running after his father's coach than in his Hallelujah Chorus. But I maintain that even this interest is better than none, at his age, and that it can possibly be directed into useful channels later.

Actual big works from the classics I have been able to take only in part, a movement here or there. (Even my music-students in a school of music only really "appreciated" one movement at a sitting.) Technical knowledge of form I introduce only in a very simple way.

Perhaps my most successful record lesson has been that on Schubert's *Erl King*. After hearing the poem the children were intently listening for the voices of the different personages, the horse's hoofs, &c.; music so dramatically allied to a vivid story naturally attracts children.

Some of the lighter Bach, Mozart, Beethoven, and Mendelssohn for piano, and Schumann's children's pieces have been very well received—but abstract, disjointed sorts of lessons on *Music—Grave and Gay, Music—Major and Minor, Sonata Form, A Symphony,* and the like, got me nowhere.

I am afraid I have written rather at length, but this subject is very near to my heart. I was a musical child, but had arrived at years of discretion before ever hearing anything really worth while (other than Handel's *Messiah*), so I write feelingly.

The Cultivation of a Liking for Music.

Ten years' school experiment in "The Teaching of Music and the Cultivation of a Liking for Music" on the part of Mr. Edgar C. Shepherd, of St. James' Church of England School, Shirley, near Birmingham, have produced the following codification of

---

[1] The principle of this chart is the scheming out of a large oblong sheet in periods of a decade, measured along top and bottom, and the placing in position, according to this scheme, of long oblongs, each containing the name of a composer, with his birth and death dates boldly displayed after the name, thus "*Schubert, 1797–1828.*" Necessarily these oblongs form a mass stretching from the left top corner to the right bottom corner and leaving blank a large space below this on the left and above it on the right. This space is utilized for the portraits of the composers (picture postcards pasted on), placed, so far as possible, on a line with their names. P. A. S.

principles and devices to be applied in the "Cultivation of a Liking for Music"—to quote the aim he states.

GENERAL METHODS.

    A. Music making. (Songs; School Violin Class.)

    B. Listening. (Gramophone; Piano.)

        A. Choice of songs from the *best*. I find Bach, Purcell, Handel, and Haydn particularly suited to the incidental introduction of simple Form to children. All the points set out on what follows arise and are dealt with over and over again in the study of songs for performance.

        B. Gramophone, as

            (*a*) Supplement to A. (Form; Instruments.)

            (*b*) Pure relaxation.

        In (*b*) the children select records they would like to hear. This free choice gives a good indication of what they have taken to.

A FEW SPECIAL POINTS.

STUDY OF FORM. This begins even in the simple song, e.g. *All through the night,* and is invariably pointed out on the larger canvas, e.g. *Where'er you walk, Lord of our Being.* (N.B. Handel particularly useful in this matter.)

Certain types of Overture can now be listened to intelligently.

Il Seraglio Overture: a simple "sandwich" form. (Chief Themes written out in staff on black paper and hung up in front of class. Sometimes these may be sight-read and hummed.)

STUDY OF BASSES. Children very interested in a good *moving* bass part, and always amused at the *cadential bass* f.r.s.s.d.[1] (Demonstrate from Handel, Purcell, Bach, Haydn.) I have sometimes compared these with *modern bass parts*—Vaughan Williams and Holst: e.g. *Let us now praise famous men* and *England my Country.*

CADENCES. I do not know if this study is common, but I have found children very interested in Cadences.

They can always spot Purcell, Bach, and Haydn by their "signatures". . . . I feel that here is an interesting field for study, and not beyond children.

    [1] English *sol-fa* symbols for *fa re so so do*. Incidentally, one doubts whether the children would have been "amused at the *cadential bass*" unless the teacher smiled. W. E.

PRACTICE IN CHORDING. We frequently practice chords and their resolutions in 2 and 3 parts, chiefly cadences, with the parts in the Treble Clef.

These simple exercises are designed to assist the child to hear an inside part.

CHARACTERISTICS OF COMPOSERS. *Mozart's* fondness for melody built on the Tonic Chord. *Purcell's* syncopation (e.g. in *Fairest Isle*). *Beethoven's* ponderous chording (*Creation's Hymn; Egmont* Overture. *Creation's Hymn* is a great favorite with children.)

MUSIC PRIZE. At the end of the year I offer a Music Prize. Entries for the Examination are purely voluntary. The paper takes broadly the following form:

A. 1. Transcription from Staff to Tonic or Tonic to Staff.[1]
   2. Naming the Composers of Works.
   3. Simple Form.
B. 1. Ear Tests.
   2. Recognition of fragments played on piano.

SUMMARY OF METHODS.

1. Study of Song Form.
2. Study of Basses.
3. Study of Cadences.
4. Practice in Chording.
5. Characteristics of Composers.

(Nos. 2, 3, and 5 above do not, I believe, usually receive attention.)

NEEDS.

1. More Gramophone records where the whole Overture or Movement is *on one side* of a record. Cuts would not matter, I feel sure.

2. More Teachers with some elementary knowledge of Harmony and Counterpoint. The early part of Stainer's little book on Harmony would repay study. I have not found a really interesting book on Counterpoint for beginners.

3. More use in schools of the great field of songs by Purcell, Bach, Handel. Every principle can be studied in these composers. (I am busy at present making a collection of Purcell suitable for schools. He is immensely popular with children.)

4. More and more records of the fine, healthy music of the great Purcell.

[1] That is to say, from Staff-notation to Tonic Sol-fa notation, or *vice versa*. See footnote, p. 260. W. E.

VERY FAVORITE SONGS.

Purcell: *Nymphs and Shepherds.*
    Fairest Isle (Novello's words, *not* Dryden's).
    Shepherd, shepherd, leave your labors.
Handel: *Lord of our Being.*
    Where'er you walk.
Bach: *Jesu, Joy of Man's Desiring* (3 part).
Beethoven: *Creation's Hymn.*
Parry: *England.*
Vaughan Williams: *Linden Lea.*

VERY FAVORITE RECORDS.

Andante from *Emperor Quartet*	Haydn
Hallelujah Chorus	Handel
Funeral March of a Marionette	Gounod
Il Seraglio Overture	Mozart
Ayres for the Theatre	Purcell
Finale of Brandenburg Concerto in F . . .	Bach

(The great rhythmic drive of Bach and Purcell is well liked.)

The salient points of the above (some of them rather striking)
will catch the eye of every reader. I comment on two tiny
matters: (1) Few of us nowadays would endorse the view that
"cuts do not matter" in records, but undoubtedly the break-and-
turn-over is a serious impediment to the maintenance of the
"atmosphere" of the music,[1] and where one-side records of a
suitable type can be found they have an additional value. (2)
Stainer's *Harmony* (perhaps the most widely-sold text-book of
its subject ever written) is surely not now the best on the market; a deaf-from-birth could be taught to work its exercises correctly: however, it will be noticed that only its "early part" is
recommended. The point here is, of course, the suggestion that
teachers require some knowledge of harmony, and this cannot
be contested. Apart from any other question, such knowledge is
a great help in the teacher's detailed analysis of form that should
precede an Appreciation lesson—whether or not the teacher in-

---

[1] A tip may be useful to less-experienced phonograph demonstrators. Winding (if by handle) should be done during the playing; at the turn-over the
machine should not be stopped.

tends, in his actual lesson, to dwell minutely on the formal side of the music.

A Teacher Who Has Qualified Himself for the Work.

Mr. R. Higgin, of Dowdales Central School, Dalton-in-Furness, Lancashire, puts us first *au fait* with his own musical position (it is, perhaps, a pity that more of my correspondents have not done this, for obviously it is the starting-point of any work attempted), then drafting a series of notes methodically based on the headings I suggested in my letter to the press.

First a personal note to give you some idea (musically) who is writing. I have no academic musical qualifications. I have taught music in Central Schools for over eight years, and very willingly. I was taught to play piano sufficiently for school purposes. I began to take an interest at large at the age of about 16 years. In this district at that time (1910 onwards) there were few opportunities of hearing good music—a third-rate Opera Company, an occasional visit of a celebrity at concerts, where now I seem to think they were picking up pin-money without really doing themselves justice. Later, I went to Manchester University and took a Science Degree and a Teaching Diploma. There I attended Dr. T. Keighley's music lectures and came out top in his yearly examination. I took the opportunity whilst in Manchester to go to the Hallé Concerts and the Brand Lane. Since then Wireless has to be my main source of hearing good music. I have a Radio-gramophone.

Thus it may be seen that I have the love of good music well developed. It is my only hobby.

Now I have attempted to teach children from 11 to 16 years (mixed classes) to appreciate good music. The problem bristles with difficulties. I have had a free hand and the use of gramophone and wireless. I will deal with the various points of investigation in the order mentioned in your letter, in the light of my own experience.

1. Best Methods of Gaining and Keeping Interest.

Often, whilst the children are writing a little exercise, I sit at the piano and gently play snatches of tunes from the masters—say, the chief theme of the 1st movement of Beethoven's Fifth Symphony, Minuet from Eb Symphony (Mozart), a few bars of the *Pastoral* Symphony, a line or two of well-known operatic airs. I often find that at least some of the pupils become curious as to "What is that tune, Sir?" Then I play it again and ask them to hum it. Then a few *casual* (apparently) words about the composer and the work from which it came. Sometimes one gets the request to hear more of it. Then you promise "Yes; sometime when we have a few minutes to spare, &c." When "Sometime" comes an appreciative audience is usually assured. *Little doses.* I find prolonged listening does not suit children. They like to be *doing.* At 11-12 years the lessons on Appreciation are infrequent and very casual (again apparently!). At 13-16 the desire often grows and one has more or less to satisfy a demand.

2. *Type of Music, &c.*

On the whole, children are not attracted by music of the type whose rhythm is not well marked. Simple operatic songs of the type which might stand condemned by the "musician", such as *In happy moments, Yes! let me like a soldier fall,* and (further up the scale) *Toreador's Song, Largo al Factotum* (in English) prove acceptable, especially if a brief verbal sketch of the character and circumstance of the song is previously given. Children can learn to sing and enjoy *Harvest Home Chorus (Faust)* and *Pilgrims' Chorus (Tannhäuser)* simplified. Later, I have found pupils come to school with a gramophone record of the very thing. Thus, one is given an opportunity to explore Opera. Mozart's Minuet from the E♭ Symphony, the Minuet from Haydn's *Clock* Symphony, and the slow movement from the *Surprise* have proved acceptable. Schumann's *Träumerei* is useful: children like to hum it while it is being played and I never discourage this habit, within reason.

Band (Brass and Military) records are acceptable. The word "band" means much more to a child than the word "orchestra." The "Miserere" (*Il Trovatore*) captures children's imagination. Piano music must be used sparingly. A little Chopin in brilliant mood can be interesting.

3. *Instances of Successes and Failures.*

I find that each occasion is a success for some children and a failure for others. I once heard a teacher try to get fifty children (11-16 years) to listen to Act I of the *Pirates of Penzance* on records. As is usual with opera the words were almost unintelligible and the company of children got restless and soon bored. Too big a dose—especially of opera, where the appeal to children would be the story!

4. Biographical Explanation and Analysis.

This is undoubtedly useful, *but* I find that it must be mentioned merely incidentally to the music being performed. Analysis is often useful—*after* the performance when an interest is perceived. Otherwise, just the main theme and its various "dressings and disguises" are sufficient. The whole thing has to be intimate: the teacher must be one of the class in order to bring in biography or analysis.

5. Effective Use of the Gramophone.

Leaving out such things as choice of well-recorded pieces, and choice of the actual items to be rendered, it is necessary to be careful to use the gramophone as the actual performers. By suggestion the children can be made to picture the singers (say) or the bandsmen with their instruments, and so on. Unless this is accomplished the best effect is for the most part lost. Winding up, changing records and needles can be terrible moments for destroying the atmosphere unless one talks them off. Another point for the teacher: appear to, and actually you will, enjoy the performance. A carefully inserted remark at a moment when the music needs it, or when it may appear to be temporarily rather dull, keeps the interest going. I do not know whether all this sounds revolutionary, but from my own experience I know it pays. Encourage children to bring records from home to play in school. They like it and other children get interested too. Moreover, often the child takes more interest in the home collection of records than he did previously.

6. Any Devices, &c.

Encourage children to cut out photographs, &c., relating to music and composers and to paste them into their music exercise books. Also keep a "scrap" book yourself and hand it round amongst the children at appropriate moments. Never be afraid of retailing anecdotes (true or traditional) to heighten the impression of a composer's personality or to suggest how certain pieces of music came to be written. e.g. *Surprise* and *Farewell* Symphonies, and the *1812* Overture. The whole subject has to *live,* and I think it is rather useless a teacher attempting it without an enthusiasm which he or she can, at least in some small measure, hand on to the children.

Finally, a few observations! It is useless trying to get children to listen to good music just because it *is* good. It is no use *telling* children that this and that is *good* music and this and that is trash.

The cheap, raucous gramophone and equally cheap records of

jazz, &c., are our greatest enemies; also homes where the popular Jazz bands of the Radio, &c., represent the height of musical achievement. There is no doubt that, musically, the average person is a very poor specimen. We can only aim at giving the children the *knowledge* that good music has an appeal; at letting them know where they can find it, and at giving them a foundation on which they can build. Consequently, expositions of whole symphonies, &c., are out of the question. Give the child the striking feature of the movement and leave the rest to the interest which will arise in due course.

Wireless concerts for children are of doubtful value. I know that with a large number of children in a concert hall the novelty and mass suggestion can make it rather effective. Children up to fourteen, at any rate, cannot listen for long unless the piece has a very superficial interest.

Sometimes we have a boy who plays in a Brass Band. We encourage him to bring his instrument along and play it, and the children can examine it. This can be made to lead to a talk on kinds of instruments and the reason for and use of their characteristic tones.[1]

Just one trivial comment may be made on this. Surely the loss of "atmosphere" while the "gramophone" is receiving its fresh supply of energy, &c. (American readers will be shocked to see that electric phonographs are not everywhere in use in Britain) could be avoided by detailing a deft-handed child to tend that piece of machinery—with instructions to do it as unobtrusively as possible. However, so elementary a suggestion to so experienced a teacher seems rather impertinent. Doubtless there is some impediment.

Work Among the "Middle-Aged" of the School Community.

Principles and devices put into practice in a school for boys and girls of eleven and over are set out, in businesslike fashion, by Mr. W. E. Wilkinson, of Billingham-on-Tees, Durham. It will be seen that the general idea here is an expansion of the old-type singing lesson, and an enrichment of it.

[1] If proof were needed that the good teacher of Musical Appreciation need not be a professional musician, we have it here. His paragraphs 1 and 4, and the latter part of 5, are particularly discerning. W. E.

1. The following are features found to serve most efficiently in the maintenance of interest in the Music Lesson.

(*a*) The lesson to be as informal as conditions allow.

(*b*) Occasional changing of the routine of the lesson.

(*c*) Learning songs that the *children like.*

(*d*) Singing songs selected by children during the lesson.

(*e*) Encouragement of individual singing of songs by children.

(*f*) Use of child conductor.

(*g*) Encouragement of child pianists, &c., to bring and play their own pieces before the class.

(*h*) Interesting facts or stories relative to composers of songs used.

(*i*) Memorizing of short classical melodies that appeal. e.g. Braga's *Serenade;* Mendelssohn's *Spring Song.*

(*j*) Building up on blackboard of melodies by the children singing them.

(*k*) Introduction of theory incidentally and in simple, attractive style.

(*l*) Occasional attractive music played by Teacher.

(*m*) The homely, artistic atmosphere of the Music Room.

2. *Types of Music.*

Naturally, a great part of the Music Lesson should be taken up with the singing of songs.

It is my experience throughout the school that songs of the old masters are welcomed and enjoyed.

With the younger children folk and traditional songs predominate. Attractive modern compositions are also taken. In the higher classes, whilst songs of younger days are still rehearsed, more scope is given to the learning of classical and modern items.

With regard to the selection of songs, I find generally that children prefer songs that have a "continuous melody" with simple and attractive phrases. If the song can be learnt quickly, say, in one lesson, it is generally welcomed. Having laborious effort in the learning of a song tends to detract from whatever beauty it may possess. It is sometimes good to scrap songs that the children don't like—'tis true, that often these songs are those that "Teacher likes."

Children love to sing melodies set to poems they have learnt in the English lesson. Wherever possible I find such items and in case of failure have attempted to create such melodies myself. I have purposely made the melodies simple and continuous and have found them acceptable.

As examples of the last-mentioned device, Mr. Wilkinson sends me effective simple settings, by himself, of Yeats' *The Lake Isle of Innisfree* and Wordsworth's *Daffodils*.

A Three-Years' Course Outlined.

The following three-years' scheme is sent by Mr. Edgar Smith, Head Teacher of the Church of England Boys' School, Chipping Norton, Oxfordshire. Here we have the necessarily rare case of a school principal who is also a trained musician, possessing a professional diploma of the Royal College of Organists, and having the use of the parish church organ, a modern instrument of forty stops.

We may take it for granted that the general musical training of this school is over average, and that by the time the pupils reach the upper classes they have received a sound grounding in ear-training and sight-singing, as well as having done a good deal of general "appreciation" work. For the last three years of school work Mr. Smith has drafted and is carrying out the following syllabus. He says it is "the result of previous experimental work, and is constructed with the object of developing an intelligent appreciation of the art, with a bias towards 'absolute's music as opposed to 'program' music."

First Year—FORM IN MUSIC

Musical phrases and sentences; cadences.
Simple Binary or two-part form.
Simple Ternary or three-part form.
Expansion of Ternary form—minuet and trio.
Rondo form.
Sonata or First-movement form—exposition, development, recapitulation, and coda; use of introductions to first-movement form, e.g. Beethoven's sonatas.
Variation form; ground basses.
Counterpoint and canon.

Fugue: definition—written in voices, subject and answer, real and tonal answers, counter-subject, exposition, middle entries, stretto, subject in augmentation and diminution.

Illustrations and examples on pianoforte and organ [1] from Bach, Haydn, Mozart, Beethoven, &c.; examples of choral fugues from oratorios, boys being encouraged to follow various entries whilst the score is played.

Second Year—THE ORCHESTRA

The string group—violin, viola, violoncello, and double-bass; compass of each instrument; how sound is produced and pitch varied; double-stopping; C clef for viola; the mute.

The wind group—wood and brass; reeds; compass of each instrument and its distinctive tone.

Instrument of percussion—drums, triangle, and cymbals.

Additional instruments sometimes used in orchestra—the harp, piano, and organ.

Solo instruments and instruments in combination; concerto work.

Note how string group, wood-wind, and brass each form complete harmony; compare with vocal score.

Use gramophone records for illustration of all lessons and exhibit actual instruments under discussion, or photos of same.

Third Year—LIVES OF GREAT COMPOSERS AND THEIR INFLUENCE UPON THE ART OF MUSIC

The English Madrigal School; Handel, his oratorios and suites; prelude, allemande, courante, sarabande, and gigue—binary form predominant.

Bach and contrapuntal music; compare suites of Bach and Handel; Bach's preludes and fugues.

Haydn and Mozart and the development of instrumental music.

Beethoven and the perfection of the sonata.

Chopin and the pianoforte.

Wagner and opera; the combination of music and poetry in the music-drama.

Elgar and his music.

(Musical illustrations on the pianoforte, organ, and gramophone.)

---

[1] At the moment when this syllabus was drafted the school possessed no phonograph but was expecting to get one (the nature of the second year work of course demands it). P. A. S.

Mr. Smith comments on his syllabus as follows: "I need scarcely state that the method adopted in working the syllabus is of paramount importance. For example, in approaching form it is essential to demonstrate its necessity, and then children are keenly interested in its evolution. At the end of the course they should be able to state the form of a composition heard on any instrument or combination of instruments and should have come to distinguish between good and inferior music."

Mr. Smith invites my comments, and I can only say that I think his scheme excellent, given the conditions of previous musical work and an awakened interest in music and of sufficient class time to carry out so thorough a scheme. It is quite evident that these children at the age of fourteen will have a general grasp of music such as many a university student might envy, and that, indeed, this very scheme, treated in a way suitable for the adult mind, might very well form a part of the course for an arts degree.

In practice Mr. Smith may just possibly find parts of his course a little too thorough for the age of the pupils (take his treatment of Fugue as an example), and in any case there is obviously a demand for genuine teaching power in order to maintain interest throughout. His remark above quoted as to demonstrating the necessity for form and then treating it from an evolutionary standpoint shows that he is alive to the human aspect and gives one confidence in his power to adapt himself to the receptive powers of his pupils, which, as every experienced teacher knows, may turn out to be greater than one expects in some parts of the course and less than one expects in others. In carrying out such a thorough course as that, one would, of course, be constantly on the watch for any sign of decline of interest, prepared immediately to change one's methods or one's musical examples so as to restimulate.

It may be suggested that a slight extension of the Third Year's syllabus would bring in music of a more "modern" type. The working to a climax with Elgar is admirable in a British school, but from a listener's point of view the line Beethoven-Wagner-Elgar is a line of natural continuation and a jump into another field might be suggested. Thus Debussy might be coupled with Elgar as the culmination of the course, or (alternatively) Debussy, Ravel, and even Stravinsky might be drawn on occasionally to illustrate the syllabus of the Second Year.

The point is tactfully to destroy the narrow feeling (shown by so large a proportion of the Radio public) that what we may call the Beethoven style and its later manifestations are the only ones yielding real enjoyment to the listener.

Some of the Danger Points.

Mr. Arthur Goodchild, L.R.A.M., Music Master of Woodlands Senior Boys' School, Gillingham, Kent, gives his views as follows. I have set out in italics one particular passage that seems to me to be worth our special attention. Mr. Goodchild devotes himself first to listing some of the "Dangers of Musical Appreciation."

During the past twelve years I have devoted most of my school time and practically all my spare time to the cause of musical education, and, of course, I have formed many conclusions on the appreciative aspect. Here are a few conclusions which came uppermost in my mind.

(1) The danger of promiscuity and the prolific record catalogue. It is useless to play any piece of music to children once only. Rather than bewilder pupils with ten different examples, it is always better to play one good example say ten times, discovering some new feature at each successive playing, until "all the juice has been sucked out of the orange." The coarseness of the metaphor is excused when I say that care must be taken that the orange is a juicy one in the first place. I have conducted a class of "dull and backwards" from a state of apathy to one of alert enthusiasm by this method, and over as abstruse a matter as the first movement of a Bach sonata for violin and keyboard.

(2) The danger of omniprescence and the passive attitude. *In these days when, in nine houses out of ten, the radio is switched on as a background for conversation and other noises, the "appreciationist" will have achieved his object if he has formed in his pupils the habit of intensive listening, irrespective of what they are listening to; for he who listens intently to jazz must very soon switch it off!*

(3) The danger of program music. A very little of this will suffice to make children reject all music which does not "tell a story."

(4) The danger of "instrument spotting." All music is not orchestral, and anyhow, even Queen's Hall audiences are not wholly concerned with the identification of the players of solo passages. Again, how many recordings are so perfect that even an expert would feel safe to indulge in this sort of detective work? And after all, what's it got to do with the music? Only a little, perhaps.

My realization of dangers 3 and 4 has led me into the realms of chamber music for most of my appreciation work, with very gratifying results—though you might not believe it.

(5) The danger of the watertight compartment. "Appreciation" is not a subject apart from the general music course, but the appreciative attitude (i.e. the attitude of alert criticism and appraisement) should be cultivated throughout every music lesson until even the scales sung for voice training are so carefully listened to that their effect is musical.[1] That is why I personally prefer to scrap the words "Appreciation" and "Aural Training" in favor of the more general term, "Listening."

Correlation, both within the music course and outside it (e.g. History and Literature lessons), provides an excellent means of overcoming the watertight compartment danger. For example, a class who were studying the Napoleonic period and early nineteenth century in their History lessons were introduced to the songs of Schubert. They learnt the *Cradle Song* and *The Trout*. The school violinists played them some *Rosamund* music. The individual instruments of the string quartet were introduced via suitable records, and the whole thing culminated in a fairly detailed study of the *Trout* piano quintet.

(6) The danger of poor "gramophone technique." Record changing, needle changing, and winding should be done with the minimum of ostentation. The attention of boys in particular is very easily deflected from the beauties of music to the mechanics of sound reproduction.

Do teachers realize how very delicate are such things as soundboxes and records, despite the claims of the manufacturers? The school piano is universally known to be anything but a musical instrument, but I strongly suspect that in many schools the gramo-

[1] *Cf.* footnote, p. 185. W. E.

phone and its equipment are equally bad, though there is little reason why they should be so.

Records should be stored and dusted with religious care and should be replaced immediately they begin to show signs of wear. Needles should *never* be lowered on to the middle of a record. Personally, I favor non-metallic needles, as I have always found the scratch of the metal variety very annoying. The result, of course, is on the soft side, but if this causes a greater listening effort, it is all to the good.

So much for "dangers." Now for one or two other points that occur to me.

I have tried the biographical method but have discarded it as largely waste of time. Children are always interested in a story as such, but I have found from subsequent testing, that the story of a composer's life is not linked up in the child's mind to the music, and I am sure that time thus spent might be better devoted to learning more music. Of course, it is essential that a composer should be historically placed. By all means let us tell the children that Haydn wore a pigtail when he was in the choir *if it is going to make them listen harder*. Personally, I've found that it doesn't.

The method I have found most successful is one whereby I tell as little as possible and elicit as much as possible. A piece of music is played the first time entirely without comment. At its conclusion every pupil is expected to have *noticed* something (e.g. vocal or instrumental, rough form, time signature, a feature of expression, &c.—very simple, perhaps, but enough to prove they've been listening). I then mention something that I should have liked them to have noticed. The piece is played again and a show of hands indicates whether the point has been discovered. Further enlightenment and further playing, and so on. Questioning and comment are strongly encouraged and only insincerity (e.g. "It sounded like prim-roses in Spring") is discouraged.

A careful reading of this letter impresses me with the necessity of remembering that not only do not all pupils respond to the same treatment but, also, that not all teachers can successfully apply the same methods. We all have our own temperaments, and our work has to be done in such a way as to conform to these. I do not doubt that this teacher's plans (the result of twelve years' experience) are the best for him and that parts of them can be adopted by all of us. Some of his findings differ from those of other equally experienced teachers in similar schools, but they represent what is truth *for him*. He can apply the "orange-squeezing" principle; many teachers would ruin their work if they attempted it. He finds he must use program music very sparingly; some teachers can use it more freely without the bad results he has experienced. His views on "instrument spotting" in orchestral music would not be confirmed by all good teachers, nor could all good teachers use chamber music so successfully as he. The biographical approach, which to him is of slight value, has been found of high value by some others whose experiences I reproduce here. Most of us are quite accustomed to lower the needle on to the middle of a record, and, provided we do it gently, have noticed no ill effects.

The lesson of all this is *Quot homines, tot sententiae*. There are, it is true, general educational principles we must all accept, but as for what we may call the "devices" of education, rather than the principles, each of us has to select those which suit his constituency and suit *him*.

It is to be hoped that heads of schools and inspectors fully recognize this principle, as otherwise injustice may be done in expecting from one able teacher the following out of a scheme that has proved successful with other able teachers but which may not suit his individuality.

An Experiment in British Columbia.

The Rev. W. Arthur B. Clementson, of Horeham Road, East Sussex, writes a letter that is interesting as showing common sense at work, in an informal way, to find the entry to unprepared minds.

I am not a teacher by profession, but for several terms I had the opportunity of making some experiments with a gramophone in two country schools in British Columbia, namely at Keremeos and Cawston. The courses were continued longer and more thoroughly at the latter place. The children, boys and girls together, were aged between 10 and 13, though at Cawston sometimes some of the younger ones were allowed to come in and listen. . . .

My aim was first of all to get the children to believe that good music was worth listening to. Canada is a very unmusical country, and most of the children had only heard the crudest kind of music at dances or popular music on very imperfect radio sets. My theory was that many people do not appreciate good music because they do not listen to it, and they do not trouble to listen because they don't enjoy it—a vicious circle. So I set out to show the children How to Listen—some of the things to listen for, in order that they might *enjoy* more and more what they heard. This musical knowledge, such as I was able to impart, was entirely secondary to enjoyment. I used the blackboard freely and asked questions and got the children to ask me questions, but made no attempt to cram them with *facts,* either musical or biographical. I would sometimes tell them the name of the composer and, if there was anything interesting to children, something about his life, but was careful not to overdo biographical details. I exploited shamelessly the children's love of stories. I invariably found that the pieces that told some kind of a story, or were somewhat descriptive, were the most popular. It is perfectly true that such an interest might be entirely unconnected with the music and rest simply on the story, but in most cases the story actually helped the children to listen to the music and to notice the themes and moods, &c. I found then that Program Music was definitely the most popular.

One little girl asked me one day to put on "the piece about the golden ring, where they went over a bridge" (*The Entry of the Gods into Valhalla*). A small boy said he liked the "one about the guy in the vault" (Finale of *Aïda*).

I should say from my experience that children are more broad-minded in their taste than uncultivated adults. The latter like something that sounds familiar. Children, however, are quite ready to welcome something very new and strange provided that it appeals to the imagination.

I was very surprised to find how many of them voted for *La Cathédrale Engloutie* (Debussy).

I found that great interest was excited if I let them vote at the end of the lesson which piece they liked best. The program was written on the board, and each piece numbered. At the end each child wrote down the number of the piece he liked best. There was no copying the opinion of others; each had to decide for himself. This practice made them very attentive to each piece in order to decide which was liked best; it was also interesting to the teacher to study the results.

Next to imaginative pieces, I should say pieces with a rousing melody and a quick rhythm were the most popular. Orchestra was preferred to solo pieces, though some songs were liked well. String quartet music, even if tuneful and simple, was not appreciated. Symphonic music, as distinct from opera and program music, was found too difficult, though many liked Schubert's "Unfinished." I was glad to find that the children were quite unanimous in preferring the lovely second subject in the first movement (entering on the 'cellos) *in its original form* to the popular "waltz song" version, "The Song of Love" in *Blossom Time* (which was, I believe, an American version of what we know as *Lilac Time*).

I found them very interested in the instruments of the orchestra and in picking out the principal ones. For this purpose I used some records, "The Instruments of the Orchestra", giving each instrument separately, and some picture cards supplied with them by the Canadian Victor Co. (H.M.V.). As an introduction I played them the Prelude of *L'Arlésienne* Suite (Bizet), which interested them from the start by its lively rhythm: the first tune here is repeated four times with different orchestral tone color each time. Delius's *On Hearing the First Cuckoo in Spring* was a great favorite, chiefly, no doubt, from the fun of listening for the elusive cuckoo (clarinet).

Some of the best loved pieces, as far as I can remember (not a few of which benefited from your *Second Book of the Gramophone Record*) were as follows:

Peer Gynt Suite.	One record by Yehudi Menuhin.
Casse Noisette Suite.	*William Tell* Overture
Carmen, Overture and Entr'actes.	Some records from *Lohengrin*.
Selections from *Pagliacci*.	*Le Cygne* (Saint-Saëns).

One day, by way of teaching them to distinguish good tone quality, &c., in singing, I pretended that the children were to give me a singing lesson. I took a simple song sung by the baritone, Werrenrath, and played it through. I then repeated one verse myself, several times, taking care to make some mistake in words, rhythm, or tone color. The children were told to hammer on the desks if they noticed anything wrong, in which case they had to tell me what I was doing wrong. In this way I showed them the difference between a "white tone", "a throaty", "a nasal tone", &c., by comparison with our good model.

Then we had records of different types of voices, all of the best, singly and in combination. It was easy after that to trace the analogy between the voices of different instruments and the human voices, and to show how it was possible for different voices to sing different tunes at the same time and yet to secure a pleasing result, leading up to simple polyphony. One pointed out some of the more striking examples in some of the Wagner records, which some of the children, at any rate, were quite capable of appreciating.

It is impossible to estimate the result of these lessons. They were at any rate very popular, and I am sure that not a few of the children afterwards would listen more intelligently to music, when they had the chance. One tangible result was that, after I left the district, the Cawston School managers bought a gramophone for the use of the school and some records (I don't know what), so that any teacher who was musically inclined could carry on on similar lines, but what has actually been done since then I do not know.

The children mentioned above were just the ordinary school children at the government schools, children of farmers and fruit growers, not specially well educated, but mostly rather brighter than the children of English farm laborers, &c.

Thirty Years' Experience Summarized.

London musicians (and British musicians generally) know of the fine organizing work and the stimulating influence of a London school principal, Mr. G. Kirkham Jones, M.B.E. In asking Mr. Jones to give me some notes of his views I have begged him to put modesty aside and incorporate a statement showing the solid body of actual experience, of various kinds, that forms the basis of those views. This he has kindly done.

I. Foreword.

The most frequent organization of London Elementary schools is as follows:

Infants—3 to 7 years old.

Juniors—7 to 11 years.

At 11 scholars, as the result of the Junior Scholarship Examination, proceed either to—

Secondary Schools (the best in academic attainments).

Central Schools (the next best).

Senior Schools (the remainder).

At 12½ a small section go to Trade Schools for Technical Vocational Training.

All sub-normal children (physically or mentally) go to Special Schools.

By far the largest proportion of pupils are of average ability and attainment and enter the Senior Schools at 11 and leave at 14 years of age.

It will be assumed that all schools have an official graded syllabus in Music with formal training in Vocal and Aural Musical Work. Most of them have Instrumental classes, i.e. Violin Bands, Percussion Bands, and a few have Brass Bands and Reed Pipe Bands. Nearly all have Rhythmic Work such as Folk and Classic Dancing.

A few schools have wireless sets. Large numbers have modern gramophones. All have pianofortes.

Most schools have a regular morning service and other special assembly occasions (Empire Day, May Day, &c.) when music of one form or another plays a prominent part.

By common consent, no real success in so-called Musical Appreciation is possible without a solid foundation of Vocal and Aural Training. No unworthy music of any kind should be heard or sung or played at any time in any school (except, perhaps, as "the awful example"). Undue precocity in any one branch of school music is to be deprecated; a well-balanced syllabus is the ideal.

The broad musical road and not the long narrow path leading to dizzy heights of exceptional attainment is the one for the elementary school child.

II. *Personal Views and Opinions, Founded on Actual Experience.*

As an assistant master, I have had many years' continuous musical teaching practice in London elementary schools; I have been a Headmaster since 1916. I have acted as Inspector for the Board of Education, and have been a member of many official advisory committees on school music. I have given talks on music in schools and colleges of all kinds in many parts of the country and for three years gave the broadcast talks at children's concerts on Friday afternoons. I have served as adjudicator many times at competitive festivals. I was the inaugurator of the Battersea Concerts for School Children in school time and Chairman for the ensuing year of the London Schools Music Association. And I am the author of many articles, descriptive music rolls, &c. It is interesting to recall that I first used a Phonograph in a school music lesson in the year 1900 at Hatfield Street School, Blackfriars.[1] I have, therefore, had exceptional opportunities and experiences on the "Listening" side of Musical Teaching, and have probably made more mistakes than any other teacher with regard to so-called Musical Appreciation, but I have never feared to revise my opinion as the result of daily intimate contact with elementary school children and their *apparent* reaction to music.

I dislike intensely the word "Appreciation" and prefer Intelligent Enjoyment. I have found the former word so often means dull, boring lecturing at inordinate length on the mechanical structure of the form and texture of musical examples very often most ill-chosen.[2]

Speaking generally, music which makes more appeal to the performer than to the listener, to the intellect rather than to the emotions, music of merely historical interest, &c., is not entirely suitable to the immature child mind. This must not be taken to mean that the simply constructed music of past generations is more acceptable to children than the more elaborate, intricate, and "fuller" music of more modern times. Wagner and Tchaikovsky often make more appeal than Bach and Mozart. Essentials are brevity and variety, rhythmic vitality and melodic beauty—not necessarily "bright" music, for children often love mournful strains.

It is imperative that the performance should be "first class"; this cuts out actual performance by most teachers and means the use of wireless, gramophone, and pianola (in the future, the sound film), and visits to central concerts by reputable artists, or (in rare cases as far as elementary schools are concerned) small-scale performances at the schools themselves by these artists.

In any case, school children should be allowed to "wallow" in good music without any explanation as often as possible from their earliest school days.

I have found it necessary to break down in the minds of teachers and scholars the idea that Music, especially "heard music", is a thing

[1] I suggest that this stamps Mr. Jones as "the father of all such as handle" that valuable adjunct to Appreciation work. P. A. S.

[2] Here, as Chairman, I venture to intervene. Will a change of name for a subject rule out "dull, boring lecturing" on it? P. A. S.

apart in a "water-tight compartment." I have therefore tried to make music enter into nearly every aspect of school life (*vide* six articles in *The Teachers' World*, which I wrote in the Autumn of 1933).

Every Music Lesson (generally [1] called a singing lesson) must be a lesson in Musical Appreciation.

1. By wise Choice of Material—good choice of song.
2. By Voice Exercises chosen from the classics.
3. By a very simple Chat on the Musical Form of the Song, &c.
4. By a simple Chat about the Composer and his Period.

Make a collection of portraits of the great composers and pictures from the great masters dealing with musical subjects, e.g. *The Lute Player, The Concert, The Village Philharmonic, Boyhood of Handel,* &c. Get them as large as possible, frame them well, hang them in prominent view, often chat about them, make them "familiar in our mouths as household words." Why are so many school portraits merely of soldiers, sailors, courtiers, kings, &c., many of whom are better forgotten?

Make children familiar with the look and sound of musical instruments by picture and record and by "action song." And make them familiar with an instrumental score by easy stages from the percussion band onward.

There is a great wealth of interesting material in the lives and times of the composers; this should be incorporated in the History, Story, and Reading Lesson.

Also by easy stages and from the earliest times make the children familiar with the terrifying words to be found on any music program. This is where the skilful teacher comes in and the advanced academic musician goes out. How to do it is a matter of personality and not so much of profound learning.

This must be nearly always a cumulative process, e.g. children must learn to feel and not merely to know what a fugue is, by means of many jolly games such as the singing of many rounds and canons, spotting the hidden tunes, &c., and then by playing a complete fugue many times and getting the class to spot one thing at a time. Finally, divide the class up into sections, each to represent one feature in the fugue, e.g. subject, stretto, &c., letting each one spring

---

[1] This bit of basic truth will be warmly welcomed by many teachers in the United States. May every Musical Appreciation Lesson also be, as it is with Mr. Jones, a Music Lesson! W. E.

into appropriate action as and when each entry takes place. A little ingenuity will make inversion, &c., a reality and not an abstraction. Of course, many playings without action or remark, in strict silence and concentrated attention, must round off all teaching devices. The idea is to make them laugh at the often clumsy nomenclature of the musician.

For heaven's sake don't give them an essay to write afterwards or make them answer examination questions about these things. I try to make them feel and love beautiful music, not to dissect, describe, analyze, and hate it. Above all I try to get them to have their own opinions, likes and dislikes, and not to become hypocritical little prigs—to hum, whistle, and sing lovely tunes of their own accord and to persuade mother to buy a gramophone record other than a jazz tune.

It is frightfully difficult to get to know what children really think and it can't be done by the written question and answer method. Informal chats are the nearest approach to it. Draw attention to any musical event, e.g. a wireless program, the band in the park, even the music at the cinema, and then have a pally chat about it; and never crush an apparently honest opinion, however crude and unexpected it may be. Be prepared for many blanks and few prizes, all kinds of surprises and reversals of anticipations.

Applause, especially at massed scale concerts, is very deceptive—often merely physical relief and rebellion against enforced stillness. The tense silence of an audience of 1,000 children when thoroughly gripped by a fine performance of fine music is unmistakable and unforgettable.

Many children, especially girls, are too polite and grateful to tell the whole truth and some are incurable sycophants. Quite a few givers of appreciation concerts have been taken in by these little darlings. The B.B.C.[1] has been nicely led up the garden by letters and essays. I should be surprised if more than 5 per cent. of a child audience is really "appreciative" of the music as such. My aim is to increase this percentage by steady, patient effort in the future.

It is necessary to increase the children's opportunities for hearing the best music well played. They must hear the best *over and over again*.

When they go to a large-scale concert, they must be prepared beforehand (as a rule) and refreshed after by gramophone records

[1] The British Broadcasting Corporation.   W. E.

and a *little* but good talk. They must be fairly well aware of the technical names on the programs. At the concert itself, a few brief introductory remarks are absolutely essential—*brief and attractive,* about fifteen minutes in all to about forty-five minutes net playing time.

Sometimes a totally new and unexpected item "rings the bell." There is no cast-iron procedure.

III. *What Every School Needs.*

I should like to see in every school—

A really good "Pianola." A modern Gramophone. A Radio set.

A set of readable books on the lives of the composers and the interesting side of musical history.

A fine set of musical pictures and portraits.

A central core of records, &c., supplemented by those on loan from a circulating library.

Every district should have its school music association to encourage and hold music festivals and appreciation concerts, featuring every aspect and activity of musical education, and to arrange for specially gifted teachers to pay occasional visits to schools and give music chats.

And it should also have a group of fine players, permanently engaged by the Local Education Authority to give, on demand, say half an hour's music at any particular school, i.e. peripatetic listening lessons.

I am convinced that a gramophone, preferably a radiogram,[1] is absolutely necessary in every school.

(B) BOYS' SECONDARY SCHOOLS

A School Principal's Experiences.

The following lively description of varied and fruitful activities comes not from a musician but from a Headmaster, Dr. J. R. Kinnes, of the Secondary School for Boys, Stockton-on-Tees. Accompanying them is a program of the school's Speech Day which happens to have appended to it a list of the Examination Results and "Old Boys' Successes" of the year—one of such a character as to suggest to me that activity in music is no impedi-

---

[1] A duo radio-phonograph. W. E.

ment to steady work in other branches, but rather a stimulus
to it.

Let me say at the beginning that the whole of this extensive and
populous district is dead so far as good music is concerned. When I
first came to Stockton, there was certainly a Chamber Music Society,
but, after struggling along painfully for a year or so, it came to an
inglorious end when, at the last Concert it gave, we had to ask the
Artist if he would be so good as to take part of his fee on account,
and accept the balance after we had made a whip-round amongst
ourselves!

It is true that in Middlesbrough we have an annual series of some
half-dozen International Celebrity Concerts, but they are rather ex-
pensive, and, personally, I no longer go, simply because of the fury
inevitably aroused within me by the chattering ill-behavior of the
majority of the audience. I don't want to seem cynically "high-
brow" in this respect, but it seems to me that the women (and most
of the audience is female) go there not for musical but for sartorial
reasons; pea-hens, so to speak, and not song birds! The result is
that, apart from the wireless and gramophone, most of the 400 boys
in this School have never had the opportunity of listening to music,
and it was thus obviously part of my job to try, in some measure
at least, to make good the deficiency.

We have, like most other Secondary Schools, a Music Master who
is responsible for the ordinary class singing, but we are, I know,
especially fortunate in that our man, Mr. Gavin Kay, is an excep-
tionally good teacher. His name is well known in the North as an
excellent Choir Master and Choir Trainer, and, in consequence, our
school singing is particularly good. The only regrettable feature is
that, as he is a very busy man, he can come only twice a week to the
School, and so the senior Forms have no actual singing lessons. Just
on that account I make a point of never shelving his periods. I mention this because I was struck by the number of Music Teachers
whom I met at a recent music course who complained to me that
their subject was *the* subject to be dismissed if and when any short-
ening of the time-table had to be made for one reason or another; it
seems to be taken for granted in not a few schools that the Music
period is of secondary importance as compared with that, say, of
French or Mathematics, and can, therefore, be interfered with quite
cheerfully and unhesitatingly.

We are especially lucky here in having on the staff two men who are as capable as they are enthusiastic with regard to music. When, therefore, I embodied a course in Musical Appreciation and asked them to carry it out, they were only too willing. This course I am hoping gradually to increase; at present it is confined to the senior Forms—those, in fact, which do not have singing lessons. For the present, however, I must be content, for the two Masters in question have their usual work to do as well. But we are going to have a new and larger School in about two years' time and then, with a larger staff, I shall be able to extend the Musical Appreciation Course to the junior Forms as to the senior.

Perhaps I should remark at this juncture that the Durham County Council are wise and generous in their outlook upon educational requirements. Our pianos, for example, are good ones, and are properly and regularly tuned; requisitions for Music, Gramophone Records, Gramophone Needles, &c., as well as for books dealing with Music are always granted. Naturally, I ask for nothing outrageous; I would never try to bounce them into giving me a Bechstein Grand when an ordinary Rogers Upright does quite as well! But what we do ask for and get is well used and cared for. Our Music Library is something of which we are justly proud.

These courses in Musical Appreciation are easily one of the most popular subjects in the curriculum, and they are doing, I am perfectly convinced (and with all due deference to Ernest Newman), a great deal of valuable work. A lot, of course, depends on how such courses are carried out; I suppose any subject can be made a weariness to the flesh if its exponent is as dull as ditch-water. In our case, however, it is by no means infrequent that bursts of happy and appreciative laughter punctuate the lesson. Only yesterday, when I happened to look in for a few moments, I myself, a Scot though I be, and hence one who, I suppose, "jokes wi' deeficulty", guffawed loudly at the remarks being made about—dare I say it?— Ravel's *Bolero*. These two Masters, you will understand, treat Music as something human, and not as something mysteriously esoteric, to be mentioned only with a grimly solemn countenance.

Well, the logical sequence to this theory work seemed to point to the necessity for practice, so it is that we have, every Wednesday afternoon after School, a Concert open to any boy who cares to come. When the idea was first mooted, my two Masters wanted, and I think quite rightly, no kind of compulsion brought on any boy to attend.   No roll is called; you sit where you like and leave when you like and above all, we try not to make attendance "the thing to do."

Perhaps as a result of this, we have big audiences each time, and it is noticeable that the same boys always turn up, that is to say, boys fond of music welcome the chance given.   And if I may say so, these weekly Concerts are well worth turning up to.   Local musicians and friends have been extremely kind and we get all sorts of music —Piano Recitals, String Quartets, Song Recitals, &c., &c., and, of course, the School Orchestra.   Will you think me absurdly boastful if I declare that in all this district the only place where good music, well performed, can be heard, is in our School Hall, each Wednesday afternoon?

The School Orchestra involved a good deal of time and trouble to form.   It is a strange thing that so many boys have piano lessons as opposed to tuition in some other instruments.   At the beginning of each term I go round the School to find out how many boys have private music lessons; the answer is always the same—boy after boy learning the piano.   Now, at the start of each session, when I hold a meeting of parents, I urge them to consider the claims of the violin or of the 'cello; the response is not all I should like it to be, but so far it has been good enough to allow us to keep the Orchestra going.   (I am now trying to form a violin class on the Bonner system.   It's stiff going, but it's dogged as does it!)

You will rightly understand how difficult the matter is.   For each new session means the loss of a certain number of members of the Orchestra, and this loss has, of course, to be made good.   At present we have 18 violins, 2 violas, 3 'cellos, 1 double-bass, 1 cornet, and 1 flute (the last two cannot be used very often) and, of course, as many pianos as ever we want!   And apart from one or two appearances at our Wednesday Concerts, its first public appearance this term will be on Speech Day.   I am enclosing a Program in which the Orchestra appeared positively for the first time in its existence; a great occasion it was; I could hardly sit quietly in my chair, bursting as I was with sinful pride!

Lastly, we have our own Annual Inter-house Musical Festival.   One friend of the School presented us with a silver cup and early in December we have a proper field day.   The proceedings are carried out in proper style; an outside Adjudicator is present and no results are made known until the end of the day, when the cheering and counter-cheering gives ample evidence of the general enthusiasm. Singing, solo or otherwise, instrumental playing, &c., &c., figure in the Syllabus, and one of the funniest, as well as most delightful things to see, is the way in which Smith minor, for example, aetat 14, conducts his choir of eight youngsters in some part-song, or the ill-suppressed fury of Smith major when one of his string quartet breaks a fiddle-string!

Intensive Work with a Senior Class.

Here is a fine example of the kind of work that can be done with a class of seniors who, by analogy with their serious study of literary texts in various languages, can be brought to see the value of similar study of a masterpiece of music. The writer is Mr. A. F. Milner. His experience in definite Appreciation Class work with young children is certainly not that of some other teachers, and here I am tempted to say that he has somehow not yet "found the way." But when it comes to work at the top of the school I feel that few or none of us have anything to teach him.

I am Director of Music at the Royal Grammar School, Newcastle-upon-Tyne (about 800 boys), and have held other similar posts ever since I was demobbed in 1919. Almost from the commencement of my career as a schoolmaster I have made various attempts to provide more music than is expected from the usual time-table, with varying results. I firmly believe that the best way to "appreciate" music is to *do* it, especially with young children, and my first step to increasing interest has always been to form a voluntary choir which meets outside ordinary school hours.

Concerts of music provided by really able artists have proved very successful and greatly enjoyed by the children; and such concerts afford an opportunity of going over the program beforehand in such a way as to prepare them for what they are to hear. I have found that compulsory appreciation classes with very young children (8 to 13 years of age) are only of slight value. At that age children are too restless to take the matter seriously enough to derive much benefit from them. They will sing all day and enjoy it but do not seem so interested in the "works."

The most successful class I have ever had, and I still have it, is the VI form (one section which is free for a period on Monday mornings) at the Grammar School. This class consists of boys ranging in age from 16 to 19, and a very earnest lot of boys they are, too. I always tell them at the outset of the course that the lesson is not going to be a pleasant way of filling in three-quarters of an hour listening to nice sounds, but something that will require their active co-operation mentally if they are going to get anything from it. The course proper commences with a very concise survey of musical history (with copious illustrations, all fully explained): this is followed with three to four lessons (the hardest part of the course to the class) explaining *at the keyboard* the meaning of various musical terms which everybody ought to understand. Such explanations include:

(1) A thumb-nail sketch of Harmony. I find this can quite easily be done, as all members of the class have been through my hands when they were juniors and are able to do the usual staff-reading of the standard customary in secondary schools. With this foundation and with the aid of the music-blackboard, it is quite simple to show how our system of harmony is built upon a series of superimposed thirds, to explain suspensions, modulation, passing notes, &c. I have always found classes very interested in this part of the work, and singularly quick in grasping the essentials.

(2) An explanation of "counterpoint" and "contrapuntal" by homemade examples (e.g. a tune well known to the class first of all played with a plain harmonic background and then with a second accompanying voice in free counterpoint).

(3) The meaning of various terms such as "augmentation", "diminution", "canon", &c.

(4) "How the Composer works"—a short summary of the varied devices by which a composer builds up a movement out of his germinal idea or ideas. I have found that this part of the course gets home best if I take a tune well known to them and show them the ways in which it might be extended by elementary development. (I enclose specimen of this type founded upon *The British Grenadiers*.[1] From this it is a short step to more serious examples from

---

[1] This is an ingenious treatment well calculated to serve the purpose in mind. I remember that my friend, the late Sir John McClure, LL.D., D.Mus., Headmaster of Mill Hill School, composed a symphonic movement, using the Coster Songs *Liza* and *Knocked 'em in the Old Kent Road* as his two subjects. I got his permission to use this as an illustration of Sonata Form in my *Listener's Guide to Music* (1919), but found it did not reduce well to a piano arrangement, and so abandoned it. It was a moving composition! P. A. S.

the works of great masters. (I always find them very interested in
an analysis of Brahms' Intermezzo in E minor, Op. 119, as an instance of a movement evolved from a single germ—especially in the
major mode metamorphosis in the middle section.)

When this ground has been covered I proceed to Form proper and
take them through Binary and Ternary, Rondo, Fugue, and Sonata
form. All the work is done by analysis at the keyboard: if I can beg,
borrow or steal enough copies of Beethoven's sonatas (or if any
members of the class can bring copies from their homes) so much
the better. But I am convinced that the work can only be truly
beneficial when students have the music in front of their eyes.

The next stage is a short course of score-reading. Here I have the
advantage of a remarkable Headmaster (Mr. E. R. Thomas), who
has obtained the permission of the Governors for me to order practically anything I require for my work. In my department's library
I have many works in miniature score (including all the Beethoven
Symphonies)—*not less than six copies of each*. These are handed
round the class, and the boys are taught how to follow a score during performance. I generally start with a Mozart Symphony. I have
seen various writers advocate the use of string quartets as a first
step to acquiring facility in score-reading, but I believe that a quartet
with its overlapping of the violin parts (and others, too, occasionally)
and its homogeneous timbre is much more difficult to follow for a
tyro than an early Symphony with its clearly-marked differences of
tone-quality in wind and strings. So Mozart generally opens the
ball (at this year's course it was the G minor Symphony).

As soon as the boys develop reasonable ability to understand the
score, we proceed to the analysis and study of as many great masterpieces as it is possible to crowd into the remainder of the course.
For instance, during last Term, and so far in this, we have analyzed
in detail the above-mentioned Mozart, Beethoven's Eighth, and
Brahms' Variations on a Theme by Haydn. They are first analyzed
at the piano and then played over on the gramophone, section by
section: after which a complete performance is given without further
explanation, but with the scores in front of the boys.

If we have any important concerts in the town I generally go
through the principal items beforehand with them: last week, for
instance, we had the London Philharmonic Orchestra (Beecham)
doing Beethoven's Third and Sibelius' *Tapiola*. I dealt with both
these works beforehand, though in the case of Sibelius we were

handicapped by having no scores (there are no miniature scores available, and I didn't feel like imposing on the generous good-nature of the Headmaster and Governors by ordering half a dozen full scores at 30s. each): the Beethoven scores were already in the library.

I don't suppose you want any information about the School orchestras (we have two, numbering about seventy all told), as their work is rather outside the scope of the subject. But one matter arising from them I feel does come under the heading of "appreciation": whenever we have a well-known conductor in the neighborhood I always try to arrange for the members of my school orchestras to attend a rehearsal. The Headmaster is always very willing to grant permission for this, providing the conductor is of the same mind. We have attended several rehearsals in this way, including two with Sir Henry Wood, who came over to speak to the boys before starting, and was very pleased to see a number of miniature scores in evidence.

Musical Work in a North Irish Public School.

Four years' experience in an important North Irish school of about 300 boys (80 of them day boys, the rest boarders) are recorded in the memorandum that follows. The author of this is Mr. A. E. F. Dickinson, of Campbell College, Belfast (his really admirable book, *Musical Experience: what it is and what it might be,* must be known to many readers). I the more seriously ask for a careful reading of Mr. Dickinson's account of his experiences since some of the views on which his general scheme is based are not quite my own. This memorandum, in some degree, indeed, serves as a set-off to the thesis of my section, *Hearing and Doing*—to which the reader may care to turn again after reading what follows:

(When I went to Campbell, my predecessor modestly informed me that so far as appreciation was concerned, I should find virgin soil. This was not true. He had provided two concerts a year, all first-rate in material and mainly home-grown. But the *general* musical interest did centre round the performances of a well-trained choir and band, and less upon the music itself. So I decided to start as if at scratch.)

Although I had had the great opportunity of watching the late

A. H. Peppin [1] revolutionize the musical taste of at least an intelligent majority, as mere listeners, I soon discovered that an interest in thinking in sound demanded a higher standard of general intelligence [2] than I found at Campbell, and that education must come chiefly through sensitive performance. This has not ceased to be the general situation. The most cultivated musical minds are all performers, and the nucleus of interest in music comes always from the orchestra, the pianists, and the choir. I therefore attach first importance to what is done to promote the wide existence of ultimately experienced performers, from whom an intelligent grasp of certain music is chiefly communicated to the rest, by the usual process of personal infection, if at all. The less regular and far less intensive experience which is offered to non-performers can only supply a flavor, not a vital presentation, of music.

Appreciation Through Performance.

1. The ORCHESTRA contribute one substantial piece to each of the two School Concerts of the year, besides accompanying the choir. In the third term they usually rehearse part of the program given by my outside orchestra, both with a view to three preparatory concerts and with a view to the final concert. They thus thoroughly study an overture and part of a symphony, and probably part of an oratorio; and "swim in" a larger program (the orchestral concert). I have introduced new composers gradually, and when introduced, rather intensively. Haydn, Mozart, Schubert, Beethoven, a little Wagner, Elgar, Holst, and Vaughan Williams, have been the principals so far (the orchestra has been going three years).

A realization of the distinctive qualities of different music naturally comes into rehearsal, and the structural interest of music receives attention in the preparatory concerts.

Most of the unquestionable musicians are in the orchestra. Even capable pianists who play an orchestral instrument tend to give up the piano rather than the orchestra.

The BAND (Military Band) also contribute one or two pieces, generally arrangements of Purcell, Handel, &c., and in the third term tend towards lighter stuff. They are not all musical or even fond of music, but they learn to play in time, and with a reasonable

---

[1] Mr. Peppin was at Clifton College and then at Rugby. Mr. Dickinson was under him at the latter. P. A. S.

[2] "No, musical intelligence!" (a boy critic). A. E. F. D.

tone-control, also the value of inner parts. The orchestral wind are naturally recruited here.

In addition, Band and Orchestra deputize for the organ every day, in a hymn. They thus develop at an early stage all the essentials of personal musical experience, and imbibe on a large scale good and well-harmonized melody.

2. PIANISTS and other soloists are encouraged to play off each piece to another music-master, if not at a junior or senior concert; to read regularly, and to take an interest in music beyond their own noses. A good many seem to arrive at a vital stage of experience, even if they are unskilful. It has been difficult to find time for chamber-music, but occasionally this has taken place.

3. The CHOIR annually rehearse (1) a cantata or part of an oratorio, (2) unison songs of all sorts, (3) unaccompanied music. Purcell, Handel, Haydn, Bach, Parry, and Vaughan Williams have provided the nucleus of the last four years.

It is easy to be in the choir. I exclude from the treble classes (in school) only the utterly voiceless. Trebles on the descent are accepted as altos, tenors, or basses, and I never refuse any boy who wants to join (as bass or tenor). A large portion of the school (rather less than half at any given moment) thus enter from the inside the realm of folk-song, oratorio, and madrigal, and learn to appreciate the different features of different styles, as well as the sensation of singing in parts. In addition, I give (still rather experimentally) a modicum of historical instruction to the treble (in school) classes. In their first year I am chiefly occupied in explaining a few processes such as the evolution of different styles at successive ages. In their second year (if their voices hold out) I can go deeper. Any such irrelevancies would be resented in the alto, tenor, and bass practices, out of school.

4. The NON-CHOIR (or more strictly the non-choir led by the choir) sing a hymn daily, and have two practices a term for this. In addition, they sing a group of unison songs at the end of each school concert. (When I first arrived, I tried the non-choir in a part of the oratorio, &c., in a school concert. The musicians protested, the seating conditions were revealed as objectionable, and, most of all, the number of tenors and basses in the choir increased 50 per cent. a year later, and again a year after that. I therefore judge that all who are capable of taking any real part in an oratorio are already in the choir, and that the singing feeling, if new, is sufficiently sug-

gested in the unison songs which are *a priori* much more suitable communal material.)

Appreciation Through Trained Listening.

1. CONCERTS WITHOUT COMMENT. Chiefly the two school concerts, an orchestral concert and an outside recitalist. The school attends (besides its own non-choir rehearsal) the rehearsal of the school concerts; program notes (one page on the whole program) supplied. For the orchestral concert, fuller and musically illustrated notes.

The gradual introduction of new composers and new styles seems to work well. Vocal items are naturally the most popular, but these include oratorio-selections, and there is no rooted objection to an orchestral overture or movement. Chamber-music not yet arrived, nor even a good piano recital—for the enjoyment of the many.

Modern music (i.e. post-Parry) not popular. Handel, Beethoven, and Schubert the chief winners. Some Brahms, Haydn, Mozart, Wagner, Mendelssohn, Parry, Vaughan Williams (folk-song side). Usually the school makes a good audience, as a whole—as schools go.

2. CONCERTS WITH COMMENT, i.e. the three preparatory concerts to the outside-orchestra concert. Analysis by *playing* in bits, or by program-notes. Little talk. Chiefly familiarizing in sound. Response doubtful. Few except the orchestra and a few pianists interested enough to want to hear the final concert in advance.

3. Appreciation-classes, called INFORMAL MUSIC. Odd music played by myself weekly, with occasional comment. Little attended. No inference possible, except that no one will or can give up the necessary time.

4. A MUSIC COMMITTEE to whom I can explain myself and who can offer suggestions.

Some Inferences as to the Most Promising Environments.

1. The appeal of the familiar is a very strong one, and its absence a strong hindrance. But the unfamiliar may fairly quickly become numbered amongst familiar things if it is tactfully presented and, once unrejected, persevered with. Thus, at the time of writing (after four years' experiment), Mozart is fairly certain of a hearing, in one movement; *a fortiori,* the more rhythmic Beethoven (orchestrally) and the more tuneful Schubert, Mendelssohn, Handel; *a fortiori,* the more dramatic appeal and singing tone of oratorio; *a fortiori,*

the direct simplicity of *Loch Lomond,* at once melodious, well-constructed, rhythmical, and emotional in an easily apprehended way. "Program" music always constitutes an appearance of the familiar. *The Marriage of Figaro* is more congenial than "G minor", and a song recital than a piano recital. Any piece over 5-7 minutes will not make itself at home to non-performers, unless it has a program basis. The appreciation of the representative element is not, of course, the essential part, but it makes an easier starting-point than purely formal relations.

2. Regular performance is far the best approach to encourage. Singing is most popular (less time and less to pay, *inter alia*); blowing the next (the next to nature?); thumping and bowing third. But permanent results come from the hardest instruments, i.e. piano and orchestral instruments. (By permanent I mean in after-life. I am able to observe old boys more than usual, as many live in Belfast.)

3. Mechanical performances of previously unheard works never very convincing unless there is a mechanical interest (an unfamiliar instrument or instrumental effect).

4. Biographical information never attempted, unless this includes the musical origins of a work (patrons, fashions, &c.) or contemporary criticism. Musically historical information, very briefly set out, useful.

Attention to the "program" interest, if any, can easily be secured. (But this needs much more careful handling than I have observed in many school "programs", which are aesthetically most misleading; it is far too commonly assumed that given music "exactly expresses" this and that emotion of waking life—and nothing more of importance. The approach from waking life at the expense of aesthetic satisfaction should never be encouraged; it will arise enough without that.)

Analysis always difficult going in a crowd. It remains a cardinal necessity, and no sound rising musician seems to deny this.

5. The approach to aesthetic experience sufficiently vital to lead on and on and on from the school starting-point must always greatly depend on the personality and resulting methods of the official musician, headmaster, and others. The critical progress from an indulgence in various gregarious impulses to genuine aesthetic satisfaction depends on a happy co-operation of the headmaster, jolly school concerts, &c., on the one hand, and of sound musical direction

on the other. Concerts where roars of applause (or even of "singing") are the chief feature point to a lack of this second factor.

With all due modesty I must record that Campbell has produced
distinctly more critical boys than when I first went; critical in my
way even (i.e. more of the music and what I consider relevant
features than of other things). I am satisfied that my main concentration on the performer does not lead to aesthetically very barren
experience, and *never need if the hypothesis of the teaching of performance is a musically inspiring experience.*[1]

As I have hinted above, I do not wish to comment in detail
on the very interesting detailed report. I would like to say two
things, however: (*a*) that the last fifteen words of the report
(which I have italicized) are of importance as bearing on all that
has preceded them; and that (*b*) one way of testing the report
would be to translate all its terms, so far as possible, into those
of the teaching of English Literature and to consider to what
extent the curriculum and methods laid down would then be
considered satisfactory, as offering a sufficient initiation. Admittedly everything done at this school is excellent, and the only
considerable subject for debate that I suggest to thoughtful
readers is as to whether, on the *normal boy* leaving the school,
he takes with him *all* one could give him. It would be very
interesting if we could look ahead and know whether Mr. Dickinson's views and methods will be just the same after four years'
further experience, i.e. after four years of building *on a foundation laid by himself.*

Support from the Poets and Philosophers.

Mr. Arthur Baynon, well known as a composer, sends particulars of the work done under his direction at Caterham School for
Boys, Surrey. This is a school of 200 boarders and 120 day boys.
At least one period a week is devoted to music in every form
except the sixth (confined to boys who have passed their University Matriculation Examination, of which boys there are about

[1] The thought expressed here in italics is basic. Not only performance, however, but every branch of musical education, including Musical Appreciation itself,
should take for its hypothesis the provision of a musically inspiring experience.
Much argument would be silenced were this well understood. W. E.

forty in the school, indicating, of course, a high standard of teaching throughout).

Mr. Baynon's letter concerns the Musical Society, which meets fortnightly, and constitutes a climax to the work done in the music classes. Membership of the society is free and voluntary. The meetings are held on a week evening during the winter term and on Sunday evening during the summer term. They are not open to the juniors. The attendance of those qualified to be present·rises as high as 90 per cent. in the summer. The attendance and the keen listening of the boys (of whom visiting artists always speak as "a good audience") is taken as the criterion of the school's musical work in general.

A study of the large number of programs sent shows a very high standard. Songs, Madrigals, String Quartets, Piano Solos, Orchestral Compositions are all of the highest class, and it is only on scrutiny that one realizes the care that has been taken to choose from the repertory such works as can be expected to make a special appeal to the boy mind. This combination of the highest standard of artistic excellence with special suitability to the audience is, of course, the ideal to be aimed at in performance to young people. The *big* long things are included, but they are skilfully interspersed with lighter, shorter things. In general the programs are mixed ones, i.e. there are few one-man or one-medium programs.

A feature of the printed programs is the appearance at the bottom of each of a passage commendatory of music from some standard author. The cumulative effect of such quotations must have value, as showing the appreciation of the art by minds not devoted to music in any specialist way. A few examples are here given, as suggestive to others who have to compile such programs.

It need hardly be pointed out that meetings of the kind described (fortunately increasingly common nowadays) have one advantage denied to the Appreciation Classes to which they form so desirable a complement. Being extra-time-table and voluntary the atmosphere is entirely unacademic.

Music, thou queen of heaven, care-charming spell,
That strik'st a stillness into hell;
Thou that tam'st tigers and fierce storms that rise,
With thy soul-melting lullabies;
Fall down, down, down, from those thy chiming spheres
To charm our souls, as thou enchant'st our ears.

(Robert Herrick.)

There is in souls a sympathy with sounds,
And as the mind is pitched the ear is pleased
With melting airs of martial, brisk, or grave,
Some chord in unison with what we hear
Is touched within us, and the heart replies.

(Cowper.)

Music resembles poetry; in each
Are nameless graces which no methods teach
And which a master hand alone can reach.

(Pope.)

There are few delights in any life so high and rare as the subtle and strong delight of sovereign Art and Poetry; there are none more pure and more sublime. To have read the greatest works of any great poet; to have beheld or heard the greatest works of any great painter or musician is a possession added to the best things of life. (*Essays and Studies,* by A. C. Swinburne.)

Among all the sciences this (Music) is the more commendable, pleasing, courtly, mirthful and lovely. It makes men liberal, cheerful, courteous, glad and aimable—it exhorts them to bear fatigue, and comforts them under labour; it refreshes the mind that is disturbed, chases away headache and sorrow, dispels the depraved humours, and cheers the desponding spirits. (Bede.)

All the Arts are brothers; each one is a light to the others.

(Voltaire.)

Preposterous ass, that never read so far
To know the cause why music was ordained!
Was it not to refresh the mind of man
After his studies or his usual pain?

(*The Taming of the Shrew,* Act iii, Sc. i.)

He that would his body keep
From diseases must not weep;
But whoever laughs and sings
Never he his body brings
Into fevers, gouts and rheums.

(Beaumont and Fletcher.)

Music, the greatest good that mortals know
And all of heaven we have below.

(Addison.)

Some Experiences in Phonograph Teaching.

The following practical remarks come from Mr. W. W. Johnson, of the County School, Gillingham, Kent, whose writings on this subject, in the journal *The Gramophone* and elsewhere, are well known.

From my own experience, boys *are* easily bored by the gramophone (not the music). And the reason is not merely that musical reproduction by gramophone and loud speaker is plentiful, but that there is a serious glut of it which tends to destroy our taste for it. In my opinion, unless the musical educationalist can supply reproduced music *at least* as good as the *average* loud speaker in the homes, however good the music he has to present, it is likely to be belittled. In my own case I am not over-keen on listening to music on other people's gramophones if their machines are not as good as mine. And I am sure that this is equally true of the young pupil. So I feel it should be stressed and stressed again that schools must possess good and up-to-date machines if pupils are to listen. Otherwise there is a danger of falling into habits of "awareness" that music is being played (not listening, by any means, and a step below even *hearing*)—habits that more than 50 per cent. of the population are acquiring simply because wireless is turned on in the morning, and in some cases left running all day. We were not up against this problem five years ago, but we are to-day; and goodness knows what will have happened in another five years!

So we not only have to make the music interest the pupils, but we have to see that the reproduction is really good.

The more music I come into contact with myself, the harder it is to choose music for pupils. Some of the most excellent examples I have come across have in practice been failures. *My* tastes do not seem to satisfy my pupils. I regret to say I am compelled to spend much valuable time "trying out" records. "This modern music", which often terrifies us, often greatly attracts children. For this reason, I append a list of records which have interested 90 per cent. of the boys between 11 and 15 years on whom they have been tried:

Honegger, *Pacific* 231. Saint-Saëns, *Carnival of Animals.* Rimsky-Korsakov, *Flight of the Bumble Bee.* Schubert, *Erl King.* Sibelius, *Swan of Tuonela.* Daquin, *The Cuckoo.* Rameau, *La Poule* (Harpsichord).

All the above for Descriptive Qualities.

Mozart, *Pastoral Variations & Cadenza* (Harpsichord). Dohnanyi, *Variations on a Nursery Tune.* Arensky, *Basso Ostinato.* Purcell, *Trumpet Voluntary.* Schubert, *Marche Militaire.* Grainger's recorded works. Lambert, *Rio Grande.*

The above for Form.

With reference to illustrations of musical instruments for use in conjunction with lessons on the Orchestra, I have now adopted the new Victor Talking Machine Co.'s set of *colored* diagrams (price 15s.). These are better than some other sets because each instrument is on a separate sheet. Moreover, there is a text-book, valuable in many respects, but in others most inaccurate (e.g. Elgar photographed at about the age of 30, is placed among the great *conductors* of the world!).

My scheme for the teaching of FORM, which, as you know, has been the subject of many articles in *The Musical Times* recently, is entirely my own, and, if I may be allowed to judge my own work, has been of interest as well as successful. A bare outline of it, which to my mind is psychologically sound, is as follows:

Begin with PURE REPETITION.
1. Of Melody.
    a. "On top."
    b. In an inner part.
    c. As a bass (Ground).
2. Of Rhythm.
3. Of Harmony.

Thence to REPETITION WITH CONTRAST (Binary form leading to TERNARY FORM).

Thence by further expansion to the RONDO FORMS.

And by internal expansion to MINUET and TRIO and SONATA FORM.

For the FUGUE, which I leave till last, I begin with ROUNDS and CANONS, then your "Camouflaged tunes", then "Messiah" choruses, and finally Bach Clavier and Organ Fugues—not forgetting to end up with the amusing Berner's C minor Fugue for Orchestra. I have heaps of examples for my lessons on Form, but have no room to mention them all here.

Reverting to lessons on the Orchestra; whether you intended it or not, your *Columbia History* is providing excellent material for illustrating each instrument—piano, oboe, clarinet, flute, drum, &c. I am hoping that future volumes will contain examples of the bassoon, French horn, viola, &c., while carrying out their prime historical functions.

For the past four years I have given an appreciation test to boys who have had a two-year course with me. My test piece, which I find excellent for the purpose, is Pierné's *Entrance of the Little Fauns* —not a masterpiece in itself, but not generally known, and therefore very suitable. I set about fifteen questions, involving such matters as date or period, title (suggested), adjectives describing it, pattern, a question on the formation of the coda, time, rhythm, phrase-lengths, instruments (solo and accompanying), orchestration, modes or scales, &c. The boys find it most fascinating, and though they rarely score more than half-marks, work like Trojans to arrive at conclusions. If you don't know the record, which is Columbia 9518, I commend it to you. It is interesting and intriguing.

(C) GIRLS' SECONDARY SCHOOLS

A Complete Scheme.

"*I should have failed in my duty if . . .*" Miss Annie O. Warburton of the Manchester High School for Girls, sends a most thoughtful description of her plans there, as follows:

In this school I am fortunate in having all girls up to the age of 14 for two periods a week, including Singing. After that girls who decide to take music as a subject in the School Certificate examination are adequately catered for with three periods a week (more in the VIth form). For the rest there is a singing lesson, in large groups from sixty to a hundred, and extra activities such as dinner-hour concerts for those who wish to go, but no more regular general music lessons. As, owing to time-table difficulties, only a few girls join the School Certificate Class, and those not necessarily the most musical, the bulk of the girls have no more definite training after the age of 14. I believe this state of affairs is very general in Girls' Secondary Schools, even where the music is good.

Now I should feel that I had lamentably failed in my duty if those girls left school unaware of what a symphony is or how to listen to it, or of the significance of such figures as Bach and Beethoven. I consider that they would be musically uneducated—and this in a world of wireless and gramophone where they cannot escape symphonies if they wish to do so. If they are going to hear them in any case, surely it is better to help them to listen intelligently than to let them join the mass of listeners to whom symphonies are unintelligible, and therefore not to be tolerated.

Yet I am sure it is unwise for children to hear large-scale works. They are beyond their intellectual and emotional grasp and may inculcate a distaste for Classical music. In my early days of teaching I made this mistake, though I think, even so, that a feeling of the greatness and significance of the work often came through. I frequently meet old girls who remind me in glowing language of some music they heard in class and tell me how much it has meant to them—though probably I have forgotten all about it! I remember in my early days taking the first movement of Beethoven's Fifth Symphony with most classes in the school. Even the eleven- and twelve-year-olds sensed its rhythmic drive and appreciated it tremendously in their own way. Yet nowadays I would not take a movement as long as this at such an age.

I will outline my solution of the problem respecting the Symphony. In the IVth forms (ages 12 to 13) I make first mention of the symphony, but practically all they learn about it is that it is a big piece of music written for orchestra, generally in four movements; quick, slow, minuet or scherzo, quick. I take as illustration Mozart's *Kleine Nachtmusik* and I want to stress that I go into no formal detail at all. They sing the themes before hearing the movements, and I give them a very rough, non-technical outline of the general plan. The listening is "listening in the large."

At one time I dealt with separate movements and with sonata form before dealing with the symphony as a whole. I am convinced that this is the wrong way round and only creates confusion. But note that my example has been very carefully chosen, and is simple, short, and charming music well within the child's power of understanding. (Perhaps I ought to state that the children have been discovering "how composers build pieces" right up the school and know about phrases and sentences and such simple terms as binary and ternary, episodical and rondo. But all examples have been very short and simple. Also this Mozart example is, of course, only part of the IVth form work.)

In the Upper IVths (ages 13 to 14), the last year in which I have all the girls, this side of the work culminates in a set work which we study just as they might study a Shakespeare play. Again I choose a short and simple work well within their understanding, and have found Haydn's *Clock* Symphony excellent for this purpose. We study it throughout one term in considerable detail and the outline of Sonata form is now given. We get to know the music thoroughly. I tell the girls that if they know one symphony really well they will know how to find their way about when listening to others. I warn them that they will find other symphonies longer and more complicated, but make them understand that the essential principles will be the same.

My present solution of this difficulty, then, is to let the girls know the main facts which will help them to listen intelligently, but to illustrate with simple music not beyond their powers of understanding, in the hope that they will apply their knowledge to more complex works as they grow older. One can only grow the seeds of understanding; it is quite impossible, as well as unwise, to study an extensive literature of masterpieces. I consider that my introduction of a set work to complete the junior Appreciation scheme is one of the best innovations I have ever made in my school work.

All Appreciation work is done in the Aural Training lesson, and I spend from ten to twenty minutes every fortnight with an occasional whole period in the more advanced stages.

This letter is already very long but I should also like to say a little about the use of the gramophone.

If I were one of those unfortunate teachers who could not illustrate at the piano I should certainly use the gramophone in preference to having no music at all. But as I can play I use the gramophone very little in the lowest forms. I have studied this matter carefully and I have come to the conclusion that it is unwise to let children hear an orchestra on the gramophone until they have heard the real thing, though I know this is a counsel of perfection for those who do not live in a town. But even a pier performance on a holiday has *some* value.

A gramophone reproduces in miniature. The musician, with his knowledge of the orchestra, unconsciously turns the miniature into a large-scale painting, but the child cannot do so. I believe that a good pianist can give a truer picture of the grandeur of an orchestral work on the piano than a gramophone can do. And there is certainly no question which the children prefer.[1] They leave the room after listening to the piano feeling that they have had a treat. The gramophone is merely the gramophone. Also if the work is at all noisy or complicated the gramophone miniature will be a confused one. I myself have had the experience of listening unmoved to a record of an unfamiliar work, and of then hearing a performance of it; on re-hearing the same record afterwards it has seemed most moving and magnificent. How much more so must this be with children!

I do not mean to imply that I could do without a gramophone— it is unthinkable. For teaching something about the various instruments, for preparing for a concert, and for all advanced work, it is invaluable. But I believe I get the best use out of it by using it discriminately in the lower forms. There is also the further point that a gramophone undoubtedly tends to make the teacher lazy!

The following comments may be offered on this valuable statement.

1. For American readers it may be explained that the School Certificate Examination is a school-leaving examination conducted by a University, and if passed at a certain standard serving also as a University Entrance, or Matriculation Examination. The optional subject of Music in this examination has of late years come to be taken more seriously by school authorities. For some years I myself, as it happens, occupied the position of Examiner in Music for this examination of London University, and at that time it was perfectly clear that many schools were entering pupils in the subject on very slender preparation or even none at all. Now, apparently, Music is taken more seri-

---

[1] A discussion in the *American Editor's Preface* is recalled here. In the light of it the disinclination of this teacher to use the phonograph *in lower forms* is interesting. But the modern electric recordings have banished this bugaboo. W. E.

ously. The value of the examination as a stimulus to better musical work in schools depends largely on the syllabus; in my own judgment, any lingering traces of the thoughtless assumption that this examination is a preliminary to further musical study in the university should be removed from the syllabus. The idea should not be to treat this examination as the entrance to a new course in Music (which it can be for only a very tiny percentage of pupils) but to make it the culmination of the musical work of the whole school life. While it should certainly call for a final year's strenuous work in Music, there should be eliminated from it any tests that require special preparation in branches of Music that otherwise would not be thought necessary or suitable as a part of the school curriculum. It should, in fine, look back and not forward, and so doing should exert a stimulating influence on the musical work down to the lowest classes.[1]

2. I should like, in the strongest fashion, to endorse the paragraph beginning "Now I should feel that I had lamentably failed in my duty. . . ." That puts the big general case for Appreciation in a nutshell.

3. I do not quite understand the feeling this writer has against the practice of treating Sonata Form before treating the Symphony as a whole. Taking her admirably chosen Mozart example, it is clear that in earlier years of school life she has initiated the pupils into the essentials of form and even into all the forms, other than Sonata Form, that are found in this particular work. She is now, in effect, introducing Sonata Form in its logical order, and, apparently, with pupils of 12 to 14. I see no reason why she, as a pianist, might not have taken Sonata Form still earlier, and I do not grasp why, when it is taken, the movement illustrating it must necessarily be associated with these other movements (could not a Mozart or Beethoven overture have served—a complete symphony then following?). In fact there is a point here that clearly eludes me, but perhaps some

---

[1] The matter of this paragraph has wide application. Secondary schools in the United States are struggling to emancipate themselves from a "preparatory" curriculum for the hosts who should pursue a culminating course. W. E.

readers with experience more similar to that of the writer I am quoting may better understand her intention. Anyhow, I see nothing *against* her practice.

4. The idea of studying a "set work" in the way in which, in the English class, a Shakespeare play is studied, has a great deal to be said for it, but it must be remembered that insufficiently skilful teachers of English are every year prejudicing thousands of children against Shakespeare (or so we are often told), and any music teacher not quite sure of his or her power to maintain the interest of a class throughout a course of detailed study may still do fine work by treating a larger number of compositions somewhat more briefly and lightly. Of course the principle of "knowing one symphony well" as a means of knowing how to "find the way about others" has, in itself, considerable attractions.

5. The points about the phonograph (gramophone) are interesting but do not quite convince me. To be candid I am left wondering whether the particular phonograph in use at this school is quite as good an instrument as its teacher deserves! The personal experience mentioned seems to me to *be* a personal experience, and, moreover, the deduction drawn is not the only one possible, for we may take it for granted that with a new and unfamiliar work the third hearing would in any case have much more significance than the first. Then I do not quite realize how the phonograph makes a teacher lazy; to prepare (with the score) a good phonograph lesson on a symphony movement means some hours of intensive work. However, I feel that all that this experienced and obviously very thoughtful teacher tells us is worth our closest consideration, and my own opinions on it are put forward somewhat tentatively.

6. I see in this letter no attention to the historical side of Appreciation work, but we may assume that this is not neglected. Probably it receives incidental attention throughout the course, and in that case two or three lessons devoted to assembling logically in the pupils' minds the individual facts accumulated would be very valuable. Perhaps such lessons are included.

"Opening All Possible Doors."

Experience gained in a girls' secondary school of the highest class is set out in the following by Miss Gwendolen M. Webster, of the Streatham Hill High School, London:

1. *Best Methods of Gaining and Retaining Interest of Pupils of All Ages.*

Works for young listeners should be short and there must be more playing than talking. Very young children like to take part. They can beat, clap, sing suitable portions or begin to use percussion instruments. The band must be used carefully and must never become more important than the music they try to perform, therefore let drums and the louder instruments be in the minority.[1] After the age of 9 or 10 I think bands are not suitable.

2. *Singing Classes.*

All songs must be of real musical worth—folk, national, or modern ones, of which there are so many of highest merit. Hymn tunes should be carefully chosen.

3. *Old Dance Forms* are universally popular. Minuets from Haydn, Mozart, or early Beethoven, sonatas, or symphonies, are known and loved even by small children.

4. *Biographical Information.*

I find with younger children this comes best after the music has been heard. With older ones it naturally forms part of the study. Some children gain their first interest through this side and in a large class it is always worth while opening all possible doors to the understanding of the music.

5. *Analysis.*

Analysis will keep many alert who otherwise have nothing to hold on to, but first and last the music must be presented unspoilt by comment of any sort. Here I am repeating this, but I so firmly believe in trusting the works of great masters to find their way into children's minds and affections that I am always loth to spoil the music by too many explanations and directions. It is hard some-

---

[1] In Appendix F (American edition) the use of percussion bands in teaching Musical Appreciation is treated more fully. W. E.

times, though, to strike the happy mean between this and letting a class sit passively hearing sounds poured into their ears.

6. *Use of Gramophone.*

As a general rule an actual performance, even a pianoforte arrangement of an orchestral work is of far greater value than a record. When a class has its interest aroused and is ready for more detailed study, then is the time for a gramophone. If scores can be followed, however vaguely at first, much good is done. We generally manage to secure one or two full scores and possibly a solo or duet arrangement and find great interest is aroused, eye and ear being co-related.

For detailed study of quartets or symphonies or before a visit to an orchestral concert the value of the gramophone is incalculable.

With older classes I find discussions of wireless programs of interest. I think the ultimate effect of broadcasting will be that more listeners will want to perform themselves for their own pleasure.

The sentence in the above that I would like to stress is: *"It is always worth while opening all possible doors to the understanding of music."* This is a reminder to us of the danger of narrowness in our methods; necessarily there is an element of "hit or miss" in all education, and what may miss one child may hit another. The views as to the relative positions of piano and phonograph are, of course, those of a fluent pianist; for many teachers (especially in elementary schools) they are obviously not valid. The linking of school appreciation work to home radio listening is very sound indeed, and the opinion expressed as to the "ultimate effect of broadcasting" is cheering in view of an opposite opinion often heard.

A Definite Syllabus Outlined.

A typical syllabus of the treatment of music in the better English secondary schools of to-day is that of the Girls' High School, Wakefield, Yorkshire, sent by the organizer of its music, Miss Louise M. Dawe, A.R.C.M. It will be observed that in what follows there is no mention of vocal work (beyond a little sight-singing); we may assume, then, that this is done in a separate series of classes.

I outline here the scheme of "Musical Appreciation" in this school. The weekly class in this subject has proved of the utmost benefit to the school. The forms are graded according to ability, so that the more musical girls are placed together as far as possible, for a 40-minutes' lesson. Beginning with a few minutes in Singing at Sight, using the Folk Song Sight-Singing Series (Oxford University Press), the class proceeds to practise in Dictation, Melody Building, Phrasing, Modulation, and Form in Music, including Opera and Oratorio. A graded Syllabus is planned for the whole year (I append a copy).

The Gramophone is used freely, and we use the *Columbia History of Music*.

We find great interest taken in works such as the Dance Movements of Bach's French Suites, or the Older Rondo Form as exemplified in a Mozart or Haydn Sonata, after the children have understood the *form* of such works.

Almost always towards the end of the class a talk on the Orchestra and its instruments is given (including the showing of a violin, viola, clarinet, or bassoon by the leader of the School orchestra); or a short sketch of the life of a composer, with a movement played from some of the aforesaid composer's works. We find that amongst others the following are of proved interest.

Bach. Two-part Inventions.	Schumann. *Kinderscenen.*
" French Suites.	Schubert. Impromptu in A flat.
Handel. Water Music.	Tchaikowsky. *Nut-cracker* Suite.
Mozart. Sonatas.	Debussy. *Little Shepherd.*
Beethoven. Sonatas in F minor and C major.	MacDowell. *Woodland Sketches.*
	Dunhill. *Pied Piper.*
Schumann. Album for the Young.	Balfour Gardiner. *Noël.*
	Grieg. *Peer Gynt* Suite.

We notice too, that the children come and ask us what music was played as a Voluntary just before our Morning Prayers, also tell us with enjoyment that such and such a work "was heard on the wireless last night"; also that they are made keen to take up the playing of an instrument to join the school orchestra. We are glad too to have a Library of standard works for the girls, which they may borrow and take home to read.

The syllabus leads one gradually to Fifth Upper work, i.e. the Music Syllabus for this subject in the School Certificate of the Northern Universities.

It is, of course, difficult to find enough time for all this unless the Headmistress (as is the case with us) is sympathetic towards Music as a school subject.

Syllabus.

Kindergarten and Form I. Recognition of Time-names.[1] Tonality. Pitch. Conducting. Percussion Band.[2] Stories of Composers.

Forms II and III. The same, and in addition Phrasing and Knowledge of Binary and Ternary Forms. Lives of Bach, Handel, Mendelssohn, Schumann.

Forms IV Lowers. Mental memorizing of melodies. Melody-making. Binary and Ternary Form. Orchestral Instruments. Dictation. Lives of Composers and some knowledge of works of the same composers.

Forms IV Middles. Invention of Melodies. The setting of sentences of poetry or two short lines to a rhythm on *one* note. The Older Dance Forms.

Gramophone Records. Folk Music of different nations. Compositions and their composers.

Forms IV Uppers. Modulation to related keys. Intervals. Rondo Form. The Sonata. Musical History—style, personality, period. Composers' lives and works.

Forms V Lowers. Advanced Tonality. Rhythmic work. Memorization. Dictation. Harmony with primary triads. Music from an historical standpoint.

Work in Girls' Private Schools—and in Some Others.

The following notes come from Mrs. G. F. Hilton, L.R.A.M., A.R.C.M., whose varied experiences have included Abbot's Hill, Hemel Hempstead; Hermitage House, Bath; and the Manchester Training College—amplified by work with Percussion and Pipe Bands [3] and other devices in private practice as a piano teacher.

---

[1] A system of syllable names for rhythm-forms. The name for a one-beat note is *taa;* for a two-beat note *taa-aa;* for two equal notes in a beat, *taatai;* for notes 1½ and ½ beats *taa-aatai.* The system was originated in France by Aimé Paris, was adopted by John Curwen in his Tonic-sol-fa method, and has been widely used in England. W. E.

[2] See Appendix F (American edition). W. E.

[3] The pipes are made by the children from lengths of bamboo. Because of the comparative ease of their manufacture and the quality of the music that may be obtained from them they probably represent the best form of such

Experience in Private schools has shown that the teacher of Appreciation is usually responsible for the piano lessons also; so that instead of having time to meet each class separately, it is necessary to group several together. The division has been as follows:

(*a*) Kindergarten . . ʌges 4– 6 years
(*b*) Transition . . . " 6– 8 "
(c) Forms I and II . . " 8–10 "
(*d*) * Forms III and IV . . " 10–14 "
(*e*) * Forms V and VI . . " 14–17 "

(*a, b, c*) KINDERGARTEN, TRANSITION, FORMS I AND II.

Although these classes are taken separately, in three groups, the work of all consists of:

(i) Singing of simple Nursery Rhymes and Folk Tunes (dramatized if possible).
(ii) Free Rhythmic movements to express character, time, or shape.
(iii) Band of Percussion instruments for rhythm and color.
(iv) The addition of a Pipe band for Form II.

The Child and the Masterpiece may be brought together in the Kindergarten by the singing of traditional airs, free movements to simple music of Bach, Schumann, Mozart, &c. (in addition to the purely rhythmic music of Dalcroze and others), and the playing of Percussion instruments.

Music used is of strong rhythm and contrasted tone in the early stages. (See list.)

There was failure with the youngest children, when an effort was made to do more advanced Band playing than they were capable of at this stage.

A successful device was that of a child conductor choosing instruments to suit his music (King, Queen, &c., in *Sing a Song of Sixpence*).

In Kindergarten and Transition no talk about composer or music was given but sometimes one would begin with "Here's a jolly tune", or "Is this music sleepy or wide-awake?" &c.

creative work. They are now widely used in England and have received high educational endorsement. Dealers in music and music supplies advertise materials and tools for making them and much excellent music arranged for them. W. E.

* These two groups have only one 40-minute lesson a week, which has to be shared with Aural Culture.

With Forms I and II any short story about the composer of music being used was given. The children are unconsciously learning Form in Band playing [1] and in some of the rhythmic movements.

I have not used gramophone at this stage, but children listen to Nursery Rhymes, &c. on their own gramophone at home.

Dramatization of short scenes to suitable music is valuable, e.g. *Bethlehem* (carols), *Pied Piper* (dances), *Alice in Wonderland, Flower Scenes* (movements of arms, head, body). Suggestions come from the Children as to what the music tells them to do.

The difference in the three classes is that the work in the Kindergarten is purely unconscious. The Band in the later classes develops from playing pulses only, through various stages to the reading of pieces from individual scores. (See *The Percussion Band,* by Yvonne Adair, 1s., and *Children's Percussion Bands,* L. E. de Rusette, 3s. 6d.)

Music is used from Handel, Schubert, Mendelssohn, Purcell, Beethoven, &c., as found in the *Rhythmic Band Series,* arranged by Ernest Read. The Pipe playing for the children of 9 and 10 years can be used for many of the Folk tunes and arrangements of classics.

Some Music used at Stage I (Kindergarten, Transitional, Forms I and II): *Songtime,* M. Shaw. *March and Dance Album,* Somervell. *British Marches for Schools,* M. Shaw. *British Nursery Rhymes,* Moffat and Kidson. *English Folk Songs for School,* C. Sharp. *National Song Book,* Stanford. *Album for the Young,* Schumann. *Lyric Pieces,* Grieg. *Ecossaises,* Beethoven. *In Cheerful Mood* and *Valse Miniature,* Rebikof. *Rosamunde* (2nd Entr'acte), Schubert. *Gavotte* (Five Pieces), Balfour Gardiner. *Country Gardens,* Grainger.

In addition, music by contemporary composers for rhythmic movements, percussion band, and songs.

(*d*) FORMS III AND IV: AGES 10–14.

Use is made of *A Child's Path to Music,* by E. A. Allen (Forsyth Bros. 3s.), for method of approach. Music illustrations given in this are imaginative, with strong melodic outline; others deal with the beginnings of form. They are for piano and gramophone.

Music with a story background, such as Grieg's *Peer Gynt* Suite, is always successful. The children are at the story age, and this gives them something definite to listen for. Using story music is danger-

---

[1] One is disposed to think that the fact stated here seldom receives the emphasis in thought to which, by reason of its importance, it is entitled. W. E.

ous, unless it be given in addition to music chosen for beauty of form, which should be analyzed. (See list.)

These Ten Steps in Appreciation are followed by *The Complete Book of the Great Musicians* by P. A. Scholes. Music is chosen which applies to the lesson.

The Piano is mostly used for illustrating (because of lack of funds); the gramophone for a few orchestral pieces.

A large colored chart has been used which shows musicians in their centuries, together with artists and writers.

Some Music used for Forms III and IV: *Forgotten Fairy Tales* and *Woodland Sketches*, MacDowell. *Noël* and *London Bridge*, Balfour Gardiner. *Shepherd's Song*, Roger Quilter. *The Swan*, Saint-Saëns. *Golliwog's Cake Walk*, Debussy. *Valse Triste*, Sibelius. *Scenes of Childhood*, Schumann. *Norwegian Bridal Procession*, Grieg. *Spring Song*, Mendelssohn. *First lessons in Bach*, Books 1 and 2, Carroll.

(*e*) FORMS V AND VI: 14–17 YEARS.

Lessons with definite analytical teaching (the teacher using Dr. Carroll's *Notes on Musical Form*, Macpherson's *Form in Music*, and Macpherson and Read's *Aural Culture and Appreciation*, Books 2 and 3 for this). The lessons deal at the same time with the effect of the period on the composer; nationality in music and so on (*Learning to Listen* [1] by P. A. Scholes, Parry's *Great Composers*, Colles's *Growth of Music*, Walker's *History of Music in England*, and latterly P. A. Scholes's *Listener's History of Music*, Vols. i, ii, and iii, for reference).

Modern music and the Romantic School of composers are preferred, and in this order: for orchestra, piano, or voice.

The class is inclined to mistake brilliance for beauty, and to follow the personal preference of the teacher. The amount of keenness shown by students at an orchestral concert or opera, quite justifies the time spent on Musical Appreciation.

The expense of gramophone records means that without a big outlay on the teacher's part it is not possible to procure as many as are needed.

Some of the best pianists illustrate (arrangement of concertos for 2 pianos, Bach Chorales, &c.), also singers.

Discussion is encouraged, and comparisons with art and literature are drawn.

[1] Out of print. P. A. S.

Some Music for Forms V and VI: *Preludes*, Scriabin. *Berceuse, Dragon Fly*, and *Finnish Lullaby*, Palmgren. *Dance for Harpsichord*, Delius. *Towing Path*, Ireland. *Witches' Dance* and *Sea Pieces*, MacDowell. *La Cathédrale engloutie* and *Clair de Lune*, Debussy. *Lullaby*, Bax. *Bavarian Highlands*, Elgar. *Chorale*, Bach-Rummel. *Jesu, Joy of Man's Desiring*, Bach. *Pastorale Variée*, Mozart. *Études*, Op. 19, No. 1, Poldini. *Romance in A flat*, Arensky. *Prelude in F*, Pachulski. *Chanson Simple*, Glière. *Berceuse*, Illynsky. *Valse in A flat*, Tchaikovsky. *Waldesrauschen*, Liszt. *The Juggleress*, Moszkovski. *Intermezzo* (*Carnival*), Schumann. *G minor Ballad*, Brahms. *3 pieces for Harpsichord*, Robert Jones. *Italian Concerto*, Bach. *Water Music*, Handel, arr. Harty.

And any of the well-known pieces of Bach, Handel, Haydn, Mozart, &c.

Some Gramophone Records used in Forms V and VI: *Now is the month of maying*, Morley. *Silver Swan*, Gibbons. *He shall feed His flock*, Handel. *Surprise Symphony*, Haydn. *Nutcracker Suite*, Tchaikovsky. *Unfinished Symphony*, Schubert. *Peer Gynt Suite*, Grieg. *Prize Song*, Meistersinger, Wagner. *Midsummer Night's Dream Overture*, Mendelssohn. *Pomp and Circumstance*, No. 1, Elgar. *Linden Lea*, Vaughan Williams, and other songs.

When taking classes for Musical Appreciation in Elementary Schools (boys and girls), Private Schools (girls), and Training College, the method differed according to the conditions.

The keenest listeners were found in the Elementary Schools, where (in the early days of Appreciation) there was no tradition to follow, the child bringing an unprejudiced mind to the lesson.

In the Elementary Schools a piano only was used; in the others, a gramophone also, when available (when it was not, a series of dinner-hour concerts at a small charge supplied half the cost of an instrument, college funds doing the rest; this was in a Training College).

The students were taken, at a reduced fee, to local concerts, opera, and Bach's Passion music, after lessons on the particular work in question. They were encouraged to join Public Libraries, where (as in the case of the Henry Watson Library, Manchester) there was plenty of available music to be taken home and studied.

In schools use was made of wireless programs to be heard after school hours, reference being made at the lesson to coming music of interest and themes played where possible.

The taking of *Music and Youth* (now *The Music Student*), together with the formation of one of its "Music Clans", spurred the interest of the younger members of the school, and the use of music notice-boards (one for current musical news, the other for pictures of musicians, &c.), were helpful.

In boarding-schools which were out of reach of good concerts, the girls heard recitals of piano, violin, singing, and old instruments by visiting artists, as well as fortnightly recitals, or music lectures given by the resident staff. There were three open practices a term of their solo work. The school chapel helped to provide music of a different type, such as plainsong, and in addition, an orchestra, singing classes, and Eurhythmics were further means of Appreciation. There were no regular class lessons in this subject.

Informal Ways of Working Up Interest in Music.

Less formal ways of cultivating a living interest in music, and of providing a definite basis of musical knowledge, are briefly described by Miss Jessie Cruse, of the Central Secondary School for Girls, High Storrs, Sheffield.

1. I found the girls had no general knowledge of composers and the periods in which they lived. It was impossible to do much in the regular lesson, with its aural work, sight-reading, &c., so I have begun using *The Book of the Great Musicians*. We use vol. 1 in the First Year, as a home reading book, and follow it by vol. ii in the Second Year. Occasional questioning shows whether the work has been understood and the girls in general are very much interested in the books. By the time the Third Year is reached, when the girls can specialize in music if they wish, they have some foundation of music history on which to build.

2. The younger girls are encouraged to make "music books", pasting in cuttings, portraits, &c. The work is quite voluntary, but some of the girls have made quite interesting books.

3. We have formed a Music Circle, which holds meetings fortnightly after school; pieces are played by the girls (this week they are giving dance tunes, &c., from Bach's suites), or we have a gramophone recital, illustrating different types of music.

4. We are forming a Music Library, so the girls can have plenty of music to browse in, if they wish.

5. I try to encourage the girls to take the monthly journal, *The Music Student*. Ten girls are now taking it.

(D) SOME SPECIAL EXPERIENCES, EXPERIMENTS, AND VIEWS

The Teacher's Own Mental Attitude.

Mr. G. A. Stanton, L.R.A.M., A.R.C.M., Supervisor of Music in the Montreal Protestant Schools and formerly Lecturer in Music at Macdonald College, P.Q., sends me the following thoughtful reflections arising out of his long experience.

The success of a lesson depends greatly upon the teacher's own mental attitude. There is a distinctive slant of mind peculiar to each subject, which is the secret of efficient thinking in that subject. You cannot teach French well in a geography disposition of mind, nor poetry from the arithmetic angle. A well-designed time-table is a sequence of psychological "moods and tenses", not a patch-work of subjects. Of course all the subjects are more or less related, but each has its own unique mental or emotional twist which is auto-matically assumed by the teacher and unconsciously adopted by the class.

Subjects in which emotion and imagination are chiefly engaged, in which cold facts are of secondary importance, suffer most from an unfavorable teaching bias. Facts in literature, drawing, poetry, and music must be taught accurately, but the main issues are far beyond, in the realm of ideality. Too many lessons in the "cultural" subjects are so concerned with the bare facts that intrinsic values are lost. Our children cry for bread and we offer them a stone. In teaching music the intellectual difficulties often obscure the aesthetic objective. Music has its roots in the cool soil of reason, but its fruits grow only in the sunlight of beauty. *Sursum corda*: "Lift up your hearts!" The aim must be idealistic, the method artistically business-like (a seeming paradox), and the spirit of the procedure consistent with both. These are not stated in order of importance. Purpose, method, and spirit, like the sides of a triangle, form one design. Let us briefly consider them separately.

1. *Aim*. Music is an art. The purpose of a music lesson is essen-tially artistic. It must seek to develop the aesthetic susceptibilities of the pupil through lovely tonal impressions; to convince him that

good music is a vital manifestation of man's higher nature, a vision of the beautiful, the good, the true, the infinite. This is the impressional phase. On the expressional side, the aim of music teaching is to enable the pupil to express his ideality through a musical medium, voice, or instrument. Technical training with all its problems is here involved—a perilous sea in which many a barque of musical promise has foundered, but which must be crossed nevertheless. The gaze of the pilot-teacher must be steadily fixed upon the beacon, *Ideality,* for guidance. For what shall it profit a student if he gain a whole world of technique and lose his artistic soul in the process? [1]

2. *Method.* Music and method have a curious affinity in some minds. Pianoforte, violin, vocal, sight-singing, theory and similar music "methods" are legion. While most of them have their good points, a teacher who relies entirely upon some ready-to-wear system would be better employed in a dry goods store. A good method is a useful tool in the hands of a skilful teacher; but when it becomes a mechanical routine, a frictionless groove, or is in danger of adoration as a fetish, its discard is overdue. As teachers you are accustomed to judge methods by their results. In music the most manifest results are often misleading, for imposing superficialities are obtainable by sadly miseducative means. The most worthwhile results are imponderable. There is no adequate test for growth in aesthetic enjoyment, musical insight, refinement of taste, broadening and deepening of sympathy, and other marks of progress in artistry. A method which balances the technical and the artistic, with a very decided leaning towards the latter, is worth consideration. The wise teacher will preserve an open mind towards new ideas. Out of his experience in proving different systems he will evolve a method of his own, partly eclectic, partly original. Objectively there are two distinguishing marks of a good method: it is in complete accord with the aesthetic character of the subject, and it accomplishes its purpose by the most direct means.

3. *Spirit.* Even with the best intentions and a satisfactory method the music lesson will be a failure unless it is animated by the right spirit. Like all the arts, the true function of music is to express beauty. I have sometimes defined music to children as "beautiful ideas in beautiful sounds." The spirit of beauty must pervade our

---

[1] The discussion in the *American Editor's Preface* of perceptive as contrasted to intuitive attention comes to mind in connection with this page. W. E.

music teaching. Does it? Are we always careful to invoke this delightful but evanescent spirit? It is easily banished by any sort of ugliness, such as inartistic material, drill-sergeant repetitions, lack of insight, an irritable or hectoring manner. Children love music; but when it is associated with unpleasantness, distaste is engendered, a consequence to be avoided at all costs. We are all very tired of hearing about the ideal virtues of the perfect teacher, that de-humanized paragon who in the flesh would probably be shot on sight. Therefore, instead of drawing up a futile decalogue of class-room ethics I will suggest merely one practical hint. It is in regard to the correction of errors, a prolific source of trouble. Mistakes will occur, and frequently too. An error should not be treated as a criminal offense, an outrage, and least of all as a personal affront. Without a doubt, children always want to do the right thing. Give them credit for an honest motive, and try the plan of correcting errors in (shall I say?) a sportsmanlike way. Some musicians like to be thought temperamental. When it is not a mere pose it is just temper, and deplorably a-mental! The teacher who is thoroughly imbued with the spirit of beauty will make every lesson a beautiful experience to the children.

Without claiming any originality or finality I venture to submit a formula as the basis of music teaching, in the hope that its principles and their implications may serve to raise our school music teaching to a higher artistic plane: (1) an aim which is idealistic; (2) a method which is economical, adaptable, productive, consistent with the aim; (3) a process in which the spirit of beauty breathes into each lesson the breath of life.

A Blind Musician's Views.

I call particular attention to the one contribution that comes to me from a blind teacher with blind pupils—and to be a Blind Leader of the Blind is no disqualification in the country of the ear. The following has been received from Mr. H. V. Spanner, B.Mus., F.R.C.O., whose fine musicianship and musical memory are the admiration of those who know him. To say that he can play you at demand anything whatever from the whole "48" and most of the organ works of Bach is to give but one tiny hint of the range of his musical memory and his close acquaintance with the musical repertory, and I mention it here merely for its bearing on some of the remarks he makes below.

I trust that what Mr. Spanner says will be very carefully considered by the reader, since he is in the position of being compelled to get his own "appreciation" almost entirely through the bodily organ nature supplied for the purpose and to appeal to his pupils through that organ also.

I. *Aural Training.* The fact that blind children are compelled to use their ears, in place of eyes, in order to get about by themselves, results in an early development of the habit of "listening", and the aural discrimination between sounds becomes much easier for them. The difference between the pitch of notes is easier for them to recognize in consequence; and I consider that when they know the sol-fa notes of the scale, with *fe, taw, maw,* and *law,*[1] they know all that is necessary as a foundation. The power to recognize the four cadences, and to trace simple modulations to related keys, should be easily. enough acquired by them—and in my experience it *is.* Time seems to be a difficulty with many of them; but time is not merely an aural acquirement, but a mental one; and since the Braille music notation is simply the application of the Braille reading system to new purposes, it can easily be understood that a remarkable gift of intelligence is needed to carry both in the mind at once—for the child, at least. Blind children are not, as is sometimes conveniently supposed by the ignorant, more musical than seeing children; they have *not* better memories; they have *not* an uncanny power of insight into things that seeing children find difficult to learn; what they *have* got is the power to "listen" with all their ears (if they want to—not otherwise), and to discriminate sounds rather more readily at first than most seeing children.

It has been said that aural training should be based on musical appreciation, but this is putting the cart before the horse, and in consequence the cart has been built far too large. The fact is that if aural training is to be thorough (and I am not convinced of the invariable necessity of such thoroughness) it must be taken as a separate subject, like physical training, and the pupil must face hard work.

I am convinced that, however careful one is, any deliberate teach-

[1] According to usage in the United States: fi, te, me, le (Italian pronunciation). W. E.

ing of this subject to children is decidedly near the edge of boredom. It is all very well to say that ear-training must be the result of musical experience; but directly you get to actual music, you get to something like fairyland for the child (I believe it should be so with us all), and I feel that it needs the very greatest care to prevent the finding of notes of the scale, modulations, cadences, and what not, in a fine bit of Beethoven from becoming something like disillusionment for the child under sixteen—so much care in fact, that the benefit is hardly worth the risk.

I said that I am not convinced of the need of a thorough course in ear-training as a guarantee of the ability properly to listen to music. Which knows most about real music—the person who cannot tell what time or key a piece is in, but will make a personal sacrifice in order to have the money for a Bach or Beethoven concert; or the gold medalist who has the whole thing at his finger's ends (literally and figuratively), and then turns, "fed-up", to jazz for his real recreation? The test of a man's literary education is not his proficiency in analysis and etymology, but his power to read, write, speak, and understand when he is spoken to. And how did he lay the foundations of that education? Not through the text-book, but by the conversation of his family and associates, and by the reading of good literature for himself. So it is with music. In the days when the Appreciation movement was started, musical performances were something of a luxury; now every one can have them wellnigh free, and music can do its own teaching far better than any of its votaries.

II. *Musical Appreciation.* I have tried, as far as I can, to follow this line with my children. I believe in being systematic, but beyond this, I fancy it does not much matter what the plan is for children between the ages of eleven and sixteen, so long as the music is always good. Long pieces should be avoided at first; but apart from this, complex counterpoint or straightforward harmony seem to appeal equally, so long as I put them forward in an interesting setting. I am taking selections from the first three albums of the *Columbia History of Music,* together with *The First Book of the Great Musicians* (which is unfortunately not in Braille yet); and my children enjoyed Weelkes's "Fantasia for a chest of viols", *The King's Hunt, The Silver Swan, Rejoice in the Lord, Jesu, Joy of Man's Desiring,* and the first movement of Haydn's *Drum-roll* symphony, with equal relish. I have familiarized them with the sound of the harpsichord and the virginals, the choir and the orchestra; I have given them a clear, if general, idea of two- and three-part form, and even of first-movement form and the air with variations; and they know not only some stories of the lives of the composers we have taken, but a little about the difference between these composers as men—and I am sure they look forward to the class.

It is likely that these children would need special preparation for examinations; but examinations are not yet a passport to human life; and the examination candidate must face hard work. Examinations in musical analysis are the best possible antidote for genuine musical appreciation; so that, where possible, I keep examination work entirely out of my mind in teaching (or rather trying to inspire) this ability.

III. *Performance.* Finally, sight-singing, piano-playing, &c. are no guarantee in themselves to the would-be "listener." Their help in this respect only lies in the fact that they *may* familiarize the pupil with more music than he is likely otherwise to hear. But even that benefit has gone now, thanks to the wireless and gramophone; and the hard work of practise by itself simply makes the child tired of the piece practiced, unless he has the love of it beforehand, or unless the teacher can inspire him with that feeling. The study of performance is excellent in and for itself, and every one should be able to play or sing music, just as every one should be able to write and speak as well as read and listen. But, once more, we learnt to speak and understand chiefly through the speech of others, heard and read; and the time is fast coming when the clumsy methods of aural training now practiced can give way to the natural perception of the child, and music can teach itself.

Securing an Initial Interest with a New Constituency.

Mr. S. Hodgkinson, B.Sc., writes as follows from the Battersea Central School for Boys, London.

At this school where I am a Mathematics Master, it has long been customary for masters (and visitors occasionally) to give lectures to the whole school on Friday afternoons from 3 to 4 o'clock. These lectures are usually accompanied by some form of picture—either slides, or photographs reproduced by epidiascope, or cinema. Also the lectures usually illustrate some part of the lecturer's own teaching subject.

My own subject, mathematics, hardly lends itself to lecturing with a popular appeal, so, although not the music master at this school, yet being very definitely interested in music (and a fair pianist) I decided to try the effect of an Appreciation lecture when my turn came.

My first lecture I gave by merely selecting a number of pieces, which I played on the piano, giving a little informal chat about each in very simple language—any stories about the pieces also finding a place.

Considering that I was lecturing (quite alone) to about 400 boys, many of whom must have had very limited ideas about music, I was not discouraged by this experiment. One fact, however, emerged very clearly, i.e. that boys very definitely like the martial type of music. Elgar's *Imperial March* seemed really to stir them.

I gave another two lectures on this plan and the results were similar in each case. It was obvious, however, that something further was needed to make the effort a real success. So I hit on the following plan. Before describing it, I should like to make it quite clear that the *sole aim* is to *interest boys,* hence the *exaggerated* pictorial and descriptive ideas. It is essential to arouse *interest first,* so it seems to me, even if the road one has to travel is not very true to musical principles as understood by the musician.

I proceeded as follows: I took a number of pieces, four of them, all in an approximate A B A form (very approximate, but the aim has succeeded if *any* idea of form gets home), wrote a short leaflet about them and duplicated a hundred copies, sufficient for one between two boys (I had previously persuaded the headmaster to let me have the school in two halves of 200 boys each, a junior half aged 11-13 and a senior half aged 13-16).

Then I prepared four charts or diagrams, one for each piece, consisting of a color strip (color chosen with some regard to the type of music). This strip, I divided up proportionately to the length (in bars) of each section of the music; the B (middle) section I differentiated by coloring a darker shade of the same color. Superimposed on this I drew a graph which, by rising and falling, by thickness of line, by sudden rises or falls, indicated the emotional progress of the music—and occasionally the rise and fall of the notes in addition. All of this, had, of course, to be very carefully and simply explained to the boys.

When actually tried out, the experiment seemed a great success, so much so that I was encouraged to prepare another talk *On Listening to Music* and a further one to be given shortly, *Seven Pictures in Music.*

In order that I could show my idea easily and quickly to any one interested I prepared the little booklet enclosed with this letter.

The booklet mentioned is in manuscript, and as its value depends mainly on its ingenious colored diagrams, I cannot draw upon it. The whole scheme strikes me as a good one for its purpose—to secure an initial interest, to awaken the first stirrings in the hearts of the heathen! It does not carry Musical Appreciation very far, but it certainly makes an excellent "entering wedge", and to put the eyes at the service of the ears is, of course, good strategy.

An Attempt at Connecting Music and Color.

The following has been sent me by Miss D. D. Sawer, formerly Art Lecturer at the Diocesan Training College, Brighton, and author of *Everyday Art at School and Home,* published (with foreword by Sir Michael Sadler) by Batsford, London.

In an Elementary school with children of 6-8 years, being the end of the term before Christmas, I took two classes for experimental drawing; about 80 children. The children had their water colors and plenty of paper.

I asked them to listen while I played, and then paint what the music made them think of; they could paint either the picture they had thought of or the colors only. I played a few bars several times over of different types of music; between each the children had time to paint.

They listened quietly and painted industriously for some time after each piece of music; scarcely any were restless; apparently they could nearly all explain what their colors meant, though it was impossible to question each child with so large a number.

With a Minuet some painted children dancing, some made a pattern. After playing a few bars of the "Moonlight" Sonata (first movement) I found a little girl who had painted a grey mass going to a peak at the top, with black strokes projecting from it; she explained that the music made her think of a regiment of soldiers marching over a mountain.

All the children seemed interested and happy to work.

I had been taking these children once a week for color work for some little time.

With Training College students, I have often played short passages of music, and asked them to put down what colors the music suggested.

The same color scheme would be shown all through the class of about twenty-five students, gay rapid music producing orange, red, and yellow, sad music purple, dark green, grey, and so on; the idea was to use music in connection with expression and imaginative painting, and also to try to show connection with Poetry and Literature. Later pictures were painted to express the music.

The students were always interested and worked; some of the results were good, but the object was to rouse thought and give outlet for emotion rather than to produce a picture.

When drawing autumn leaves the beauty of curves was especially studied and connected with rhythm; a few students would take a curve or group of curves, and from the rise and fall or shape found in the leaf, find notes that could be worked into music.

I found that even to think of the rhythm of the shapes in this way roused interest in a wide field of beauty that is seldom observed.

I have had students who would design music from the colors found in their plant study.

Correlation with Language Teaching.

The following is of interest as suggesting one means of awakening an interest in the German Lieder. It comes from Mr. W. Lamb, master of the King Edward VI Grammar School, Aston, Birmingham.

For a number of years it has been the custom at our school for boys who take German to learn a number of songs which they sing in that language. We begin with two or three simple folk-songs and then proceed to Schubert and Schumann. Last year the boys in Lower Va (aged 14-15) learnt the following songs:

Heidenröslein	Schubert	*Mein*	Schubert
Das Wandern	"	*Liebesbotschaft*	"
Wohin?	"	*Erlkönig*	"
Meeresstille	"	*Die beiden Grenadiere*	Schumann

The most popular song (probably on account of its subject-matter) is, I think, *Die beiden Grenadiere; Mein* and *Liebsbotschaft* have been criticized as sentimental; *Erlkönig* I am inclined to think is too difficult.

My part, as an assistant master, is merely to teach the German words, the boys being taught the music by Mr. Dunnill, whom the school is very fortunate to have as its visiting music master.

I can testify to the sincere enthusiasm which the boys show for what they call "German Singing."

Dancing as a Means of Familiarity with Great Music.

Classical Dancing as a means of familiarizing the pupils with fine music . . .? It does not seem a very direct approach—nor a complete one. That dancing should be done to good music, not poor, and that the familiarity with good music thus established is in itself a considerable gain, we can at least admit. That comment made, I reproduce with pleasure a brief letter from Miss C. D. Hodgson, of the Holly Hall Senior Mixed School, Dudley.

We venture to believe that "the actual bringing together of the child and the masterpiece" is being done effectively in this school with selected girls (aged 12 to 14 years) by means of the teaching of classical dancing.

The gramophone has been used throughout and the following records give some idea of the music selected.

Minuet in G minor—Beethoven	*Sylvia Ballet*—Delibes.
Waltz in C sharp minor—Chopin	*The Blue Danube*—Strauss.
Dance of the Hours—Ponchielli	Ballet from *Faust*—Gounod
Unfinished Symphony—Schubert	

In order to perfect the dancing the record is heard, of course, dozens of times and becomes really familiar so that when heard by chance among other pieces on the wireless or at a picture house the child quickly picks it out and can follow it in her mind (I have been told eagerly several times of this experience). We are hoping that in after years when this music is heard it will still be recognized, and because of its association with the joy of active expression in school days will be listened to carefully and perhaps interpreted afresh by the mature mind. Thus the musical side of these lessons will be of value long after dancing days are over.

The Study of the Composer-Mind.

Mr. Horace Middleton writes from The Bennett School, South Millbrook, N.Y. This is a private girl's school, the ages of the main body of the pupils ranging from 14 to 20. Apart from special classes in Harmony, History, Appreciation of Music, &c., there is a weekly evening of the whole school devoted to music, and Mr. Middleton tells of an experiment in the introduction, by means of this evening, of the composer's point of view.

This has always interested me very much; nominally a class in "Appreciation", that is what it really is, and it has covered musical and non-musical alike. Also I have always had a free hand to experiment in any way that I thought best. It began before I came here seventeen years ago and still continues. I am able to look back on some degrees of gratifying success—and much failure. The various experiments have included two-piano, eight-hands playing of symphonies, overtures and miscellaneous items; ditto with four hands on two pianos; piano concertos with orchestra on second piano; two pianos, eight hands, plus Mustel organ; a long period during which the gramophone bore most of the illustrations; musical memory contests (carried on in the usual way, I suppose); sol-fa singing class; general singing rehearsals; &c., &c. All this of course illustrating short lectures. Of the typical kind, no doubt, but I have always dealt much more with the work (its structure, and so forth) than with the composer—biography hardly touched on, except in so far as it helped to elucidate the work in question. I would not bother you with all this as it is all in the usual run of things. But last year I made a very interesting venture, with unusual and surprising success, and of this I know you will be interested to hear.

I am a composer. In my long teaching experience it has gradually but convincingly dawned upon me that the composer regards music (or, rather, the material of music) quite differently from the ordinary musician, and even more the music student, and, descending again, the average layman.

One's teaching must be rather hopeless if one does not realize this sooner or later, and try to benefit one's teaching thereby. Anyway this fact (so obvious when obvious!) at last dawned upon me, and I decided to try to present the composers' point of view in my Monday evenings to the entire school. I feared for the result, and I hardly knew how to proceed. I fumbled my way along, taking them candidly into my confidence, and asking for their help. I discussed with them, one by one, the various factors of music as drawn upon by the composer *for expressive purposes.* I did not talk down to them, but treated them, by and large, as fellow musicians. In fact I had no alternative, even had I so wished. But I make it a general rule for my guidance *not* to "talk down" at any time. (Of course this rule must be tempered with common sense: technical terms when unavoidable must be explained. What is the use of gabbling a trade jargon to the uninitiated?) But in this case, because of the nature of my subject, I had to make the highest demands upon their intelligence. I need not detail, to you, the course I followed. I covered the ground pretty thoroughly, though more time would have enabled me to have presented more illustrations. The great success of the experiment was unquestionable. A great number of girls were interested, and those much more interested than usual. Also I am convinced that they were enabled to take more than an initial peep into the great world of music.

At the end of the year, feeling that a minute analysis of something or other illustrating the lines we had followed was highly desirable, I took a work of my own (my analysis of that work would certainly have the authority of a voice *ex cathedra!*) and spent three evenings on it. One evening was filled with a detailed analysis of *only two pages,* another evening in a general skipping about touching on certain useful passages, and the third and last in a quicker and less detailed consideration of a whole movement. The work was my music to the *Iphigenia in Tauris* (Euripides-Murray) which the drama department of the school was just then performing. Our Greek Festival is an annual spring event and the performances are public.

It is difficult to realize how Mr. Middleton's treatment could differ greatly from that adopted in the normal Appreciation Lesson, except in *attitude.* We are accustomed, in Appreciation work, to take a composition as an existing fact, and then, as interestingly as we can, to analyze it: [1] presumably Mr. Middle-

---

[1] Perhaps the difference is in whether one puts himself within the music and rebuilds it with infinite thought, or whether he regards it from the outside,

ton would do what we might all of us do more often than is usual, perhaps—work upward from the prime intention of the composer and the first germs of his composition.

Weekly Test Papers as a Stimulus.

The name of Ernest A. Dicks, F.R.C.O., is well known in English musical circles. Mr. Dicks sends me some of his experiences "as a teacher and coach of nearly fifty years' standing." The special feature in his work that attracts my attention is his practice of giving weekly papers, graded to follow the course of the teaching—"It is surprising what pleasure it gives when marks go up; ambition is fired at once." Now this is a practice to which some of my correspondents would greatly object, as creating "the wrong attitude", and I would emphasize again the subjective nature of many of the principles laid down. What works badly with one teacher or one class of pupil may be found, surprisingly, to work well with another.

Musical Appreciation in a Pianoforte Teaching Practice.

The following letter, from Miss Irene Martin of Bradford, is of particular interest as showing Appreciation work elsewhere than on school premises:

I am just an ordinary private music mistress and am not connected with any school, and have now taught from thirty to forty private pupils a week for about eighteen years in my own studio, where I have a grand piano, a music board, a gramophone, and a Phillips all-mains wireless set.

I give each of my pupils one hour lesson a week or two half-hours to the younger and more irresponsible people, and I also ask for (and usually get) attendance at one class a week, for which I charge 10s. 6d. per term in addition to the fees charged for ordinary lessons. There is very little music teaching provided in our two Grammar Schools, beyond a weekly Singing Class, so I don't get much help from school music, and as my pupils have to travel to and from school

as something finished which is to be pleasurably received. The more complete, experience must, in such case, come from sharing the "inside" point of view. That both methods begin with a motive and work to the completed composition does not affect their relative values. W. E.

each day, and then have practicing, homework, and games, they have very little spare time to give to music, but I do try to make them love great music, and to give them as much of the tremendous joy of playing and hearing it as I can.

I have now three of these Classes each week. One for children up to 14–15 years of age, one for definite preparation for School Certificate or Matriculation music, and the third for those studying for diplomas, L.R.A.M., A.R.C.M., and L.T.C.L.[1]

I am now starting a Music-Making Circle for little children of 6–7 years of age.

In Class 1, where attendance is generally for two or three years, the work done includes Theory up to the standard required by the Associated Board in their Rudiments of Music examination. We have Ear-Training, Elementary Harmony (mostly Aural), talks on Form—the building up of sentences and phrases and talks about the Orchestra with gramophone illustrations and pictures of the various instruments. Then about three times a term we have a "musician", which is very popular. I give them a few biographical details if these are likely to be interesting, but more about the work he did, the times he lived in and the kind of instruments then used. We have illustrations, mostly on the piano but sometimes the gramophone comes in useful.

This class is one of the brightest spots of the week and is very popular. My people love "Theory Class" as they call it, and hate missing it; this class has also formed itself into the "Jolly Clan" of the Music Makers' Guild,[2] and once a month we carry out the program set, adapted to my own individual people.

The children all have their music note-books which are very interesting; they will listen to anything I provide, and usually prefer the music I think is best; they watch me play and follow in the music and squabble as to who shall turn over. A little while ago I played them three funeral marches, Beethoven, Chopin, and Mendelssohn, and asked for a vote for the one they liked best. They love Bach and have heard several of the Preludes and Fugues, the English Suites, Myra Hess's arrangement of *Jesu, Joy of Man's Desiring*, the

---

[1] Licentiate of the Royal Academy of Music; Associate of the Royal College of Music; and Licentiate of Trinity College of Music, London—three professional diplomas. I explain this for the benefit of American readers. And, by the way, the Grammar Schools just mentioned correspond to the American High Schools. P. A. S.

[2] A national activity carried on by the journal *The Music Student.* P. A. S.

Fantasie in C minor, *Mortify us* (Rummel's arrangement) &c. I use also the Giles Farnaby pieces, Arne sonatas, Handel Suites, Mozart and Beethoven, Schumann (very popular), Greig, MacDowell, Debussy, and some of the Russian people (I am not very good at modern music, but they love *Till Eulenspiegel* and *On hearing the first Cuckoo in Spring,* and Percy Grainger's *Londonderry Air* and *Shepherd's Hey*).

I met a girl who was in this class for a year when she was seven. I have not seen her for fourteen years and she greeted me with "Do you remember playing *The Bee's Wedding* to us? I always think of Theory Classes when I hear it", so it had evidently made an impression.

Very occasionally, if they have more or less finished at 5.25 or so, we turn on the wireless and listen to Henry Hall and the B.B.C.[1] Dance Orchestra, as our tastes are very liberal, and I think a contrast is a good thing in education.

One of my difficulties in a class like this is that of combining all ages and stages; at present the youngest member is nine and is doing Primary Division, and the eldest is fourteen and is doing Intermediate.[2] There are new pupils practically every term and often the older ones go to boarding school for a year or two, so the work cannot be altogether graded; but after about three years in this class the children have a thorough grounding of theory, their ear-training is fairly good and they know quite a lot about Fugues, Sonatas, Symphonies, and Operas.

We attend any orchestral concert we can and we have been twice to see *Hänsel and Gretel,* once to *Hugh the Drover,* once to *Falstaff, The Barber of Seville,* and *The Bohemian Girl* (which they didn't like, much to my joy), once to *The Mikado,* and once to *The Gondoliers.*

After this they go into the School Certificate Class[3] and here the program is much more definite and limited by the syllabus. Their musical history and the study of set works needs time, and they have much more ear-training.

---

[1] British Broadcasting Corporation. P. A. S.

[2] For the benefit of American readers I must explain that these are grades in the examination scheme that conditions so much pianoforte teaching in Britain. P. A. S.

[3] A class in preparation for the subject of music as a part of the school-leaving examination. P. A. S.

I have sent pupils in for this examination for some years now and have never had a failure; usually about 70 per cent. of them get credit and "Good" and an occasional Distinction, and the others pass, and they usually love the work and even the ones who do not take up music in after life are very glad they chose that subject and enjoy working for it. After this about two years is needed for definite L.R.A.M. preparation and this is a great joy to us all. One of my pupils has just gone as a student to the Royal Academy after taking L.R.A.M. and A.R.C.M. and she writes, "I realize more and more how very wonderful my musical education has been." She has been with me for seven years and done just this program.

If any of this is helpful to you, please use it, and I shall be grateful for any suggestions to improve and make my work more efficient. I know there must be lots of loopholes in a scheme which is perforce somewhat sketchy.

The reply to the modest request with which this letter ends is that as much seems to be done as the circumstances permit, and that if, as is surmised by the writer, improvements are possible, she is certainly capable of finding the opportunity for making them. She has evidently effectually succeeded in destroying the one-sidedness that is so often a feature of pianoforte study.

Boys v. Girls.

A woman teacher who happens to be occupied in both a Preparatory School for Boys and a High School for Girls (both of them famous institutions of the first class) sends the following discriminatory remarks:

Only one 45-minute period per week is allotted to me for each singing class, so I can do very little in the way of Appreciation. I do, however, give up about two lessons a term to gramophone records.

I have got some of the *Columbia History of Music* records and among them the plainsong *Veni Sancte Spiritus*. After a short introductory talk I put this on for the oldest boys—10's and 11's. They listened to it entranced, and asked to hear it again and again. I put this record on for the First Form at the Girls' High School and they were faintly bored, and asked if I knew a piece called *Country Gardens*. I played the record for some of my older pupils who listened politely and described it afterwards as "queer."

I find the boys much more enthusiastic in every way—even to the extent of foregoing voluntarily their mid-morning lunch of milk and biscuits before a singing lesson, as they found it difficult to sing after they had had them.

They listen intelligently to music on the wireless and ask me questions about the music they hear and the composers, a thing quite unknown in the girls.

And yet I know the girls enjoy their music, and in a way enjoy listening to records and learning about it.

I cannot give you any hard and fast rules about the sort of music they like. Vigorous, jolly music they both like, such as Bach's G major Brandenburg Concerto and the boys love such things as Dukas' *Sorcerer's Apprentice.* The girls like Delius's *On Hearing the First Cuckoo,* while the boys have no use for it. I don't pretend to understand them.

A Phonograph Library for the Schools of a City.

A very valuable contribution comes from Mr. Herbert Wiseman, M.A., who has for some years had the oversight of the music in the Edinburgh schools and whose success there is well recognized. Instead of writing us anything special Mr. Wiseman sends me an official document just issued, which I propose to reproduce intact, with the suggestion that it may be taken as a model series of practical suggestions to rank-and-file school teachers who, while lacking the technical training of the professional musician, can yet be enabled to do excellent work if generously encouraged and wisely guided. It will be seen that the occasion of the issue of the document is the provision by the Education Committee of a carefully-planned central loan collection of Phonograph Records, and that the document consists of hints on the use of this collection by teachers in the different types of school under the Committee.

I cannot help the fact that Mr. Wiseman mentions some of my own publications. It would be false modesty to pretend I am not pleased to find these recognized as of service, and to cut out all references to myself would be difficult. I have done so in the case of some communications, but in this one the result would be incompleteness; so I just let the allusions stand.

I have added in footnotes indications concerning any records mentioned such as the reader might have difficulty in tracing.

A lending library of Gramophone Records has been instituted as part of a scheme to help teachers to give their pupils experience of music which is beyond their own powers of performance. The nucleus of the collection, of which the catalogue has been issued, provides a representation of most aspects of musical activity. Historically, it ranges from early plainsong to works of contemporary composers, and, in complexity, from simple nursery rhymes and folk-songs to complete symphonies. Teachers should therefore be able to select records to illustrate any particular phase of music which they desire to study with their classes.

It should be noted that what may be called "general utility" records such as those of folk-dances, marches, &c., have not been included. They are outside the scope of the library and it is felt that schools which desire records of this type will probably be prepared to get them for themselves. The records, from their very nature, would, moreover, probably be so much used that they would soon become too worn for lending purposes.

Every class music lesson, even at the most junior stages, should be to some extent a training in musical appreciation.

In the INFANT ROOM, the children should learn through their own singing, the first principles of musical form, the value of beautiful tone, tonal variety, expression and color. All these are important and too often neglected points in the teaching of appreciation. As, however, music is a harmonic as well as a melodic experience, attention must not be focused solely on the tune. The feeling for harmonic background can be engendered by the pianoforte accompaniment which, it is hardly necessary to state, should always be played in as musical a fashion as possible. If this accompaniment contains any imaginative features, these should be brought to the notice of the children, and, even at the earliest stages, an endeavor should be made to teach the children to sing their tune as a unit in a larger tissue. Harmony and counterpoint can thus be made familiar even to the very youngest.

Rhythmical training can be fostered by means of exercises on eurythmic principles, by clapping, tapping, walking, running, skipping, &c., and by means of Percussion Bands, provided that they are used as an aid and not as an end in themselves. (There is a distinct danger that performances by Percussion Bands may degenerate into "stunts" and so their musical and educational purposes may not be achieved.)[1]

Gramophone Records in the Infant Room must, of necessity, be limited to those of music which is within the pupils' powers of comprehension.

As at all other stages of school work, their use should be regarded as a pleasant and, one might almost say, necessary "extra", but not as a substitute for the class singing lesson with all that that implies in the way of ear-training and sight-reading.

In the catalogue, records B. 1 [2] and B. 2 [2] will give the children a chance of listening to nursery rhymes which they know and which they sing. The records should not be introduced until the children can sing the songs. They can be followed by a record such as D. 47—Quilter's *Children's Overture,* which shows the use which a composer can make of well-known melodies.

It is fatally easy to imagine that, merely because a gramophone record is being played, the children are really listening. All teachers know that, in other subjects, the attention of little people flags unless something is done to keep it on the alert. From time to time, therefore, the listening should be tested. Many devices for so doing will suggest themselves to the experienced teacher. In the case of the *Children's Overture* with its frequent changes of time, the children may imagine themselves to be conducting the Orchestra and adapting their beat to these changes (any rudimentary form of beating time will do).

As this Overture is built on familiar nursery rhymes, another plan might be to suggest a tune for the appearance of which a special watch should be kept. The children, listening with closed eyes, might be asked to raise their hands when they hear say *Paul's Steeple* or *Sing a Song of Sixpence.* If they are listening intently for the appearance of any one tune, they will be absorbing the others.

Other records which may be useful in Infant Rooms include B. 19 and 20—settings of some of A. A. Milne's Poems; [3] and D. 42 and 42a—Nursery Rhymes for Orchestra,[4] very suitable for use with Percussion Bands. (In schools which have no Percussion Band material, these two records will serve a useful purpose if the children

[1] See Appendix F (American edition). W. E.
[2] Traditional Nursery Rhymes, sung by Annette Blackwell (Columbia).
[3] Sung by Dale Smith (Columbia).
[4] *Nursery Rhymes Medley* (Columbia).

are encouraged to sing the tunes and to express the rhythm by some
form of bodily movement.)

Some of the orchestral records will be found useful in awakening
the imagination of the children. It is hardly necessary to state that,
at this stage, no reference to details of musical form or conduct
should be made, but, in cases where the music tells a story, the
preparation for listening should be made by calling attention to any
picturesque features in the music.

For instance in the slow movement of Haydn's Symphony, *The
Clock* (D. 1), the lower instruments keep the "ticking" going, while
the higher instruments sing lovely tunes. The first item in Greig's
Peer Gynt Suite (D. 13–D. 14) paints a lovely picture of morning
with a gradual increase of light, the waving of trees and the singing
of birds. The last movement of this suite is a grotesque *Dance of
the Elves.*

Elgar's *Nursery Suite* (D. 15–16) was specially written for Princess
Elizabeth and gives musical pictures of experiences which are known
to every child.

The Ride of the Valkyries (D. 21), though extremely complicated
from the point of view of a student of orchestration, has yet a simple
basic rhythmical drive in its main tune, which can be sung even by
very small people.

The Spring Song and *The Bee's Wedding* (D. 31) and *The Flight
of the Bumble Bee* (D. 34) have an irresistible imaginative appeal
and the excerpts from the *Casse Noisette* Suite give a chance of
thinking of foreign lands.

In all cases where there is a singable tune, the children should be
encouraged to sing it and to mark the rhythm by "conducting."

It need hardly be said that the teachers should themselves study
the records before playing them to a class, and should know the
important points to which reference is to be made. The best way to
carry through such preparation is to follow the record from a score:
even a piano score will do. Reference may be made to some very
interesting condensations of full scores made by James Easson in the
Book of Great Music (Oxford University Press). It is hoped, in
course of time, to add a certain number of miniature orchestral scores
to the library.

The use of the records named above will not, of course, be confined to the Infant Room. A student of composition would find
much to study in them, but attention is drawn to them here because

their beauty does make a great appeal even to the youngest pupils and because they are records of good music which does not become stale through repetition. Indeed, it is only through repetition that they will become part of the child's life, and as pupils grow older, they will find new beauties in them.

In the PRIMARY SCHOOLS generally, it should be said that the teaching of musical appreciation should be linked up with the teaching of class-singing. As in all other branches of teaching, progress should be made from the known to the unknown. If the children have learned to sing some Scots Songs, they will be interested to hear the Scots selection (H. 2).[1] If they have sung sea chanties, they will listen with joy to B. 18 and to H. 1.[2] If they have been studying folk-song, they can learn much from the records (B. 4 and B. 5)[3] of Clive Carey, a great exponent.

On another side, if, for instance, the class has been singing any of Schubert's songs, the teacher should take the opportunity of saying something about Schubert's life and works and of letting the children hear some other examples of his songs sung by Elizabeth Schumann or Elsie Suddaby (B. 11 and 12).[4] Whether these are sung in German or English has little bearing on the case. A short general explanation of the meaning of the song will explain the words, and for our present purpose, it is the music which matters. Similarly a class which has sung Mozart's Lullaby (Clarendon Song Book IV) will receive inspiration from the perfect rendering of it on B. 9,[5] and can go on to make the acquaintance of other lovely specimens of the composer's genius such as B. 10, D. 35, D. 17, and D. 18.[6]

When *Come, see where golden-hearted spring* has given a class some idea of the great tunes which Handel wrote, something should be said about the commanding genius of the composer, and the *Hallelujah Chorus* and *I know that my Redeemer liveth* (C. 10) with some of the smaller items on D. 43, 44, and 45 [7] will serve as apt illustrations.

[1] *The Thistle* (Columbia).
[2] *Shenandoah, &c.* sung by John Goss and Male Voice Quartet (H.M.V.), and *Songs of the Sea Medley,* played by Grenadier Guards Band (Columbia).
[3] Columbia.
[4] Both H.M.V.
[5] By Elizabeth Schumann (H.M.V.).
[6] *Batti, batti,* by Elizabeth Schumann (H.M.V.). Minuet in D, by Squire Octet (Columbia), *Kleine Nachtmusik,* by British Symphony Orchestra (Columbia).
[7] *Handel Series,* by Light Orchestra, conducted by S. S. Moore.

The record of Morley's *It was a lover and his lass* (B. 13) is an excellent example of diction and breath control, and Stanford's *Songs of the Sea* (B. 14, 15, and 16) will be found very attractive, and useful as settings of well-known poems by a more modern composer.

Choral music is represented by some well varied specimens and the record of Purcell's *Nymphs and Shepherds* (C. 11) is an example of fine singing by a choir of elementary school children.

Teachers may find the following books useful:

The Growth of Music—H. C. Colles.
The Listener's History of Music—P. A. Scholes.
The Book of the Great Musicians—P. A. Scholes.
Music—W. H. Hadow.

Copies of these are in the general library.

Other aspects of music which can be studied at this stage are (*a*) form, and (*b*) tone color.

With regard to the former, simple forms (binary or two-part form, or, to use a formula—AB, and ternary or three-part form—ABA) can be studied by means of the folk-songs which the children know. From these progress can be made by such easily grasped things as the Marches and Minuets of Handel (D. 43, 44, and 45),[7] the Purcell Suite (F. 21)[1] played on a harpsichord, and by the gigue from the Bach Suite (F. 1 and 2).[2] Rondo form can be introduced by the last movement of the Haydn Trio (E. 9)[3] and the Mozart Minuet (D. 35)[4] may serve as an introduction to the more extended minuet and trio form (ABA-CD-ABA). The Toy Symphony of Haydn (D. 38), even though it was written in jest for toy instruments, contains the kernel of symphonic form.

A book which deals very simply with this aspect of music is *The Listener's Guide to Music* by P. A. Scholes and further help may be obtained from *Music and its Appreciation* by Stewart Macpherson.

Instrumental tone-color can be studied by means of A. 6-9, four records which give an opportunity of hearing the instruments of the orchestra played separately. Once these have been studied by frequent re-hearing, "guessing competitions" can be held, the teacher dropping the needle point gently on to different sections. (The

[1] *Columbia History of Music.*
[2] In A minor, played by Harold Samuel (H.M.V.).
[3] In G major, played by Cortot, Thibaud, and Casals (H.M.V.).
[4] J. H. Squire Octet (Columbia)

Columbia records are the better for this purpose, as on them the instruments are playing the same tune, and so there is no fear of the children associating a certain fragment of melody with a certain instrument.)

These records of separate instruments have been included in the catalogue as specimens. They are, however, the type of records which should be in the possession of schools and should be used frequently enough for the children to become thoroughly familiar with the tone-colors. One or two hearings are not enough. Many adults find difficulty in distinguishing between the tones of an oboe and a clarinet because they have not sufficient opportunities of hearing these instruments singly. They have heard the tunes they play as part of an orchestral mass of tone without troubling to consider the quality which differentiates the one from the other. By means of these gramophone records, children's ears are enabled with comparative ease to sense differences in quality, and a new and fascinating type of ear exercise ought to be added to the more common tests for pitch and time. When proficiency is reached a fresh world is conquered and a new joy is added to the experience of hearing an orchestra.

When the instruments can be "spotted" with accuracy when playing separately, actual compositions should be played and attention concentrated on instrumental tone-colors rather than on form or any other aspect. The effect of strings alone can be heard in *Eine Kleine Nachtmusik*—Mozart (D. 17 and 18); and exchange of conversation between the wind instruments in the slow movement of Schubert's Unfinished Symphony (D. 9); the lightness of the flutes in the Scherzo from the *Midsummer Night's Dream;* the splendor of the trombones in Prelude to Act III of *Lohengrin* (D. 21); the mellow tones of the horn in the Nocturne from the *Midsummer Night's Dream* (D. 30). A beautiful flute solo will be found in Gluck's *Orpheus* Ballet (D. 33), and other examples, too numerous to mention, will be found in nearly all the other orchestral records.

The sound of a string quartet may be introduced to pupils by the two movements by Schubert (E. 6)[1] and the evolution of the tone of the modern piano shown by contrasting a record for clavichord and one for harpsichord in the *Columbia History of Music*, vol. ii (A. 11) with the record of Liszt's *Hungarian Rhapsody* No. 2 (F. 5). A short description of the mechanics of tone production on these

[1] Minuet and Moment Musical, No. 3, played by Lener Quartet (Columbia).

three instruments and a demonstration of the action of the school piano will create a lot of interest and enhance the value of the records.

Here, as at all other stages, it is necessary to test the listening of the class. The children should be questioned as to the instruments, should raise their hand as they hear oboe, horn, &c., and should be encouraged to discuss with the teacher the music after its performance.

For more advanced work in INTERMEDIATE AND SECONDARY SCHOOLS, the catalogue provides a wide choice. Some teachers may decide to make the teaching of appreciation incidental to the work of the singing class, in which case the methods suggested for Primary Schools can be applied with an appropriate enlargement of horizon. Others may decide to set aside a certain amount of time once a week or less frequently for a systematic course.

The attention of all may be directed to the admirable historical survey of the whole field of music which is provided by the four volumes of the *Columbia History of Music*. The outstanding and far-sighted enterprise of this well-known recording company, in conjunction with the Oxford University Press, has provided not only a series of booklets dealing with the earliest facts of the history of music and written by Percy Scholes, but also records which illustrate the developments which the books describe.

This might well be made the basis of instruction and the records in it should be supplemented by others chosen from the rest of the catalogue. The various styles, forms, and periods are already well represented. From time to time additions will be made and teachers are asked to show their interest by calling attention to any omission and by suggesting titles of records which they think ought to be added.

All sorts of ideas suggest themselves as to possible treatments of the subject at this stage. The points of good singing can be studied from records to the great advantage of the performance of the class itself. The history of keyed instruments and the construction of the modern pianoforte can be dealt with in greater detail than in the primary schools. The development of musical forms should be shown to find its point of greatest expansion in the symphony and the concerto. The use which composers make of short themes, as, for instance, the "fate" theme in Beethoven's Fifth Symphony, should be studied. More attention can now be paid to the development of themes in the middle sections of the first movements and in such a work as the *Enigma* Variations (D. 24–7). The contribution of individual composers to the general story of music can be indicated and some idea of style can be inculcated. The study of the string quartet should be begun. Music can be linked up with other studies, literature, history, geography, religious instruction, &c.

The main object, however, of all teaching of this type is to stock the pupils' minds with beautiful music. As, after the English classes, we expect the pupils to know something of the works of standard poets and authors, so from the music classes we should expect to find pupils coming with a certain amount of knowledge of the great composers and of their works.

In these days of wireless the children cannot avoid music in their homes; it should be our aim to teach them to listen with intelligence and to recognize as old friends at least a few of the world's great musical masterpieces.

(E) THE EXAMPLE OF A GREAT ENGLISH CITY

Nothing has given me greater pleasure when preparing this book than the study of what has been accomplished in Manchester, and nothing in my book will, I think, give my readers greater pleasure.

It will be known to all that this city is one of the comparatively few in the British Isles that have organized their school music on the system to be found in all the cities of the United States and some of the cities of Canada—that of a chief musician with a staff of musicians under him, responsible for the organization of the music in all the schools, doing some of the teaching but necessarily making use of the services also of members of the regular staffs of those schools.

I have said that this system is to be found universally in the United States, but to spare British susceptibilities I will add that I am by no means sure that it is American in its origin. In some of the British cities where it is found it dates back a long way; I can remember that something like it existed in my native city at least forty-five years ago, and I doubt if it was very novel then. It sprang up independently in the two countries, and then the

Americans, with their passion for organization and specialization, developed it to the higher point. It is my impression that in Britain it came in as a result of the enthusiasm for school music generated by the work of John Curwen and his proof of the possibility of teaching every child to sing. Our early Music Supervisors (not called by that name, however, which *is,* I think, purely American) were all keen Sol-faists, with qualifications obtained through study under the egis of the Tonic Sol-fa College, and looking upon it as their duty to encourage as many Elementary School teachers as possible to acquire such qualifications. Probably, in the main, the few cities that in those days acquired officials of this kind still possess them, and a few other cities have in recent times appointed them[1]. It is, of course, much to be desired that the system should be generally adopted, and, indeed, without it we can never give the children of the nation what they have a right to receive from us in the way of a sufficient and efficient initiation into that art which, for a child, is obviously the most generally accessible of the arts.

So much by way of preamble. Now for the facts as to Manchester.

In the year the Great War ended that city, famous for its orchestra, its great choir, and its College of Music (all, by the way, let us admit, built upon the native Lancashire love of music by the enthusiasm and organizing ability of a foreigner, Hallé, and largely fostered by other foreigners such as Richter and Brodsky), appointed what it called a "Musical Adviser" in the person of Dr. Walter Carroll, at that time Lecturer in Music at Manchester University and Professor of Harmony, Composition, and the Art of Teaching (he must have been the very first to "profess" this subject in a British musical institution) at the Royal Manchester College of Music. Dr. Carroll, after two years during which his appointment was a "part-time" one, abandoned other positions and focused his energies upon the duties of the new one.

---

[1] The following are known to me to possess such officials at the present date—Bradford, Hull, London, Manchester, Sheffield, Stoke-on-Trent, Sunderland; Aberdeen, Clackmannan, Dumbartonshire, Dundee, East Lothian, Edinburgh, Fife, Inverness. (There are probably others.)

To my request for a general statement as to his experiences, Dr. Carroll sends me the following—in which, as will be noted, I have ventured to italicize the passage that has, for my present purpose, the greatest importance, as a complete support of the thesis of my book.

Manchester, a great industrial city, has large areas of slum dwellings and of congested conditions generally. Music in a commercial city offers one of the few opportunities for the spread of something beautiful among a people whose conditions are, to a large extent, of a sordid character. I have not waited for the full development of an ideal system of aural training, nor for an ideal supply of Elementary School teachers capable of carrying out that training. The regular teachers of the schools, with considerable credit and great earnestness carry on the teaching of Vocal Music, including Voice, Ear-training, Sight-singing, and Songs. These subjects are presented as well as is possible under the conditions of education to-day. But in addition to this, life and beauty have been brought into our schools by a special staff of full-time Assistants all of whom are excellent musicians, fine pianists, and sympathetic teachers. In this way our senior school children receive benefits in music comparable to those enjoyed by their visits to the Parks and to the Art Galleries. It is not considered necessary, in the case of the Parks, that the children shall know the details of all plants and flowers. It is not felt necessary that before visiting an Art Gallery they shall be familiar with all the rules of color and perspective. It is not convenient to take children, in a similar way, to concerts during school hours. The Manchester Education Committee, therefore, brings the music of the Great Masters to the children for their enjoyment, for the uplifting of their minds and for such benefits as they may receive through absorbing something beautiful and elevating.

In my view, the presentation of beautiful music to the children, with a few simple and very human remarks about that music, is of the utmost value, in spite of the fact that, technically, their musical knowledge may be unequal to the analysis and full understanding of all that they hear.

It is a significant fact that out of 144 schools constantly receiving this subject as a regular part of their curriculum at least 142 write at the end of every session asking that the course may be continued. The odd cases which occur occasionally are usually due to some re-

arrangement of time-table. This has been going on since 1918 and I cannot believe that Headmasters and Headmistresses and their staffs would have been so utterly mistaken as to retain Music Appreciation, carried out on these principles, in their schools if they were not convinced of its real and lasting value.

In 1930 the City of Manchester Education Committee published a booklet called *Music in Manchester Schools, 1918-1930* (Offices of the Committee, Deansgate, Manchester, 1s.). Dr. Carroll has kindly sent me this as his contribution to my symposium. It surveys and records experience over the whole field of musical activities and may be warmly recommended to all interested in the subject. I extract the passage of immediate relevance:

The provision of effective training in modern methods of teaching vocal music was one of the earliest and most important features of the scheme. The child's desire for self-expression through Song is natural and its encouragement lies at the very root of interest and progress. No system of education in music would be sound if it failed to recognize this fact. Children love to sing, and it is the duty of the educationist to see that they are trained to sing well; but the old plan of keeping the child's musical experiences entirely within the confines of the school song was obviously wrong. Music, with its wonderful power over Mind, is something too great and noble to be encompassed by the voice alone. Outside the domain of Song there lie wide and fertile stretches of Music—regions in which the child may roam without taking part as an active worker; regions which may be visited and explored and enjoyed with the utmost pleasure and benefit. It is this opportunity for association with music in its fuller sense which is the true aim of the Music Appreciation class. The Manchester Education Committee was one of the first Authorities to provide the children of the Elementary Schools, as a regular subject of the curriculum, with a systematic course of training in Musical Art, the lessons being given by musicians appointed as special teachers by the Committee for this purpose. The term "Musical Art" is here used in its wider significance, and in contrast with the term "Music" which still, in primary education, is usually a synonym for "Vocal Music."

The Education Committee's scheme of Music Appreciation teaching preceded the advent of the domestic wireless by about two years. Some seven years later Sir Walford Davies, in his highly valued wireless talks, demonstrated the necessity for such training of intelligent listeners among all sections of the people. The welcome accorded to his work was sincere and unanimous, and vindicated in no uncertain manner the wisdom of the movement which, as a regular subject of Elementary Education, had its inception in Manchester in 1918, and which has made possible a greater and more discriminating enjoyment of Broadcast Music in thousands of northern homes to-day.

In September, 1919, the actual work of teaching Musical Appreciation in the Manchester Elementary Schools began, one special teacher being appointed to take charge of the subject in 36 departments. The children in this first group of classes numbered, in all, some 3,000. The attitude of the school staffs, and of the children, has from the outset been one of lively interest and pleasure. Before the end of the first term applications for the course were received from many additional schools, and in January, 1920, another special teacher was appointed, the total number attending the lessons being now increased to 6,000 from seventy-two school departments.

Interest in the work continued to spread and requests from other schools were numerous. By September, 1920, a third teacher was found necessary and the number of departments able to benefit by the course rose to 108. At this time 9,000 children were in attendance—a remarkable result obtained in the short space of one year.

A difficulty now arose which threatened very seriously to delay the expansion of the work. One of the vital factors in Music Appreciation teaching is the piano, which, to give effective help, must be good in tone, touch, and general condition. It was found that many Voluntary Schools [1] were entirely without pianos, while others were handicapped by an instrument the tone of which precluded any possibility of artistic use.

A census of pianos was taken and plans were made for a large number of new instruments to be supplied and for others to be thoroughly renovated. Piano tuning and repairing, a matter of primary importance both musically and economically, was completely

---

[1] For American readers this term must be explained—"Voluntary Schools" are schools which, though under public control, are provided, and in part sustained, by other than the public authority; the system dates back to the time when religious bodies largely made themselves responsible for the country's education, and such schools are still the property of such bodies. P. A. S.

reorganized on a systematic basis. In due course the difficulty was overcome and every department of every school was the possessor of a piano, regularly tuned and in good condition. This result was achieved by active co-operation between the Education Committee, the School Managers, the Musical Adviser, and the teaching staffs of the schools. The Appreciation Course was further extended. A fourth teacher was appointed in 1927 and took charge of 36 additional schools, bringing the number of departments up to 144 and the children in attendance to 12,000, figures which represent the position as it now stands in 1930.

Most of the schools which had waited so long for suitable instruments were in very poor districts, where the need for the influence of beautiful music was greatest. The delight with which the new subject was greeted, and the welcome accorded it by children and teachers alike, were ample compensation for the long and difficult task of providing the necessary musical equipment.

Though musicians and educationists are in agreement regarding the desirability of a knowledge of the Art of Music which shall extend beyond the activities of the singing class, marked differences of opinion exist as to the means whereby such knowledge should be made accessible to the child. Teachers of the academic type would build, step by step, upon a basis theoretical or historical, making their appeal mainly through the analytical or chronological aspects of the subject. This method is usually adopted by teachers who, by temperament, are followers rather than leaders. Rules and facts reign supreme, but Music's message of joy and loveliness is often lost in a maze of theory and verbal exposition. At the opposite extreme are those who are opposed to any attempt to train systematically the faculty of listening. "Let music convey its own message in its own way" is perhaps the best, as it is also the commonest, indication of this attitude. From the same source comes that other slogan, "Let the children sing like the birds" (*kinds* of birds not stated). Such views are not rare among artists, who, possessing special gifts themselves, are often unable to assess the difficulties and limitations of normal people.

Appreciation teaching as established in the Manchester schools is the outcome of independent thought and original research. Its first purpose is to provide examples of beauty from among the masterpieces of music. These are played or sung to the children, who are encouraged to make their own adventures in the byways of melody and rhythm by humming or tapping the more prominent phrases. In the early stages the pieces selected are short and picturesque; the smaller compositions of Schumann and Grieg may be named as types which make simple and direct appeal to the youthful mind. Gradually it becomes possible to draw upon longer and less obvious forms of musical expression and to pass, by easy steps from what may be termed the rational, or narrative, mode of approach to the deeper and more spiritual side of the art. Every piece of music given must be a perfect specimen of its kind; one which makes a real call upon the intelligence of the listener without exceeding such powers of concentration as are possessed by the average child.

It has already been said that four special teachers are engaged in the work, the 144 schools are included in the scheme, and that 12,000 children are regularly in attendance. Some further reference to the actual working of the classes may be of interest.

A lesson is given once in every three weeks, the full course lasting three years. The children's ages are from eleven to fourteen. The lesson lasts forty minutes and the number in the class varies from eighty to one hundred. A quiet room of moderate size is better than a large hall, and a piano in good condition is, of course, essential. The teacher must be a very good pianist; if a fairly good singer or violinist too—all the better. Broad training and experience are not enough; the teacher needs these and much more. A knowledge of Education and its aims; a love of children; the gift of story-telling; a sense of humor; clear and ready speech; charm of manner; buoyancy of spirit—these and other attributes go to make up the Music Appreciation teacher's equipment.

A lesson includes—(a) a few questions on the previous lesson; (b) a brief talk upon some new point; (c) musical illustrations, aptly bearing upon that point, played or sung by the teacher; (d) experiments in which the children take active part, including melodies and rhythms from the pieces played; (e) music, by the finest composers, played or sung to the children as a means of developing a love of music, musical taste and intelligent listening; (f) the occasional use of other instruments and of the gramophone.

For the planning and presenting of the lessons the personality of the teacher is allowed complete freedom. In a subject so dependent upon the subtle influence of temperament a set syllabus, officially prescribed for uniform application, would certainly be obstructive and probably disastrous. Many earnest people have failed through the attempt to standardize Appreciation teaching. Sense of ease and consciousness of freedom are factors of first importance to the teacher who would successfully unfold to children the wonder and beauty of music, rousing the spirit of emulation and the desire for the beautiful, both of which are strong in childhood.

Closely connected with the general musical growth of the child, begun in the singing class and amplified in the Appreciation class, is the provision of facilities for the hearing of the finest choral and orchestral works of the Great Masters of music. Contact with the creations of genius is as essential a stimulus in music as in pictorial art. It is, however, far more difficult of achievement for, in its true presentation, it is costly and demands personal collaboration of a high order. As early as 1916 Manchester was one of the few cities engaged in pioneer work of this kind. In October of that year was formed the Children's Concert Society. The enterprise began under the direction of a committee of private citizens several of whom were associated with the schools, the chairman himself being a member of the Education Committee. Seven concerts (September to March) were given each year, each being attended by some 1,500 children from the schools of Manchester and Salford. The meetings were held in the Central Hall on Saturdays from 3.0 to 4.30. Solo, ensemble, choral and orchestral music was represented in fair proportions, and the expenses were entirely met by the charges for admission—minimum threepence, maximum sixpence. Arrangements with the schools were made through the Director of Education. These concerts, which received excellent support, continued for ten years, and from 1918 onwards the Musical Adviser, who was a member of the Children's Concert Committee from the first, was able to link up the Concerts with the new school music scheme. In 1926 the original society ceased to function, but its work and influence were now well grounded, and, as will presently be seen, were destined to merge into an enlarged sphere of usefulness.

The origin of this transition from the Central Hall to the Free Trade Hall is interesting as showing that between the old régime and the new there was no break; indeed, for a short time they actually overlapped.

On December 21st, 1923, the Hallé Concerts Society generously gave an orchestral concert to the school children of Manchester, Salford, Stockport, and Stretford. The concert was greatly enjoyed by the 2,400 scholars present, and it was noteworthy that the favorite piece was the finest composition in the program—Mozart's *Serenade for Strings.* A second concert was given a year later and, as on the former occasion, no charge was made for admission. The Society, by these two gracious acts, enabled the children to hear some of the finest music played by one of the world's great orchestras, and initiated a new force in Manchester's musical life.

An event of outstanding importance was the decision of the City Council, in 1924, to engage the Hallé Orchestra for a series of Municipal Concerts to be given during the winter months. This valuable addition to the existing facilities for the hearing of good music came at an opportune time and arrangements were made for five hundred children from the Manchester Schools to attend the concerts, each child paying sixpence for admission. As the result of an experience extending over six years the Musical Adviser has made careful records regarding the attitude of the children in relation to the excellent programs of music performed under the direction of Sir Hamilton Harty. Some extracts from these observations may be of interest, among general conclusions being the following:

(1) That the children responded more fully to the advanced music of the Municipal Concerts than they did to the simpler music given at the original Children's Concerts (disbanded in 1926).

(2) That the child mind in relation to art is still but little understood, and is probably capable of assimilating effects of beauty and refinement far beyond the limits of what has been deemed "suitable for children."

(3) That notwithstanding the fact that the music of Wagner is of a type most subtle and involved it is nevertheless true that the Wagner evening at the Free Trade Hall is, to the children, the supreme event. Unconscious of all external things, spellbound by some call we cannot comprehend, they appear to experience a peculiar joy and satisfaction of their own, seldom quite equaled at any other concert.

(4) That the music of Bach appears to make a very direct appeal to the power of attention and the sense of happiness. This is possibly due to its perfect rhythmic symmetry—rhythm being an element of music which touches one of the most primitive instincts of humanity.

(5) That children greatly appreciate being with grown-ups at an evening concert *not* specially prepared for children.

(6) That in the presence of fine music, played by a fine orchestra, a speaker or lecturer is unnecessary. Verbal explanation at the time is undesirable, though previous preparation in the school is valuable,[1] and a few well-chosen words printed in the program may be helpful at the concert.

(7) That attempts to simplify the music, to put words to instrumental themes, and especially to suggest feeble or facetious words with a view to aiding memory, are tricks which must be unsparingly denounced. They are an insult to the child's intelligence.[2]

The aspect of the Free Trade Hall at the special concert given by the Hallé Orchestra every Christmas, filled to overflowing by 2,500 boys and girls from all parts of the city, is a reminder that such occasions do not merely serve the cause of music alone but give to the children a sense of community—their first real experience of growing citizenship and of civic pride.

To all this it does not seem necessary that I should add anything—except the remark that doubtless in other cities in Britain and the Dominions where a fine musician and educationist has been appointed to direct the educational development admirable work is also going on. The logic of this "supervisor" system is such that it must inevitably in time become universal throughout the British Empire as it is in the United States. It offers the only possible opportunity for the application of what we may call a *statesmanlike policy,* as distinct from sporadic effort.

[1] The second clause deserves to be italicized. W. E.

[2] The most prominent British exponent of this device has been Dr. Malcolm Sargent, conductor of Mr. Robert Mayer's admirable London Concerts for Children. It may be interesting to see his defense of the practice.

"I have been criticized because I have on occasion set words to musical phrases and musical themes which were not intended by the composer. I think probably the criticisms have come from people who were not at the concerts, because what I do is really quite harmless. It is simply that where a piece is written in a very definite mood it is easier for the children to remember the tune if some suitable words are put to it. They have only to sing it once, or they can hum it through, and they will recognize it whenever it occurs on any particular instrument and interest is immediately excited." (*The Listener,* 29 July 1931.)

Here, then, are "doctors differing"—which leaves us free to form our own opinions. The subject is, of course, one that has been widely (and sometimes heatedly) discussed in the British musical press.

FINALLY . . . !

Having gone through the foregoing accounts, by practical teachers of their own work, and of the views they have been led to develop in the course of it, the reader may be advised to go through them again in a spirit of careful comparison. One feature of the collection that will then inevitably strike him is the considerable measure of difference of experience in the details of the work (and hence of resulting opinion) as between one writer and another. Here are a few of the questions on which different writers will be found to give different answers:

1. What is the value of "Program Music" in Appreciation work?
2. Does Chamber Music appeal to the young?
3. What is the value of biography and anecdote? If used, should it precede or follow the hearing of a piece of music?
4. Are thorough courses desirable or is a light-handed approach the best?
5. Is direct Appreciation teaching the most successful method, or does incidental teaching connected with the pupil's own performance offer the better approach?
6. Do "big" works appeal to children or is it more desirable to use simple movements very carefully chosen as within their capacities of understanding? Is the lighter (Haydn-Mozart) style or the heavy (Beethoven-Wagner) style more appealing to children?
7. How much should one rely on the phonograph and how much on the piano?
8. At children's concerts is the presence of a speaker desirable?
9. What is the proper relation of "Aural Training" to Appreciation?

The existence of marked divergence of view on such matters as these is doubtless largely due to the fact that Appreciation training is still in its infancy and that teachers (more in Britain than in the United States, perhaps) are still engaged in working out their own plans. Other factors tending to produce divergence are, (*a*) the varied character of the schools or classes mentioned (varied in age and sex of pupils, social class and general culture of the homes from which the pupils come, greater or lesser innate musicality in different parts of the country, &c.), and (*b*) varieties of temperament in the teachers.

I have already, and several times, drawn attention to the importance of the last factor. Undoubtedly a plan or device or type of music which proves a failure in the hands of one teacher may prove quite a success in the hands of another. Yet equally undoubtedly we human beings are all of us apt to generalize from our own personal experiences. I suggest that one big lesson that we can learn by the careful collation of personal experiences is the lesson that experiences *are* personal, and that a large liberty should always be left to a teacher, so that he may find *his own best way*.

We are to judge methods by their results. And what is the criterion? There is really only one! I conclude this section of my book by a quotation from the official summary of an American doctoral thesis that lies before me: [1]

"THE EFFECTIVENESS OF MUSICAL PEDAGOGY IS TO BE JUDGED
BY THE RESIDUE OF MUSICAL INTEREST IN THE ADULT"

[1] *Problems of Experimental Didactics in School Musical Education*, by Leonard Elsmith, Ph.D. (New York University).

APPENDICES

APPENDIX A

THE APPRECIATIVE SIDE OF MUSIC IN SCHOOL-LEAVING EXAMINATIONS

THE musical work in the higher forms of secondary schools is necessarily much conditioned by the regulations of external bodies conducting school-leaving examinations. These bodies now include music within their requirements (as an optional subject, of course). The following gives a brief survey of the position of the appreciative side of music in their examination syllabuses in the year 1934. Necessarily this side is directly represented chiefly by a study of history and form, but, in addition, tests are now usually included implying considerable training in the aural recognition of pitch and harmonic elements, which, of course, has its indirect (but important) bearing on appreciation: what is listed below, then, represents usually only a small portion of a pretty comprehensive examination syllabus of a type that existed nowhere a few years ago.

It is outside the scope of the present book to discuss the regulations in general; otherwise it could be shown that some of them (in their requirements for harmony and elementary composition especially) seem to assume not that the candidates are closing their period of formal musical study (which is necessarily the case with most of them), but rather that they are intending to proceed to the further examinations for a degree in music. A general reduction of the requirements in compositional elements and an increase in the appreciative elements (history, form, knowledge of the orchestra) seem to be called for if these examinations are fully to serve the valuable purpose of directing the teacher's attention to the kind of instruction that the student will in after life admit to be repaying.

It may be suggested that the proper criterion of a school-leaving examination in music is not *"Does it look forward to further and more intensive technical study on the part of the candi-*

date?" but *"Does it look back to a comprehensive and solid general grounding carried on throughout the whole school life?"*

1. UNIVERSITY OF OXFORD (Regulations of 1934).

SCHOOL CERTIFICATE EXAMINATION. The demand is for:

An elementary knowledge of musical history (the Paper will be divided into two sections, viz. Section A up to 1759, Section B from 1759 to the present day. Candidates may choose their questions from either Section or from both).

The "two-section" arrangement seems undesirable, but at all events each section covers a good long stretch of history and, moreover, the permission to choose questions from both sections allows the modern-minded teacher to avoid juvenile specialization.

2. UNIVERSITY OF CAMBRIDGE (Regulations of 1934).

SCHOOL CERTIFICATE EXAMINATION. The regulations require *the outline of Musical History and study of a specified musical work*. This seems entirely satisfactory. A special paper of instructions more closely defines the work required. It is disappointing in that "the outline of Musical History" is now whittled down by the recommendation of a volume that covers only the comparatively brief period of the classical sonata.

Outline of Musical History. A choice of simple questions will be given. Colles' *The Growth of Music*, vol. ii, is recommended.

Study of specified works. Detailed study of any *one* of the following prescribed works:

(*a*) A work for pianoforte solo.

(*b*) A work for solo instrument and pianoforte.

(*c*) A work for voices in not more than four parts.

Copies (with numbered bars where necessary) will be provided in the examination room. Questions will embody points of construction, context, and historical circumstances.

The works prescribed for 1934 are:

(*a*) Beethoven, Pianoforte Sonata in C minor, op. 10, no. 1.

(*b*) Mozart, Sonata for Violin and Pianoforte, no. 14.

(*c*) Mendelssohn, *Hymn of Praise*, omitting nos. 2½ and 5 (Novello).

3. OXFORD AND CAMBRIDGE SCHOOLS EXAMINA-TION BOARD (1934 Regulations).

(*a*) SCHOOL CERTIFICATE EXAMINATION (Syllabus I).

A. General questions testing musical taste and knowledge.

B. General elementary knowledge of the outlines of musical history.

C. Study of a set work (elementary). For the examination in 1934 this will be Haydn, Pianoforte Sonata No. 7 in D Major.

(*b*) HIGHER CERTIFICATE.

A. Questions in musical history, with special reference to 1700–1800.

B. Study of a set work. For the examination in 1934 this will be: Grieg, Violoncello Sonata.

This seems to be a nearly perfect arrangement—to demand first an outline knowledge of the whole range of musical history (with, however, intensive analytical work on a single example of composition), and then, for students who proceed further, to prescribe concentration on a special period. (With analysis of a work outside this period. Is this last a debatable point, perhaps?)

What about questions "testing musical taste"? They must be rather difficult to frame!

4. LONDON UNIVERSITY.

(*a*) MATRICULATION EXAMINATION (Regulations issued September 1933).

The candidate will be required to give a concise analysis of a movement in sonata form, written for the pianoforte.

N.B.—The term "sonata form" shall signify First Movement form only, and no knowledge of Rondo or Rondo-Sonata form shall be implied.

To show some knowledge of musical works and their composers. The questions to be set will include:

(i) The identification of short extracts from British National songs or from well-known instrumental works;

(ii) An acquaintance with the outlines of musical history within a specified period, which will be set for each year's examination. [For 1934: The Renaissance Period (*circa* 1625–1700).]

N.B.—Detailed biographical information will not be required.

This is very unsatisfactory. A candidate may get full marks who has been coached in the happenings of seventy-five years; these years are not very important ones in the history of music, moreover, falling somewhat between the close of one great period and the opening of another, and, anyhow, the logical objection to test of specialization without test of previous general study is a strong one.

The regulations then go on to state that "in and after 1935" the following will be substituted:

To show acquaintance with certain prescribed chapters of *The Summary of Musical History* (Parry, published by Novello).
For Examinations held in 1935, Chapters VI–VIII. For Examinations held in 1936, Chapters IX–XII.

This is worse still. Parry's book is, unfortunately, little more than a "cram" book; it has its value as a convenient conspectus for use by adult readers, in revision, but is not in the least suitable for school use. Chapters VI-VIII cover practically the ground defined in the previous regulations just quoted. Chapters IX-XII cover a period that may be roughly defined as Beethoven to Wagner—with the addition, however, of a quantity of later *names* of composers and works, down to Stainer's *Daughter of Jairus,* Bridge's *Callirhoë,* Gray's *Arethusa,* and the like. An intelligent and well-informed teacher will doubtless dish up the material of these chapters in his or her own way, warning the pupil against burdening himself with information about Felix Draeske, Lindpainter, Hugo Brückler, F. J. C. Schneider, &c., and also Corder, Lee Williams, and others who certainly do not come within the legitimate purview of the pupil of 15 to 17 years of age. It is natural for examination candidates and less intelligent (or less daring) teachers, who see definite chapters of a text-book prescribed, to think that what is to be found in these chapters must be known. In 1936 this would mean knowledge of about 130 composers (and perhaps 400 of their works), all of one period of about a century; yet the examination could be passed by a candidate who had never heard a Madrigal or a work of Purcell, Bach, Handel, Haydn, or Mozart. Is this common sense?

Then what a retrograde step we observe in the omission of actual analytical contact with a piece of music. This appears in 1934 and then drops out, as does also the "identification" test, which at least tended to induce the teacher to see that the candidates actually heard a good deal of music and became intimate with it.

Here, then, is lost ground! Who is responsible?

(*b*) GENERAL SCHOOL EXAMINATION (Regulations of 1934).

There is nothing in the regulations that demands any knowledge of a single piece of music. After a number of aural tests and tests in rudiments and harmony (good in themselves) we come to the one touch of recognition of music as a literature in the following:

To show acquaintance with certain prescribed chapters of *The Summary of Musical History* (Parry). For the year 1934 Chapters I–V are prescribed.

This is as unintelligent as can be imagined. The prospective candidate "swots up" Hucbald, Otger, Guido d'Arezzo, Léonin, Perotin, Robert de Sabillon, Tinctoris, &c., and proceeds to push forward to Bach and Handel—but only to "*Oratorio* in the Time of Bach and Handel", the instrumental music of these composers (and that of many of their predecessors) falling into Chapter VI, which is not prescribed.

Surely it is unnecessary to condemn a syllabus that requires knowledge of Willaert and Cyprian van Rore (however important they may be) and none of Bach's Fugues or Suites, or any of the works of Mozart, Haydn, Beethoven, Chopin, Wagner, &c. Who will institute an Examination for Examiners?

(*c*) HIGHER SCHOOL EXAMINATION.

Here we find the following:

Identification of extracts from well-known works (vocal or instrumental).

Simple questions on the general outlines of musical history.

N.B.—The questions will be designed to test a candidate's knowledge of the general course of musical history, and will involve neither criticism of works nor detailed biographical information.

This is admirable (save for the omission of any analytical test). But quite clearly the examinations of London University are standing on their head, since the earlier one demands heavy specialization on short periods and the later demands generalized "simple" knowledge. Is there no board or official charged with the duty of correlating these syllabuses?

5. JOINT MATRICULATION BOARD OF THE UNIVER- SITIES OF MANCHESTER, LIVERPOOL, LEEDS, SHEFFIELD, AND BIRMINGHAM (Regulations for 1934).

(a) SCHOOL CERTIFICATE EXAMINATION.

The study of *three* prescribed works in relation to the life and work of the respective composers.

Prescribed for 1934.

(i) J. S. Bach, Preludes and Fugues in C major and C minor, Nos. 1 and 2 (Book I of "Forty-eight").
(ii) Haydn, Sonata in E flat [defined here in music type by its opening notes].
(iii) Schubert, *Moments Musicals*, Nos. 1–6.

The absence of any requirement of a general outline knowledge of the history of music seems to be a weakness. However, three distinct periods are represented, covering a period of about a century and a third.

(b) HIGHER CERTIFICATE EXAMINATION.

Musical History. The study of a prescribed period.

Prescribed for 1934.

Haydn and Mozart and their contemporaries.

Prescribed for 1935.

Beethoven and Schubert.

This specialization would be all right if the School Certificate Examination, taken about two years earlier, had demanded wide general outline knowledge of musical history. But it did not!

6. UNVERSITY OF DURHAM (Regulations of 1934 and 1935).

SCHOOL CERTIFICATE EXAMINATION.

History and General Musical Knowledge: Three groups of three questions each will be set on the substance of the following portions of P. A. Scholes' *The Listener's Guide to Music* (Oxford Press): Chapters III, IV, V, VI, VII, VIII, XI, XII, together with the Glossary at the end of the book.

Three questions on the general form, character, themes, and place in history of a work specially studied.

For 1934—Beethoven, Symphony No. 1 in C major (Op. 21).

For 1935—Mozart, Symphony in D major (the "Haffner") K. 385.

These should be studied from the following: Miniature score, Philharmonia edition; arrangement for either Pianoforte solo or Pianoforte duet, Peters' or Augener's edition; Gramophone records, Columbia Nos. L 1889–92 (Beethoven) and Nos. L 1783–5 (Mozart).

The chapters in question of *The Listener's Guide* are as follows:

   III. What the Listener really needs to know.
   IV. How the Composer works.
    V. On the Principle of Design in Music.
   VI. How small Instrumental Pieces are made.
  VII. On the Mysteries of "Sonata Form."
VIII. On the Sonata or Symphony as a whole.
   XI. On the Song, on Oratorio, and on Opera.
  XII. The Orchestra and its Instruments.

It seems a pity that it has been felt necessary to omit Chapter IX (on the Fugue), but presumably this has been done in order not unfairly to overburden candidates. Apart from this the requirements are as comprehensive as could be expected or desired at the stage of culture represented by a school-leaving examination. The inclusion of the Glossary seems a highly practical point (and apparently unique in examination syllabuses): as this Glossary includes the technical terms found in over 300 annotated programs of the Queen's Hall Promenade Concerts it will be seen that a solid basis of knowledge useful to the future concert-goer is demanded. This is typical of the regulations as a whole, which, as should surely be the case in such an examination, are wide in their range rather than deep at any one point in a specialist way. The complete regulations can be obtained from the University, price 6*d*.: they are well worth study *because they obviously represent an endeavor to direct the attention of the teacher, throughout the years of work culminating in this examination, to the inclusion of what will be directly useful to the pupil in after life,* and so many school-leaving examinations largely overlook this.[1]

7. UNIVERSITY OF BRISTOL (1934 Regulations).

FIRST SCHOOL CERTIFICATE.

The relevant part of the regulations reads as follows:

The outline of Musical History. Candidates will be expected to know something of the styles of music prevalent in different periods, the effect on music of the invention and improvement of instruments, the growth of musical form, &c.

(The study of Ethel Home's *Short History of Music* is recommended.)

The study of *one* of the following works:

1.   Pianoforte Sonata, Beethoven, No. 5, Op. 7.
2. * Mozart. Clarinet Quintet in A, K. 586. (First movement only.)
3. * Fifth Symphony, Beethoven. (Andante con moto.)

Copies of the Music will be provided at the examination.

At least ten days notice of the work selected should be forwarded to the Registrar.

* For the study of these works the use of miniature scores and gramophone records is recommended, for (2) L. 2252 Columbia and for (3) C. 2023, D. 1151 H.M.V., and L. 1881 Columbia. Copies of the scores will be provided at the examination.

---

[1] I am in a rather delicate position, perhaps, in commending this syllabus. It was a pleasure to me, on sending for it, to find that one of my own books had been adopted as its basis. However, altogether apart from my appreciation of this solid compliment, I feel admiration for the *spirit* of the whole syllabus, which clearly embodies more *practical thinking* than many of its fellows quoted here.

This seems almost perfect—(*a*) Generalized study, not specialization, (*b*) Actual and intimate contact, by use of score and phonograph records, with a selected work.

(*b*) Higher School Certificate Examination.

As an alternative to the Harmony Section of the examination the following may be taken:

Study by means of miniature scores and gramophone records of specified works: simple harmonic analysis, form, style, and general artistic criticism.

This is certainly as valuable as the working of harmony exercises, however well devised, and the only point to regret is that it has been felt necessary to treat it as a mere alternative.

A further section of the examination, however, which is *not* optional, demands a knowledge of "The Age of the Sonata." It will be seen that Bristol has things in their right order—general study of the history of music in the First School Certificate Examination, special study in the Higher School Certificate Examination.

A somewhat curious point is that schools are left to choose their own text-book of the History of Music, and are asked to inform the University of their choice six months before the date of the examination. If this plan is administratively workable it seems a good one—leaving freedom to the teacher in an important point connected with his work.

8. SCOTTISH EDUCATION DEPARTMENT (Regulations issued September 1933).

Leaving Certificate Examination.

Lower Grade

Appreciation, History of Music.—The use of the gramophone is essential in the proposed course.

Nothing elaborate need be attempted in the history of music. In every scheme, however, there will occur some works of famous composers for intensive study. The pupils will be expected to know something of the lives and works of these composers, and should have acquired an outline knowledge of the *leading facts* in the development of music since the Renaissance.

Higher Grade

"Schemes of study should make provision for" [among other items]:

Instruction in the history of music from Purcell and Bach to modern times. If possible, candidates should have some knowledge of the Elizabethan composers.

Instruction in the elements of musical form.

There seems to be an element of vagueness about these, in many ways, admirable directions, but presumably the Scottish intellect can interpret them—with the aid of past examination papers. It may be suggested that the history requirement in the two examinations covers too much the same broad general ground and that the later examination might reasonably focus historical study on a brief period, school, or even composer.

9. CENTRAL WELSH BOARD (Regulations of 1934).

(*a*) School Certificate (Matriculation Equivalent).

Here juvenile specialization is deliberately encouraged, the demand being:

To show a general knowledge of the history of Music during ONE of the following periods:

(*a*) The age of Bach and Handel.
(*b*) The Viennese period, excluding Schubert.
(*c*) The Romantic Period.

To show acquaintance with a set work for Piano, such as a suite of Bach, *or* an early sonata of Beethoven, *or* a group of short pieces by Schumann, Chopin, or Grieg.

The work set for 1934 is:

Sonata in C minor by Beethoven, Opus 10, No. 1.

(The wording offers some puzzlement here, by the way. First the candidate is led to think that he has a choice of "set work" corresponding to his choice of period, and then, apparently, he is restricted to one work belonging to one particular period.)

(*b*) MATRICULATION.

The regulations for the actual Matriculation Examination are on the same general lines, except that (strangely) nothing is said about any "set work" and an essay treatment of one question seems to have (illogically and unsatisfactorily) taken its place.

10. NORTHERN IRELAND (Regulations of 1934).

SENIOR CERTIFICATE EXAMINATION.

The following extracts from the requirements show a rational spirit. The history demanded is of a general and not specialized nature and we see what is surely the first apperance in any British examination syllabus of the aural recognition of orchestral instruments and combinations. Candidates are required.

1. To possess a general knowledge of the outlines of musical history. Candidates will be expected to know something of
   (*a*) The styles of music prevalent in different periods; and
   (*b*) The periods in which the great composers lived, and the spheres in which their influence chiefly lay;
but detailed biographical knowledge will not be required.

2. To recognize the more important instruments of an orchestra when played out of sight.

A clear gramophone record may be used, and the instruments may be played separately or in small groups of not more than three or four instruments playing together.

11. IRISH FREE STATE (Regulations of 1933-4).

(*a*) INTERMEDIATE CERTIFICATE FOR SECONDARY SCHOOLS.

The plan has been to choose a series of representative composers covering the period of about 1700-1900.

A general knowledge of the following composers:—Bach, Handel, Haydn, Mozart, Beethoven, Schubert, Mendelssohn, Chopin, Schumann, Wagner, Debussy, and Strauss—to be studied under the following heads: Period, Nationality, Outstanding Features of Life, Style and Character of Music, Principal Works.

The weak point here is that the great period of the sixteenth and seventeenth centuries is omitted. (Can there be a political reason? It was the high period of England's musical achievement.)

(b) LEAVING CERTIFICATE.

The demand is for "General Music History", then oddly defined as "The age of Bach and Handel to the present day." Thus the two examinations cover the same period, and in this respect the regulations seem unsatisfactory. A demand in the earlier examination for a genuinely "general" knowledge of history (say 1550–1900), followed by a demand in the later examination for a specialized knowledge of a definite "period", would obviously be far better. Moreover, the demands in both cases should include the making of actual contact with specified works.

These examination regulations do not, then, show the same advanced educational thought as the Program of Instruction in Music, which interested readers of the present work might well procure.

A general criticism of the treatment of music in such examinations as the above will be found in the following publication— *The School Certificate Examination, being the Report of the Panel of Investigators appointed by the Secondary School Examinations Council to Enquire into the Eight Approved School Certificate Examinations held in the Summer of 1931.* The following is the section concerned with the History of Music.

Many of the questions on the History of Music are rather far away from the "main line", e.g., "What do you know about: Orlando Gibbons, Moussorgsky, Tallis, Tartini?" "What do you know of *Musica Transalpina?*" N.B. This syllabus states that a choice of *simple* questions will be given. Colles, *The Growth of Music* is recommended. It may be mentioned that two scholarly and distinguished musicians failed to find this question simple. "Name the composer and state the nature of the following compositions, and mention one point of special interest about each:
. . . (c) *Harold in Italy.*"

A candidate catching sight of the names Mozart and Beethoven in a question may reasonably hope to do well in this; but his hopes will be dashed by looking closer at such a question as: "Do you prefer Mozart to Beethoven, or the reverse? Give your reasons." This, according to the syllabus, is a question testing musical taste, a proceeding of very doubtful value.

Elementary knowledge of the *outlines* of musical history is tested by the following really difficult question: "How have the developments of instruments helped composers?" Another example of a too difficult question is: "Name three composers by whom J. S. Bach was influenced in respect of (*a*) his organ music, (*b*) his harpsichord music, (*c*) his violin music." Calling to mind again the age of the candidates, and the time for reading at their disposal, it is not surprising that the examination is unpopular.

One cannot think very highly of the "scholarship" or "distinction" of the two musicians whose embarrassment is above recorded, but whether that question is a fair one for school pupils is another matter.

The remarks of the Panel seem to be rather elementary and haphazard. After a perusal of the foregoing analysis of the various sets of regulations, the reader will probably agree that the Panel of Investigators might have widened the scope of their remarks. However, it is something to know that such a Panel is occasionally appointed. More power to its elbow!

APPENDIX B

THE "LAUSANNE RESOLUTION"

IN 1931 there was held at Lausanne, Switzerland, the second Anglo-American Music Education Conference. For the first time at any such conference (I believe) a definite "Section" devoted itself to discussion of the subject of Musical Appreciation.[1] This Section brought before the general body of the Conference a resolution for endorsement. As somewhat

[1] The point was not considered worthy of exhaustive research, but the following facts were found recorded. In 1922 a *Section for the Appreciation of Music Literature* constituted a feature of the official program of the Music Supervisors' National Conference, meeting in Nashville, Tenn. In 1923 the same organization included *Appreciation Class in the High School* in its sectional meetings. Similar meetings have been continued in later years. W. E.

amended by that general body and as passed by a considerable majority, the Resolution read as follows: [1]

The aims of the study of Musical Appreciation, as we understand it, are (*a*) the development of a high degree of sensitiveness to the medium of the art, and (*b*) an intensive and critical study of representative examples of admitted masterpieces. This implies, first, the ability to hear music in its own terms, and not in terms of association with other experiences; and, secondly, an insight into all those factors which constitute style.

In our opinion, the development of a high degree of sensitiveness to the medium of the art represents the scope of the aural training class, and is primarily the work of the school.

Let it be clearly understood, however, that at all points in aural training actual examples of the music most appropriate for the purpose must be presented to the class. In this way, aural training and the study of the literature of music are at no time divorced from each other.

The intensive and critical study of musical masterpieces follows naturally from this foundational training, and is obviously appropriate to more mature students, and entirely unsuitable as a subject in elementary education.

It is our opinion that the best use of mechanically reproduced music in teaching is in recalling actual experiences gained in the concert room or in preparing for them. The most adequately equipped teacher of Appreciation, however, is the one who is himself a competent performer.

We believe that all that is here defined as Musical Appreciation, so far from being in opposition to training in vocal and instrumental performance, is an essential complement of all such training.

I was one of the protesting minority, and, without going again into the details of a prolonged discussion that followed in the pages of *The Musical Times*, I will give here my ideas upon the Resolution, in the shape of a suggested re-drafting of its wording, without which, to my mind, it is inacceptable. [2]

---

[1] I have the impression that there was an introductory paragraph addressing the Resolution to the attention of educational authorities.

[2] And, indeed, in many parts incomprehensible, for in paragraph after paragraph there is difficulty in discovering just what those who drafted the document had in mind.

This Conference wishes to call the sympathetic attention of all educational authorities to the importance of the subject of Musical Appreciation (under whatever name) in the curricula of both primary and secondary schools.

In the general term "Musical Appreciation" is included whatever brings to the notice of the pupils the listening side of the art, as distinct from the side of performance. The Conference holds that the educational claims of this aspect of music are much the same as those of English Literature, which have in recent years increasingly led to the supplementing of grammatical teaching and the pupils' own exercises in English composition by the provision of opportunities for actual acquaintance with literary masterpieces, under such direction as will be likely to lead to the enlargement of understanding and the growth of literary taste.

The methods to be adopted in the application of this principle to music cannot be laid down in a few words. They admit of great variety, ranging from the mere performance of suitably graded fine compositions, with little introduction or explanation, to carefully planned instruction in the history of music and the lives and aims of its composers, and systematic aural exercise in the analysis of its forms and the recognition of orchestral colors. The essential is that *attention* should be secured—that the pupils should come to look upon the listening to music not as a passive but as an active occupation. The recent enormous development of opportunity of hearing music by means of the phonograph and radio now make emphasis upon this principle an urgent educational duty.

It is the impression of the Conference that some defects at present exist in a proportion of such teaching as is given. Perhaps the chief of these lies in too great reliance upon fanciful pictorial or narrative ideas imported into the music; while a good deal of music legitimately admits of this and even suggests it by the title the composer has attached, it is an error, especially with pupils beyond the infant stage, to lay stress upon it to the neglect of the structural side of the art, which is what, in general, offers the greatest impediment to the "following" of music by the hearer.

The Conference strongly suggests that where a member of the musical profession, experienced in class teaching, is available, sympathetic and skilful treatment of the subject will be most readily secured by his or her employment. In other cases, however, a member of the school staff, with an enthusiasm for music, may do valuable work if he or she will avail himself or herself of the best of the text-books available and will devote time and thought to the gaining of a thorough acquaintance with the music to be presented. The fact that phonographic reproductions of music of all classes (solo vocal, choral, string quartet, orchestral, &c.) now exist makes it the more feasible for the non-professional musician to undertake the work, and the Conference urges that, in addition to a good pianoforte, wherever possible a phonograph and a carefully-chosen set of records (renewed and supplemented from time to time) should be looked upon as a part of the normal equipment of every place of education.

The relevant articles and letters in *The Musical Times* occur between the dates of September 1931 and March 1933. The present book takes its origin in the realization then forced upon the writer that what he considers an ordinary clear-minded view of Musical Appreciation, though prevalent in Britain,[1] has yet not been sufficiently definitely and widely adopted by the *musical profession* for the Musical Appreciation movement to exercise that influence upon the general musical interest and tastes of the country that the advent of Broadcasting (about a decade before the Conference) makes so desirable.

APPENDIX C

AN APPEAL TO WOULD-BE AUTHORS

As originally prepared for the press this book included a section that has had to be "scrapped" in order to keep the price of the book within the means of the average teacher. It was a long section and with its "scrapping" goes the result of very many weeks of extremely fatiguing work.

The vanished section was nothing less than a close examination of the *whole* of the British and American literature of the subject, classified as follows:

Books of Guidance for Teachers.

Books to be put in the Hands of Pupils.

---

[1] American members were necessarily much in the minority at a Conference held in Europe.

Books addressed to Amateurs.
History and Biography for Adults.
Books on Musical Form.
Books on the Orchestra.
Books on the Opera.
Books on Psychology, Aesthetics, &c.
Books on Music in Education; Education in Music.
Helps to the Use of the Phonograph and Pianola.
Helps to the Use of the Radio.
Guides to Particular Compositions and Composers.
Official Government Reports, &c.

It is with great reluctance that the author puts aside the results of his study of this vast literature, all of which he possesses in his own library. Possibly some means may yet be found to bring these results before the public.

Meantime the following passage from the suppressed bibliography may be salvaged in the hope that it will catch the eye of those most concerned:

The reader who goes through this list will not have got very deep into it before he will come to the conclusion that, while a very large number of most admirable books on the subject exist, they have as companions a good many that should never have been written. It really appears as though any person who feels a little interest in music feels himself *ipso facto* competent to write about it, while any bright teacher who has succeeded in interesting a class in the subject burns to show other teachers how to go about the enterprise.

Many book-publishers seem to act entirely without proper guidance in the acceptance or rejection of the works on music submitted to them and the musical public suffers in consequence from a plague of ill-informed, ill-written musical literature. Note, by the way, that this is by no means all of it definite "Appreciation" literature; every branch of musical life and thought would be represented in a wide *Index librorum prohibitorum* and every type of musical author would suffer in a public-spirited *Auto-da-fé*. We definitely need a movement towards a more conscientious treatment of music on the part of authors and publishers, and one simple hint that might be offered to the former is the following: *"The manuscript of your book completed, and your neat typescript prepared, you may take it for granted, who-*

ever you are, that you have now before you a record both of some misconceptions on your part and of some failures to express yourself clearly. You should not think of sending that typescript to the publisher without having it 'vetted' by several of your most highly-educated and intelligent friends, and then, if it be intended for the simple-minded, by one of them also so that you may discover where you have failed to make yourself clear to the particular public you have in mind."

The present writer can speak humbly and feelingly. He has a long list of books to his credit (or debit), not one of which has ever gone to press without his submitting it to one or several authorities to go through it with their particular specialist small-tooth-combs. Yet even so not one has ever proved to be totally free from slips, for when all possible precautions have been taken some element of error always remains. Frankly, if this be so with the present author, who for a quarter of a century has made his living by journalism and authorship, must it not be so with the musician or teacher essaying authorship merely for the first or second time? We should be spared a good many of the exasperating collections of blunders that go under the description of books on music if professional musicians and teachers who happen to be but amateur authors would reflect on these things.

But what are we to say of the *professional* writer who puts out books on music that are little more than a dough of half-ground thought kneaded up with lumps of misunderstood or ill-remembered history and then but half baked? There is nothing adequate to be said but by the incinerator.

It is in the definitely historical branch of writing that the worst errors exist. So many of the writers evidently know no more than they have learned (or think they have learned) from elementary text-books, and sound history cannot be written with that equipment!

The branch of Musical Form is the next worst treated: not one in five, apparently, of the people who write specifically on Form, or introduce incidental exposition of it into their writings, have actually analyzed for themselves any considerable body of musical compositions—and in those they *have* analyzed, the eye, and not the ear, has evidently often been the instrument employed. It is a great pity that our regulations for musical degrees and diplomas do not take more serious account of the candidate's background-grasp of history and form; it has become clear to me in going through both British and

American works that individuals may possess high parchment qualifications in music, with good standing in the musical profession, and yet remain pathetically ignorant of the historical and formal foundations of their art.

APPENDIX D

A POSTSCRIPT ON THE PHONOGRAPH

A PRACTICAL teacher who has seen this book in proof points out that it contains no clear pronouncement on the part of the author of his attitude on the question of *Phonograph versus Piano* (see references to this subject on pages 247, 302, and 318). That attitude can be quickly defined:

(*a*) For PIANO MUSIC, if the school piano is a good one and the teacher a good player, then naturally the piano should be used.

(*b*) For VOCAL AND CHORAL MUSIC, necessarily the phonograph must be used and for CHAMBER MUSIC and OR-CHESTRAL MUSIC it seems but the merest common sense to use it for why give such music in translation when a close approach to the original is available?

(*c*) But even when the phonograph is used for the actual performance of a composition a teacher who is a good pianist can make effective use of the piano in the process of explanation, and may find this more convenient than the performance of extracts from the record.

It will be seen then, that, on this detail of teaching procedure, the present author is not fully in sympathy with certain writers on Musical Appreciation who (themselves being excellent pianists) tend, while not excluding the use of the phonograph, to recommend the use of the piano in preference to it, even for orchestral music.

And he is frankly not in the least in sympathy with writers who have maintained that unless a teacher is a good pianist he should not attempt Musical Appreciation work, for this fiat obviously decrees the cessation of all such work in some thousands of schools.

APPENDIX E

AN EARLY COURSE THAT SOUGHT APPRECIATION

THIS course, "The Critical Study of Music," was inaugurated very near the date 1900. After it had been in operation for some six or eight years an effort was made to provide a printed text for it, and in 1909 four books of *The Master-Musician Series,* prepared by Will Earhart and E. B. Birge, with the assistance of W. S. B. Mathews, were published by C. C. Birchard and Company. The four were *Handel, Haydn, Mozart,* and *Beethoven.* In 1912 volumes on *Verdi* and *Mendelssohn* were added. The course was an "Appreciation" course, in fact if not in name, as the *Preface,* quoted entire below, will reveal. The *Preface* also shows that the course was designed for use in high schools. Possible use of the phonograph was not mentioned in the first four volumes, but was specifically recommended in the two that were issued in 1912, and specific recordings were recommended. The *Preface* fails to mention the fact that even in the first four volumes, however, a list of representative compositions for various instruments was given, available for player-piano, or susceptible of being played on piano in solo or in duet form. The lack of the phonograph, which was not yet widely accepted, made such use of the piano and player-piano necessary, even for orchestral transcriptions. The main reliance, however, as revealed below, was placed on choral music.

Preface

The Master-Musician Series consists of a number of booklets devoted to a study of the life-history and works of a group of great composers. Beginning with Handel, Haydn, Mozart and Beethoven, the series contemplates a full representation of the most eminent composers of vocal music.

Each booklet consists of

1. About thirty pages of choral selections representing the composer at his best in that particular branch of the musical art.
2. A biographical sketch of the composer.

3. A study of the composer's personality and genius.
4. A brief disquisition upon his place and authority in musical art, with an analytical study of the characteristic points in which he may be compared and contrasted with his immediate predecessors and followers.
5. A helpful glossary of musical terms, with abundant matter relating to the various musical forms and to the ideals of the composer and his times.

The end of the contrasted study of several great masters, each represented by a program showing his art at its most individual moments, must result in an appreciation of the works of these masters as well as in a deep and genuine musical culture which cannot possibly be secured in any other way.

The Master-Musician Series has grown out of a recognition of the great need of precisely this form of musical study in the High School. The editors do not claim to have originated anything novel. They have merely brought together a better and more carefully chosen selection of illustrations of the composers treated than has up to this time existed in convenient form for schools, and they have supplied, besides, much suggestive biographical and explanatory texts which otherwise would have to be compiled from widely separated books. *The Editors*
W. E.

APPENDIX F

THE PERCUSSION BAND AS AN AGENCY TOWARD MUSICAL APPRECIATION

ALTHOUGH the Percussion Band has received much more attention in England than in the United States, it is doubtful whether even there its full value in the development of musical understanding in the young child has been discovered. At any rate, the testimonies given by many able English teachers, although they include frequent mention of the Percussion Band as a factor in Appreciation courses, are not very explicit as to what values accrue from it.

Compositions of any length beyond that of very short songs, as well as all instrumental music, can enter the child's experience only through his hearing without participation, or through his hearing *with* participation. The statement implies rejection, of course, of the curious assumption that hearing ceases when participation begins; for that widely current notion, with its significant reflection upon a vast amount of teaching of "doers", certainly is not necessarily true. That a child can become acquainted with and enjoy the rich treasure of compositions that have greater length and scope than his songs, and that if he can he should do so, appears, moreover, to be the consensus of opinion. The only question remaining, then, is whether hearing without participation or hearing together with participation affords the better opportunity for such acquaintance. That there is danger, in the first case, of the attention of the child (thought of, in this connection, as being of from five to eight or nine years of age) wandering when a composition of, say, some 192 measures is played to him, is undoubtedly true. In practice, it would seem, it is found so to wander; and this is probably the reason for the fact that many teachers are driven at such a juncture to telling programmatic stories (that substitute visual for auditory imagery), or to relating anecdotes about composers—by which a musical preoccupation of mind is abandoned entirely. On the other hand, one must admit that there is danger in teaching the technique of performance; for too much directing and mechanical drilling here may cause that very lack of listening to the music in a musical way that has given rise to the widespread notion that "doing" conflicts with hearing.

But of the two dangers the latter is probably the more easily avoided. The technique of performance may readily be made so slight that it is almost subconscious, and its subordination to the stream of musical thought that is set going in the children's minds may be so complete that their performance *is* the music itself, and is their natural expression of it. In much this way, the system of Jaques Dalcroze Eurhythmics engages the absorbed and appreciative attention to music of those who take part, and at the same time calls forth their expression and interpretation of the myriad poetic moods of the music. If such responses in eurhythmics were, however, made a matter of technical instruction and military drill, the essential values would certainly be lost. To lose them in Percussion Band by the same kind of misdirected effort is quite as easy.

One factor in eurhythmics that safeguards the direction and character of attention given by the participant is the simplicity and naturalness of the responses required of him. No elaborate and highly rationalized form of technique stands between him and the music. It can flow through him unimpeded. A factor of still more basic character is the creative attitude that is (partly in consequence of the technical simplicities mentioned) superinduced. The participant is, from the outset, recreating—is repeating within himself, from the composer's standpoint, the moods, forms, and aesthetic events that preoccupied the composer. But these same factors may quite as readily characterize the activities of the Percussion Band. All that is necessary is that the music shall first be presented to the minds of the participants as a musical experience, and then that no later feature of technical performance shall become so elaborate and obtrusive that the original orientation of attention and feeling is lost. It may be that this will require some preliminary hearing that can hardly be distinguished from the "appreciative" listening that holds no thought of later action. If so, however, the appearance is deceiving. The focus and the quality of attention with which one listens to a piece of music of which he is to be the recipient only is vastly different from that which he gives to a composition which he is about to help to produce. In the one case he is likely to observe the surface; in the other he is likely to penetrate to the core. Even the adult may realize this if he fancies himself listening to a piece of music of which he is to give a verbal account with respect to form, mood, even to graces and beauties that impress him, and then fancies himself, instead, suddenly handed a triangle or a pair of cymbals with the suggestion that he employ them appropriately and tastefully in a fresh performance. (But, it must be conceded, if an instrument were handed him that required difficult technical practice, he would merely transfer attention from the surface of the music to something entirely remote from the music.)

This is not the place for a teacher's outline of materials and methods, nor does the recommended use of the Percussion Band for purposes of Musical Appreciation, entailing, as it preferably does, the improvisation of parts by the children rather than the reading of parts from printed scores, imply that this latter practice is unworthy or unimportant. It is merely considered to be more useful toward ends other than Appreciation, and less useful toward that particular end. If, with the ascent in grades, the percussion instruments are combined with such regular tonal instruments as are represented in the higher classes by players of violins, trumpets, flutes, *et cetera,* the range of compositions and the number of pupils included can be greatly extended. Every child in every group may thus be brought into participation in a creative instrumental ensemble that will add immeasurably to the experience he is able to derive from the course in "vocal music"; and there need be no fear of desecration of the music, if the compositions chosen are such as lend themselves nicely to such "scoring", and if parts for the tonal instruments are discreetly written.[1]

Rightly managed, the Percussion Band can contribute to appreciation of music much more than can be gained from any other form of *"doing"* in music; and for young children, and even with pupils up to the age of ten or twelve years, if the plan suggested in the preceding paragraph is followed, it may contribute, in application to some compositions, a warmer and more substantial appreciation than is attained through listening and reporting verbally. The translation of feelings and observations to a verbal account is not precluded, anyway, by the interposition of a form of expression that reveals observations and feelings in a language other than verbal.

By ensuring depth of absorption in the music, and maintenance of attention without effort to a composition of consider-

[1] This plan has other values apart from its specific use in Musical Appreciation. It contemplates the possibility of a course in General Music, Instrumental, that will complement the one in General Music, Vocal; and this course will depend upon developing a Schoolroom Orchestra (see all the Foreword to the Witmark publication bearing that title) which will employ all, while the small *school* orchestra continues to employ only the more advanced specialized players.

able length—and this with respect to its multiplicity of rich details as well as with respect to it as a whole—the Percussion Band lays up much treasure in the minds and hearts of the pupils. In addition, however, it becomes an excellent medium for preparing pupils for children's concerts. Its use for this purpose has long been recommended in the *Suggestions to Teachers* included in the *Instructor's Manual* for the concerts conducted by Dr. Damrosch in the course that has become noted as the NBC Music Appreciation Hour. A glance at the repertory of this course for 1934-35, discloses an astonishing number of compositions susceptible (and, again, without desecration) to such treatment. Here are a few: *Dance of the Sylphs*, Berlioz; *Farandole* from *L'Arlesienne*, Suite No. 1, Bizet; *Elephant*, and *March of the Lion*, from *Carnival of the Animals*, Saint-Saens; *Serenade*, Schubert; *Swedish Wedding March*, Soderman; *Dance of Sugar Plum Fairy*, *Dance of Toy Flutes*, and *Waltz of the Flowers*, from the *Nutcracker*, Tchaikovski. One can surely imagine that working out a lovely orchestration for these would lead the children into a warm intimacy with them that would form an admirable basis for the later hearing of them by Dr. Damrosch's orchestra. "Working out", however, implies something far more than a mere insensitive shaking and pounding of instruments with regard only to the basic beat-rhythm of the piece. Properly done it will elicit from the children attention to every feature of form and mood-effect that would receive attention and comment if they listened only, and would probably add much of fine detail besides. The only difference would be that the understanding of the children would first be expressed precisely in deeds rather than lamely in words, and only later, if at all, would find verbal statement. It is the spirit before the letter. If the letter is made to come first, instead, can we be equally sure that the spirit can be made to follow?

W. E.

APPENDIX G

THIS schedule of equipment used in the teaching of music appreciation is the work of Dr. George S. Dickinson of Vassar College, to whose courtesy we are indebted for permission to reprint this invaluable list:

EQUIPMENT AT VASSAR COLLEGE
FOR THE TEACHING OF MUSIC APPRECIATION

A. Lecture room and adjoining rooms
  1. Phonograph
     A laboratory installation, with all wiring conducted through conduits, and with the loud speakers located in a favorable acoustical position in the organ grill facing the auditorium.
     Operated from the control cabinet near the lecturer's desk.
  2. Radio unit
     Incorporated with the phonograph so as to use its amplifier and loud speakers.
     Located in and operated from the control cabinet.
  3. Recording unit
     Incorporated with the phonograph, so as to use its amplifier. The microphone, together with the phonograph amplifier and loud speakers, provides an auditorium speaker system, for the amplification of speech and music.
     For the recording of phonograph discs of class materials, ear training exercises, etc.
     Located in and operated from the control cabinet.
  4. Sound-film projector (prepared for)
     To be located in a booth at the back of the auditorium, and to use the amplifier and loud speakers of the phonograph system.
  5. Stereopticon
     Located in a room immediately adjoining the lecture stage at the back. Projects through a translux screen at the front of the stage to the class beyond in the auditorium. This location is superior to one at the rear of the auditorium for purposes of operation and servicing; it also facilitates cutting off much of the light between the stere-

opticon and screen, so that the auditorium itself need not be darkened.

Fitted with a revolving belt holding 70 slides, which are brought into position one at a time, forward or reverse, by remote control from the control cabinet.

6. Record, roll, and slide library

Located in a room adjoining the lecture stage, for convenient servicing of the stage.

Record and slide files, roll cases, and catalogue, with cataloguer's desk and equipment.

Library of records and rolls, covering much of the history of music.

Library of slides, representing pages of scores, themes, diagrams, charts, portraits, opera scenes, instruments, etc.

7. Instruments

(a) Concert grand piano for "hand-played" class illustrations.

(b) Duo-Art player piano, partially operated from the control cabinet near the lecturer's desk.

(c) Organ of 60 stops (30 more prepared for), with automatic player, operated from the control cabinet near the lecturer's desk.

(d) Harpsichord.

(e) Clavichord.

8. Special furniture

(a) Control cabinet located near the lecturer's desk.

Operates phonograph, radio, recording unit, stereopticon, and organ and piano automatic players.

Contains the phonograph turn table and tone arm, and the radio and recording units.

Lever device for a cushioned lowering of the needle to the surface of the phonograph record, without damage to the record or needle, holding it in suspense, and later resuming the playing of the record at the exact point of stop.

(b) Record truck

A truck on swivel wheels, with racks and label cards, to hold a supply of records for class use in readily visible vertical-file form.

Shelves for corresponding musical scores.

B. Music library

An extensive library of music and books about music, selected and organized for both the elementary appreciation student and for the more advanced non-special college student of music.

C. Listening rooms

A series of rooms, adjoining the music library and under its supervision, fitted with phonographs, player pianos, and record trucks.

Records, prints of slides seen in class, and music are reserved for the student's use in preparation for class, in review, and in independent study.

D. Museum

Associated with the library, and containing a revolving exhibition of music, books, prints, instruments, and instrument and action models, all connected as far as practicable with current class work.

ANALYTICAL INDEX

Permitting of a systematic review of the contents of this book and facilitating after-reference.

Where under one entry several page numbers are given any figures in italics indicate the principal treatments of the subject in question.

1. THE FOUR OBSTACLES AND THEIR REMOVAL

2. VARIOUS TEACHING DEVICES, ETC.

3. THE USE OF THE PHONOGRAPH

* This entry offers a typical example of one of the good uses to which the
Index may be put. On the pages here listed will be found some varying
opinions well worth comparison with one another. The entry "Program Music"
offers another example.

8. CHILDREN'S CONCERTS

Gauging the Value of Children's Applause, 281
Kimpton, Gwynne, 23.
Manchester Scheme, 345.

Mayer, Robert, 347.
Milton's Suggestion, 25.
Sargent, Malcolm, 347.
Weekly School Concerts, 284.

9. EXAMINATION SYLLABUSES AND MUSICAL APPRECIATION

Bristol University, 360.
Cambridge University, 354.
Central Welsh Board, 362.
Durham University, 359.
General Criticisms and Suggestions, *173, 302,* 319, Appendix A.
Irish Free State, 363.
Joint Board of Universities of Man-

chester, Liverpool, Leeds, Sheffield and Birmingham, 358.
London University, 355.
Northern Ireland, 363.
Oxford and Cambridge Schools Examination Board, 355.
Oxford University, 354.
Scottish Education Department, 361.

10. VARYING INDIVIDUAL CAPACITIES AMONG CHILDREN

Analysis of Varying Capacities, 56.
"Either a Person Is Musical or He Is Not," 43

"Hopeless" People, 46.
Problem the Same in Other School Subjects, 52.

11. COMPARISONS BETWEEN APPRECIATION IN MUSIC AND IN LITERATURE

41-2, *43, 69,* 75, 106, *138, 148, 166-170,* 198-9, 245, 251, 294, 303-4.

12. THE TERM "MUSICAL APPRECIATION"

First Use of the Term, 11-2, 17.
Misunderstandings of the Term by

Ernest Newman and Others, 66.
Proposed Substitutes, 32, 272, 279.

13. MUSICAL APPRECIATION IN OTHER COUNTRIES THAN BRITAIN

France, 81.
Germany, 79, 84.

Holland, 81.
United States, 10, 16-7, 214.

14. ANNOTATED PROGRAMS

Bad Ones, 59.
Comparable to Appreciation Lessons, *26,* 42.

History, Their, 26.
Newman's, Ernest, 101.
Stravinsky's, 102.

15. COMPOSERS AND COMPOSITIONS

Arensky, *Basso Ostinato,* 298.
Romance in A Flat, 312.

Arne, Michael, *Lass with the Delicate Air,* 236.

16. BOOKS, ARTICLES, LETTERS, JOURNALS, ETC., QUOTED OR MENTIONED

17. PERSONS

(Omitting Composers, and the Authors of Books, Articles, Letters, etc., who are included in separate sections of the Index.)

18. INSTITUTIONS, SOCIETIES, SCHOOLS, ETC.

19. UNCLASSIFIED SUBJECTS

Printed in the United States
142263LV00002B/42/A